Graven Images

GRAVEN IMAGES

RELIGION IN COMIC BOOKS AND GRAPHIC NOVELS

Edited by

A. DAVID LEWIS AND CHRISTINE HOFF KRAEMER

continuum

2010

The Continuum International Publishing Group
80 Maiden Lane, New York, NY 10038

The Tower Building, 11 York Road, London SE1 7NX
www.continuumbooks.com

Library of Congress Cataloging-in-Publication Data
Graven images: religion in comic books and graphic novels / edited by A. David Lewis
and Christine Hoff Kraemer.
    p. cm.
  Includes bibliographical references and index.
  ISBN-13: 978-1-4411-5847-5 (alk. paper)
  ISBN-10: 1-4411-5847-2 (alk. paper)
  ISBN-13: 978-0-8264-3026-7 (pbk.: alk. paper)
  ISBN-10: 0-8264-3026-0 (pbk.: alk. paper)
  1. Comic books, strips, etc.–Religious aspects. I. Lewis, A. David, 1977- II. Kraemer,
Christine Hoff. III. Title.
  PN6712.G73 2010
  741.5'382–dc22   2010015163

ISBN: 978-1-4411-5847-5 (hardcover)
         978-0-8264-3026-7 (paperback)

Typeset by Pindar NZ, Auckland, New Zealand
Printed and bound in the United States of America

CONTENTS

POSTMODERN RELIGIOSITY

Foreword
Looking for God in the Gutter

DOUGLAS RUSHKOFF

OMICS HAVE ALWAYS BEEN ABOUT mythic narratives and beings: Superman is nothing if not Godlike, the Marvel Universe is virtually a pantheon, and even Charlie Brown was everyman's Job. But recently, writers have been taking this mythic potential more literally by making comics explicitly religious: Virgin's *India Authentic*, Osamu Tezuka's *Buddha*, R. Crumb's *Book of Genesis Illustrated*, and my own *Testament*, to name just a few. Why do so many writers choose to explore their relationship to the gods through comics?

There are plenty of answers — as many as there are comics, I imagine. But really, beyond the iconic representations, the history of superheroes, or the protection offered writers in a supposedly "kids'" medium, what is it about comics themselves that make them such an appropriate venue for Bible and Upanishads alike?

The gutter.

That's right — the space between the panels. The parts of the page no one even pays attention to. Those white, empty lines separating one panel from another, one moment in comic narrative from the next. It's there in that gap that the magic of comics occurs.

In one panel, Clark Kent heads into the phone booth; in the next, he's Superman flying above Gotham City. Between those two incarnations, a simple gutter in which nothing is drawn, yet the entire transmogrification of man to superhero has taken place. It's the closest thing in comics to transubstantiation, and it happens in the unseen crack between two discreet moments. It is everything, yet nothing.

This is core premise of comics, the art of sequential narrative. Our stories and their characters do not move in a line, as in theater or even literature, but through a series of windows. Frozen instants. These are the ticks of the clock, but not the spaces between each one where life actually happens or the story actually occurs.

As such, a comic requires a leap of faith from its readers every time they move from one panel to the next. We move to the next panel and must absorb it before we even understand its connection to the panel before. Only then are we able to relate it to the narrative of which it is a component part. Picture, word, then connection.

This gives the author an amazing opportunity: to instill word and image into a reader's mind before the reader has a context for this information. This is the tremendous power behind comics' ability to generate cultural iconography — to create modern mythology.

Sure, the mere juxtaposition of word and image within panels holds a power of its own. Visual representations of characters were deemed such a coercive threat that rabbis forbade "graven images" altogether, lest the masses be drawn into the mire of polytheism or paganism.

But when the illuminated manuscript is divided into separate but related panels of text and image, something even more inspirational happens: the reader is asked to participate, willfully, in the assembly of a whole from the parts. It is the reader who makes sense of the narrative, connecting the panels and turning them from separated moments into a living story.

It's this act of reader participation — this transformation of sequence into story — that implicates readers so much more fully in the very telling of the story they think they're reading. The readers aren't just going along for the ride, but providing the propulsion forward. They are rewarded with a sense of completion and sense-making every time they move their eyes from one panel to the next, implicitly agreeing with the sense they have made.

For me, the gutter has always been such a powerful yet unrecognized element in the form that I decided to make its function explicit in my own work. For my own Bible-based comic series *Testament*, I chose to use the space between the panels as a zone for action. While my main, human characters lived in the discreet moments of the comic's panels, I placed the gods in the gutters between the panels (see Figure 1). Instead of leaving those spaces blank, I turned them into a second universe where gods fought among themselves in a war to dominate the sequential action.

Like the comic's author and readers, the gods live outside sequential

Figure 1   **From outside the boundaries of the story, Moloch and Melchizedek influence the parallel actions of events in the near-future and biblical past.** *Testament: Akedah,* 2006.

time, a dimension above and beyond the story — capable of commenting on it, seeing where it is going, even pushing the panels around. But they cannot actually enter the world of the story, at least not as themselves. If a god reaches his hand from the gutter, where he lives, into the panel itself, the hand becomes an element, like water or fire. The god can set a bush on fire, for instance, and communicate to a character through the flame — but he can never enter into the world, completely, himself.

Yes, it was a gimmick of sorts, through which I could create characters who lived beyond the story yet still had a stake in what went on. But it was also meant to reveal the power of the medium and its particular relationship to religious narrative.

Religious experience, for human beings, consists of a shift in awareness from the particular to the universal — from the mundane to the mythic or, even more precisely, from the moment to the infinite. Religion attempts to codify and transmit the eternal to creatures who are (at least for the time being) trapped in the present. It means to make human beings who are trapped within panels aware of the gutter beyond — even for just a fleeting moment, in the obscure shadows of inference.

And this is what attracts so many writers to comics as the ideal medium through which to express their own immortal intimations. The panels are winks: building blocks that, in themselves, may not amount to more than any other storytelling device, but collectively create a multidimensional rendering. Once they lock into place in the mind of the reader, they assemble, like a Kabbalistic Tree or I Ching sequence, into an informational matrix of a higher order than can be put into words.

The scholars represented in this book recognize this unique ability of comics to communicate, simulate, and perhaps even actualize transcendence. All you have to do to understand them is get over the fact that God is less likely to be found in a sacred text than in the gutter.

Introduction

CHRISTINE HOFF KRAEMER AND A. DAVID LEWIS

> You shall not make for yourself a graven image, or any
> likeness of anything that is in heaven above, or that is in
> the earth beneath, or that is in the water under the earth
> . . . for I the LORD your God am a jealous God . . .
>
> — Exodus 20.4-5, Revised Standard Version

WRITTEN THE BETTER PART OF 3,000 years ago, our epigraph warns against the power of images. An image of the divine, suggests the writer of Exodus, can be so compelling as to distract from the worship of a transcendent God, one whose nature is too vast and complex to be contained. This aniconic thread runs through all of the Abrahamic religions and has been particularly contentious in Christianity when, during the time of the Reformation, Protestant mobs rose up and destroyed "idolatrous" Catholic religious representations. Lest we think that such fear of the power of images is a thing of the past, however, contemporary debates continue to rage about the impact of images on television and film viewers, especially children. These debates reflect the implicit belief that viewing violent or sexual images encourages or causes violent or sexual behavior. Images, it seems, simply will not stay inert on the surface where they're drawn; they penetrate our hearts and minds, and to expose ourselves to the wrong images invites the worst kind of disaster.

With this background in mind, we offer this collection of essays on religion and comic books under the playful title *Graven Images*. Part of our titular choice is a straightforward homage to the historical origins of comic art: from the pictorial wall carvings of ancient Egypt, to the manuscripts painstakingly illuminated by monks of late antiquity, to mass-produced woodcut stories of saints in late medieval Europe, to the engraved books of visionary English writer and artist William Blake, sequential art with accompanying text has been a vehicle for religious storytelling in diverse cultural milieus. Modern technology may have alleviated the need to literally carve images into wood or stone, but in its fusion of words and pictures, comics is an heir to an ancient tradition of "graven images" in which artists attempted to represent the divine.

We do, however, also intend to evoke the subversive — perhaps even blasphemous — connotations of the phrase. As comics has come into its own as a sophisticated art form, one that demands high levels of both visual and textual literacy from the reader, comics writers and artists have tackled controversial religious issues: offering their own reflections on traditional religions, criticizing or satirizing those religions, or break-ing away from traditional religions in the pursuit of religious innovation. Though graphic novels now enjoy a newly won status as "serious art" in the United States, comic books in their magazine form continue to have a certain reputation for edginess: the gritty horror and crime comics that led the industry to impose its own censorship in the 1950s and 1960s, the underground comix of the 1960s and 1970s that served as satirical and often vulgar mouthpieces for a disgruntled counterculture, and the status quo-questioning superhero comics born in the 1980s. The comics medium is no stranger to subversive subject matter.

Additionally, comics rub uncomfortably against the Protestant heri-tage that so influenced the United States in its first few centuries. In contrast to Reformation-era and Enlightenment Protestantism, which prioritizes the holy Word and maintains a certain suspicion of images as being overly sensual, comics fuse words and images in complex combinations that frequently give images the final authority. Because of the aniconic threads in the theologies of Abrahamic religions (threads that are present in Christianity, but much more pronounced in Judaism and Islam), the medium can present challenges for creators practicing these religions — though such challenges are sometimes turned to their artistic advantage. Similarly, perhaps because of the problematic nature of divine images in Western culture, comics provide unique opportuni-ties for those wishing to fashion postmodern golden calves — not mere idols, but genuine religious alternatives that nevertheless reject the ideal of a wholly transcendent, unrepresentable divine.

This collection evolved from a conference by the same name that was hosted by the Luce Program in Scripture and Literary Arts at Boston University in 2008. In addition to scholarly presentations, Eisner Award-winning creator and Director of the Center for Cartoon Studies James Sturm provided the keynote address, "Finding My Religion," and creators A. David Lewis, Saurav Mohapatra, Steve Ross, Mark Smylie, and G. Willow Wilson held a round-table discussion of their works and faiths. In the "Graven Images" conference, we sought to bring scholars, comics creators, and fans together to explore the evolving relationship between comics and religion. Comics are able to blend text and image in a way that is aesthetically unique and also potentially emotionally powerful. What, we wondered, are the distinctive advantages of the medium for communicating religious messages? What religious messages are comics creators choosing to communicate, and for what audiences? Finally, what is the significance of both the traditional and innovative religious thought that is appearing in comics and graphic novels?

The conference drew a lively audience, including many Boston-area undergraduates, and we felt that the time was right to turn the conference proceedings into a book. In order to address a wider range of works and topics, we supplemented the revised versions of many of the conference presenters' papers with essays solicited from scholars and writers who had not been able to attend. Although, inevitably, significant works and religious traditions were still left out of the final product, we are proud to offer this collection as a representative cross-section of how comic books and graphic novels are handling religious issues. For the purposes of greater focus, and to avoid dealing with the very different relationships between religion, pop culture, and comics reading patterns in other cultures, we restricted ourselves to works written or translated into English that are currently being published and sold in the US market.

Following current trends in scholarship of American religion and of religion and media, we have chosen not to limit our understanding of "religion" to major world religions or traditional religious institutions. We have been guided by the work of American religion scholar Catherine Albanese, who defines religion as a creed (beliefs), code (standards of behavior), and cultus (system of practice) by which a community "orients [itself] in the world with reference to both ordinary and extraordinary powers, meanings, and values."[1] While we do not necessarily wish to assert that comics are *themselves* a religion, they are one site where individuals grapple with issues of ethics, meaning, and values; engage in ritualized behavior; and explore both traditional and new religious traditions. Particularly in light of Americans' increasing detachment from mainline churches, the religious explorations taking place in and around popular culture products should be taken seriously as one of the ways Americans express their religiosity.

We hope that readers will find this collection useful in a number of different contexts. In addition to inviting comics creators to speak about the intersections between religion and comics, we have deliberately invited a wide range of scholarly approaches (literary and cultural, religious, theological, historical) as a way to foster dialogue and to chart the diversity of possible approaches to this material. We do not seek to proselytize for any religious tradition or even for a religious or spiritual viewpoint in general; certainly some of the works analyzed here are profoundly suspicious of religious institutions and attitudes. By the nature of this book, however, we do find ourselves preaching the gospel of comics reading. In *Graven Images*, we showcase some of the medium's aesthetic and narrative capacities as well as its evolving artistic potential, particularly when turned to religious purposes. The conviction that comics can explore profound issues of meaning in provocative ways is indeed this collection's *raison d'etre*. Whether you are a comic book reader; a scholar of religion, media, or literature; or a student just beginning to discover these scholarly disciplines, we hope to share our passion for the medium with you.

This is not the first book on religion and comics — it's not even the first book on the two published in English or during the Obama administration. We are aided by the inroads cut by other scholars into this intersection (some of which are listed, with gratitude, in the bibliography). However, in many of these previous efforts, the discourse often centers on a particular faith or topic: Jews or morality, Christianity or immigrant communities, and so forth. *Graven Images* is a response to those trends: a widening of the conversation. We are very pleased, therefore, by the diversity of our contributors. In addition to representing a wide range of faiths, our writers also epitomize an array of disciplines, institutional affiliations, educational backgrounds, intellectual histories, and nationalities. *Graven Images* may have started as our brainchild at Boston University's Department of Religious and Theological Studies, but it has expanded across the US and around the world to Canada, the UK, Germany, the Palestinian territories, and New Zealand. Its disciplinary boundaries now include discourse from history, linguistics, literature, semiotics, sociology, theology, women's studies, and more. With this rich variety in mind, we hope that readers will encounter elements both familiar and strange in this volume, and that the contrast between will enhance their understanding of both.

For comic book readers, we offer the essays composed by creators as windows into how religious concerns inflect these artists' creative processes, perhaps in defiance of the expectation that comics is a secular medium. Within the scholarly contributions, fans may be especially interested in explorations of favorite works and creators. In the hands of comics readers, we hope *Graven Images* will be a tool for discussion that continues to legitimize the medium (a task that we both hope and foresee will be achieved — therefore becoming academically obvious — someday soon) and that may, perhaps, catalyze fans' efforts at comics criticism and scholarship.

For teachers and scholars, we intend the essays in *Graven Images* to provide exciting entry points for group discussions on religious issues and paths, as well as to serve as companion pieces in classes that include the study of graphic novels. More broadly, we see this collection as a historical marker for how scholars are approaching issues of religion and pop culture today, particularly the way in which religious pluralism is taken for granted as cultural context. The interdisciplinary approach of this collection demonstrates many possible approaches to comics and their subject matter; comics studies need not limit itself purely to the techniques of literary or art criticism. Finally, we hope these essays will entice students to grapple with the significance of religious issues in American culture, and that it will give them both vocabulary and space to do so.

Graven Images opens with a section entitled "New Interpretations." Here, contributors examine traditional religious themes in comic books to reveal those religions' hopes, fears, prejudices, and values. In "The Devil's Reading: Revenge and Revelation in American Comics," Aaron Ricker Parks explores the continuing influence of dispensationalist readings of the book of Revelation on superhero narratives. Parks suggests that the sadomasochistic, apocalyptic revenge fantasy that appears frequently in superhero comics is actually based on a problematic *mis*reading of Revelation, one that comics readers and believing Christians alike need to question in order to resist American culture's voyeuristic love of violence. The section then moves across the Atlantic to Emily Taylor Merriman's "London (and the Mind) as Sacred-Desecrated Place in Alan Moore's *From Hell*," where Merriman examines Moore's portrayal of London as a physical embodiment of the city's religious traditions. In Moore's narrative, the Jack the Ripper murders are an exaggerated manifestation of the patriarchal religious culture that infuses Western society; the ritualistic killings are intended to bind and control London's feminine energy. Using René Girard's theories of ritual sacrifice and scapegoating, Merriman shows how *From Hell* confronts both writer and reader with his or her complicity in acts of religiously motivated patriarchal violence.

Laurence Roth then examines the continuing influence of Jewish comics creator Will Eisner in "Drawing Contracts: Will Eisner's Legacy." Reading *The Contract with God* and related works as reflecting Eisner's sense of the creative potential of Jewish culture and religion, Roth explores Joann Sfar's *The Rabbi's Cat* and JT Waldman's *Megillat Esther* as heirs to Eisner's groundbreaking use of the medium. In contrast, the twentieth-century Catholics addressed in Anne Blankenship's "Catholic American Citizenship: Prescriptions for Children from *Treasure Chest of Fun and Fact* (1946–63)" use the comics form not to differentiate themselves, but to align with the political mainstream. Here, Catholic creators combat anti-Catholic social norms and government policies with comics that portray Catholic culture as highly patriotic and quintessentially American. Next, Graham St. John Stott parallels Roth in considering the comic book as *midrash* (a Hebrew term meaning the interpretation of religious text or tradition), but for a different faith: the Church of Latter-Day Saints. Stott considers issues of authority and translation around Michael Allred's graphic novel *The Golden Plates,* which retells the story of the Book of Mormon. In attempting to draw new readers to the Book of Mormon with his comic book, Stott asks, does Allred undermine his own work by diluting the authority of the text, even as he resists working in an interpretive mode?

From his experiences in teaching religion and comics to college undergraduates, Darby Orcutt addresses some of the religious capacity of the comics medium itself in "Comics and Religion: Theoretical Connections." Engaging Scott McCloud's theories about the reader's tendency to identify with iconic imagery in comics, Orcutt points out the similar function of symbolism in religious imagery and demonstrates how other visual techniques can be employed to communicate particular religious worldviews. These visual techniques also concern Andrew Tripp in "Killing the Graven God: Visual Representations of the Divine in Comics," specifically the problem of imaging the divine in Abrahamic traditions, where images of God are sometimes considered idolatrous.

Comics, suggests Tripp, actually avoid idolatry by continually destroying and recreating images of the divine in a process that demonstrates God's ineffability. Next, in "Echoes of Eternity: Hindu Reincarnation Motifs in Superhero Comic Books," creator Saurav Mohapatra explores reincarnation and karma as the implicit background for death and rebirth motifs in superhero comics. Mohapatra suggests that such narratives offer Westerners an entry point to essential Hindu scriptures. Tripp and Mohapatra's approaches show how comics can contribute to theological discussions, but Eriko Ogihara-Schuck's "The Christianizing of Animism in Manga and Anime: American Translations of Hayao Miyazaki's *Nausicaä of the Valley of the Wind*" proposes that theological expectations can muddle comics creators' religious messages and damage opportunities for meaningful interfaith dialogue. The dualism that Americans take for granted in Christian theology, Ogihara-Schuck argues, distorts the message of Miyazaki's animistic masterpiece when it is rendered in English translation.

In our second section, "Response and Rebellion," contributors highlight how comics provide unique opportunities to either subvert traditional religious iconography or to extend it in controversial new directions. Mike Grimshaw suggests that God is dead — yet the continuing news of his death is just more evidence of his lingering trace. "On *Preacher* (Or, the Death of God in Pictures)" explores the Vertigo title as a Generation X response to postmodern fragmentation, one that urges readers to take responsibility for the human condition fully into their own hands. Though God may be dead, Superman goes on forever for creator A. David Lewis. Resisting some critics' urge to paint Superman as a Christlike messiah, in "Superman Graveside: Superhero Salvation beyond Jesus" Lewis portrays him as a different kind of savior: an endless story who preserves other narratives within his own. In a contrasting examination of messianic themes in comics, Julia Round's "'The Apocalypse of Adolescence': Use of the *Bildungsroman* and Superheroic Tropes in Mark Millar and Peter Gross's *Chosen*" analyzes a tale of the Second Coming where a young, modern messiah figure is ultimately revealed as the Antichrist. Using misdirections and inversions, *Chosen* satirizes Christian millennial expectations, but it also undermines audience expectations about the superhero genre by blurring moral absolutes.

Moving away from the superhero genre, Clay Kinchen Smith's "From *God Nose* to *God's Bosom*, Or How God (and Jack Jackson) Began

Underground Comics" reveals the religious underpinnings in the work of one of the most influential creators of underground comics. Jackson mercilessly parodies the traditional white-bearded image of God in order to critique the inhibitions, racism, and violence of American culture — a stance that has much in common with late-twentieth-century liberal Christian theology. The comic book tropes that enhance Jackson's work, however, may interfere with the form's effectiveness when presenting other kinds of religious content. Kate Netzler's "A Hesitant Embrace: Comic Books and Evangelicals" questions whether evangelicals can successfully use comic books to spread religious messages when their religious goals do not always harmonize well with the existing traditions of the comic book medium. In limiting the artistic interaction between "Christian" comic books and other graphic works, Netzler suggests, evangelicals may be reinforcing a problematic implied dichotomy between faith and art. The section closes with a treatment of rigid dichotomies in visual form. Focusing on the visual function of Marjane Satrapi's heavy black-and-white line drawings, Kerr Houston explores the birth of adult moral individualism in "Narrative and Pictorial Dualism in *Persepolis* and the Emergence of Complexity." For Satrapi, argues Houston, moral individualism begins with the rejection of fundamentalist Islam, but it develops fully through a nuanced engagement with the religious culture in which the main character lives.

Our final section, "Postmodern Religiosity," explores fresh and innovative ways of being religious in comics. In "*Machina Ex Deus*: Perennialism in Comics," comics creator G. Willow Wilson employs the philosophy of René Guénon to explore the possibility of a primordial intellectual tradition that cyclically arises in all artistic productions, including comics. Megan Goodwin's "Conversion to Narrative: Magic as Religious Language in Grant Morrison's *Invisibles*" details the practice of Morrison's chaos magic as a postmodern spiritual path devoted to increasing human agency. For Morrison, the comic itself becomes a tool for change in the reader and the world. Similarly, in "'The Magic Circus of the Mind': Alan Moore's *Promethea* and the Transformation of Consciousness through Comics," Christine Hoff Kraemer and J. Lawton Winslade present *Promethea* as a text designed to instruct readers in the Western occult tradition. Like Morrison, Moore harnesses the visual nature of comics to increase the emotional impact of his work and perhaps even trigger altered states of consciousness.

Next, reflecting on resonances between Joseph Campbell's hero's journey and the superhero genre, creator Mark Smylie presents the mythological and scholarly sources of his polytheistic fictional world in "Religion and *Artesia*/Religion in *Artesia*." In an examination of another polytheistic worldview, Emily Ronald's "Present Gods, Absent Believers in *Sandman*" investigates the disconnection between deity and worship in Neil Gaiman's influential series. To lose worship does not necessarily lead to secularism, however; Ronald suggests that the tangible presence of deity in *Sandman* encourages an attitude of wonder toward the everyday world, one that supports a search for meaning in the immanent here-and-now. Finally, in "Tell-Tale Visions: The Erotic Theology of Craig Thompson's *Blankets*," Steve Jungkeit argues for the role of visuality in reclaiming divine Eros. Drawing on postmodern Christian erotic theologies, Jungkeit portrays *Blankets*'s insistence on the priority of images as a key element in expressing the main character's religious and sexual awakenings.

Whichever course one takes through *Graven Images*, the reader should have faith that these essays are not random selections. We feel they draw a particular strength from one another, even those that presuppose distinctly different theologies (or none at all). While all the essays are respectful of other traditions, they are not toothlessly politically correct: they have distinctive viewpoints supported by research, and they want to convince — or at least challenge — the reader. Moreover, they engage in adult frankness. Though traditional Western religions may focus on the sacred and unseen, our writers engage the profane and concrete: sex, vulgarity, violence, drugs, crime, magic, and sacrilege are all necessary, useful parts of the coming discussions (as is devout belief in the supernatural, which may equally consternate the atheists in our readership). We have held none of these topics to be untouchable; with all due respect to our Hindu and Zoroastrian friends, *Graven Images* maintains no sacred cows.

It is also worth noting that due to their intense interest in religious issues, certain comics creators are mentioned repeatedly in this collection. Alan Moore and Grant Morrison both hail from the United Kingdom and are well known for their interest in religion, magic, and the Western occult tradition; discussions of Moore's work appear in essays by Merriman, Tripp, Mohapatra, and Kraemer and Winslade, while Morrison is a subject for Tripp, Mohapatra, Lewis, Wilson, and Goodwin. Particular religious themes and issues also recur in many of the essays, including the use of comics for religious pedagogy; the relationship between the comics form and its religious function; death and afterlife beliefs; the relative authority of text and images; and the tensions among monotheistic, polytheistic, and nontheistic theologies. The reader is invited to make further connections between these essays for him- or herself and also to fruitfully problematize and sever them, distinguishing any biases accidentally woven into our material.

Inevitably, even with the marvelous diversity of the essays we have collected here, we have regrets about what was left out due to time and the relative availability of contributors. Despite the importance of Marvel Comics in the American comics industry, its series are underrepresented here, as are Japanese manga, which have become increasingly popular in the US over the last two decades. We particularly regret omitting seminal manga creator Osamu Tezuka, whose portrayal of the life of the Buddha in comics form is well known. Analyses of other provocative biblical interpretations, such as Steve Ross's *Marked!* and A. David Lewis's *The Lone and Level Sands*, would also have been welcome in these pages — but we leave those opportunities for future projects. Finally, any subsequent scholarly collections on religion and comics will necessarily have to include the increasingly important medium of web comics. Online strips such as Patrick Farley's confrontational and often hilarious *Apocamon* (a play on the words "apocalypse" and "Pokemon") represent only the tip of the iceberg when it comes to the vast potential for religiously experimental comics art in electronic form.

To that end, we have included three short appendices to outline other "hot" issues arising even as *Graven Images* goes to print. Addressing some of the early reaction to R. Crumb's *The Book of Genesis Illustrated* (2009) is the masterful — and oft-cited — Scott McCloud, taken from his online blog at www.scottmccloud.com. Further, to acknowledge the explosion of digital comics and comics scholarship, we have also included a sampling of Beth Davies Stofka's insightful online writings about religion and comics, particularly on Gary Panter's deeply intertexual *Jimbo's Inferno*. Lastly, remembering our past even as we look forward, the program for the original 2008 "Graven Images" conference has been reproduced both for readers' interest and as a jumping-off point toward new writing.

In closing, we would like to once again thank all those who made this collection possible. The "Graven Images" conference was funded by the Luce Program in Scripture and Literary Arts at Boston University, the Boston University Department of Religious and Theological Studies, the Boston University Graduate Student Organization, and the New England-Maritimes region of the American Academy of Religion. Prof. Peter Hawkins and Cristine Hutchison-Jones were major sources of moral and practical support during the planning and execution of the conference. Along with the keynote address of comics creator James Sturm, conference participants enjoyed scholarly presentations by Rene Javellana, Marla Harris, Vincent Gonzalez, Josh Cohen, and Nicholas Yanes. Steve Ross (*Marked!*) spoke on our creators panel, while JT Waldman (*Megillat Esther*) kindly provided original art for a conference logo. Our continuing gratitude goes out to the enthusiastic audience who attended the conference and encouraged us to turn the conference proceedings into this collection, as well as to Burke Gerstenschläger, who coached us through the proposal process. Finally, as always, we owe our thanks to our families and friends, whose support of our academic and artistic passions provided essential nourishment for this work.

Boston, November 29, 2009

Note
1   Catherine L. Albanese, *America: Religions and Religion*, 3rd edn. (Belmont, CA: Wadsworth, 1999) 8–11.

NEW INTERPRETATIONS

The Devil's Reading:
Revenge and Revelation in American Comics

AARON RICKER PARKS

T HE BIBLICAL BOOK OF REVELATION (also called the Apocalypse of John) is a colorful book with a colorful reception history, to put it mildly. Its hallucinatory and often violent images have made it both a popular and controversial work. D. H. Lawrence, for example, once condemned the whole book as a pandering violent mess: "[Revelation is] the work of a second-rate mind. It appeals intensely to second-rate minds in every country and in every century . . . [U]nintelligible as it is, it has no doubt been the greatest source of inspiration to the vast mass of Christian minds — the vast mass being always second-rate — since the first century."[1] In his eyes, Revelation "has in it nothing of the real Christ, none of the real Gospel."[2] While I do not share Lawrence's aristocratic disdain for "the vast mass," I agree that the book's violent imagery has a troubling kind of mass appeal. In the world of comics, as in other media, this longstanding fascination with Revelation's vengeful violence is alive and well.

Since I cannot, of course, analyze and discuss every example of sensational violence associated with the book of Revelation in comics, I will focus on one particularly illustrative example in Marvel's *Daredevil*. In one strange and pivotal scene of Kevin Smith's "Guardian Devil" series, the satanic figure Mephisto appears and quotes the Bible for Daredevil, who is looking for information about the Second Coming.[3] Unsurprisingly, the fiend misquotes his source. It's a significant moment, however, because it looks more like an honest mistake than a diabolical twisting of scripture. The simple fact that the practically omniscient Mephisto cites the book of "Revelations" seems important. Calling Revelation "Revelations" is, after all, a common error, in and out of comics. Mike Mignola, for example, makes the same mistake in *Hellboy* in "The Right Hand of Doom."[4] The banality and the narrative improbability of this mistake suggest that it is *Smith's* mistake, a probability further reinforced by the fact that the story's only other practically omniscient character, Nicholas Macabes, also calls Revelation "Revelations" in Smith's series. Mephisto even makes the common error of assuming that John the Apostle wrote Revelation, as opposed to John the prophet of Patmos.

Smith's mistakes are, for our purposes here, a good thing. They show that we are dealing in commonplaces about the Bible — in things too well "known" to bother looking up. These mistakes promise a window into comic book prejudices about Revelation, and Mephisto delivers. He assumes that Revelation is about Jesus doling out violent payback — a divine choice which, Mephisto jokes darkly, makes sense to him for once.

G. Andrew Tooze thinks this scene shows that "[b]iblical literacy pays off," because thanks to Mephisto, "Daredevil is able to unravel the mystery."[5] Assuming that Smith was making honest mistakes when he put common errors and assumptions about the Bible into Mephisto's mouth, Tooze's reaction to the scene is probably Smith's ideal reader reaction. To me, however, the scene looks like an example of biblical *illiteracy*. Not only does Mephisto get the names of both book and author wrong, he risks getting the whole point wrong as well with a superficial and sadomasochistic reading of the lion and the lamb. In Mephisto's reading, Revelation is a story of a divine victim looking for bloody payback. Mephisto's Christ allowed himself to be mistreated and murdered due to a perverse kind of divine weakness, and will return to inflict some strong sensible violence of his own. Mephisto's Christ plays victim and then victimizer. This reading is a good distillation of the kinds of garbled and selective "Christian" ideas that Barbara Rossing examines in *The Rapture Exposed*. In a chapter called "Hijacking the Lamb: Addiction to Wrath and War,"[6] she says Christians should be "outraged" that American dispensationalists are spinning the image of the Lamb's victory "as a vengeful war story, not a story of suffering love."[7] Dispensationalist Christians believe that the Bible is the key to understanding the different ages or "dispensations of grace" in God's plan for the world, including the power to predict the world's end. According to Rossing, the end that they look forward to is almost always a self-serving and bloody one, and their reading of Revelation is tailored to match it. "They preach the saving power of the blood of the Lamb," she writes,

> but it is not quite enough saving power for them. They need Christ to come again . . . not as a Lamb but as a . . . Lion . . . They crave the avenging Jesus . . . But there is no indication that . . . Revelation ever wants . . . Jesus to return as a lion. John . . . replaces the lion with the Lamb in chapter 5 and never again refers to Jesus as a lion. Only evil figures are identified as lion-like in subsequent chapters.[8]

Mephisto's reading of the Christ of Revelation is typically backwards. When the fiend jokes that he is "no literary major," he is quite right, since when he talks of a Jesus who returns to earth "as judge, jury, and executioner — as a lion, not a lamb," he seems to be working with North American conventional wisdom about Revelation more than the text itself. It should probably not surprise us, following *his* Bible lesson, that the story itself ends with a miniature sadomasochistic apocalypse, in which the sadistic bad guy and his plan are revealed and destroyed through the violent payback dished out by Daredevil, the willingly victimized hero.

To me, this situation in Smith's *Daredevil* series looks like a clear example of a comic book writer being, as antediluvian comics giant William Blake famously said of Milton, "of the devil's party without knowing it" — in the worst sense. The story invites us to join Mephisto in complicitous admiration of the "avenging Jesus," and thereby gives in to one of the most powerful and perennial temptations of reading Revelation: the addictive revenge fantasy, with its sadomasochistic Christ who submits to fatal torture on Golgotha in order to inflict it more perfectly at Armageddon. This is where Kazantzakis and Scorsese got it wrong: the Last Temptation isn't escape from the cross — it's revenge for the cross. Again, however, Smith's snuff-film reading of Revelation is not unusual. Citing examples from the *Left Behind* series, war journalism, and sermons,[9] Rossing argues that *many* Americans have a "voyeuristic desire for a violent ending to Revelation's story that [they] can both escape and also watch."[10]

The problem, however, isn't quite as simple as Rossing makes out (Bible good, American dispensationalist Christians bad). Avenging messiahs are at least as old as the Dead Sea Scrolls, which promised the coming of a purifying warrior savior in the last days,[11] and Revelation itself is clearly working within that kind of tradition, with its explicit violent imagery *and* its implicit spectator violence.[12] The text is a complicated one, though, and early Christians imagined the Apocalypse in many ways. It's a contemporary American prejudice that the end of the world always means "judgment day," and that "judgment day" always means "bodies everywhere." "Revelation," "Armageddon," and "Apocalypse" are dependably associated in the comics with sexed-up violence, especially sexily violent revenge. The *Avengelyne* series published by Maximum Press in 1995 is an interesting example. The near-naked Amazon angel Avengelyne is the leader of God's forces at Armageddon and an agent of divine judgment. Like the inversion of a lion for a lamb in Mephisto's reading of Revelation, the inversion of an "a" for an "e" here in her name makes the *evangelion* — the "good news" — into a story of vengeance.

The complexities of Revelation are swallowed up in these images of apocalypse by what John Shelton Lawrence and Robert Jewett have called "the American monomyth," in which "supersaviors in pop culture function as . . . the Christ figure"[13] who brings "cleansing" through "golden violence."[14] Explicitly religious comics are not so different. Jack T. Chick's tracts, for example, consistently refer to Revelation in terms of (lovingly illustrated) violence.[15] Like non-Christian comic book artists, and like Milton according to Blake, Chick apparently finds it easier to work with Hell than with Heaven. His pictures of the devil are rich, fascinated, even inadvertently sympathetic. God and Jesus, in contrast, are literally blanks, appearing most often as the avenging judges of Revelation. Chick's best-selling tract "This Was Your Life," for example, shows a typical American man dying and being sentenced to eternity in Hell. Its story cites Revelation explicitly when the man meets his blank-faced divine judge in Heaven, and again at the end when he is tossed into hellfire.[16]

Secular comics, for their part, also frequently feature an apocalyptically violent revenge in a story's finale. Fletcher Hanks, with typically ingenious ineptitude, offers a perfect example of this when his 1940s pulp hero Stardust the Superwizard confronts a horrible devil figure in *Fantastic Comics* #10. When attacked by the demonic villain, Stardust says, "Just what I wanted!" Duly outraged and victimized, he proceeds to do just what he (and probably most of his readers) wanted: he beats the tar out of the story's unfathomably and unforgivably evil bad guy.[17] This old story pattern appears more subtly — but only barely — in many comics, and the more the heroes are brutalized along the way, the more sympathetic the reader is supposed to be when the villains are repaid. Even stories often thought of as innovative and edgy routinely conform to this same model of the hero as victimized, vengeful messiah. Frank Miller's *Dark Knight* series, for example, enjoys the reputation of a groundbreaking, revolutionary work; critics called it "revisionary"[18] and credited it with helping comic book readers "completely rethink" the superhero genre.[19] In the end, however, it dutifully offered its readers the familiar pleasure of a clichéd sadomasochistic Christ warrior: having once again saved the day, a horribly wronged and brutalized Batman hobbles away from his dead archenemy, the Joker.[20] The message is clear: the spectacular, violent brutalization of the hero and other innocents serves to justify the villain's spectacular, violent comeuppance. In Kevin Smith's "Guardian Devil" series, it is a brutalized Daredevil who walks away in the end from a dead Mysterio, but the pattern is the same.

The voyeuristic, vengeful apocalypse described in pictures has a long history. The medieval illustrated *Biblia Paupernum*, or "Bibles of the Poor," for example, look a great deal like comics, with Old Testament scenes frequently framing New Testament scenes. In the woodcut *Biblia Paupernum* 37, Revelation gets a typical comic book interpretation: Christ as judge is set alongside King David as he hands out capital punishment, implying that the two roles are equivalent.[21] It's possible to historicize the habit of apocalyptic revenge in comic books even more precisely, however, beginning with the origin of comics as the contemporary reader knows them. Superhero comics were born just in time to be World War II propaganda, and many embraced the chance.[22] Jack Kirby, for example, created Captain America specifically as war propaganda.[23] The cover of the first issue of "Captain America" featured the patriotic hero punching out Hitler personally — and this was *before* the war! According to Joe Simon's account in *The Comic Book Makers*, the mayor of New York actually posted guards at Kirby's office to keep anti-Semites and anti-war protesters away because *Captain America* was so good at selling war with Germany.[24] Propagandizing for hawkish patriotism — and/or capitalizing on it — became an industry unto itself as imitators appeared: "American Avenger, American Crusader, American Eagle, Commando Yank, Fighting Yank . . . Yank and Doodle, the Liberator, the Sentinel, the Scarlet Sentry, Flagman, Captain Freedom,

Captain Courageous, Captain Glory, Captain Red Cross, Captain Valiant, Captain Victory . . ."[25] The Jewish and Judeo-Christian imaginations of comic book creators were instrumental here; much has been said by Will Eisner and others about the influence of golems and messiahs upon these heroes.[26] As Robert G. Weiner writes, they "resembled the Jewish messiah of apocalyptic literature coming . . . to set things right"[27] — in this case, usually by violence.

Comics were also particularly popular with soldiers, as well as with those soldiers' kid brothers. They sold well to these audiences because they were accessible and appealing to young American males in general, and offered soldiers in particular a quick, easy read whenever a distracting break was needed.[28] For this reason, being banned from army bases was sometimes enough to shut down a comics title forever.[29] A lack of patriotism was a serious accusation against a comic, so it's no real shock that many comics followed the same avenging messiah story pattern that justified the war for both Axis and Allies. Further, recurring cycles of violence fed superhero-comics sales, whose appeal frequently depended on never-ending variations on a dependable, sensational theme.[30] If the Fantastic Four decided that fighting Doctor Doom only perpetuated their problems, and instead settled their differences with the help of professional mediators in a community reconciliation circle, for example, the result would be a sales disaster and the end of an otherwise infinite storyline. A lot of time, thought, and work has gone into making Doctor Doom a recognizable and dependable threat: he is useless as a cultural commodity if he doesn't come back issue after issue, inviting and/or seeking revenge of some kind.

World War II was particularly apocalyptic in terms of the mood created by the development of nuclear weapons, and in the comics, superheroes were implicated in these anxieties. Superman associated himself right away with nuclear testing, for example,[31] since — as he says — "atomic power is the future of America."[32] Similarly, in the 1946 *All Winners Comics* #19, Captain America declares that atomic power must be kept from America's enemies because "[t]he coming Atomic Age is . . . for all mankind."[33] Superheroes became part of the millennial fever dream of the bomb's revelation — a new world of unprecedented possibilities and horrors.[34] Many Marvel heroes have their origins in radiation,[35] and Superman himself turns out to be vulnerable to radiation (from Kryptonite).[36] In Jim Starlin's *Cosmic Odyssey*, the biblical bookend worlds of New Genesis and Apokolips are both created by a doomsday weapon that is clearly inspired by the atomic bomb, a beast/weapon with seven eyes like Revelation's Lamb — the Beast, the Lamb, and the bomb hopelessly conflated through comic book logic.[37]

Interestingly, explicitly religious comics have been dreaming this same anxiety dream, only instead of reading the nuclear age through Revelation, they read Revelation through the nuclear age. In Mark Waid's *Kingdom Come*, the Spectre, the Revelation-quoting "spirit of God's vengeance," engages in an apocalyptic cliché by taking pastor Norman McCay on a tour of Earth and Heaven. Superman's return from retirement is also framed in terms of Revelation, as one reporter refers to it as his "second coming." Thanks to the ultraviolent Magog (a name from Revelation 16), Captain Atom gets split, and, in the resulting explosion, he takes a hunk of Kansas with him. When the violence escalates into what McCay calls "Armageddon," an actual nuke is dropped by the UN, and the Spectre identifies the event as God's judgment.[38] Nuclear and religious apocalypticism form a tight knot in the world of comics, as in American culture as a whole.

To conclude, then: Americans need to read Revelation carefully, because the devil is reading too, distorting the text to maximize its potential for violence. I'm reminded of Christopher Marlowe's *Doctor Faustus*. When Faust conjures Mephistophilis, he thinks — like Daredevil and Doctor Strange and, for that matter, Kevin Smith — that he's conjured a devil to use as a puppet. But Mephistophilis sees things the opposite way, and his speech in the conclusion paints a subtler, creepier picture: "When thou took'st the book / To view the scriptures, then I turned the leaves / And led thine eye."[39] Wherever a power-hungry reader opens a Bible, it seems, the devil reads over his shoulder. In particular, the violent, oppressive history of the book of Revelation — a book written by a member of an unarmed, oppressed minority — demonstrates how an initially subversive text can be used to justify the position of those in power. In particular, sadomasochistic readings of Jesus — those that read "[r]evenge as justice as entertainment,"[40] in Greg Garrett's words — need to be examined. Though Garrett claims that post-9/11, the comics industry has attempted to examine its tendency to revel in violence,[41] we as readers have a responsibility as well. Although it is easier for most of us to imagine Hell than Heaven, it is nevertheless important and possible for intellectuals and other artists to question the devil's reading, and thereby to interrogate the righteous sadomasochism that so often justifies violence in "Christian" and "post-Christian" culture.

Notes

1 D. H. Lawrence, *Apocalypse* (Toronto: Penguin Books, 1995), 66.

2 Lawrence, 66.

3 The "Guardian Devil" story arc is found in Kevin Smith, *Daredevil* Vol. 2, issues 1–8 (New York: Marvel Comics, November 1998–June 1999; republished in Kevin Smith, *Daredevil Visionaries*, New York: Marvel Comics, 2001).

4 See "The Right Hand of Doom" in Mike Mignola, *Hellboy: The Right Hand of Doom* (Milwaukie: OR, Dark Horse Comics, 2004).

5 G. Andrew Tooze, "Do Superheroes Read Scripture? Finding the Bible in Comic Books," *Society for Biblical Literature*, http://www.sbl-site.org/publications/article.aspx?articleId=614 (accessed July 11, 2009).

6 Barbara R. Rossing, *The Rapture Exposed: The Message of Hope in the Book of Revelation* (Boulder, CO: Westview Press, 2004), 135–40.

7 Rossing, 135.

8 Rossing, 137.

9 Rossing, 138–40.

10 Rossing, 139.

11 Oliver J. McTernan, *Violence in God's Name: Religion in an Age of Conflict* (Maryknoll, NY: Orbis Books, 2003), 55.

12 Scholars like Steven Friesen, Christopher Frilingos, and Tina Pippin have underlined this convincingly. See, for example, Steven J. Friesen, *Imperial Cults and the Apocalypse of John* (Toronto: Oxford University Press, 2001); Christopher A. Frilingos, *Spectacles of Empire* (Philadelphia: University of Pennsylvania Press, 2004); and Tina Pippin, "The Revelation to John," *Searching the Scriptures*, ed. Elisabeth Schüssler Fiorenza (New York: Crossroad, 1994), 109–30.

13 John Shelton Lawrence and Robert Jewett, *The American Monomyth* (Lanham, MD: University Press of America, 1988), 6–7.

14 Lawrence and Jewett, 106–25. For more on superheroes as millennial, religious symbols, see *The Gospel According to Superheroes*, ed. B. J. Oropeza (New York: Peter Lang Press, 2005), 8–9.

15 See, for example, Chick's tracts "The Beast"; "Here he comes!"; "The Only Hope," etc. See also "Back From the Dead"; "A Demon's Nightmare"; "No Fear?"; "Somebody Goofed"; "The Trick"; "Flight 144"; "The Gay Blade"; "The Great One"; "Hi There!"; "The Last Judge"; "Last Rites"; "Reverend Wonderful"; "Scream"; "This Was Your Life"; "The Trap"; "The Tycoon"; "Where's Rabbi Waxman?"; "Satan's Master," etc., available electronically at Chick Publications, http://www.chick.com.

16 Jack T. Chick, "This Was Your Life," Chick Publications, 2002, http://www.chick.com/reading/tracts/0001/0001_01.asp (accessed November 10, 2009).

17 Fletcher Hanks, "Stardust the Super Wizard," *Fantastic Comics* #10, September 1940.

18 Geoff Klock, *How to Read Superhero Comics and Why* (New York: Continuum, 2003), 25.

19 Aeon J. Skoble, "Superhero Revisionism in *Watchmen* and *The Dark Knight Returns*," *Superheroes and Philosophy: Truth, Justice, and the Socratic Way*, ed. Tom Morris and Matt Morris (Chicago: Open Court, 2005, 28–41), 29.

20 Frank Miller, *Batman: The Dark Knight Returns* (New York: DC Comics, 2002; originally published serially as *Batman: The Dark Knight Returns* 1–4, New York: DC Comics, February–June 1986).

21 See Northrop Frye and Jay Macpherson, *Biblical and Classical Myths: The Mythological Framework of Western Culture* (Toronto: University of Toronto Press, 2004), 230.

22 Chris Murray, "*Pop*aganda: Superhero Comics and Propaganda in World War Two," *Comics and Culture: Analytical and Theoretical Approaches to Comics*, ed. Anne Magnussen and Hans-Christian Christiansen (Copenhagen: Museum Tusculanum Press, 2000, 141–56), 141–9. See also Wolfgang Fuchs and Reinhold Reitberger, *Comics: Anatomy of a Mass Medium* (Boston: Little and Brown, 1972), 93–4.

23 Robert C. Harvey, *The Art of the Comic Book: an Aesthetic History* (Jackson: University Press of Mississippi, 1996), 32–3.

24 Joe Simon and Jim Simon, *The Comic Book Makers* (Lebanon, NJ: Vanguard, 2003), 42–7.

25 Harvey, 35.

26 See Greg Garrett, *Holy Superheroes* (Colorado Springs, CO: Piñon Press, 2005), 28–30, 40–2, etc.

27 Robert G. Weiner, "'Okay, Axis, Here We Come!': Captain America and the Superhero Teams from World War II and the Cold War," *The Gospel According to Superheroes*, ed. B. J. Oropeza (New York: Peter Lang, 2005, 83–101), 97.

28 Harvey, 16.

29 Harvey, 16.

30 Fuchs, 123; Garrett, 45.

31 Murray, 147.

32 Murray, 148–9.

33 Weiner, 90.

34 In the next issue, for example, Captain America must defeat Future Man and put out his atomic fire (see Weiner, 91).

35 Weiner, 90.

36 Weiner, 90.

37 See *Cosmic Odyssey Book One: Discovery* (Jim Starlin, New York: DC Comics, 1988).

38 Mark Waid, *Kingdom Come* (New York: DC Comics, 1997; originally published serially as *Kingdom Come* #1–4, New York: DC Comics, 1996).

39 Christopher Marlowe, *Doctor Faustus*, ed. Sylvan Barnet (Toronto, ON: Penguin, 1969), V.ii.101–103, p. 97.

40 Garrett, 108.

41 Garrett, 149–52.

London (and the Mind) as Sacred–Desecrated Place in Alan Moore's *From Hell*

EMILY TAYLOR MERRIMAN

E XAMINING A WORLD ON THE cusp of the mechanized nightmares of modernity, *From Hell* incorporates magic, medicine, and Freemasonry in order to condemn the late-nineteenth-century British ruling elite and its patriarchal oppression of women.[1] Created by Alan Moore and Eddie Campbell, this complex tome of text and image leads the reader on an awful, labyrinthine trip through the Victorian London where Jack the Ripper murdered five prostitutes in 1888. The graphic novel's overt purpose, however, is not to condemn, but to thrill. Yet the book is self-conscious about its ethically questionable goal of entertaining the reader with visions of suffering: murderous events that, like ritual human sacrifice, create a sense of the numinous through the destruction of lives.

Chronologically speaking, *From Hell* is set in the same London of the imagination — on the threshold of the twentieth century — where Robert Louis Stevenson's Mr. Hyde and Bram Stoker's Dracula sought their victims. Like those earlier fictions (*The Strange Case of Dr. Jekyll and Mr. Hyde* was published in 1886 and *Dracula* in 1897), it asks: what distinguishes man from monster? In chapter 4 of the book, two main characters, villains of different kinds, travel by horse and carriage around the city in a journey that is both radically subjective and geographically objective. This section of *From Hell* shows London to be a site of multiple competing forces, sacred and desecrating, sometimes both at once. Moore and Campbell's depiction of past horror that reverberates in the present, in addition to their exploration of London's religious and sacrilegious multiplicity, directs the reader toward his or her own moral and psychological self-examination.

"Sacred" as a noun or an adjective remains a notoriously slippery and contested term.[2] Emile Durkheim claimed in 1912 that the "distinctive trait of religious thought" is this categorization of the world into sacred and profane, but opinions about what should be set aside as sacred, how it should be so consecrated, by whom, and whether in fact true religious thinking avoids such dualism, continue to range widely.[3] René Girard's *Violence and the Sacred* (1972) discovers the origin of religious practice in the violent destruction of societal scapegoats. According to Girard, such acts temporarily pacify the aggression inherent in human society and then become re-enacted as ritual sacrifices: "The purpose of the sacrifice is to restore harmony to the community, to reinforce the social fabric."[4] Hence, "[v]iolence is the heart and secret soul of the sacred."[5] In *From Hell*, the Ripper's poor, urban, female victims could act as such societal scapegoats, outsiders whose destruction could be seen as symbolic of an attempt to rid the community of its internal divisions. Certainly, an uncanny, secretive atmosphere surrounds their murders. Yet, Moore interprets the consequence of their murders not as a genuine release of societal tension but as an inaugurating catalyst for further hideous acts of twentieth-century violence.

In addition to being associated with the victimization of the powerless, the sacred has been said to arise from the nexus of operations of power. In *Dimensions of the Sacred*, Ninian Smart claims that capital cities become the "most potent" sacred places "since so much national power emanates from there," and he cites the specific example of central London.[6] Smart does not elaborate on how particular national places acquire their sacred power or explore the nature of the correlations between ruling powers and sacred powers, however. Others find urban environments, especially those of industrialized Britain, not to be sacred at all but, rather, dirty, secular, unholy spaces — replete with dens of iniquity, social ills, and the worship of Mammon. Even in a text as old as the book of Genesis, cities like Sodom and Gomorrah are associated with sin, while Abraham lives a largely righteous pastoral existence. In his autobiographical poem *The Prelude*, William Wordsworth describes how he had fantasized about the magic and wonder of London (ll.77–141), but experienced the "strongest disappointment" when he actually went there and saw it (1.146).[7]

London is a place in which religious and political powers, long intertwined, have been recurrently established through the spilling of blood. *From Hell* illustrates how London's history depends on violence that could be interpreted as generating the sacred: acts of deliberate oppression as well as societal scapegoating and religious sacrifice. For example, a panel from Chapter 4 (see Figure 1) illustrates the Tower of London, whose construction was begun by William the Conqueror.[8] The Tower is renowned as a place for the exercise and display of royal power and wealth, as well as a place of imprisonment, execution, and murder.

Figure 1. *From Hell* 4.28, panel 1

From a raven's-eye perspective on the Tower buildings (the panel below consists of two ravens), the reader overhears legends about the Tower (including the importance of its ravens, associated with a Celtic god) along with a little wry religious commentary on the phenomenon of human sacrifice enacted at the site of supposedly legitimate English rule. The "tour guide" in this panel is Dr. William Gull. Gull is a fictional character based on a historical figure, one who has been represented in other works of fiction as well as in a work of purported verity. Moore's main plot is loosely based on the theories of Stephen Knight's generally discredited book *Jack the Ripper: The Final Solution* (1976).[9] Gull, Moore's central protagonist, is the Jack the Ripper murderer. In the graphic novel, he is commissioned by Queen Victoria to kill several prostitutes in order to hush up the scandal of a supposedly royal child born to a commoner and the subsequent marriage. In obeying Her Majesty's murderous command and psychotically over-interpreting his mission, Gull carries out a series of ritual sacrifices of women in the East London's Whitechapel area. He dismembers them according to his understanding of ancient Masonic practices, in order — so he asserts and believes — to reinforce the mutually supporting facets of his patriarchal vision: men's rule over women, the oppression of the female spiritual principle by the male principle, the mythological power of the sun over the mythological power of the moon, and the so-called triumph of reason over unreason.

Most of the criminal events — and most of Gull's self-motivating explanations of history and hierarchy — are set in the city of London, an ancient and now huge urban conglomeration about which much has been written and where much has occurred. *From Hell*, with its lengthy endnotes (originally an appendix to the serial), consciously participates in an eerie network of connections among texts about London: its streets, its crimes, and its passions. In the same way that a city space itself can feel haunted — as Peter Ackroyd says of London, "certain streets or neighbourhoods carry with them a particular atmosphere over many generations"[10] — texts are sometimes haunted by other texts and other writers. Moore's work operates within a self-conscious literary intertextuality that heightens the reader's impression that there are older and deeper significances to be discovered, both on the streets of London and in the panels of the volume. One especially significant haunting and haunted presence in *From Hell* is William Blake, a writer who engages with religious violence in the imagination for the redemptive goal of human happiness and freedom. For example, in the preface to Blake's *Milton*, whose words have become the lyrics for the hymn "Jerusalem," the speaker calls, "Bring me my bow of burning gold." On Gull's London tour, he passes the house where Blake wrote the poem "London," whose nightmarish vision of suffering in Britain's capital prefigures the blood and suffering of Moore's text. The reference to Blake prompts Gull both to speak on behalf of the power and glory of madness and to announce his own (stroke-induced) vision of God — in his case, Jabulon, the god honored by *From Hell*'s Freemasons, who has commanded him.[11]

As several critics have noted, Blake's visual and verbal art, and especially his combination of the two, are significant precursors to the graphic novel in English. With reference to Moore's graphic novel *Watchmen*, John Whitson has written about how the author deliberately picks up on Blake's notion of "fearful symmetry."[12] Ron Broglio's essay on Blake and the contemporary graphic novel doesn't consider *From Hell* specifically, but he analyzes the usefulness of thinking about Blake the revolutionary poet and printer in relation to the graphic novel in general. Broglio's core assumption that "William Blake is the poet of transformation"[13] is a notion to which Moore himself subscribes wholeheartedly. Here, Moore articulates both Blake's importance for his own text, and his understanding of how Blake transforms London:

> I . . . studied [Blake] seriously when I was researching *From Hell*, my book about Jack the Ripper, which has lots of references to Blake; him seeing a spectre at his house in Hercules Road, for example. Blake represents the visionary heroism of the imagination. He was living in a London which was not much more than a squalid horse toilet, on which he superimposed a magnificent four-fold city and populated it with angels, and philosophers of the past. Art at its best has the power to insist on a different reality.[14]

To call London a "squalid horse toilet" may sound like an exaggeration on Moore's part, but a mid-nineteenth-century scientific study determined that around one hundred tons of animal dung were dropped on London every day.[15] Such statistics also contextualize the muddy streets of Victorian novels, like Charles Dickens's *Bleak House*. In that novel, the city turns young Jo, the dung-removing crossing sweeper whom the authorities are always telling to "move on," into a human animal, a goat being chased out of town, and eventually out of existence. As he is "moving on," even though he has nowhere to go, Jo stops at the base of St. Paul's Cathedral. Dickens's novelistic description is of St. Paul's at dusk, a similar image to the one with which Moore concludes the chapter 4 journey around London of *From Hell* (see Figure 2). Moore and Campbell show St. Paul's from an aerial view — a gull's-eye view — while Jo, Dickens's representative figure of London's hopeless underclass, sees it from below.

The perspectives provided by Moore and Dickens are different,

Figure 2. ***From Hell* 4.38, panel 1**

From Hell © Alan Moore and Eddie Campbell. Published by Top Shelf Productions. Used with permission.

and Dickens is able to include color, but both texts place everyone in the encroaching dark. Here is Dickens's passage, which treats social religious power with irony. It directs the reader's attention first to Jo himself:

> And there he sits, munching and gnawing, and looking up at the great Cross on the summit of St. Paul's Cathedral, glittering above a red and violet-tinted cloud of smoke. From the boy's face one might suppose that sacred emblem to be, in his eyes, the crowning confusion of the great, confused city; so golden, so high up, so far out of his reach. There he sits, the sun going down, the river running fast, the crowd flowing by him in two streams — everything moving on to some purpose and to one end — until he is stirred up and told to "move on" too.[16]

The ceaseless, mindless movement of the city, and the crowd flowing by Jo, reappear in T. S. Eliot's *The Waste Land* (1922), in which a "crowd flowed over London Bridge, so many." As Eliot's own footnote points out,[17] the line alludes to the souls in the vestibule of Hell in Dante's *Inferno*, Canto III, a work that Moore mentions later in his own *From Hell* (whose title comes from an letter written to the police by someone purporting to be Jack the Ripper).

The London from Hell in Moore's work partakes in the same dramatic irony that Dickens highlights by focusing on the "sacred emblem" that is the cross on St. Paul's. This central Christian symbol represents crucifixion, a cruel and violent means of punishing criminals and reinforcing social power, and specifically the self-sacrifice of the Son of God for the redemption of human beings. For Jo, who is to be sacrificed on the altar of societal indifference, it represents only the confusion of the city that creates and then mirrors the confusion in his own mind. In terms of the text, Jo's situation reflects in personified microcosm the confused union of violence and the sacred. London is revealed by these works of literature to be a site of millennia's intertwining of religion and violence, construction and destruction. In his review of *From Hell*, entitled "London Kills Me," Richard Gehr speaks of "Moore's ongoing spiritual archaeology of London and its environs."[18] But, as the author himself is well aware, Moore is far from the first to explore the sacred and desecrated dimensions of the city. These constitute aspects of a city's psychological atmosphere, historically generated, that have been of interest to a group of thinkers who engage in what is termed "psychogeography."

In its origins, psychogeography was a subversive cartographic method developed by the Situationists, a group formed in 1956 to explore a "nascent and collective fascination with urban geography."[19] According to Peta Mitchell, the Situationists deliberately reworked the journey of the "bourgeouis flâneur" into a more radical, creative, subjective, and non-rational urban experience that involves a drifting controlled by the forces of the city. In this experience, however, the person who moves through the urban environment refuses to see the physical aspects of the city merely as concrete manifestations and instead perceives them as social constructions.[20] While the Situationists have faded, psychogeography became popular in London in the latter part of the twentieth century. A hilarious, hat-pin definition of the phenomenon was printed in London's *Time Out* magazine in 2006.[21] This piece mentions novelist and poet Iain Sinclair as a particular renowned high-level practitioner, and in fact Moore credits Sinclair's influence in leading him to the study and incorporation of psychogeography into his text.[22]

Of particular relevance to *From Hell* is Sinclair's novel *White Chappell, Scarlet Tracings*, first published in 1987, which plays with Gull's possible role in the Jack the Ripper murders. Thus, the labyrinthine connections of the London imagination that these authors establish are not just geographical but also textual. For instance, Sinclair mentions "an inscribed copy of Peter Ackroyd's *Hawksmoor*"[23] as well as Stephen Knight's book, *Jack the Ripper: The Final Solution*.[24] Sinclair's narrator, a character in the non-linear, fragmented, time-travelling plot and himself given to meditation on the past and present of London, declares to a sceptical friend, "We must use what we have been given: go back over the Ripper text, turn each cell of it — until it means something else, something beyond us."[25]

Such an interpretive activity suggests a quasi-psychogeographical approach to reading itself. The standard early definition of psychogeography is that it consists of the "study of the specific effects of the geographical environment, consciously organized or not, on the emotions and behavior of individuals."[26] Moore speaks of it in very similar terms, describing psychogeography as "recognizing that how we see the landscape that we live in makes us what we are." Moore gives some examples that suggest both the religious and political elements of psychogeography: "If you're living in a gorgeous temple, you're thinking,

'Hang on — I'm in a temple, I'm probably a god!' But if you put somebody in a tower block, and it's a shitheap, you're gonna subconsciously
take in the message: 'Hey, I'm living in a shitheap, I'm probably a shit.'"[27]
(Or, as in the case of Dickens's Jo described above: the city doesn't
want me and I don't understand it; I must be an animal, not a citizen.)
Moore, who has also written psychogeographically about his hometown
of Northampton in *Voice of the Fire* (2003)[28] and in the forthcoming novel
Jerusalem,[29] finally sums it up: "Our environment, and our response to it,
creates us."[30] The texts that we read constitute part of our environment,
and what we read and how we respond to our reading also "creates us."
In fact, as textual scholars, this phenomenon of audience response
sometimes becomes an object of our study.

The graphic novel is a particular kind of text. Examining *From Hell*
among other graphic texts in "London Khoragraphic," Julian Wolfrey
argues, "Something is clearly at work in the graphic novel, having to do
with the visionary evocation of what we are tempted to describe as the
spirit of London."[31] This spirit of London finds its way into *From Hell*
itself. It's a huge, heavy, dark tome of a book in its final collected form
(although it was originally published in installments in the comic series
Taboo between 1991 and 1996).[32] In its Top Shelf edition, it weighs nearly
three pounds. As Peter Ackroyd says of Blake's poem "London," which
he terms an "urban lament": "Thus the experience of London becomes
deep and sonorous."[33] *From Hell* reveals London to be a sacred space,
or, rather, a site of competing sacred spaces overlaid on one another in
multiple dimensions, including geography, archaeology, architecture,
image, text, and intertext.

One striking consequence of this multidimensionality is that the
graphic text itself becomes a site of religious resonance and dissonance,
to which the reader must pay close, even self-conscious attention if she
is to make sense of what is going on. Alan Moore claims in interviews that
his own moment of religious, or "magical," awakening happened as he was
writing the text for a panel of chapter 4 (see Figure 3). Moore said:

> One word balloon in *From Hell* completely hijacked my life. A character
> says something like, 'The one place gods inarguably exist is in the
> human mind'. After I wrote that, I realised I'd accidentally made a
> true statement, and now I'd have to rearrange my entire life around
> it. The only thing that seemed to really be appropriate was to become
> a magician.[34]

Figure 3. *From Hell* 4.18, panels 1–3

From Hell © Alan Moore and Eddie Campbell. Published by Top Shelf Productions. Used with permission.

As with Augustine, the text itself (although in this case the author's own creation, not the Bible) acts as a catalyst for conversion. Moore's most elaborate discussion of what leads up to his conversion moment can be found in his interview with Eddie Campbell, printed in *The Disease of Language*, whose title comes from Aleister Crowley's definition of magic.[35] The relationship between religion and magic is notoriously difficult to articulate, and it remains highly dependent on personal worldview. Graham Cunningham says that "the sacred" is a term that can be used to describe both, but we haven't thereby elided the terminology problem, as different people will still have different notions about what constitutes "real" religion or "real" magic.[36] Objects and practices sacred to one group may be abominations to another. Even for supposedly neutral scholars of religion, definitions continue to elude. Moore's text seizes, at least momentarily, on one way of understanding the relationship between the individual psyche and the real power of supernatural entities.

The panel discussed here (Figure 3) appears almost exactly in the middle of chapter 4 of *From Hell*, on a page facing a map of London. The title of the chapter is biblical — "What doth the Lord require of thee?" — and is excerpted from a prophetic verse, part of which is inscribed on the real William Gull's grave: "He hath shewed thee, O man, what is good; and what doth the LORD require of thee, but to do justly, and to love mercy, and to walk humbly with thy God?" (Micah 6.8). Yet, what the William Gull of Moore's book believes the Lord requires of him is a far grander and more gruesome enterprise than this scripture would suggest.

In the chapter, the reader encounters some of London's supposedly sacred places, as well as its history of consecration, sacrifice, desacralization, and desecration. It is an integral part of the larger work that shows how human and non-human forces imagine and sometimes actually create these religious phenomena. This demonstration is all filtered through the imagination of the graphic novel's creators, who work with a changing urban environment where many gods have been worshipped and where many real human beings have encountered violent deaths. In this chapter, previous to the murders, Sir William Gull drives around the city with his coachman, John Netley. Gull takes Netley (and Moore takes the reader) on a disturbing journey, a circling and disorienting ride through the end of matriarchy and the significance of Freemasonry, of architecture, and of magic. All this is sketched out in Eddie Campbell's black and white, energetic, restless, scored parallel lines; cross-hatchings; and blocks of black and white (see Figure 4).

In this series of panels, the reader sees Gull and Netley, dressed as an upper-class gentleman and a working-class Londoner respectively, as they travel around the city by horse and coach. Netley holds the horse's reins, but Gull controls the direction of movement, as well as the development of the conversation. Here, he argues that London, like Diana (both the ancient goddess and — in a subtle flash-forward not perceived by the characters themselves — the twentieth-century princess), is "symbol, history and myth." Diana stands in metonymically for Goddess worship in general. Princess Diana was married at

Figure 4. **From Hell 4.6, panels 4–6**

From Hell © Alan Moore and Eddie Campbell. Published by Top Shelf Productions. Used with permission.

St. Paul's Cathedral, Gull and Netley's final destination, and once pos-sibly the site of a temple dedicated to the worship of the goddess Diana.[37] In his dialogue with Netley, Gull employs a range of rhetorical strategies, including the use of rhetorical questions, parallels, genuine questions to his audience, and an ominous coerciveness in his insistence, "you'll agree." On the next page, Gull continues to expound on the powers of London (see Figure 5).

Echoing Sinclair's narrator in *White Chappell, Scarlet Tracings,* Gull proclaims the possibility of creating new works out of old texts — just as Moore himself is doing precisely that. The physician (and the novel writer) combine the persuasive power of Latinate, scientific vocabu-lary ("veritable," "formulating") with the straightforward strength of monosyllabic Old English words. The words of panel 1 here also invert normal English syntax so that the rhetorical question can end on the resonant weight of the name of "London": "Do you begin to grasp how truly great a work is London? A veritable textbook we may draw upon in formulating great works of our own!" Another reason for this inver-sion is that it enables Gull, and Moore, to establish a subtle incantatory iambic rhythm:

$$x \quad / \quad x \quad / \quad x \quad / \quad \quad x \quad / \quad x$$
Do you begin to grasp how truly
$$/ \quad x \quad / \quad x \quad / \quad x$$
great a work is London?

Figure 5. ***From Hell* 4.9, panels 1–3**

From Hell © Alan Moore and Eddie Campbell. Published by Top Shelf Productions. Used with permission.

```
x  / x / x   /   x   /
A veritable textbook we
  x   /  x  /  x  /  x /  x
may draw upon in formulating
  /    /   x  x   /
great works of our own!
```

The exception to the iambs is the spondaic reinforcement of "great works," which picks up on the key word "great" with its indication of Gull's maniacal obsession with personal greatness. The phrase "Great Work" is also the alternative title for a published version of Masonic rituals,[38] as well as a term used in ceremonial magick to refer to the "culmination of all magickal work . . . the process of refining the mind and soul to create as perfect and effective a human as possible."[39]

Gull's primary aim throughout the novel is to gain access to masculine power. In order to achieve this, he first turns the city into a cryptic religious text that he can decipher by associating its stones with symbols and also with syllables (see Figure 6). Gull's claim, "Encoded in this city's stones are symbols thunderous enough to rouse the sleeping Gods submerged beneath the sea-bed of our dreams,"[40] derives its own encoded power partly from the fact that it is a disguised but perfect iambic tetrameter quatrain, whose familiar rhythm, sometimes known as ballad meter or hymn meter (employed in Blake's "London," for example), works on the reader's unconscious:

```
x  /  x  /  x  / x   /
Encoded in this city's stones
x  /  x  /  x  / x  /
are symbols thunderous enough
x  /  x  /  x  /  x   /
to rouse the sleeping Gods submerged
x  /  x  /  x  / x   /
beneath the sea-bed of our dreams.
```

Such snippets of verse continue to appear. In one instance, as Gull explains the mythological significance of Cleopatra's Needle to Netley, a sequence of mostly rhyming alexandrines appears — certainly not great poetry, but effective nonetheless:

Figure 6. ***From Hell*** **4.19, panels 4–6**

From Hell © Alan Moore and Eddie Campbell. Published by Top Shelf Productions.
Used with permission.

> He who'd wield it would the BEST of tailors be,
>> To do its work; increase the Sun God's sovereignty . . .
>> . . . call down the sun itself: touch Earth with Atum's purifying light
> that all might know his majesty.[41]

The single epigraph to chapter 4 indicates that Moore was well aware of
the impact of his subtle insertions of verse into his text. The epigraph's
lines are excerpted from one of the first texts on architecture, written
by Vitruvius in the first century BCE:

> Writing on architecture is not like history or poetry . . .. Poetry, with
> its measures and metrical feet, its refinement in the arrangement of
> words, and the delivery in verse of the sentiments expressed by several

characters to one another, delights the feeling of the reader, and leads
him smoothly on to the very end of the work.[42]

Moore, through Gull, equates stone with symbols, and declares, "Their
language speaks direct to our unconscious mind."[43] Speaking of
Hawksmoor's London churches, he equates architecture with poetry:
"THERE's magic, . . . Aye, and Poetry! As true as any bard he spoke
his soul, in syllables of stone reverberating down the centuries."[44]
Such claims resonate with those of Peter Ackroyd (author of the novel
Hawksmoor), who in *London: The Biography* writes about the mystery of the
city's name, and declares, "With its syllabic power, so much suggesting
force or thunder, it has continually echoed throughout history."[45]

Large parts of *From Hell*'s fourth chapter constitute a rare medium, for
which the true precursor is Blake: graphic poetry, conceived architectur-
ally, "with its measures and metrical feet," its own morbid "syllables of
stone." Its rhythms carry the reader along hypnotically — "delight[ing]
the feeling of the reader, and lead[ing] him smoothly on to the very
end of the work." The reader is subtly seduced by Gull's rhetoric, even
while the absurdity, the misogyny, and the violence of his narrative repel.
Caught between these forces of attraction and repulsion, the reader is
forced to read actively in order to resist the undertow of the linguistic
unconscious. Reading the chapter is like being at sea in London, a city
built where the sea once was. The intense hybridity of the text (architecture, history, fiction, art, verse), and the multiple directions of its visual
lines that send the reader's gaze in conflicting directions, enhance this
effect. Reading it gives you motion sickness; it is nauseating. Netley complains of feeling sick, and Gull suggests that "these stones and symbols'
morbid airs [have] afflicted you. Their language speaks directly to our
unconscious mind."[46]

Indeed, Gull and Netley's journey, and Moore and Campbell's chapter, conclude with Netley vomiting on the pavement of London while
Gull declares that Netley's "destiny" is "inscribed" there.[47] In other
words, fate is written on the stones in partially digested kidney and
human bile.[48] Blood, vomit, horse-dung, and ink run together. The
horrible power of this sequence, prefiguring the greater horror of
the murders themselves, is engraved in its images and incorporated
into the language. The syllables of this text and the stones of Nicholas
Hawksmoor's and Christopher Wren's churches all become associated.
Is the text itself then asking us to support Gull, as Netley does, on his

supposedly God-given mission to murder and mutilate women? No, obviously it is not — but it is pushing its readers towards a conscious consideration of this horrible question.

From Hell requires the reader to be a better, more *comprehending* reader than Netley, who is illiterate ("uh, with respect, sir . . . I can't read"[49]), but it also warns us not to be an overinterpreting, *gullible* reader like Gull. It turns out that Moore is writing a subtle morality tale: read a text, and read the world; understand them as deeply you can, but don't see things that aren't there. Don't swallow other people's fanciful interpretations, and do not force your own interpretation on anyone else. In tandem, the text also implies: don't be naïve about the power of religious history and the power of the gods in the human psyche, but don't force your gods on other people. (Moore takes for his own object of veneration a pre-Christian snake god, Glycon — in origin apparently a fake, a puppet — and he is clear that he doesn't want his magic religion to have any other followers.[50] As Brian says to the hordes hungry for their prophet's teachings in Monty Python's *The Life of Brian* (1979): "Look. You've got it all wrong. You don't need to follow me. You don't need to follow anybody! You've got to think for yourselves. You're all individuals!" Of course, they respond in collective union: "Yes, we are all individuals!"[51]) In his own exemplification of the necessary balance between skepticism and acuity, Moore has spoken about the pentacle that Gull inscribes on a map of London, outlining the magical shape that the places he has visited create when the dots are joined:

> It struck me when I got around to the London pentacle and I actually had people saying, 'Is that real?' And I was saying yes and no. Those sites are really there, they do line up like I say they do, they do have the significance that I apply to them. Do I believe that a group of Freemasons got together to map London into the shape of a diabolical pentacle? Of course not. I don't believe bollocks like that. Do I believe that the pentacle has meaning and relevance? Of course I do.[52]

Julian Wolfreys argues that the graphic novel about London with its pentacle and other spatial mappings of city space, complete with gaps, produces "the uncanny." He acknowledges that this phenomenon is, by its very nature, impossible to pin down, but it can be defined as "a representation of a mental state of projection that precisely elides the boundaries of the real and the unreal to provoke a disturbing ambiguity, a slippage between waking and dreaming."[53] Lisa Coppin conducts a psychoanalytic reading of how *From Hell* creates "the uncanny" through its manipulation of the characters' vision and the reader's gaze.[54] This technique is the graphic novel's equivalent to free indirect discourse. When one sees the world, natural and supernatural, through Gull's eyes, one is seeing through the eyes of a madman and a murderer. Unless she simply puts down the book and refuses to take it up and read it again, the reader recognizes the power of evil in her own imagination. That evil can take different forms: it may seek power over the Other, like Gull, or it may abdicate responsibility and follow orders, like Netley the coachman. Manifested in the extreme at the personal level, such evil can lead to serial killings or at least complicity in them. Manifested in the extreme at the societal level, such evil leads to genocide. Chapter 5, which follows upon Gull and Netley's journey, begins with the conception of Adolf Hitler and his mother's premonition of horror. Moore ties in this episode with the graphic novel's examination of both anti-Semitism in late-nineteenth-century Victorian London and the part it played in the Jack the Ripper investigations.

If read with the requisite combination of empathy and awareness, Alan Moore and Eddie Campbell's work brings home to the reader the reality of cruelty and its human abode within each person, including oneself. This graphic novel, like many horror books and movies, is at least partially intended to thrill the reader or viewer by providing a voyeuristic satisfaction through the witnessing of violence. At the same time as entertaining in this ethically dubious way, *From Hell* condemns the murders and points toward both writerly and readerly complicity in them as well as in human violence of all kinds. This human tendency towards violence is also the force that René Girard sees as central to social dynamics and the operations of human religious practice. Yet Moore's presentation of Gull's activities can be read as illustrating the ultimate ineffectiveness of sacrificial scapegoating; the death of the victims does not prevent hideous future violence.

In *From Hell*, an examination of London's bloody history illustrates how the urban landscape, its confluences of the violence and the sacred, can influence the lives and minds of those who come to inhabit it. More profoundly, it shows how the landscape of the imagination, including the literary imagination, affects the lives of those who enter there — including its authors. Asked by Eddie Campbell himself about the importance of psychogeography in *From Hell*, Alan Moore acknowledges that it led him "further into the realm of magical thinking and magical ideas" culminating in the revelation he had as he wrote the panel about gods existing in the human mind.[55] This graphic novel, in postmodernist fashion, renders unstable the boundaries between fact and fiction, world and text, natural and supernatural, the real and the imaginary, the sacred and the desecrated, and even the awesome and the awful. These deconstructions necessitate the reader's own moral self-examination. As Moore says, in reference to Blake, "Art at its best has the power to insist on a different reality." It also may also insist, as *From Hell* does, that the consumer of the art consider her own role in the reality that is, and the better reality that may be.

Notes

1 Alan Moore (w) and Eddie Campbell (a), *From Hell* (Marletta, GA: Top Shelf Productions, 2000).
2 See, for example, Matthew T Evans, "The Sacred: Differentiating, Clarifying and Extending Concepts," *Review of Religious Research* 45:1 (2003): 32–47 and N. J. Demerath, III, "The Varieties of Sacred Experience: Finding the Sacred in a Secular Grove" (Presidential Address): Society for the Scientific Study of Religion, November 6, 1999. Boston, MA).
3 Émile Durkheim, *The Elementary Forms of Religious Life*, trans. Karen Elise Fields (New York: Simon & Schuster, 1995), 34.
4 René Girard, *Violence and the Sacred*, trans. Patrick Gregory (Baltimore: Johns Hopkins University Press, 1977), 8.
5 Girard, 31.
6 Ninian Smart, *Dimensions of the Sacred* (Berkeley: University of California Press, 1996), 142.
7 William Wordsworth, "Residence in London," *The Prelude* (1850), Book Seventh (London: Oxford UP, 1932), 221–5.
8 Moore, Campbell, *From Hell*, 4.28, panel 1.
9 Stephen Knight, *Jack the Ripper: The Final Solution* (New York: McKay, 1976).
10 Peter Ackroyd, *London: The Biography* (London: Vintage, 2001), 504.
11 Moore, Campbell, *From Hell*, 4.22, panels 1–3.
12 Roger Whitson, "Panelling Parallax: The Fearful Symmetry of Alan Moore and William Blake," *ImageTexT: Interdisciplinary Comics Studies* 3.2 (2007), http://www.english.ufl.edu/imagetext/archives/v3_2/whitson/ (accessed April 5, 2008).
13 Ron Broglio, "William Blake and the Novel Space of Revolution," *ImageTexT: Interdisciplinary Comics Studies* 3.2 (2007). http://www.english.ufl.edu/imagetext/archives/v3_2/broglio/ (accessed April 6, 2008).
14 Quoted in Neil Spencer, "Into the mystic: Visions of paradise to words of wisdom . . . an homage to the written work of William Blake," *Observer*, October 22, 2000, http://books.guardian.co.uk/departments/classics/story/0,,386024,00.html (accessed April 5, 2008).
15 Henry Mayhew, "Of the Horse-Dung of the Streets of London," in Charles Dickens, *Bleak House* (New York: Norton, 1977), 904–6.
16 Charles Dickens, *Bleak House* (New York: Norton, 1977), 243–4.

17 TS Eliot, *The Waste Land, Collected Poems* (New York: Harcourt Brace, 1963), 71. Footnote to line 63.

18 Richard Gehr, "London Kills Me," *Village Voice*, February 29, 2000, http://www.villagevoice.com/books/0009,gehr,12715,10.html (accessed April 4, 2008).

19 Peta Mitchell, *Cartographic Strategies of Postmodernity: The Figure of the Map in Contemporary Theory and Fiction* (New York: Routledge, 2008), 118.

20 Mitchell, 118–20.

21 Peter Watts, "Bluffer's Guide: Psychogeography," *Time Out*, September 5, 2006, http://www.timeout.com/london/features/1940/Bluffer-s_guide-Psychogeography.html (accessed May 2, 2009).

22 Alan Moore (w) and Eddie Campbell (a), *A Disease of Language* (London: Knockabout, 2005), 116. See also Alan Moore, "Eroto-Graphic Mania," Interview by Peter Murphy, *New Review* (2006), http://www.laurahird.com/newreview/alanmooreinterview.html (accessed April 5, 2008).

23 Iain Sinclair, *White Chappell, Scarlet Tracings* (London: Penguin, 2004), 12. I have an inscribed copy of Ackroyd's *London: The Biography* on my desk as I write this.

24 Sinclair, 47.

25 Sinclair, 181.

26 "Definitions," *Situationist International Anthology*, ed. Ken Knabb (Berkeley: Bureau of Public Secrets, 1981), 45. Originally published as "Définitions," *Internationale Situationniste* 1 (1958).

27 Moore, "Eroto-Graphic Mania."

28 Alan Moore, *Voice of the Fire* (Marletta, GA: Top Shelf Productions, 2003).

29 Nic Rigby, "Comic legend keeps true to roots," BBC News, Northampton, March 21, 2008, http://news.bbc.co.uk/2/hi/entertainment/7307303.stm (accessed July 3, 2009).

30 Moore, "Eroto-Graphic Mania."

31 Julian Wolfreys, "London Khorographic," *ImageTexT: Interdisciplinary Comics Studies* 1.2 (2004), http://www.english.ufl.edu/imagetext/archives/v1_2/wolfreys/ (accessed April 4, 2008).

32 Grand Comic Books Database, http://www.comics.org/series.lasso?SeriesID=13561.

33 Peter Ackroyd, "The London that Became Jerusalem," *Times Online*, March 3, 2007, http://entertainment.timesonline.co.uk/tol/arts_and_entertainment/books/biography/article1461686.ece (accessed April 5, 2008).

34 Steve Rose, "Moore's murderer," *Guardian*, February 2, 2002, http://books.guardian.co.uk/departments/sciencefiction/story/0,6000,643500,00.html (accessed April 5, 2008). See also "Alan Moore Interview" with Brad Stone, *Comic Book Resources News*, October 22, 2008, http://www.comicbookresources.com/?page=article&id=511 (accessed April 5, 2008).

35 Moore, Campbell, *A Disease of Language*, 112–13.

36 Graham Cunningham, *Religion and Magic: Approaches and Theories* (New York: New York UP, 1999), vii.

37 There is another odd life/plot coincidence here. Princess Diana, still alive at the time of Moore's writing, was a woman who bore children to a prince, the son of the Queen, and who — according to generally discredited conspiracy theorists — was murdered by the secret orders of the Royal Family to prevent a scandal.

38 Albert Pike, *Magnum Opus or the Great Work* (Kila, MT: Kessinger Publishing, 1992). Facsimile of 1857 edition.

39   Paul Tuitéan and Estelle Daniels, *Essential Wicca* (Freedom, CA: Crossing Press, 2001), 358.

40   Moore, Campbell, *From Hell*, 4.19.

41   Moore, Campbell, *From Hell*, 4.21.

42   Vitruvius, *The Ten Books on Architecture* (Cambridge, MA: Harvard, 1914), 129, http://www.gutenberg.org/files/20239/20239-h/29239-h.htm (accessed October 21, 2009).

43   Moore, Campbell, *From Hell*, 4.23.

44   Moore, Campbell, *From Hell*, 4.26.

45   Ackroyd, *London*, 11.

46   Moore, Campbell, *From Hell*, 4.23.

47   Moore, Campbell, *From Hell*, 4.37.

48   And Gull is not incorrect; Netley will eventually die bloodily upon London's streets.

49   Moore, Campbell, *From Hell*, 4.9.

50   Moore, Campbell, *A Disease of Language*, 114, 126.

51   Except for one ironically non-conformist conformist who says he is *not* an individual.

52   Alan Moore, "The Alan Moore Interview," with David Kendall, abbreviated version, *The Edge* Old Series #5, http://www.theedge.abelgratis.co.uk/mooreiview.htm (accessed April 5, 2008).

53   Wolfreys, "London Khorographic."

54   Lisa Coppin, "Looking Inside Out: The vision as particular gaze in *From Hell*," *Image & Narrative* (January 2003), http://www.imageandnarrative.be/uncanny/lisacoppin.htm (accessed April 5, 2008).

55   Moore, Campbell, *A Disease of Language*, 116.

Drawing Contracts: Will Eisner's Legacy

LAURENCE ROTH

[Editor's note: An earlier version of this essay appeared in the *Jewish Quarterly Review* 97.3 (Summer 2007): 463-484.]

ON JANUARY 5, 2005, THE *New York Times* published its obituary for Will Eisner, one of the most lauded figures in the world of comics and graphic novels, who had died three days earlier in Fort Lauderdale, Florida, after quadruple bypass surgery. On January 6, the *Times* ran the following correction: "An obituary of the innovative comic-page illustrator Will Eisner yesterday included an imprecise comparison in some copies between his character The Spirit and others, including Batman. Unlike Superman and some other heroes of the comics, Batman relied on intelligence and skill, not supernatural powers."[1] One can only imagine the torrent of e-mails from comics fans pointing out this crucial difference, one that makes even more apt the comparison between Bob Kane's dour, night-stalking, masked detective and the dapper, night-stalking, masked detective who made Eisner famous in the early 1940s. Both were human rather than superhuman heroes, and so exemplified a different kind of balance between the "archetypal" and the "typical" — Umberto Eco's terms for the mythic and the mimetic dimensions of comic book characters.[2] Weighted more toward the mimetic, they intimated, even in their earliest incarnations, that comic book protagonists and stories were capable of transcending stereotype and reflecting temporal progression and psychological depth.

Eisner retired *The Spirit* in 1952, tired of the demands of a formulaic comic strip. His subsequent turn to educational and commercial work in the 1950s and 1960s was, in a sense, a waiting period — waiting for comic books to catch up to him, waiting for the right opportunity to explore characters and stories in a more innovative manner. That period ended in 1972 when, inspired by the protest and social ideas of underground and adult comics of the 1960s and early 1970s,[3] Eisner took up specifically Jewish characters and topics in a new comics form, for which he employed the name "graphic novel." As he says in the introduction to *The Contract with God Trilogy*, W. W. Norton's 2006 collection of his first three graphic novels, Eisner employed that term in homage to the "serious" wordless picture novels produced by Otto Nückel, Franz Masereel, and Lynd Ward, and as a sales tool to pitch his work, unsuccessfully as it turned out, to a mainstream publisher.[4] Eisner, of course, was not the first to use "graphic novel" to describe comic books that employ the narrative strategies and character development of full-length literary fiction, but he was quick to recognize how to capitalize on the possibilities that literary comic books presented. Such a new mode of popular literature provided the right vehicle through which to tell stories about the world of his childhood, and it offered him a belated opportunity to address the challenges of both cultural and formal change.

The Contract with God Trilogy illustrates how he tackled that opportunity and so prompts this essay's consideration of his legacy. While neither Joann Sfar's *The Rabbi's Cat* nor JT Waldman's *Megillat Esther* owe any specific visual or narrative debt to Eisner's work, they both exemplify his legacy in that they use the creative potential inherent in the comics medium as analogous to, and a commentary on, the creative potential inherent in contemporary Jewish culture and religiosity. Eisner was the first to show how that could be done; he used his own experiences as the son of Jewish immigrants to show how the language of comics art — of "sequential art" as he called it — could not only give voice to complex, socially aware characters and stories, but also marshal powerful arguments about collective self-representation.

This is not to say that Eisner's experiences or his work exemplify how a subterranean Jewishness infiltrated the form and social functions of the graphic novel, nor do they illustrate the genealogy and aesthetics of a "Jewish graphic novel." The graphic novel, after all, is no more Jewish than the novel is Spanish or English or Russian. To appreciate how Eisner and contemporary Jewish graphic novelists employ the language of comics for literary ends, one needs to avoid the old trap of simply arguing for the special case of Jewish writers or the special status of Jewishness within cultural products. As Stephen Burt has pointed out, the ideal model of comics criticism — one not all that different from the ideal model of literary criticism — takes form as well as content into account, and must "acknowledge both the exceptional and the typical, exploring both writers' choices and commercial or cultural meanings, without neglecting comics form."[5] Eisner's melding of the vocabulary of comics with film noir composition and social commentary in *The Contract with God Trilogy* and in *To the Heart of the Storm* evidences a visual critique of the American exceptionalism — the cultural chauvinism that fueled the rise of superhero comics — and of a Jewish exceptionalism hard pressed by the immigrant experience.

In other words, the special contracts promised between America and its citizens and between Jews and their God are redrawn by Eisner as distinctly unglamorous and unfulfilled agreements. Eisner's signal accomplishment as an American Jewish writer/artist is his fortuitous and unique yoking of subject matter to form: in order to survive in an ever-changing open market, he seems to argue, both comic books and Jews must progress beyond heroics and toward aesthetic, cultural, and social renegotiation and redevelopment.

A Contract with God (first published by Kitchen Sink Press in 1978 and republished in 2006 by W. W. Norton as part of *The Contract with God Trilogy: Life on Dropsie Avenue*) is a series of four interlocked short stories — "A Contract with God," "The Street Singer," "The Super," and "Cookalein" — that revolve around the residents of 55 Dropsie Avenue. The title story concerns the tenement owner, Frimmeh Hersh, who as a young orphan in a Russian shtetl is selected by the village elders to go to America because of his many good deeds and because he is thought to be favored by God. On his way to the seaport, he asks his guardian whether God is just and whether He knows that Hersh has been good. Assured that God knows everything, Hersh decides to write a contract with God on a stone, a none-too-subtle redrawing of the *shnei luchot ha-berit*, the two tablets of the covenant given to Moses and Israel at Mt. Sinai.

In America, Hersh finds a home within the Hasidic community and continues to do good deeds, one of which is adopting a baby girl left on his doorstep. He loves her dearly, but when she dies Hersh considers his contract with God broken; he is no longer obligated to be an observant Jew, and he tosses his stone out the window. Looking out only for himself and cutting every moral corner there is, Hersh becomes just another immigrant on the make in New York City. He takes a *shikse* mistress whose drinking, card playing, and offers to convert reflect the shabbiness of his secular life. Unhappy, he decides to draw a new contract, promising himself, rededicated, that he will "make a new life."[6] Almost immediately, Hersh has a heart attack and dies. In the story's epilogue, however, Shloime, a young Hasidic Jew living in 55 Dropsie, finds the contract and exclaims, "I will keep it!"[7] The final full-page panel pictures Shloime sitting on the front steps of the tenement, his face in deep shadow, the steps lit in bright contrast by the glare of a streetlamp. The play of light and dark suggests that Shloime will repeat Hersh's battle.

Eisner acknowledges in the Norton preface that the story reflects the loss of his 16-year-old daughter Alice to leukemia eight years before, and that its creation "was an exercise in personal agony."[8] Hersh reflected Eisner's anguish, and "his argument with God was also mine."[9] Read in light of Eisner's Depression-era adolescence and acknowledgment that his favorite writers were Maupassant, Gorky, and O. Henry,[10] this tragedy illuminates Eisner's hard-boiled take on life and religion, and it helps explain why his story evokes literary realism, even a kind of naturalism. In *Contract*, life is a matter of conflict and survival, and humans often behave as if they were only higher order animals. Through Hersh, readers learn, as Eisner claimed all people learned during the Depression, "how little control we have over human destiny — despite our technology and innovation."[11] As for God and Judaism, Eisner observed in an interview that "most religions I'm familiar with assure us that there exists a compact between man and deity under which each has certain obligations. Well, so far I have yet to be convinced that both parties have truly lived up to and delivered on this agreement."[12] Hersh exemplifies the fallibility of the human partner in this compact, as does Eddie the street singer, Mr. Scuggs the ironically named "super" (both gentiles), and Benny the Catskills Lothario, all of whom fall short in their moral and ethical obligations.

Eisner's book quite literally casts a dark shadow on the meaning of heroism in comics and among immigrant Jews. The rain-soaked chiaroscuro, the vertical emphasis, and the off-kilter point of view of Eisner's street-scene and tenement panels, borrowed from film noir, were similar in kind, if not in style, to depictions in superhero comics of Gotham City or Metropolis. In *Contract*, however, the urban setting limits the characters' horizons, traps them (see Figure 1); it is not a backdrop or

Figure 1

foil for a larger-than-city-life protagonist. There is no one to save the day in Eisner's stories, no one who speaks for truth or justice, and the American way is simply to accrue capital and social prestige. Those characters who do good, like Hersh and Herbie the medical student in "Cookalein" who helps a rape victim, are depicted as eventually betrayed by life or as nobodies whose "heroic" conduct is the product of self-interest or neighborly concern — but not any special relationship with a Jewish God.

By focusing on the unexceptional about America and Jews, on the commonality of disappointment, powerlessness, and provisional success, Eisner fashions his graphic novel as a medium with which to explore the vernacular and the everyday. Others were taking comic books in similar directions — Harvey Pekar's *American Splendor*, first published in 1976, also visualizes an anti-heroic Jewish everyman in American life. But as *A Life Force* (1988) illustrates even better than *Contract*, Eisner contributed to the deepening of comics characters and narratives by making public and private memory — of the Depression, of Jewish acculturation, of the Bronx — a subject of his stories because it is an indispensable predicate for survival.

Chapter 1, "Izzy the Cockroach and the Meaning of Life," introduces readers to the main protagonist of the book, the carpenter Jacob Shtarkah. After five years building a study-hall for his synagogue, Shtarkah is fired upon its completion. On his way home, he suffers a mild heart attack that brings him, in an obvious homage to Kafka, face to face with a cockroach that has also fallen on its back. Asking what constitutes the difference between a man and a cockroach, Shtarkah meditates on the reason for life in a way that, through the use of bold-face typography, translates into English a rhythm-memory of vocalized, singsong Yiddish and Talmudic reasoning (see Figure 2): "If . . . *man created God* . . . then the *reason* for life is only in the *mind* of *man!!* . . . *If*, on the other hand, *God created man* . . . then the *reason* for living is still *only* a *guess!* . . . After all is said and done . . . *who* really *knows* the will of God?? *So*, in *either* case, both *man* and *cockroach* are in *serious trouble!*"[13] Though Shtarkah comes up with a reason for *dying* when he protects the life of the cockroach from an unmindful, quickly angered passerby who nearly steps on it, the opening chapter ends with no answer regarding their difference. Both man and cockroach pick themselves up and walk away, linked together "because staying alive seems to be the *only* thing on which *everybody* agrees."[14]

Figure 2

Using Shtarkah as a focal point to show what is necessary for survival, Eisner leads readers through eleven chapters of family conflict, grudging compromises, and inventive collaborations. The penultimate survival story in the book is that of Shtarkah's rescue and courtship of a long-lost girlfriend trapped in Nazi Germany. The initial exchange of letters between him and Frieda Gold brings back memories of Shtarkah's youth in Germany and of all the possibilities for the future that are now closed off to him. Using his new network of connections, including gentile son-in-law banker Evan Shaftsbury and the local mob boss, Shtarkah brings Frieda over and gives her a job as secretary and bookkeeper at his lumberyard. Though she initially resists his advances, Shtarkah persists, explaining that with a daughter marrying out of the religion and a wife with whom he shares nothing, "just existing . . . day to day,"[15] he and Frieda have a chance to start over and make a new future together.

As in *Contract*, such a new start proves a chimera. Shtarkah asks his wife for a divorce and leaves her, but his first night with Frieda is sexually disappointing. When Frieda later receives a letter from the Jewish Agency saying that her daughter has made it to Palestine but is ill and needs her mother's help, Frieda insists on going alone. She must remain a dream for Shtarkah, who will have to settle for a future of maybes, which is, as he says, "*more* than a cockroach has!!"[16] Returned to his overbearing and demanding wife, Shtarkah is reminded by her, "we still got *cockroaches* in the house!!"[17] He then throws his insect familiar out the window and prepares to pick himself up once again, though, as the facing page suggests with its flat description of the cockroach's life cycle, the question of what separates a man from a cockroach — a question now shadowed by memories of the Depression and the Holocaust, and so more appropriate here than in the frontispiece — still remains. The issue also begs another, final question about Eisner's immigrant Jewish everyman: is a Jacob Shtarkah a *shtarker mentsch*, a strong man wrestling through the night, or, taking idiomatic Yiddish as our guide, just another *shtarker*, another mindless brute muddling through life?

Remembering, renegotiating, surviving — this is the pattern inked by the life force moving through Eisner's Bronx. The relation of that pattern, and of Eisner's redrawing of contracts, to comics art is given overt illustration in *To the Heart of the Storm* (1991). The book is Eisner's thinly disguised autobiography and a work that addresses the question of why those on the edge of the storm of hatred in Europe — American Jews and Americans in general — went to war against fascism. The book opens with Willie, the young Will Eisner, on a troop train headed to a training camp; the chapters that follow are flashbacks recounting his and his father's life stories, as well as the varieties of anti-Semitism they encountered. Willie draws to escape from these slights and outright insults, but in the end Eisner pictures Willie in the dark of a comic book studio, surrounded by the haze of speech balloons that have drifted into nothing.[18] Superhero comics are fantasies, and the only recourse for real action against prejudice and bigotry — and for ensuring survival — is to take his place in the army, to head in to the heart of the storm. Willie is no hero in this respect; this is simply the unexceptional imperative of the times. By implication, the graphic novel as Eisner envisioned it, in and through which his critique is made possible, must also take its place in history. Indeed, the "graphic novel" (or "literary comic" or "graphic narrative") as a form of mimetic literature would be hard to imagine were it not for this very memory of the inadequacy of superhero comic books.

Eisner's graphic novels are complex examples of the ways that form and content feed off each other and illuminate the cultural work of comics innovation. He created an instructive analogy in them: the intelligent protagonists of his graphic novels must continually renegotiate and redevelop their fictional worlds, just as comics writers and artists must continually renegotiate and redevelop their medium. That the fulcrum for his analogy is Jewish life in America puts him in company with contemporaries such as Saul Bellow, Herman Wouk, Bernard Malamud, Grace Paley, and Philip Roth.

Yet Eisner addressed the acculturation of immigrant Jews using both narrative and visual culture, a different perspective from that of his more "literary" peers and one that focuses attention on the ideological work of comics. Though Eisner's graphic novels critique and redraw the contracts between America and its citizens as well as between Jews and their God, they never abrogate those contracts. Eisner's works teach a contradictory sort of social and cultural accommodation, one that flirts with political consciousness (the relationship, for example, between toxic bigotries and various forms of reactionary politics), but that settles for promoting an enlightened civic consciousness — Eisner's valorization of the neighborhood as a "fraternity held together by memories,"[19] a small-scale arena for the exercise of community bonds and duties. Unlike Bellow's old system, wherein a sentimental humanism lends dignity to the absurdity of religious and social contracts, or Paley's loudest voice, whose shouted agreement with the terms of those contracts prods laughter at them, Eisner's neighborhood, focused on survival, is a place of restraint, not parody, and limitation, not philosophical skepticism.

That is a legacy of the Depression-inspired superhero comic, in which serving the greater good involves the conservation of private property and consists of many local acts of neighborly virtue. Both Richard Reynolds and Bradford Wright have noted this aspect of superhero comics,[20] but Umberto Eco puts it most succinctly when he asks: why is it that Jerry Siegel and Joe Shuster's Superman primarily fought gangsters and urban supervillains, never using his superhuman powers to make radical changes in world politics — even when fighting fascism — or to redirect wealth to the poor? Eco's answer is that the creators of superheroes adapted to, and modeled in small, "a concept of 'order' which pervade[d] the cultural model in which the authors live[d]."[21] In the cultural model of 1930s consumer capitalism, evil, Eco observes, is any offense to private property, and good takes the form of charity — of helping the "common man" survive, as Bradford Wright says.[22] Thus, for all of his innovations in character and narrative and despite his interrogation of heroism from comic books to immigrant Jews, Eisner's work remained indebted to and dependent on the civic ideology of the early superhero comics in which he started.

Perhaps that origin accounts for the wide range of comics writers, artists, and fans around the world that help keep Eisner's work in print. His graphic novels remain appealing to fans of *The Spirit* and superhero comics, and *The Spirit*, given its own formal experimentation, remains appealing to fans of *A Contract with God* and literary comics. Rather than the fans, the publishing industry is primarily responsible for maintaining a distinction between Eisner's early and later work. While highbrow Norton is busy laying claim to his graphic novels — an arrangement that obviously increases their cultural capital — *The Spirit* continues to be reissued by presumably lowbrow DC Comics in their series *The Spirit Archives*. Fittingly, it was Pantheon's publication of *The Rabbi's Cat* by French Jewish writer/artist Joann Sfar in late summer of 2005, just as the publicity machine for Norton's trilogy shuddered into motion, that coincidentally highlighted Eisner's legacy for the smaller subset of comics writer/artists who specifically address Jewish renegotiation and redevelopment.

Sfar is the author or illustrator of some 26 books of comics art in France, books that evidence a wide range of interests including philosophy (*La petite bibliothèque philosophique de Joann Sfar*), music (*Ukélélé, Harmonica, Klezmer*), classic literature (*Socrate Le Demi-Chien, Le Miniscule Mousquetaire*), and the gothic/supernatural (*Troll, Le petit monde du Golem,*

Petit Vampire, Merlin, Grand Vampire). Up until 2005, Sfar was best known in the US for his Little Vampire books, *Little Vampire Goes to School* and *Little Vampire Does Kung Fu!*, which were marketed as children's books but are really graphic novels. With the publication and commercial success of *The Rabbi's Cat*, however, Sfar's reputation in the American comics market shifted. The quick translation and appearance in 2006 of *Klezmer, Book One: Tales of the Wild East* tied that reputation even more firmly to Jewish concerns and stories.

As with Eisner, Sfar's turn to Jewish stories opened creative opportunities that *The Rabbi's Cat* best illustrates. What is most evocative of Eisner in that work is the deft interplay between form and content, as well as the book's focus on the vexing challenges of day-to-day life and the survival of Jewish community. Set in Algeria and Paris during the 1930s, *The Rabbi's Cat* is drawn in a cartoony style and computer colored. The contrast between the wobbly, often densely shaded drawings and the sharp colors thereby underscores the thematic contrast in the story between design (the sketch-work that gives provisional shape to images and ideas) and finish (the colorful rendering that binds together), bringing to life what was previously suggestion. The cat of the story, a philosophical skeptic and provocateur, helps both his master Rabbi Abraham and the readers see how the densely shaded design of Judaism is colorfully rendered through the everyday practices of Jews.

In the first chapter, the cat asks to convert to Judaism and have a bar mitzvah.[23] The cat's *pilpul* (Talmudic reasoning and disputation) with the rabbi's rabbi, who opposes the conversion, reveals that rabbi as dogmatic and cold-hearted; he wants to drown the cat for blaspheming God. But the cat's *pilpul* with Rabbi Abraham about the nature of Western and Jewish thought reveals that rabbi as a more generous thinker. While Westerners "want to resolve the world," Judaism, according to Rabbi Abraham, tries "to turn multiplicity into oneness" not through synthesis but through an ever-expanding acceptance of all antitheses to the original proposition.[24]

This is a hard *midrash*, a difficult interpretation and teaching, to act on in everyday life. It prompts the recognition that, whatever a Jew's level of knowledge, all are perplexed and in need of a guide. Witness one of Rabbi Abraham's students, a narrow-minded young man given to disquisitions on the immodesty of Western fashion and the relation of female purity to a proper Jewish home. The cat describes the student as a "braggart who doesn't know a thing but thinks he does and talks loudly and interrupts people and wants to marry my mistress,"[25] Rabbi Abraham's beautiful daughter. Following the student one day, the cat spots him sneaking into a whorehouse in an Arab neighborhood so that his fellow Jews will not see him. Oddly, however, "Now that I know him to be two-faced and hypocritical," says the cat, "now that I've seen him struggle between his hormones and his beliefs, I love him."[26] Perplexity, the cat discovers, is what makes one both Jewish and human.

The rabbi's *midrash* also nicely sets up the logic of the story's plot, which in chapters 2 and 3 concerns the arrival from Paris of a young, newly minted rabbi who grew up in a highly assimilated Algerian Jewish family and who marries Rabbi Abraham's daughter. In chapter 3, "Exodus," Rabbi Abraham journeys to Paris to meet the in-laws and spend the Sabbath with them, and he learns at their doorstep that the father "doesn't do Shabbat too much."[27] Faced with an unexpected antithesis, Rabbi Abraham bolts. As he wanders the urban desert of Paris, he sleeps in a church, indulges in a non-kosher feast, and accompanies his nephew to a demeaning audition at a Paris cabaret, each an object lesson in how to apply his assertion about the capaciousness of Jewish thought.

The audition is a particularly good lesson. The nephew Raymond Rebibo is not, as Rabbi Abraham assumes, a singer at the Théâtre du Grand Guignol, but a street performer outside it. He dresses in a djellaba and fez and entertains those waiting in line with an Arab minstrel show. The rabbi is appalled, but his nephew explains that this is how he earns enough money to survive in Paris, and he pretends to be an Arab because "to play a Jew you have to have a Polish accent, and I don't know how to do it. Playing a North African Jew just doesn't work, people aren't interested, it's too complicated for them. The public, Uncle, doesn't like things that are complicated."[28] Despite this, Rabbi Abraham convinces Rebibo to play traditional Algerian tunes for an important audition, and predictably the cabaret booker is bored witless. The audition is nearly a disaster until Rebibo breaks out his minstrel routine. The booker immediately hires him with the advice, "Write me a dozen songs in that vein and your fortune's made, my friend."[29] Rabbi Abraham realizes that, for his nephew, "it's hard to break through,"[30] and that, in an "imperfect world,"[31] ethnic stereotypes offer at least a starting point from which to embark on social and cultural redevelopment.

That recognition carries over to Rabbi Abraham's meeting with Armand, his new brother-in-law; explaining himself, the Rabbi ends up deconstructing his and Armand's stereotypes of assimilated and religious Jews. On the final page of the book, readers see Rabbi Abraham back home in his synagogue, giving a Sabbath evening's sermon about Armand, an irreligious man who ate pork, smoked on the Sabbath, and never prayed, but "I don't think he lived less well than I do."[32] Admitting that he doesn't know why Jews ought to observe all the precepts in the Torah, Rabbi Abraham then recites the *Kiddush* and symbolically welcomes both the Sabbath and philosophical doubt into his community. As the final panel suggests (drawn from the cat's vantage point on the woman's balcony and so locating the inspiration for the Rabbi's view), the most important precept is *shalom bayit*, keeping the extended Jewish family together in peace.

Thus, Rabbi Abraham, a genial patriarch for modern times, illustrates and teaches how Jews ought to respond to ideas and situations that bring them face to face with cultural and religious antitheses. Like the protagonists in Eisner's work, Rabbi Abraham shows readers how to safeguard community without heroics, while aesthetically Sfar's book provides a running commentary on how finish invigorates design. Judaism is a philosophically rich and complex faith tradition, Sfar seems to argue, and an open-minded Jew, like a good artist, should be ready to entertain a new perspective or develop a new role for the self to play in order to enlarge the meaning of family.

JT Waldman's *Megillat Esther*, published the same year as *The Rabbi's Cat*, similarly urges readers to consider a fresh viewpoint and provides another provocative example of a future direction for Eisner's legacy, a direction particularly amenable to comics writer/artists interested in redeveloping the tired narratives and stale images of American Jewish religious texts. "Megillat Esther — The Graphic Novel," as Moshe Silberschein calls it in his introduction,[33] shuns the simplified Sunday-morning Hebrew-school retelling of the book of Esther, too often the default for translations aimed at a broad, young audience. In that abridged version, the tale speeds from Vashti's bad decision, to King Achashverosh's lust for the surreptitiously Jewish Esther, to Esther's feast, to evil Haman's downfall, and then to a happily-ever-after in which Esther and her uncle Mordechai are fêted for saving the Jews. A Philadelphia native and graduate of the University of Michigan who is just starting out in comics, Waldman includes the entire narrative. He takes advantage of comics' potential for formal experimentation by incorporating Hebrew calligraphy, traditional and scholarly commentary, and his own embellishments in order to heighten both the story's mysteries and the strangeness of a famously complicated plot.

Like Eisner, and many other comics writer/artists these days, Waldman does not box his story into a rote arrangement of panels, but he instead employs the whole page as a vehicle for the narrative and allows the themes of the story to suggest ways of dividing and managing the text. Although that technique occasionally leads to confusion over where and how the eye should follow the narrative, Waldman turns this potential shortcoming to his advantage by making the lushness of his black-and-white design and the sensual feel of his lines integral to the story's atmosphere. Hebrew and English languages, Persian and Judaic images jostle and intersect on almost every page, an interwoven pattern of allusion and exposition that Waldman leaves to readers to sort out on a second, or third, or even a fourth reading (see Figure 3). One is reminded of Arthur Szyk's highly detailed caricatures and illustrations (particularly in his illustrated Bible stories of the 1940s) on the one hand, and on the other, of the Hernandez brothers' curvaceous female figures and magic realism in *Love and Rockets*.

Waldman takes as his design cue the root of the word "Esther," *s-t-r* ("hidden"); his dense yet attractive artwork invites readers to search out the many levels of interpretation that he has drawn into his retelling of the story. He opens *Megillat Esther* with a wordless picture prologue that recounts the initial rejection and then acceptance of Timna, Amalek's mother, into the tribe of Israel. No doubt some readers will be surprised to learn that the mother of the eternal enemy of Israel (and ancestor of Haman) was a Jewish convert, though a greater number may be aware that he is Esau's grandson and thus Isaac's great-grandson. Waldman, however, is intent on foregrounding the interfamily rivalries and oppositions that drive Judaism's secret history — secret, that is, to many secular or acculturated readers. For those unfamiliar with esoteric rabbinic and mystical commentaries or with more recent scholarly explorations of the sources for and motifs in the book of Esther, the contrast between Timna and Esther (one renounces her royal status and embraces Judaism, the other gains royal status and hides her Judaism), the rivalry between Rachel and Leah and their descendents (Rachel's line will lead to Mashiach Ben David, Leah's to Mashiach Ben Joseph), the power struggle between Saul and David, and the cultural opposition between the warrior Joshua and the artist Bezalel will all, like the book's design, provoke confusion but also a productive curiosity. The

Figure 3

book's appendices offer a helpful armature of resources for readers: an explanation of *midrash*, Rabbinic sources, and unusual words; a list of Rabbinic citations; authorial notes that "serve as clues toward uncovering more of the mystery surrounding the story of Esther;"[34] and a six-page bibliography.

The book's signature feature is that it flips page orientation at the turning point of the story — one literally has to turn it upside down — where Ahasuerus is reminded of Mordechai's discovery of a plot against him and determines to grant Mordechai a belated reward. This material expression of the Jews' reversal of fortune is laudably imaginative, though something of a gamble. It challenges readers to negotiate the story, from that point onward, not only upside down but also backwards, and those willing to spend a little time figuring out how to navigate the next few pages will find their patience well rewarded.

Waldman's strategy forces readers to rethink the meaning of "overturning" in the falling action of the story. Collectively, the destruction of Haman and his family as well as the raising up of Mordechai and Esther is obviously the triumph of good over evil, but less clear are the implications of the way in which that triumph furthers a cosmic design for the Jewish family and the Jewish future. In a story where God is Himself hidden (His name never appears), there is no way to know, definitively, what will follow the reversal of Mordechai from wise supplicant to feared vizier, of Esther from modest Jewish beauty to a Judaized Ishtar, and of the Judeans from a powerless to a powerful community — reversals that overturn the image of Jews from victims to avengers (see Figure 4). How will and how should these contradictions be resolved?

Like Eisner, Waldman yokes his Jewish subject matter to comics form, using one to comment on the other in order to stir cultural and theological discussion among readers. By the end, learning how to read Waldman's comics text becomes analogous to learning how to read a classical Jewish text in the original, because the one is as strange as the other to many contemporary readers. His *Megillat Esther* nudges readers away from approaching classical Jewish texts as texts to be conquered and consumed. Instead, it proffers reading as a dizzying, often topsy-turvy negotiation, a familiar trait of comics and a reason why they are never "easy reading." As Peter Scheldahl observes, reading comics, "toggling for hours between the incommensurable functions of reading and looking — is taxing."[35]

In that light, Waldman's *Megillat Esther* can be interpreted as a kind

Figure 4

of allegory for the creative potential inherent in learning to read new modes of literature. It reintroduces the pleasures of the (Jewish) text in that it slows us down and asks us to reread, to question how we are reading and looking, and to enjoy the very physicality of the text. Reading *as* formal and cultural experimentation: the ostensibly modern reading skills that Waldman's experimental graphic novel both requires and teaches, reintroduces and updates, are a traditional mode of Jewish reading.

This is a surprising but effective way to make classical Jewish texts new — or known at all to uninformed audiences. Programs to improve American Jews' religious literacy and facility with Hebrew, Aramaic, and other Jewish languages are well established and have certain if sometimes sluggish effect. Imagine, however, if more classical Jewish texts were double translated in the fashion of Waldman's *Megillat Esther* — from Hebrew to English (in side-by-side or linear translation) and from word-tethered narrative to comics art. How would such a re-emphasis on the materiality of the book change reading habits? What might be the result of such renegotiation and redevelopment of Jewish literacy?

These questions may read like fan mail speculation, but the comics medium is a site of continual revision, adaptation, and surprise. While Eisner may have felt that, for him, superhero comics ultimately led to a creative dead end, his own example shows the tenacity of that genre's hold on the comics imagination. Its resurgence and current dominance is a reminder that it is still a fruitful and useful genre. Like any formula literature, comics are capable of both reactionary and progressive formulations, as well as a wide range of ideological work, not all of it nefarious. Nevertheless, as Waldman's *Megillat Esther* shows, when it comes to Jewish cultural production the heroic has long been a troubling category, especially in its political adaptations (see, for example, Paul Breines' *Tough Jews*, or the work of Israeli post-Zionist scholars that critique the classic, heroic Zionist self-image). The comics medium, still in the process of discovering its creative potential, is uniquely suited to explore and critique that category — for the medium's practitioners, that is the primal scene to which they must return in order to break away. As Eisner intuited, the development of the graphic novel as a new mode of popular literature offers Jewish writer/artists a formal correlative for their projects of cultural rediscovery and renegotiation, for their redrawing of the religious and social contracts that accompanied Jews into modernity. Such tentative projects do not inspire the certitude of heroism, and the doubts that hover over Eisner's, Sfar's, and Waldman's books shadow the Jewish covenants they illustrate. But in registering that, their books present instructive cases for the future of comics that draw contracts rather than enforce them.

Notes

1 *The New York Times*, January 6, 2005, News Summary section, 2.
2 Umberto Eco, *The Role of the Reader: Explorations in the Semiotics of Texts* (Bloomington, Indiana University Press, 1984), 108–10.
3 Will Eisner, "Getting the Last Laugh: My Life in Comics," *The New York Times Book Review*, January 14, 1990, 27.
4 Will Eisner, *The Contract with God Trilogy: Life on Dropsie Avenue* (New York, London: W. W. Norton, 2006), xiii–xiv.
5 Stephen Burt, "'Blown To Atoms or Reshaped At Will': Recent Books About Comics," *College Literature* 32.1 (2005), 168.
6 Burt, 51.
7 Burt, 60.
8 Burt, xvi.
9 Burt, xvi.
10 Will Eisner, interview by Stefano Gorla, *Famiglia Cristiana #38*, September 23, 2001, reprinted at <http://www.willeisner.com/shoptalk/shoptalk4.html>.
11 Eisner, *Famiglia Cristiana #38*, <http://www.willeisner.com/shoptalk/shoptalk5.html>.

12 Eisner, *Famiglia Cristiana #38*, <http://www.willeisner.com/shoptalk/shoptalk4.html>.

13 Eisner, *The Contract With God Trilogy*, 200.

14 Eisner, *The Contract With God Trilogy*, 200.

15 Eisner, *The Contract With God Trilogy*, 296.

16 Eisner, *The Contract With God Trilogy*, 318.

17 Eisner, *The Contract With God Trilogy*, 319.

18 Will Eisner, *To the Heart of the Storm* (New York: DC Comics, 2000), 199.

19 Will Eisner, "Introduction," *Dropsie Avenue: The Neighborhood* (Northampton: Kitchen Sink Press, 1995).

20 Richard Reynolds, *Super Heroes: A Modern Mythology* (Jackson: University Press of Mississippi, 1992), 15; Bradford Wright, *Comic Book Nation: The Transformation of Youth Culture in America* (Baltimore and London: Johns Hopkins University Press, 2003), 22–6.

21 Umberto Eco, *The Role of the Reader*, 124.

22 Wright, 10.

23 Having eaten a parrot, he can talk, though the first thing he says is a lie.

24 Joann Sfar, *The Rabbi's Cat* (New York: Pantheon Books, 2005), 25.

25 Sfar, 43.

26 Sfar, 46.

27 Sfar, 106.

28 Sfar, 122.

29 Sfar, 133.

30 Sfar, 134.

31 Sfar, 134.

32 Sfar, 142.

33 JT Waldman, *Megillat Esther* (Philadelphia: Jewish Publication Society, 2005).

34 Waldman, 163.

35 Peter Scheldahl, "Words and Pictures: Graphic Novels Come of Age," *New Yorker*, October 17, 2005, 162.

Catholic American Citizenship:
Prescriptions for Children from *Treasure Chest of Fun and Fact* (1946–63)

ANNE BLANKENSHIP

URING THE DECADES FOLLOWING WORLD War II, Catholic parochial schools introduced a new type of educational text to the classroom: the comic book. *Treasure Chest of Fun and Fact* consisted of over 500 issues, containing puzzles, crafts, adventure stories and religious and historical lessons.[1] However, the comics did more than just entertain. *Treasure Chest*'s storylines taught persuasive social lessons as children read about parochial students like themselves and cheered on exciting moral heroes like Squanto, a Native American convert, and nuns in the Wild West. Through vivid representations of cultural and social values, religious leaders illustrated how to become perfect Catholic American citizens. Stories within *Treasure Chest*'s covers articulated what it means to be an American and the essential responsibilities of every citizen, children and adults alike. Their progressive lessons challenged social norms and even government policies — a remarkable stance for a minority group already coping with discrimination.

Resolute prescriptions for children appeared throughout the issues; some comics taught proper manners, offered homemaking lessons for girls, or gave tips on choosing a future career. The most prominent theme, however, was that of American citizenship. Repeatedly, stories modeled behavior or explicitly stated what children must do as responsible American citizens. I will explain how the writers and illustrators portrayed America at this time and then look at specific prescriptions. The comic regularly defined America by freedom, democracy, and multiculturalism. Playful narratives taught the value of ethnic diversity and caring for one's neighbor, while the stern, threatening resolutions of "This Godless Communism" trained children to become resolute defenders of democracy.

The combination of text and images within comic books contains many layers of interpretation, providing a rich source for research. A material culture approach is particularly efficacious for studying American Catholicism because Catholics have used images to educate laity for nearly 2,000 years. Comic books are, in a way, a natural medium for the church, particularly as an educational form intended for students. Children acknowledge the form as something created specifically for them, granting it additional authority. The agency of children was highlighted in every issue of *Treasure Chest*, the tone increasing in urgency in later issues on communism, a threat viewed as insurmountable without the help of every child and adult. The church still uses this medium — comic and coloring books — to reinforce critical messages to children today.

This essay will focus on the issues presented in *Treasure Chest* before Vatican II to isolate a particular moment in American Catholic history. Though church burnings and legalized discrimination against Catholics did not occur after World War II, Catholics still faced more subtle forms of prejudice in the United States. Many Protestants feared that Roman Catholicism inhibited democracy and individualism, and it would even dampen capitalism and scientific development. They believed the hierarchical structure of the church limited creativity and any fundamental curiosity about the world. They further worried that growing up in a Catholic home could stunt a child's psychological development as a result of an extreme emphasis on obedience, possibly leading to fascist sympathies.[2] In the mid-1960s, Vatican II implemented perhaps the greatest changes to church policy and worship practices in the history of the church. This transformation increased dialogue with non-Catholics and ultimately decreased tensions between Catholics and Protestants in America. This essay reflects the social atmosphere before Vatican II, when American Catholics faced greater discrimination. Additionally, the original publisher of *Treasure Chest*, George Pflaum, died in 1963, so this periodization will isolate his influence on the publication.

At the encouragement of Catholic educational organizations, George Pflaum's publication company produced *Treasure Chest* to be distributed in Catholic parochial schools. Pflaum designed *Treasure Chest* to educate Catholic youth and provide an alternative to the behavior and mores depicted in popular comics. The first issues appeared in 1946, just as comic book burnings and boycotts brought the public's attention to an ongoing censorship battle. Pflaum's strategy of providing an edifying alternative was not the first in this direction. *True Comics*, a publication of *Parents' Magazine*, and *Classic Comics*, which retold classic literature, sold on newsstands, while the Catholic Church distributed *Picture Stories from the Bible* in Sunday schools and the nonfiction *Topix Comics* in parochial schools.[3] *Treasure Chest* distinguished itself from these comics by its success. It ran several decades longer and produced far more total issues. Its distribution through parochial schools provided a large readership, and the comic thrived when teachers began using it in the classroom. Unavailable to the public, parochial school teachers sold individual subscriptions to their students. When parochial school enrollment fell in the late 1960s, subscription rates fell and production finally ceased in 1972.[4]

Treasure Chest presents Catholics as true, patriotic Americans eager to show newcomers the American way of life. Considered outsiders since colonial times, Catholics struggled to balance their religious and national identities amidst frequent discrimination. Internal and external debates about their patriotism and loyalty to the United States continued through the centuries but significantly dissipated after World War II, when the GI Bill improved their financial standing. With greater acceptance came impulses to provide the next generation of Catholics with a strong civic education and a more generous acceptance of Catholics outside of the center — new immigrants and racial minorities. *Treasure Chest* shows Catholics serving as moral stewards for newcomers, teaching them about America, and modeling perfect American citizenship. While many series show true citizenship as seemingly secular behavior, others reinforce its Catholic characteristics and foundations as well. The comics show that not only are Catholics true Americans, but also they might be better Americans than anyone else.

What is America?

Treasure Chest addresses the question "What is America?" in several series, often through a framework of Catholic parochial school students introducing new immigrants to the freedom, democracy, and multi-culturalism of American society. These newcomers are DPs, displaced persons from communist countries, providing the story with a clear contrast between their different types of government and citizenship. Frightening descriptions of communism define America by what it is not. These stories emphasize the characteristics and importance of freedom and democracy, while others focus on America's multiculturalism as readers learn about the myriad — though mostly European — origins of American culture.

"It Happens Here: A Story of Young Citizens" opens with a picture of a blond boy gazing at the Statue of Liberty from the deck of a boat. A policeman, the dominant central figure in this frame, stands taller and larger than the immigrants, showing his power and authority. He asks the boy if he knows the statue's meaning. The boy looks up at him, stating, "My father told me the Statue of Liberty welcomes us to a land of freedom. Here we shall be free and happy. I will be able to pray and learn more about my religion and democracy."[5] This short introduction demonstrates the eagerness of young Catholic immigrants to embrace and celebrate defining characteristics of the United States: freedom and democracy. Over the course of the year, the immigrants learn that policemen are helpful and friendly, that American citizens have a right and responsibility to protest injustice, and that it is important to always vote for the best candidate.[6] The DP must grow accustomed to such differences as he struggles to trust authority figures. His behavior calls attention to the fears of people living under a communist regime. In contrast, the American children are relaxed and carefree, assured of their safety and protection from dangers they can hardly imagine.

In a similar series nine years later, two refugees from Hungary tell their stories of communism as classmates show them the ropes at a Catholic parochial school. The first panel reads, "In Hungary there was no such thing as freedom of thought about anything. You had to think their way, and training to think their way began in the schools." A Hungarian teacher repeats, "I told you yesterday, I tell you today, and I'll tell you tomorrow: What the communist party says is true, what it does is right. All loyal citizens believe this."[7] This comparison highlights characteristics of America that readers might overlook, assuming them to be universal. The book's characters learn about the contrasting values and ways of life of communist Hungary and democratic America within a Catholic parochial school, the very place non-Catholics accused of fostering undemocratic leanings.

These series introduce the ambiguous role of authority figures in *Treasure Chest*. The comics often fit the stereotype of Catholic faith in and obedience to power hierarchies — but not always. *Treasure Chest* never undermines the intellectual and moral superiority of priests, for example, but several series depict Catholic children guiding the actions of adults. Others criticize the government's poor racial policies, labor laws, or church-state disputes, teaching readers how to fight or cope with the results of misguided politicians. But generally, civil employees and other leaders serve as honest, kind, dependable foils to treacherous communists. The visual representations of infamous communists startle viewers with their bulbous, squat, ugly bodies, but in America, innocent-looking leaders, like librarians and teachers, can harbor communist sympathies. While the challenges to hierarchies between adults and children, and a government and its citizens, illustrate the difficulties of being a Catholic in America, the portrayal of communists disguised as trusted authority figures reveals the chaos that communism threatens to unleash.

"We Built America," a series sponsored by the Commission for American Citizenship, reveals America's multicultural aspects. The thin plotline narrates a group of parochial students' investigation into the national origins of a new family. On the first page, a girl observes, "It may take them a little time to get used to the American way of life," and a boy quickly responds, "Remember it was people who came here from foreign countries who made *the American way of life*." Under the auspices of their civics club, the students arrange a series of dinners. The new kids are taken to each of their homes to introduce the "new" American way of life in hopes that their unknown heritage will be revealed along the way. Here, as in other series, good Catholic children model an attitude of acceptance and celebrate diversity with the contingency that immigrants adapt to new ways as well. A sister-teacher steps into the panel to agree that "the *American* way of life is not a solid color, but rather a *pattern* of different tones of color."[8] This voice of authority validates the opinions of the students and reinforces the concept of diversity strengthening America.

Each evening constitutes a separate story in which the older members of the family explain the many contributions their ethnicity brought to America. Spanish, Italian, German, British, Chinese, Irish, Polish, and Scandinavian cultures are explored before the students discover that their new friends are Native American. This revelation is delivered as a punch line, but also reminds readers that "those who were already here have also helped to weave the American pattern."[9] Each episode relates a group's important role in American history and their culture's contributions of food and vocabulary. No characteristics are specifically Catholic, but that is largely beside the point. Citizens are united through their identity as Americans, not by their religion.

The necessity of acculturation, specifically "Americanization," appears in several series. The popular concept of a melting pot entailed absorbing the best attributes of immigrant cultures into a generic American culture where everyone would have the same values, cultural metaphors, and civil religion after assimilation.[10] Following their economic success after World War II, many Catholics saw themselves within this milieu and, by 1950, used this type of rhetoric approvingly.[11] *Treasure Chest*, however, modified the usual interpretation of the melting pot metaphor. Cultural contributions *and* distinctions are acknowledged and lauded alongside encouragement to assimilate, to accept American values and honor America's symbols and ideals. In other words, the immigrants must accept a degree of assimilation to become American, but they need not sacrifice their previous traditions. By naming multiculturalism as one of the major components of America, *Treasure Chest* creates a place for Catholic immigrants and embraces a welcoming ethos of diversity. This unwavering stance promotes a positive, idealistic perspective of the United States and directs the next generation to accept newcomers. This progressive message generally runs counter to the actions of both Catholics and Protestants in America, who excluded most new immigrant populations. The popular comic *Wonder Woman* offers a neat comparison between *Treasure Chest*'s melting pot and general cultural expectations for immigrants. Matthew J. Smith's article, "The Tyranny of the Melting Pot Metaphor: Wonder Woman as the Americanized Immigrant," tells how Wonder Woman instantly speaks only English upon her arrival, slides into American gender roles, and never refers to her old country except to confirm America's superiority over the paradise she left.[12] George Pflaum's civic involvement helps explain the origins of *Treasure Chest*'s progressive ideology.

In addition to publishing educational materials for Catholic children, Pflaum co-founded the Catholic Civics Clubs of America, an organization associated with Catholic University of America's Commission on American Citizenship. In the mid-1940s, the Commission approached Pflaum's company to publish *Treasure Chest* and produced several series within it. This involvement helps explain *Treasure Chest*'s emphasis on patriotism, citizenship, and parochial school civics clubs. The Commission had one central goal: educate American Catholics about proper citizenship from a young age. The organization designed curricula, dispersed information to educators, and published a series of textbooks called "Faith and Freedom" that was used in over five thousand Catholic schools.[13] The books aimed to prepare "young people for the task of thinking and feeling and acting in such a way as to keep alive in American society the spirit of democracy."[14] A glance through these books quickly overturns popular notions of Catholicism's incompatibility with democracy. Their teaching methods rooted the impetus for good citizenship in Catholic doctrine, but they made clear that charity and understanding were for all people, not just Catholics. *Treasure Chest* advocates these ideals of equality and caring for one's neighbor, particularly when charging children with the responsibility of protecting the true spirit of America.

How Do We Keep America This Way?

How did *Treasure Chest* inspire readers to protect the freedom, democracy and multiculturalism of America? Later issues address the critical issue of resisting communism, and earlier series show *Treasure Chest* readers how to answer this final question through the activities of parochial school civics clubs. Regular community involvement, charity, voting, and racial tolerance are the answers most commonly presented in the comic book.

A story in "It Happens Here" presents the most straightforward answer. Civics club students run about town to find out what makes a good citizen. A Hungarian student answers, "It's doing whatever the government says to do, without a question." The children, knowing America stands for independent thought, immediately dismiss the new immigrant's answer and search for an alternative. They first ask the mayor, who tells them, "A good citizen is someone who obeys laws, pays taxes, votes in all elections, and, if he holds office, he does his duty honestly." The editor of the local paper answers, "He's the fellow who pays his bills, sweeps the snow from his sidewalk, and joins clubs that help the community." Unsatisfied with these answers, the students ask their priest. He explains, "The good citizen is one who loves his neighbor" and shows it "not by words alone, but by deeds . . . Justice to everyone; charity to all

Figure 1.   **The story of the Good Samaritan (4 April 1950). "It Happens Here, Vol. 5, No. 16,"** *The Treasure Chest of Fun and Fact.* **American Catholic History Research Center and University Archives, Catholic University of America, Washington, DC**

who need it, but first and last, a good citizen obeys the laws of God. He loves God and loves his neighbor."[15]

The most compelling element to this story is not the answers themselves, but rather whom the students ask and who offers the ultimate answer. A politician seems to be the most obvious source for a question about community obligations, followed by a newspaper writer, someone committed to communicating public information. These men fail to explain the central root to all citizenship, but their priest knows it lies in their faith. The strip visually prioritizes the final answer. Previous frames were noticeably busier than almost any other found in *Treasure Chest*. One page shows 21 distinct figures and another 18, but the final frame (see Figure 1) presents the students and their priest as black silhouettes gazing at a portrayal of the priest's answer: the Good Samaritan. The muted silhouettes negate the individuals to prioritize this solution. The first answers were not inaccurate, but this ultimate answer is holy, delivered by a higher power. The story of the Good Samaritan teaches children to always show kindness to others, the core of every action described by the other community leaders. Roman Catholics — or at least Christians — hold the key to a more perfect America. This story teaches children the fundamental value of loving your neighbor and provides many examples of this, all while demonstrating the supreme knowledge and guidance of the Catholic Church.

Several other series follow the actions of civics clubs, modeling good behavior for fictional companions and real-life readers. Whether the task is fixing up an old playground, convincing neighborhood stores to stop selling "bad magazines," or collecting funds and donations for orphans,[16] students take charge and improve their community. Students tend to know right from wrong and act accordingly, emphasizing action over discussion. Merely talking about injustice or any other problem is explicitly criticized, and students quickly rally to solve the problem at hand. Most do not reference Catholicism apart from the parochial school setting, but this does not necessarily express a lack of Catholic influence. It shows a confidence that these students, raised in Catholic homes and given a parochial school education, naturally ask the right questions and reach sound conclusions on their own or by asking appropriate authority figures. *Treasure Chest* characters demonstrate the agency and capabilities of both children and good Catholics.

One civics club series explains distinctively Catholic positions. A page of citations from priests, cardinals, popes, and the Baltimore Catechism reinforces ethical solutions in "Where Do We Stand?" These references and the more frequent delivery of prescriptions by authority figures strengthen the weight of the texts. "Where Do We Stand?" gave children tools to defend Catholicism while encouraging patriotism and commitment to American ideals. Several topics, like voting responsibilities, promote participation in the democratic system. Characters volunteer on political campaigns and hold elections to emphasize the importance of voting regularly.[17] Another story tells students that no one should vote for a candidate simply because he is Catholic,[18] a concern often voiced by non-Catholics. After studying the series, students could explain why Catholics excelled at American citizenship — because their religious doctrines and traditions instruct them to hold the same values.

Because many series show students acting autonomously from adults, when clergy do instruct, their message is more powerful. A lesson about racism comes from a sister-teacher who echoes the priorities of Pflaum and the Commission on American Citizenship. She reminds the students, "we're all created in the image and likeness of God, but when we talk about Negroes or Jews or any other group of people, we forget it." The students question why the Catholic Church would operate segregated schools and orphanages and the sister answers, "Sometimes we must follow local customs and laws — even though it is wrong . . . If we didn't take care of [Negro orphans] this way, we shouldn't be able to take care of them at all." In other words, the church allows segregation "in certain cases to prevent greater evil."[19] This story and others suggest that the United States government limits the benevolence of the Catholic Church to teach readers two things: First, that by following a system of Catholic ethics, they are conforming to American ideals more faithfully than the country's leaders — a huge statement for a minority group to make. Second, they teach students how to act within a restrictive situation: do what leads to the greatest good.

When discussing communism, however, *Treasure Chest* never differentiates between Catholic and national aims. A 1950 story first addresses the threat of communism and begins to suggest the necessary roles of American children. The strip makes an example of a naïve woman, fooled by men urging people to sign the Stockholm Peace Proposal, which other students know to be a communist ploy. The woman shrugs, "Communism would be all right if it didn't fight against religion and belief in God." The boys lean toward her in disbelief, or perhaps anger, to correct her false impressions. After a DP tells of his experience, most of which does concern religion, the boys continue their lesson until she agrees with their views.[20] While this comic strip is not explicitly prescriptive, it warns children to be suspicious of certain organizations and, in turn, reinforces the importance of knowing one's enemy. The comic does not tell students how to investigate such a group, but it still cautions them to be wary. The tone of this strip, while more aggressive than those on other subjects, is still much lighter than ones addressing communism ten years later.

By the 1960s, series about communism became explicitly prescriptive and more direct, urgent, and aggressive. America needs charity and good citizenship, but its very survival is at stake in the series about communism, and the children must learn to resist and fight it. In 1961, *Treasure Chest* ran a jarring series entitled "This Godless Communism." The cover bears a large red hammer and sickle encompassing a white arm and torch of the Statue of Liberty upon a blue background, rendering the traditional patriotic colors malevolent (see Figure 2). A letter from J. Edgar Hoover prefaces the series, urging children to be vigilant and learn all they can about communism as it "represents the most serious threat facing our way of life." This message granted agency to children to fight communism and charged them with the responsibility to learn how to "recognize and detect the communists as they attempt to infiltrate the various segments of our society."[21] This intentionally frightening message precedes a similarly scary story that exposes the real fear of communism in America during the 1960s. American Catholics opposed communism with exceptional zeal, but this unease was felt across the nation.

The initial storyline of "This Godless Communism" describes what would happen if communists won the Cold War and the country became

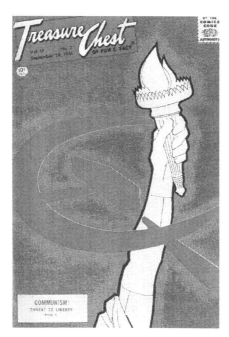

Figure 2. **Cover from the debut issue of "This Godless Communism" (28 September 1961). "This Godless Communism, Vol. 17, No. 2,"** *The Treasure Chest of Fun and Fact.* **American Catholic History Research Center and University Archives, Catholic University of America, Washington, DC**

the Union of Soviet States of America. A Catholic boy sees lawyers and clergy members sent to labor camps and the loss of property rights and freedoms of speech, press, and worship. Since the new government does not "believe in families," the father is sent to a labor camp and the mother is "[freed] from the home and put . . . to work" in a factory. Government schools and nurseries raise the children and tell them there is no God or heaven, only the "all good and all-powerful" communism. An image shows the symbolic unmanning of America with the destruction of the Washington Monument (see Figure 3). The familiar phallic building is drawn mid-collapse, limply bending downward as a manly, uniformed Soviet soldier thrusts down the trigger for the explosives.[22] The comic does not belittle America's enemy; Soviets are strong and fierce and will rapidly transform the entire landscape of America if permitted.

Fear tactics continue in subsequent issues that chart the history of communism.[23] The story begins with "the greatest dangers . . . to the

Figure 3. **The Soviets unman America (28 September 1961). "This Godless Communism, Vol. 17, No. 2,"** *The Treasure Chest of Fun and Fact.* **American Catholic History Research Center and University Archives, Catholic University of America, Washington, DC**

world that have ever existed" coming to the mind of Karl Marx[24] and ends with the failed Hungarian revolt. The penultimate series shows Khrushchev's plan to "win the world without firing another shot" and the extent of communist infiltration around the world. Innocent-looking people, a librarian, a university professor, and a labor union organizer gather in an average American living room, plotting to remove anticommunist books from their respective libraries.[25] The images instruct readers that communists can look just like anyone else and hold positions of authority. Several frames also discuss the people of Russia to remind readers that they are suffering victims and do not necessarily support this system of government.[26]

At the conclusion of "This Godless Communism," an American girl and boy ask their priest what they can do to stop communism. His immediate response, "Pray, it is our greatest spiritual weapon," correlates with most texts, including a teacher's guide, about defeating communism. Prayer is rarely shown as a solution to other challenges, but the evils of communism seem to have an unnatural power (perhaps due to its atheism) that necessitates supernatural help. The comic emphasizes the responsibility of its young readers to respond to the communist threat. A serious-looking priest stares directly from the final panel of the series, arresting the viewer with his gaze, and says, "Pray hard and work hard, for the success of the battle may well be up to you."[27] An immense responsibility! The emphasis on prayer parallels the national discourse at this time; Eisenhower repeatedly affirmed the superior power of religion over the atheism of communism.

Parochial school teachers are not left out of the strategy. *Treasure Chest* tells teachers that communism must be fought at every level, by children and adults, again stressing its urgency. It explains in a teacher's guide, this "diabolical conspiracy . . . is not *coming* to the United States . . . it is *already here.*" The "world crisis" is "a plot against the Creator of the universe," suggesting a nearly unimaginable attack against not only the United States, but also God.[28] The guide reminds educators of the importance of teaching students how to fight communism through love and by living "God-centered lives."[29] But the series for children primarily teaches through fear, not love. The high expectations for teachers, couched in militaristic language, stress children's role in America's defense.

Educating children through alternative media has not ceased in the Catholic Church. In the United States today, concerns about Catholics are most likely to relate to the priest abuse scandals rather than proper citizenship, and this new fear is discussed in a similar format. In 2007, the New York Archdiocese distributed the coloring book *Being Friends, Being Safe, Being Catholic* to young children and a comic book on molestation to older children in 700 parochial schools. These materials talk about sexual abuse, caution children to never be alone with a priest or any other adult, and provide a list of trustworthy adults.[30] Just as *Treasure Chest* approached questions of citizenship decades ago, American Catholics today address concerns through the medium thought most likely to appeal to children. This use of comic books is less innovative today, but its intent and approach remains the same. It is a medium that children recognize as designed and intended just for them.

While many scholars analyze textbooks, they generally overlook comic books due to their association with children and designation as low culture. However, comics reflect cultural norms and expectations just like other forms of popular media and have even greater room for creativity than many other sources. *Treasure Chest* issues operated as textbooks, but they held greater appeal to children. Serious historical tales or moral prescriptions were palatably illustrated and interlaced with games, amusing stories, and activities. While textbooks remained largely static, the monthly production of the comics allowed for the inclusion of current, pressing issues like communism. Contemporary settings within many series also facilitated flexibility. Teachers' guides supplemented the books, suggesting ways to use the comics in history, reading and civics classes.

The exceptionality of *Treasure Chest* becomes even more apparent when compared to the pedagogy of contemporary secular comics. DC Comics placed one- or two-page strips within popular comic books, rather than showing superheroes enacting a moral tale. This enabled them to retain their central stories while satisfying parental desires for a more edifying product. However, the primary comic often propagated contrasting values. The public service inserts in DC Comics talked about tolerance and diversity, but the main text never starred an African-American character or even drew one in the background.[31] *Treasure Chest* was unique in abiding by its own moral standard. A variety of skin tones appear in most series, regardless of the topic, and a later issue even portrays a black presidential candidate — the very first public, popular portrayal of an African-American presidential nominee.[32]

Treasure Chest of Fun and Fact both taught children that individual initiative and patriotism are essential traits among Americans and offered models of good citizenship through stories of community-oriented parochial school civics clubs. It illustrates how all Catholics can become true Americans by utilizing a vision of a melting pot in which immigrants adapt to America's democratic ideals but also contribute to American culture by retaining their old traditions. America's diversity strengthens the country and reinforces its democratic ideals. Contradicting common stereotypes about Catholics, *Treasure Chest* declares that American Catholic children have more grounds and capacity than anyone to be the best American citizens.

Notes

1   Frank M Borth, Interviewed by Maria Mazzenga and Jordan Patty (Newville, PA: May 2006), Catholic University of America. In 1966 and 1967, Pflaum also published six summer editions.
2   John T McGreevy, *Catholicism and American Freedom: A History* (New York: W. W. Norton, 2003), 177–80.
3   Amy Kiste Nyberg, *Seal of Approval: The History of the Comics Code* (Jackson: University Press of Mississippi, 1998), 7–8. Mike Benton, *The Comic Book in America: An Illustrated History* (Dallas: Taylor, 1989), 97. David Hajdu, *The Ten-Cent Plague: The Great Comic Book Scare and How it Changed America* (New York: Farrar, Straus and Giroux, 2008), 72.
4   Borth.
5   "It Happens Here," *Treasure Chest* (20 September 1949).
6   "It Happens Here," *Treasure Chest* (18 October 1949).
7   "Let Freedom Ring," *Treasure Chest* (25 September 1958).
8   "We Built America," *Treasure Chest* (23 September 1954).
9   "We Built America," *Treasure Chest* (2 June 1955). "America: The Melting Pot" (1962/1963) taught multicultural lessons with similar content and attitudes.
10 Think the Borg on *Star Trek: The Next Generation.*
11 Philip Gleason, "Pluralism, Democracy, and Catholicism in the Era of World War II," *The Review of Politics* (Spring 1987): 215.

12 Smith persuasively argues that super hero comics "served as vanguards of conservative representations . . . and traditional values," suggesting that *Wonder Woman* accurately represents contemporary cultural norms. Matthew J. Smith, "The Tyranny of the Melting Pot Metaphor: Wonder Woman as the Americanized Immigrant" in *Comics and Ideology*, Matthew P. McAllister et al. (New York: Peter Lang, 2001), 132.

13 Timothy Walch, *Parish School: American Catholic Parochial Education from Colonial Times to the Present* (New York: Crossroad, 1996), 131–2.

14 George Johnson, "The Commission on American Citizenship of the Catholic University of America," *Journal of Educational Sociology* (February 1943): 382.

15 "It Happens Here," *Treasure Chest* (4 April 1950).

16 "You are Citizens Now," *Treasure Chest* (24 October 1957 and 16 January 1958). "It Happens Here," *Treasure Chest* (2 and 30 May 1950).

17 "Let Freedom Ring," *Treasure Chest* (20 November 1958).

18 "Where Do We Stand?" *Treasure Chest* (15 February 1951).

19 "Where Do We Stand?" *Treasure Chest* (23 November 1950).

20 "Where Do We Stand?" *Treasure Chest* (18 January 1951).

21 "Letter from John Edgar Hoover to the Readers of Treasure Chest, Date March 13, 1961," *Treasure Chest* (28 September 1961).

22 "This Godless Communism," *Treasure Chest* (28 September 1961).

23 "This Godless Communism" focuses on the Soviet Union and its history, but a separate series, "What About Red China?" explained the origins of communism in China the following year.

24 "This Godless Communism," *Treasure Chest* (12 October 1961).

25 "This Godless Communism," *Treasure Chest* (10 May 1962).

26 "This Godless Communism," *Treasure Chest* (7 June 1962).

27 "This Godless Communism," *Treasure Chest* (7 June 1962).

28 A Murphy, "Teacher's Edition: Why Teach Communism in the Elementary School?" *Treasure Chest* (28 September 1961).

29 "Teacher's Edition: A Question of Approach," *Treasure Chest* (14 September 1961).

30 Jessica Bennett, "Coloring outside the Lines," *Newsweek* (10 December 2007): 16. "Being Friends, Being Safe, Being Catholic" (New York: Archdiocese of New York, 2007). Patrick McGuire, ed., *Archangel* (New York: Archdiocese of New York, 2007).

31 Bradford W Wright, *Comic Book Nation: The Transformation of Youth Culture in America* (Baltimore: Johns Hopkins, 2001), 61–5.

32 The Catholic University of America Office of Public Affairs, "1960s Comic Book in Archives Depicts Black Presidential Nominee" (12 March 2008).

Gold Plates, Inked Pages:
The Authority of the Graphic Novel

G. ST. JOHN STOTT

Comic Book as *Midrash*

"I guess you think you know this story," Roald Dahl teases in the first line of his "Cinderella," only to disabuse us he moves quickly to the truth: "You don't. The real one's much more gory. / The phoney one, the one you know, / Was cooked up years and years ago, / And made to sound all soft and sappy / Just to keep the children happy."[1] This is one way to define the relationship between a retelling and the story retold — to claim the status of the *real* story (the authority of the first telling) for the work one has in her hands, and to dismiss any other version as derivative and therefore phony. Of course, even if people take Dahl at his word, they find that they cannot really forget the version already known;[2] no matter how hard they try, there is an "almost unconscious prioritizing" of the text with which they are already familiar.[3] However, by assuming the high ground in this way, Dahl points us in a healthy direction. A retelling should be considered on its own terms. Dahl's own "Cinderella," Michel Tournier's *Vendredi ou les Limbes du Pacifique*, Woody Guthrie's "The Ballad of Tom Joad"[4] — such works should not approached through a discourse of loss.

This much is generally granted to reinterpretations of texts — except, it seems, when the retelling takes the form of a comic book. Then, parity seems out of the question. Pictures are presumed to be less serious than words; graphic novels are presumed to have less significance than works in prose (in Anna Healy's summary of the charges, to be "lacking depth and any form of intellectual rigor"[5]), and, that being so, comic book versions of literary works are usually dismissed for offering inadequate summaries of textually rich originals. Of course, as David Hajdu has shown, factors other than *lèse majesté* have contributed to the fear and loathing with which comics have been seen[6] — but a lack of respect for the classics has clearly been part of the bill of charges. Delmore Schwartz's concern, that replacing a descriptive paragraph with a comic book panel creates a "debased" and trivialized work, is far from unique.[7]

Such concern for trivialization, all too common when the work adapted is a literary classic, is compounded when it comes to comic book versions of scripture. In such cases, there is not only the fear of triviality and a predictable discomfort over the changes that come with the adoption of a new narrative form for a well-known story; there is also uncertainty as to the authority of such a work. Is a Bible comic as authoritative as its source? The question begs the further question of what is meant by authority, and, in what follows, I will offer a definition. But for now, it is enough to wonder if a comic book or graphic novel could be thought of, by believers, as being a guide for "teaching [. . .] and training in righteousness" like its scriptural original.[8] Does the reader lose something by reading one rather than the other?

At first thought, the answer seems obvious: Even the most conservative comic book authors edit the words of their source, "drawing out what is implicit already within the text itself [. . .] and bringing it into explicit form in the visualized medium."[9] ("Changes are *inevitable* the moment one abandons the linguistic for the visual medium," George Bluestone noted in his discussion of film adaptations of literary texts,[10] and the same is true with comic book adaptations.) That being the case, if it is accepted that "every detail [of a work] has, at least in principle, a point,"[11] then it would necessarily follow that different details signal a different work. What does not necessarily follow, however, is that this new work is a lesser one.

Consider the suggestion of David G. Burke that comic books on biblical themes are like *midrashim* in the way that they offer a "drawing out" of what is implicit in their source. Although there are problems with Burke's approach, the comparison is attractive. A *midrash* — offering, in Chaim Milikowsky's words, "the rabbis' reconstruction of God's word to the Jewish people" (a re-presentation, that is to say, rather than a reproduction of their source) — could usefully serve as a precedent for the work of graphic novelists[12] and allow one to read a comic book expecting insight rather than fearing loss. There are two problems with this approach, however. One, to which I will return, is that the model of the *midrash* misdirects our attention to the relationship between the comic book and its source, when that between the work and its original is far more fruitful. The second is that not every comic book can be seen as *midrash*. Unlike the rabbis described by Milikowsky, some comic book authors *are* interested in gaining insight into what they believe is a known (or knowable) past and are not (consciously) interested in going beyond a common-sense interpretation of their text.[13] A broader definition of the relationship between comic book and source is necessary.

The Golden Plates

As an illustration of a work that does not fit the midrashic mould, consider Michael Allred's *The Golden Plates* (2005), a multi-part graphic novel retelling the story of the Book of Mormon. As a committed Latter-Day Saint (LDS) and successful comic book author, Allred wanted to create a work that would introduce the Book of Mormon to new readers.[14] The task he set himself was challenging. The Book of Mormon was published in 1830 by Joseph Smith Jr. (1805–44) as the translation of a history from Ancient America — a record engraved in a "reformed Egyptian" script on plates that had "the appearance of gold."[15] The lengthy sermons and extended chronicles of warfare that we find in Smith's work do not readily translate into graphic imagery, and, to give animation to its characters, Allred had to go beyond his source. Nevertheless, despite this need to illuminate or bring out the hidden implications of a text,[16] he was not particularly interested in working in a midrashic fashion.

Note, for example, the way Allred handles the killing of Laban. Lehi, the patriarch who, at the beginning of the Book of Mormon, leads his family out of Jerusalem, sends his sons back to the city they have left to obtain from a relative, Laban, a family genealogy and a "record of the Jews" inscribed on brass plates.[17] For Lehi, these plates are a necessary resource for the faith and worship of future generations, but Laban refuses to surrender or sell them. Frustrated twice by Laban's trickery,

Figure 1. **Nephi encounters Laban (1 Nephi 4.5–10).** *The Sword of Laban*, 15.

Lehi's third son, Nephi, approaches Laban's house alone by night, "led by the Spirit, not knowing beforehand the things which [he] should do."[18] As he does, he comes upon Laban, lying on the ground drunk (see Figure 1). Apparently acting without premeditation, Nephi pulls Laban's sword from its sheath and admires its workmanship — and he is troubled to feel the Spirit constrain him to kill the man lying there.[19] He feels reluctant to act, but the Spirit persuades him that what has happened is a working out of God's purposes — that, in putting Laban at his mercy, the Lord made it possible for the plates to be obtained. Nephi is persuaded, and taking Laban by his hair, he smites off his relative's head "with his own sword."[20]

This is a story that leaves many modern readers uncomfortable — it is a "horrendous" beginning to the Book of Mormon, one author has written[21] — but Allred does not address the concerns of the faint-hearted[22] or even bother to clarify Nephi's motivation for his readers, whatever their reactions to his protagonist's act. And yet one would expect him to do so, for there is a gap that needs to be filled in the Book of Mormon narrative. Although the logic and psychology of Nephi's action once he had Laban's sword in his hands is understandable, his reasons for drawing it from its sheath are not. Nothing is said in Allred's source that would explain this first step to murder, and it is noteworthy that he makes no effort to fill this gap. He shows Laban propped up by a wall with an amphora of wine next to him, some of the wine spilled, and the sword leaning against the wall, easy for Nephi to see and examine,[23] but he gives no answer as to Nephi's motives in picking it up. We as readers might guess at prudence, lest Laban awaken and become drunkenly violent, or an aesthetic delight in fine workmanship, or greed — the hilt was, after all, made of pure gold. Yet Allred does not say. Although he breaks the connection between Nephi's admiring the sword and the impulse to kill Laban (replacing Smith's "and it came to pass," implying continuity, with *suddenly*, suggesting discontinuity),[24] he makes no other attempt at clarification.

This is not to say that Allred never adds to what he finds in his source. He readily invents details that can be taken for granted, given human nature (as in the moments of tenderness one finds in Nephi's courtship of his wife, a part of the story not described in the Book of Mormon — see Figure 2), or Mormon doctrine (as in Figure 3, where the couple kneeling across an altar seem to be following LDS practice).[25] More interestingly, when Nephi interprets a dream of his father for the

Figure 2. **Nephi's courtship. *The Liahona*, 69.**

Figure 3. **Nephi's marriage (1 Nephi 16.7). *The Liahona*, 70.**

benefit of his brothers, he and they are shown to be within the scenes he describes (see Figure 4).[26] In the first panel, all three admire the fruit of the Tree of Life; in the second panel, all three are beside the rod of iron that leads to this tree[27] — but then the brothers are separated. In the remaining panels of the page, Laman and Lemuel are standing in dark and murky water (a river that symbolizes the gulf separating the wicked from the love of God), while Nephi is on the bank. The narration of what is a rather dry theological exchange in the Book of Mormon is imaginatively presented in graphic form.

However, Allred takes no such liberties in his handling of the murder of Laban. To do so would call for a theological rather than visual elaboration and, as noted already, he is not writing a commentary; *The Golden Plates* is no *midrash*.[28]

Figure 4.   **Nephi explains his father's dream (1 Nephi 15.23-28).** *The Liahona,* **68.**

A Constellation of Texts

If that is the case, how might we describe *The Golden Plates?* An easy answer would be *translation* (intersemiotic translation, in Roman Jakobson's typology).[29] As Christiane Nord points out, translations "enable communication to take place between members of different culture communities" (the emphasis on culture rather than language is important here),[30] and this definition fits well with the idea of comic book versions of scripture. Seeing his work as a translation would allow one to recognize Allred's achievement without worrying whether every detail of his original has been carried over into his work.

To suggest this, *The Golden Plates* as translation, might seem counter-intuitive, for talk of translation usually brings with it a concern for detail. Yet, it does not always do so. Translating, Nord argues, is an action carried out in order to achieve a purpose,[31] and that purpose need not involve strict fidelity to a source.[32] A more helpful approach is provided by André Bazin's suggestion that a work can be viewed as a constellation of texts. In such a constellation, the various versions of a work would each be thought to be of equal worth, for each would be a retelling of an original not to be identified with any one of them. Discussing the book, play, and film versions of *Of Mice and Men*, Bazin suggested that one thinks "not of a novel out of which a play and a film had been 'made,' but rather a single work reflected through three art forms, an artistic pyramid with three sides" — and one might view a comic book retelling of the story as providing a fresh face to the figure, creating a cube.[33] Or again, to revert to an earlier example, one could see Dahl's wonderful version of the Cinderella story (the gory but "true" story found in his *Revolting Rhymes*), the phony version he disparages (Perrault's sanitized "Cendrillon, ou La Petite Pantoufle de Verre"), the rather sadistic comic book in which the ugly sisters are pecked to death by crows, and a thousand other texts held together by their common theme as part of the same constellation.[34] And, as Dahl would have very well known, one would not really be truer than another.

The "work," Bazin argued, is not to be identified with any of the faces of the figure,[35] but is thought to exist at "at an ideal point," independent of each. In the present case, *The Golden Plates* would be one face of a figure representing the history Nephi and his descendants, the Book of Mormon another; but neither would be the history itself — Bazin's single work.

Artifactual Authority

Bazin's argument might be granted in general and yet leave one feeling uncomfortable when applied to scripture. Isn't there something different about texts that present themselves as the word of God? I would suggest not, but in arguing this, I need to consider the other problem noted above: that, in focusing on the relationship of a comic book to its *source* (the text that is used by the comic book author), one might overlook the work's relationship to its *original.* Any retelling of a story — any member of a Bazinian constellation — lacks what Walter Benjamin called "aura": the authority inherent in a work's uniqueness, the authority that is only found in the original work. "The authenticity of a thing is the essence of all that is transmissible from its beginning," Benjamin noted, associating a work's authority with its testimony "to the history which it has experienced." "[W]hat is really jeopardized when the historical testimony is affected is the authority of the object."[36]

In the case of *The Golden Plates,* the original work would be the record inscribed in "reformed Egyptian" on metal plates reportedly translated by Joseph Smith.[37] Talk of such plates is, of course, controversial, and polemicists have not hesitated to point out that there is no evidence for their existence. However, that does not matter in the present context. All that I am concerned to do here is note that, if one takes Smith at his word, then it would be unimportant how closely Allred followed the Book of Mormon text: his work would not possess the artifactual authority of the plates. Remember here Nephi's testimony that the record that he leaves for posterity can be trusted because he was the one who engraved his story on metal plates. "I know that the record which I make is true," he writes, "and I make it with mine own hand; and I make it according to my knowledge."[38] If the importance of such testimony is granted, then it follows that no mechanical reproduction of Nephi's words would have the same claim upon us. As Benjamin notes, "The presence of the original is the prerequisite to the concept of authenticity."[39]

This forensic location of a work's authority in its provenance might be thought problematic. For us to recognize a work as a *true* record, one might object, we need to know more than the circumstances under which it was written.[40] Nevertheless, whatever else one might want to say about the reliability of historical witnesses, from the point of view of the authors of the Book of Mormon, it is appropriate to appeal to artifactual authority in the way that Nephi does. As they believed that

God was with them as they wrote, the plates they engraved were a testimony to his presence. Hence Nephi's words and the importance of
King Benjamin's testimony (some 480 years later) that the plates in his
possession really are "the plates of Nephi, which contain the records
and the sayings of our fathers from the time they left Jerusalem, until
now."[41] For the authors of the Book of Mormon, that is to say, there was
an authority inherent in a nexus "of Creator, creature, and creativity"[42]
that was evidenced in a physical artifact.[43]

The same claim could also be made for the original manuscript
of the Book of Mormon, remembering Smith's insistence that he
translated the work "by the gift and power of God."[44] The idea that he
did is controversial, of course, but if Smith's inspiration is allowed as a
premise, it is possible to apply Beckman's description of manuscripts of
mystic experience to the original record of his text: "Divine authority
inscribes itself into [the] very book."[45] And this brings me to the heart
of the matter. Allred's work is not a Reformed Egyptian text engraved
on golden plates, and it is not the text in English that Smith dictated,
but then neither is any edition of the Book of Mormon to which one
might turn. There is no artifactual authority in the printed text (the
first edition of 1830 or any of the subsequent editions) or even the
manuscript (a copy of the original) used for printing. As it happens,
accidents of copying in the latter and paratextual elements of the former
mean that they have to be considered different texts; but, even if they
were identical, they would still be merely the products of a technology
of reproduction, *not* Beckman's "material objects where one meets the
living presence of God."[46] No version of the Book of Mormon that one
can read or respond to has this artifactual authority, and that being so,
both translation (*The Golden Plates*) and source (the published Book of
Mormon) have equal authority as a response to the text Smith dictated.
Different responses would have different canonical status, but they
would have equivalence as mechanical reproductions, as well as members of a Bazinian constellation.

Biblical Comics

Could the same be said for comic book versions of the Bible? It might
be thought not, as one cannot point to an artifactual original for the
Bible in the way that one can for the Book of Mormon. As James Barr
has observed, the Bible did not "just drop from heaven, a divine book

ready-made by God."[47] It was formed by a long process involving oral transmission and scribal copying. And yet, it can still be helpful to think of it as a text inscribed by God. After all, despite the complicated history of the biblical books, one can posit that there is an "original" form of these texts — the first writing down of an oracle, say, or the first framing of a history — and that (to state the obvious) these originals had authors. And once authorship is allowed for in this way, remembering the reflections of the novelist and poet Gilbert Sorrentino on the process of writing allow one to reasonably point to an artifactual authority in originals so defined. Although Sorrentino argues that the artifact produced by an author has little importance as a text,[48] it has, he stresses, significance as evidence of creativity — a "recollection of [the author] in the act of writing."[49] Once again, it will be noted, there is a conjunction of creativity and artifact. Whether or not we choose to add a divine afflatus to the mix, there would be an authority — an aura — to this original text that would be lacking in subsequent revisions and expansions.[50]

Of course, as it was noted above, artifactual authority cannot be transmitted. One must approach graphic novels on biblical themes in the same way as one did *The Golden Plates* — granting them both respect as translations of their source and equivalence to other works with respect to a putative original. Although biblical comic books do not have the authority of a text "spoken by the Word of God" (this was Irenaeus' second-century account of the Bible's authority),[51] neither do the editions and translations of the Bible used in study and worship. One might well prefer to trust their insights, as doing so places one in the church's interpretive tradition. Yet just as Allred's work is part of the same constellation as its source, so a graphic novel treating a biblical theme is part of the same constellation as a Bible translation and — no less than the latter — is a representation of Irenaeus' spoken Word. Contrary to those first impressions, Bible comics do not call for a discourse of loss. They are not to be dismissed as simplifications of a verbally complex source but, instead, accepted as retellings of the stories that had also inspired the authors of scripture.

Notes
1   *Revolting Rhymes* (1982; London: Puffin, 1995), 5.
2   Dahl himself has fun with this in another of his *Revolting Rhymes*, when his Wolf protests that Little Red Riding Hood has forgotten to comment on his teeth (37).

3 Imelda Whelehan, "Adaptations: The Contemporary Dilemmas," Deborah Cartmell and Imelda Whelehan, eds, *Adaptations: From Text to Screen, Screen to Text* (London: Routledge, 1999), 3.

4 Michel Tournier, *Vendredi ou les Limbes du Pacifique* (Paris: Gallimard, 1967), a retelling of *Robinson Crusoe*; Woodie Guthrie, "The Ballad of Tom Joad," *Dust Bowl Ballads*, RCA Victor, 1940, a retelling of *The Grapes of Wrath*.

5 "Visual Literacy: Reading and the Contemporary Text Environment," *Literacies and the Learners*, ed. Rod Campbell and David Green (French's Forest: Prentice Hall, 2000), 32.

6 *The Ten-Cent Plague: The Great Comic-Book Scare and How It Changed America* (New York: Farrar, Straus & Giroux, 2008).

7 "Masterpieces as Comic Books," Jeet Heer and Kent Worcester, eds, *Arguing Comics: Literary Masters on a Popular Medium*, Studies in Popular Culture (Jackson: University Press of Mississippi, 2004), 52–62.

8 2 Tim 3:16 (NIV).

9 Review of A David Lewis, *The Lone and Level Sands* (Arlington, VA: Caption Box, 2005), *SBL Forum*, online: http://www.sbl-site.org/Article.aspx?ArticleId=451.

10 *Novels into Film* (Baltimore, Md.: Johns Hopkins University Press, 1957), 6.

11 Alexander Nehemas, *Nietzsche: Life as Literature* (Cambridge, MA: Harvard University Press, 1985), 165.

12 Chaim Milikowsky, "Midrash as Fiction and Midrash as History: What did the Rabbis Mean?," *Ancient Fiction: The Matrix of Early Christian and Jewish Narrative*, ed. Jo-Ann A Brant, Charles W Hedrickand and Chris Shea (Atlanta, GA: Society for Biblical Literature, 2005), 125; cf. Jacob Neusner, *Midrash as Literature: The Primacy of Documentary Discourse*, Studies in Judaism (Lanham, MD: University Press of America, 1987), 14; one might think of *The Lone and Level Sands*, the work which provoked Burke's response, where Lewis retells the events of the Exodus from slavery in Egypt through the eyes of Ramses II, or, on a smaller scale, the way in which Elijah, pouring water on his altar in Alan Close's *Fire from Heaven* (Grand Rapids, MI: Dust Press, 2007), 17, is pouring water and blood on the stones. Examples could be multiplied.

13 I am not pretending that one can approach a scriptural text without theological presuppositions (the impossibility of doing so is laid out in Stephen R Holmes, "Why Can't We Just Read the Bible: The Place of Tradition in Theology," *Listening to the Past: The Place of Tradition in Theology* [Grand Rapids, MI: Baker Academic, 2002], 6–7); nevertheless, I would still distinguish between those who set out to reinterpret a text and those who (perhaps naively) merely seek to present in a new form.

14 For Allred's motivations, see Eric Nolen-Weathington, ed., *Mike Allred, Modern Masters 16* (Raleigh, N. C.: TwoMorrows Publishing, 2008), 64–7. To date three volumes of the project have been published: this paper focuses on *The Golden Plates — Volume One: The Sword of Laban and the Tree of Life* (Lakeside, OR: AAA POP, 2004) and *Volume Two: The Liahona and the Promised Land* (Lakeside, OR: AAA POP, 2005). References to the Book of Mormon are to *Book of Mormon: Another Testament of Jesus Christ* (Salt Lake City, Utah: The Church of Jesus Christ of Latter-day Saints, 1981).

15 A good introduction to the Book of Mormon can be found in Terryl L Givens, *By the Hand of Mormon: The American Scripture that Launched a New World Religion* (New York: Oxford University Press, 2002).

16 This is James L Kugel's definition of *midrash*: see his *In Potiphar's House: The*

Interpretive Life of Biblical Texts (San Francisco: Harper, 1990), 247, 251. For problems with the Book of Mormon narrative when it is read as literature, see Neal Chandler, "Book of Mormon Stories That My Teachers Kept From Me," *Dialogue: A Journal of Mormon Thought*, vol. 24, no. 4 (1991), 30, 23.

17 1 Nephi 3.3 — the records contain the law and a selection of the prophets.

18 1 Nephi 4.6.

19 In the Book of Mormon, although "constrain" can have the meaning of being forced (Ether 6.25) or obligated (Alma 60.10), it is just used by Nephi to refer to the milder experience of feeling led or inspired to do something (1 Nephi 7.15, 2 Nephi 4.14, 28.1).

20 1 Nephi 4.18.

21 Andrew Bolton, "Anabaptism, the Book of Mormon, and the Peace Church Option," *Dialogue: A Journal of Mormon Thought*, vol. 36, no. 1 (2004), 86.

22 Others take the killing of Laban in their stride as an inevitable consequence of his refusal to surrender or sell the plates (John W Welch, "Legal Perspectives on the Slaying of Laban," *Journal of Book of Mormon Studies*, vol. 1, no. 1 [1992], 132). Arguably, if those who divert Israel from true religion should be put to death (Dt 13:5) then so should Laban, because of his indifference to the fate of Lehi's posterity. (Nephi's assuming the authority to determine this might still be thought problematic; the story presents difficulties, however we approach it.)

23 Allred, *The Sword of Laban*, 15.

24 1 Nephi 4.10; Allred, *The Sword of Laban*, 15.

25 Allred, *The Liahona*, 69–70. For LDS temple marriages ("sealings"), see Douglas J Davies, *An Introduction to Mormonism* (Cambridge: Cambridge University Press, 2003), 214.

26 Allred, *The Liahona*, 68; cf. 1 Nephi 15.21-29.

27 Readers familiar with the Book of Mormon will notice the significance of it being only Nephi who *grips* the rod, which represents God's word.

28 This should not be attributed to a lack of theological imagination: see, for example, Allred's exploration of the struggle between good and evil, which draws on LDS formulations but is not captive to them, in *Madman Comics 4: Waning of the Weird* (Milwaukie, OR: Dark Horse Comics, 1994), 8–9.

29 "On Linguistic Aspects of Translation," *On Translation*, ed. RA Brower (Cambridge, MA: Harvard University Press, 1959), 232–9.

30 *Translating as a Purposeful Activity: Functionalist Approaches Explained* (Manchester: St. Jerome Publishing, 1997), 17. "What does it mean to be a church of the Word in a visual culture?" asks Jérôme Cottin (*Le regard et la Parole: une théologie protestante de l'image* [Geneva: Labor et Fides, 1994], 7), going on to suggest that we might "know and understand God" by studying his representation in images (319).

31 In German, *Skopos* — hence the labeling of this approach *Skopostheorie*.

32 Although Allred's project might be better thought a "textual adaptation" (Katherina Reiss suggests using this term when a translation addresses an audience with different needs from that of the source: *Translation Criticism: The Potentials and Limitations* [1971], trans. Erroll F Rhodes [New York: American Bible Society, 2000], 103), but for our purposes "translation" is still an acceptable term. Also helpful is the concept of "remediation," as developed by Jay David Bolter and Richard Grusin: *Remediation: Understanding New Media* (Cambridge, MA: MIT Press, 1998).

33 "Adaptation, or the Cinema as Digest" (1948), in Bert Cardullo (ed.), *Bazin*

at Work: Major Essays and Reviews from the Forties and Fifties, trans. Alain Piette and Bert Cardullo (London: Routledge, 1997), 50. As it happens, there is no comic book version of *Of Mice and Men* listed in The Comic Book Database (http://comicbookdb.com), but one could illustrate Bazin's argument with other works: *I Am Legend*, for example — with a constellation formed from the Richard Matheson novel (New York: Fawcett Publications, 1954), the Steve Niles and Elman Brown graphic novel (San Diego: IDW Publishing, 1991), and the movies: *The Last Man on Earth* (API, 1964), *The Omega Man* (Warner Bros., 1971), and *I Am Legend* (Warner Bros., 2007).

34 Charles Perrault, *Histoires ou contes du temps passé* (1697), Petits Classiques Larousse (Paris: Larousse, 1999); Joe Tyler and Ralph Tedesco, *Cinderella*, Grimm's Fairy Tales 2 (Abingdon, PA: Zenescope, 2005). In the Jacob and Wilhelm Grimm version, the sisters are merely blinded: Maria Tatar, *The Classic Fairy Tales: Texts, Criticism* (New York: W. W. Norton, 1999), 122.

35 What one might see as a polyhedron, with the number of faces corresponding to the number of instantiations.

36 "The Work of Art in the Age of Mechanical Reproduction" (1936), *Illuminations: Essays and Reflections*, ed. Hannah Arendt, trans. Harry Zohn (New York: Schocken Books, 1968), 221. In the context of these thoughts, Benjamin's criticism of the valuation of a work's aura is irrelevant. One might remember here Nelson Goodman's definition of the autographic work (*Languages of Art: An Approach to a Theory of Symbols*, 2nd ed. [Indianapolis, IN: Bobbs-Merrill, 1976], 113; to do so is, of course, to resist his definition of literary works as merely allographic.

37 Plates that "had the appearance of gold" — hence the title of Allred's work.

38 1 Nephi 1.2. There are multiple definitions of truth in Smith's work, and Nephi's words point to just one aspect of a complex whole. Elsewhere in the work, truth is thought of as experiential (even covenantal) — something to be discovered through the experiment of living a life of faith in Christ (Moroni 10.6). Clearly one does not need any evidence for the provenance of the plates, or indeed any evidence of the plates' existence, for truth defined in this way to be evident.

39 "The Work of Art," 220.

40 Though we might remember that provenance is not unimportant in the New Testament, where we read that the word *handed down* is trustworthy (1 Tim. 1.15).

41 Mosiah 1.10.

42 The phrase is borrowed from Patricia Zimmerman Beckman.

43 "The Power of Books and the Practice of Mysticism in the Fourteenth Century: Heinrich of Nördlingen and Margaret Ebner on Mechthild's Flowing Light of the Godhead." *Church History*, vol. 76, no. 1 (March, 2007), 61–83. Beckman's interest is in medieval manuscripts of mystical works "which were, and were experienced as, Word" (63), but as the Book of Mormon plates were reportedly inscribed by revelation her words could also be applied to them.

44 *Book of Mormon*, Title Page. Some sheets and fragments from what is claimed to be the original manuscript still exist. See the discussion in Richard P Howard, *Restoration Scriptures: A Study of Their Textual Development* (Independence, MO: Herald House, 1969).

45 Beckman, 68.

46 Beckman, 71.

47 *The Scope and Authority of the Bible* (Philadelphia, PA: Westminster, 1980), 58.

48   "The act of writing has, for the writer, little to do with the product that issues forth from it: for him, the act itself is the product." Gilbert Sorrentino, "The Act of Creation and Its Artifact" (1981), *The Review of Contemporary Fiction*, vol. 19 (1999), 8.

49   Sorrentino, 8; cf. the reflection in Italo Calvino, *If on a Winter's Night a Traveller*, trans. William Weaver (London: Vintage, 1998), 190 — "the truth of literature consists only in the physicality of the act of writing."

50   A fuller account would need to allow for creativity in the evolution of the text, but even in such an account we would have to distinguish between the manuscript that would have revealed the author "in the act of writing" from subsequent copies.

51   *Against Heresies*, in *The Ante-Nicene Fathers: Translations of the Writings of the Fathers down to AD 325*, ed. Alexander Roberts and James Donaldson, 10 vols (1885–97; Peabody, MA: Hendrickson Publishers, 1994), 2.28.2; cf. the account of scripture as "god-breathed" in 2 Tim. 3.16.

Comics and Religion: Theoretical Connections

DARBY ORCUTT

OME FORM OF COMICS EXPRESSION exists within the broad context of nearly every major contemporary religious tradition. For example, the Association of Jewish Libraries provides three different recommended resource lists of "Jewish Graphic Novels."[1] Christian examples range from sympathetic comic book biographies of Pope John Paul II to the fundamentalist tracts of Jack Chick, likely the most widely distributed comics creator in the world. The extremely popular comics series *Amar Chitra Katha (ACK)* has carried the teachings of Hinduism to entire generations in South Asia and to South Asian children in diaspora, replacing the traditional passing of stories from grandparents to grandchildren as family structures and proximities have changed. Even in the Islamic context, a tradition generally wary of images and wherein representations of God or Mohammed are forbidden, comics traditions thrive.

Advocates of comics within these traditions often value this format for its simplicity. Typical testimonials for Chick tracts laud their ease of comprehension and their cross-cultural understandability, evinced by their use and appeal worldwide. According to religious comics' boosters, even children can understand them due to their pictorial and textual nature. Popular Islamic comic strips take advantage of this characteristic, providing moral guidance to children using human and funny animal cartoon characters. These and other comics exude a "magic in word and pictures" that not only appeals to children and youth, but also promotes understanding and retention of teachings, an experimentally demonstrated effect of *ACK* comics.[2] Religious communicators value comics for their easy engagement of audiences with their message.

But scholars are only beginning to truly understand how comics are "read"; the reading experience is much more complex than that of text alone. Readers are engaged in interpreting not just linguistic signs, but also visual signs and cues as well as hybrid visual and linguistic content (e.g., text integrated into the artwork rather than merely side-by-side in a caption or word balloon). Visual literacy in comics relies on icons, colors, graphical perspective, stock cartoon "vocabulary" (e.g., wavy lines to indicate a strong smell), and much more. Reading comics requires proficiency in interpreting text, images, and their interaction.

By their very nature, therefore, comics constitute "multimodal" texts, those necessitating and facilitating understanding through multiple approaches to meaning-making. Intended to be the easiest-to-understand comics, where verbal and visual elements seek simply to reinforce one another, even the instructions included with "some assembly required" products demand at least some linguistic and visual attention. These instructions may further elicit readers' embodied involvement in laying out parts and tentatively fitting them together in order to fully grasp meaning. While their sensory grounding is nominally visual, comics narratives evoke such multi-sensory experiences. They prompt readers to imaginatively "hear" sound effects and dialogue, to "smell" strong odors, or to "feel" the tactile sensations of characters (be it cold weather or the impact of a villain's punch). Comics can mimic virtually all modes of human perception, physical or mental; for example, attention to a physical object may be expressed using a close-up view or via high detail within an otherwise less-detailed panel.

Religious experience is similarly multimodal. By any definition, religion is a complex phenomenon or set of phenomena. Religions are necessarily shared, socially constructed understandings — and religious expression is largely comprised of symbols and symbolism. According to anthropologist Clifford Geertz's frequently cited definition, "A religion is a system of symbols."[3] Religious traditions include beliefs, rituals, texts, morals, and more, expressed by means of speaking, writing, performance, prayer, meditation, music, art, and so on. These symbolic texts, images, acts, and other means of religious expression, like comics narratives, involve and evoke multiple ways of interpreting and understanding, and they reflect a grounding in sensory perception that may be either more concrete (e.g., the "smells and bells" of traditional liturgical Christianity) or more strictly metaphorical (e.g., the nearly universal religious language of "seeing," "feeling," "hearing," or even "tasting" the divine).

Icon

The iconic nature of comics is evident, first of all, in comics' common use of the cartoon as an ideal form: a spare visual representation for which readers must fill in the details. A few lines drawn with just a basic sense of perspective become, say, a table in the mind of the reader, through an interpretive process that seems nothing short of amazing. Depending on the visual cues presented, furthermore, the "table" imagined by the reader may be either more or less "fleshed out" or abstract; in other words, it may be a specific kind of table (e.g., heavy, ornate, antique, wooden) or a more generic "table" (e.g., a basic notion of something on which objects may be placed). In his seminal *Understanding Comics*, Scott McCloud posits a scale of iconic abstraction and demonstrates that comics creators may utilize different levels of abstraction to particular effects. In fact, this may be accomplished even within the same comics text. (For example, in manga simply drawn characters facilitate reader identification, while more realistically drawn characters evoke a sense of "otherness.")[4]

The capacity for readers to identify with cartoon characters — including often the human inability to *not* identify with certain cartoon representations — reflects a further power of the iconic nature of comics. Perhaps the self-centeredness of humans causes us to "see" a face in a mere two dots and a line. Yet, not only do we "see" a person in simplified cartoon figures; we often "see" ourselves, identifying with cartoon characters in a very personal way. McCloud suggests that, as a highly simplified iconic abstraction, "the cartoon is a vacuum into which our identity and awareness are pulled, an empty shell that we inhabit" or "become,"[5] imaginatively and metaphorically. This easy identification with cartoon faces may, in part, stem from our own general mental images of our individual faces, versus our more detailed mental images of the faces of others.

Icons predominate in the world of religious expression. In similar ways to comics, religious traditions rely on icons to engage and promote identification of humans with them. While in certain religious traditions the term refers to a particular sort of visual representation of deity, in the present discussion "icon" may be considered most fruitfully in its broader sense as a visual symbol. Even those traditions that generally forbid representations of deity (e.g., Islam) typically have rich traditions of iconic imagery in this wider connotation. Iconic images often "stand in" for a religious tradition as a whole; for example, the Star of David for Judaism, the crescent moon for Islam, or the cross for Christianity. Iconic images often provide material for or even constitute popular understanding of a tradition. For one example, illiterate medieval Christians often learned biblical stories not by reading written texts, but via the images they saw in stained glass windows. For another example, some Hindu teachers describe their idols as "teaching tools," depictions of their gods intended not to fully represent the deity, but rather to assist necessarily limited mortal minds in apprehending some aspect of the divine.

The tremendous power of the visual icon in strongly engaging individuals and promoting identification need hardly be argued, whether in the context of particular religious communities or within the context of religious-like devotion and ritual, often referred to as civil religion. For example, sports fans often exhibit religious-like behavior in their visceral responses to totemistic images (logos, mascots, etc.). Additionally, vehement debates over flag-burning illustrate the power of visual symbols in American civil religion; Michael Welch notes that the flag is recognized, legally and popularly, as "a venerated object,"[6] and he references an opinion of Supreme Court Justice William Rehnquist "that the Stars and Stripes warrants unique status due to the 'almost mystical reverence with which it is regarded by Americans'" and "that sacralizing the flag is necessary for purposes of empowering the state,"[7] (i.e., for individuals to identify with the nation). That civil religion seeks to partake of the depth and fervor of religious devotion as created, mediated, and intensified by the visual icon attests to the power of images within religion. In many religious contexts, visual images achieve their power by becoming taken-for-granted aspects of everyday life, often hidden influences that are part of the social fabric of individual and group identity. So, for example, images of Hasidic Jews in recent photo books tacitly function to constitute generally a self-identity of "differentness" or "radical other vis-à-vis the dominant culture" for American Jews;[8] Warner Sallman's famous picture *Head of Christ* offers an "evangelical translation" of traditional depictions of Jesus[9] by presenting a gentle-faced and innately human Jesus lit by soft light, an image that begs for a personal intimacy. The more subtle the symbol's action, usually the more persuasive are its effects.

Immersive Narrative

Like the icon, narrative serves not merely as a characteristic of comics, but plays a defining role in the format. Even the seminal definition of comics, Will Eisner's "sequential art,"[10] presumes a narrative thread connecting images. This narrative thread *makes* such images comics rather than just a collection of juxtaposed pictures. McCloud's definition of comics includes the phrase "in deliberate sequence."[11] His own experimental comics illustrate that comics have the potential to simultaneously provide multiple deliberate sequences, and that the deliberateness may come on the part of the reader choosing among various paths of sequence. McCloud's "Five Card Nancy," a game in which players select the next panel from among the panels in their hand, demonstrates fully reader-driven creation of comics sequence.[12] What these extreme examples of reader-influenced narrative illustrate is true of *all* comics: readers take an active role in crafting comics narrative by acting as co-creators of their reading experience. Furthermore, this co-conspiracy of readers in comics "creation" is of a different nature than reader experiences of an exclusively textual narrative; the reader's experience of a "graphic novel" is quite different than a reader's experience of a "novel," in part because of the visual (and thus more visceral) elements, which can evoke ideas, sentiments, and identifications in ways that may seem more authentic *because* they are not linguistically mediated.

Comics narrative, by its nature, functions in an immersive fashion. Reflecting on a fondly remembered *Batman* comic re-read in adulthood, one writer remarks, "I didn't remember all of the word balloons, caption boxes, sound effects, or panel breakdowns I *must* have read as a child. What I remember, in my mind's eye, was a fluid story — much like a movie . . . *The comic seemed static compared to my memories of the story.*"[13] Comics narratives function only when readers engage in filling in the gaps: providing the ultimate flow of the narrative, sound effects, specifics of the action, and so forth. Most importantly, readers must "fill in" the gutters, the "spaces" between panels, a process that turns these otherwise static images into narrative. This process is highly demanding of readers, requiring work on their part. Part of this comes through the iconic nature of comics discussed above, as the cartoon itself requires readers to "fill in" or "flesh out" its lack of detail in similar fashion to how gutters are filled, oftentimes using very scant visual information and even without readers' awareness of their own complicity in the process. In *Understanding Media*, Marshall McLuhan notes the huge effort and investment of themselves that readers make in reading comics, as opposed to their passive involvement in many other forms of media. As he puts it, cartoons have "a participational and do-it-yourself character,"[14] provoking a "depth involvement" beyond that of most other media.[15] Those who read comics commonly experience being "sucked in" to the narrative. The format offers an imagined world for the reader to psychologically and emotionally inhabit, a world easily and quickly engaged, perhaps all the more so because its exact details are unconsciously and satisfyingly fleshed out by the reader in harmony with her own taken-for-granted ideas.

In the context of religious traditions, narrative serves many purposes; stories teach divine truths, provide moral guidance, offer exemplary models for how to behave (or how not to behave), convey history, promote common identity, and so on. Religious narratives tend to be mythic in nature, meaning that they hold or express some sort of sacred value — in other words, they somehow transcend that which is merely commonplace or everyday. The models or rules for behavior that they offer are ideal or divine ones for which devotees of a tradition should strive. The histories recounted within a religious tradition comprise larger-than-life stories, generally including the origins of the world and of the foundations of the tradition itself.

Like comics narratives, religious narratives solicit deep involvement on the part of their audiences. Religious stories necessarily address issues of identification, e.g., one's role in the universe, the relationship between human and deity, or defining the membership of the religious community. Furthermore, most myths proscribe a role or roles for the audience to play, e.g., participation in a special ritual, imitation of a holy figure, or departure on a sacred "path" or "journey." Myths advance the rational and especially emotional associations vital to religious sentiment. A religious narrative is intended to be internalized. Linguist Vito Evola notes that religious adherents reading sacred texts "universally apply a cognitive process of semantic interpretation which differs from [mere] pleasurable reading"[16] and that "recent psycholinguistic and cognitive research on metaphor has strongly proven that metaphor is a conceptual phenomenon, more governed by thought than by language."[17] Therefore, religious narrative generally connects with its audience differently — and much more deeply — than can most other narrative, in part because it partakes of non-linguistic metaphors that may "speak" more directly to the inherently metaphorical nature of human cognition: again, like comics.

Time and Narrative

By their very nature, comics represent time spatially. The passage of time in comics may be represented using *only* spatial techniques (most commonly, panel-to-panel transition), although they are often verbally reinforced (e.g., "The next day . . ."). Other narrative forms occasionally experiment with this means of presentation (e.g., certain split-screen sequences in film), but no other format by necessity relies on the spatial representation of time. Comics present images that reflect multiple moments all at once to the reader's eye. Comics pages literally display past, present, and future simultaneously. In most comics, creators make little use of this aspect, except perhaps to lay out pages such that images portraying events intended to surprise readers immediately follow a turn of the page. Some comics creators, however, take advantage of this fact; for example, Douglas Rushkoff and Liam Sharp's Vertigo series *Testament* frequently presents pages of parallel and even intermingling narratives of past, present, and future, as well as divine beings who exist in the "timeless" gutter spaces between panels.

Religious or mythic narrative also reflects a fundamental relationship to time dissimilar to other narrative modes. Rather than adhere to the familiar modern idea of time as an irreversible flow in one direction, religious narratives represent time as circular, repeatable, illusory, or even escapable. Typically, only two mundane means may transcend "normal" time: memory and imagination. Sacred means of doing so include ritual reenactment of mythic events, imitation of divine models, and profound or mystical experiences. Mircea Eliade's seminal ideas of religious myths and time in *The Myth of the Eternal Return* have since been fine-tuned by him and others. But his basic premise stands: traditional religious expression works against a modern, linear, and historicized view of time. Whether through the ritual reenactment of Jesus' last supper or the mystical participation in Christ's death and resurrection, to name Christian examples alone, "[transcendent] reality is acquired solely through repetition or participation."[18] Religious narratives, there-fore, work to make time sacred by means of repetition and participation. Repetition of traditional stories, tropes, phrases, images, and so forth infuse religious narratives and draw parallels and connections between the present time and the sacred past. Similarly, the participatory impera-tive of religious narratives solicits direct identification with the divine and makes the present time sacred through its link to a sacred past ("we believers are the new Israel"), to a sacred future ("we are ushering in God's kingdom"), or to an eternal sacred that is outside of time ("we have become one with God").

Seeing multiple "times" presented all at once in nonlinear ways seems more or less limited in modern experience to the realms of comics and the religious, in addition to their close functional simi-larities as icon-rooted, deeply immersive narratives. Unfortunately, few religious-oriented comics narratives even begin to take advantage of the expressive possibilities of how comics and religion function or can function together. The sections below offer some specific examples of the natural fit between comics and religious narrative, an illustrative and not comprehensive listing.

Chick Tracts

With more than a half-billion copies of his work published in more than 100 languages, Jack Chick has enjoyed unparalleled success as a comics creator. Although he is considered by his supporters as a frank promoter of fundamentalist gospel truth and by his detractors as an outrageously vitriolic caricaturist of non-Christian and non-conservative cultures and lifestyles, members of both camps acknowledge the high quality of craft exhibited in his comics. Chick makes tremendous use of the immersive qualities of comics, using cartoon characters with whom readers can readily identify and placing them into visual narrative worlds that readers easily and unconsciously "fill in" and thus experience as immanently "real."

Chick's "Trust Me!" tract typifies his artful blend of comics and religious narrative. Chick's common approach of offering two distinct narratives, which usually involve separate characters, is here accomplished with but one character who metaphorically lives two lives: first, as a youth enticed into an ever-downward spiral of drug addiction, crime, and suffering; and then as a poor soul who finds salvation and attains the rewards of heaven in the afterlife. Using mostly wordless panels that clearly and engagingly convey its action and emotion, the story further draws in the reader using the comics technique of a more simply drawn, cartoonish character placed within a detailed and visually complex virtual environment. Chick's main character provides what McCloud calls a "mask" that allows the reader to "safely enter a sensually stimulating world."[19] Chick's world is undeniably stimulating, although anything but safe. Within the first two panels, a bus rolls by spewing thick smoke, a poor girl is being held out the bus window, an unseen figure shoots a gun, the bus driver yells, a mean-looking cat stalks a scurrying rat, the reader sees a fence littered with various icons (including a pentagram and a peace symbol) — and all of this is apart from the main action and characters of these panels.[20]

The immersive nature of Chick's comic work plays to great effect in this tract as the reader quickly identifies with the nameless main character, who in the first panel appears as initially confused as the reader as to what's going on. Within the space of the first gutter, he begins to follow the finger that beckons him to come, as if he is simply being led, like the reader, with no true awareness of his own volition in the happenings of the story. The reader too follows the main character's path as things go increasingly badly for him, culminating with his contracting AIDS as a result of being raped in prison. At his lowest point, a pale, sickly ghost of his former self, the main character receives a Chick tract through the bars of his cell. The most immersive moment of the tract proceeds so naturally that most readers probably do not notice it consciously: the perspective switches in one panel to a point-of-view "shot" of the Chick tract held open within the hands of the main character, his thumbs in the same spots where the reader's thumbs likely rest. The page of the tract pictured is the one page that is essentially common to all Chick tracts: a text-heavy basic gospel message alongside an image of Jesus on the cross.[21] The comic has completed its work of bringing the reader into its narrative world — even to a sacred time of decision, when the reader must choose whether to continue following the main character, even through his repentance, acceptance of Jesus Christ as his savior, and departure for Heaven in the afterlife, all depicted in the comic's final three pages.[22] Through the immersive action of the comics format, this tract artfully forces the reader to a point of decision. While non-comics formats might encourage readers to act, the comics format of this tract *requires* either continued participation in the narrative or a conscious disengagement from identification with the cartoon protagonist.

James Sturm's "The Revival"

The lead story of his triptych of comics tales collected as *James Sturm's America: God, Gold, and Golems*, "The Revival" relates the experiences of early-nineteenth-century frontier families gathered to see a Christian faith healer. After witnessing the healer making a lame boy walk, a grieving mother presents her recently deceased daughter to be raised from the dead. She reacts with righteous denial when the healer instead proclaims that the child shall be resurrected "not today, nor tomorrow — but when our Savior walks among us again!"[23] Lifting the child up before the gathered masses, she prays for the Lord to "show them" his power by raising her daughter. In a brief sequence of wordless panels that form the crux of the narrative, the mother holds the dead girl close, the "camera" zooms in, and, just before the scene fades to black, the reader sees that the young girl's hand is suddenly upon her mother's arm.[24]

In the final two pages following, the reader sees that the girl has been buried. But what happened in that panel-to-panel transition? How is it that her hand was raised up? Is this a "real life" occurrence or a depiction of the mother's inner world? The comic is intentionally silent on these questions, leaving a provocative gutter for the reader to fill in. Sturm has affirmed that his intention was indeed to leave it up to the reader to ponder what may have happened here. The book is dedicated "[i]n Memory of Karen Land, Loving Guide and Unparalleled Explorer."[25] Land was a psychic healer who had been of tremendous help to Sturm, yet in ways that he found difficult to credibly express within the bounds of the scientific skepticism of contemporary culture. "The Revival" was influenced in large part by this challenge of articulation, and this particular panel transition was intentionally crafted in order to, as Sturm describes it, "carve out a space where one can talk about a person like Karen Land."[26] This in-between space of unresolved narrative possibility, a space of deep reflection on the nature of reality, is made possible by the "do-it-yourself" nature of the comics format.

India Authentic

In business for less than three years, the now-defunct Virgin Comics sought to re-envision traditional South Asian mythology and spiritual themes by appealing to more modern and international audiences. By far the most overtly steeped in Hindu mythology of the publisher's line, *India Authentic* consisted of single-issue stories that retold and modernized the "origin" stories of various Hindu deities. Following in the tradition of *Amar Chitra Katha* yet incorporating much more contemporary Western comics elements and styles, *India Authentic* stories sought to immerse South Asian and Western readers in what the series' creator, popular self-help guru Deepak Chopra, described as primal mythologies that express collective human experience.

From its very first issue — focused on the elephant-headed god and "remover of obstacles," Ganesha — *India Authentic* established itself as a new and different expression of traditional Hindu culture. While the introduction by Chopra calls upon readers to "emulate him,"[27] the comic does not promote identification with the god so much as it represents a dimension of timeless sacredness in ethical action. Most of the comic focuses on the tale of Ganesha's creation, initial death at the hands of his stepfather Shiva, and resurrection to godhood through the acquisition of the head of a dead elephant. Virtually every panel of the comic features a single primary color scheme, the bold blue, green, and red each artfully denoting a different narrative thread and mood. Although experienced by the reader all at once on the same page, the distinctive colors communicate the presence of different narratives and times simultaneously, reminding the reader (via peripheral vision, at least) of the parallel narrative structure of the story. Red and blue have even been shown to evoke differing perceptions of the rate of time's passage from the same viewer,[28] contributing to this effect.

Yet, the first and last pages of the story appear markedly different, and they are the only two pages of the comic not set in the mythic past. Bookending the interweaving mythic narratives, these two pages parallel one another visually, as well as reflect the moral thrust of the story: Ganesha, who is generally associated in Hindu tradition with the honoring of parents, here honors his elephant mother by seeking to assuage the pain of her death. These two pages alone incorporate an earthy brown color scheme, in stark contrast to the more primary colors of the mythic panels between them, visually providing a plain brown wrapper. In other words, they are the profane present within which the sacred narratives between them operate. Their own timelessness is conveyed by the very structure of the panels themselves: each of the first and last pages consists of a full-page panel into which the other panels are placed — just as these pages represent the profane eternal present into which the sacred mythic narratives are placed. This artful juxtaposition, which merges ordinary and sacred time, is impossible to imagine in a format other than comics.

Moving Forward

Once recognized and articulated, the deep connections between comics and religion will hopefully inspire further exploration by readers, scholars, and creators. For readers, this way of looking at religious comics narratives opens up an array of possibilities. How a comic functions to reflect in its very form a particular religious question or worldview could represent an entirely new dimension by which to judge and appreciate its artfulness. Recognizing the inherent iconicity and narrativity of both the format and subject matter of religiously oriented comics should lead to a greater understanding of their themes and messages.[29] Certainly, this more nuanced understanding of how religion and comics work would assist their audiences in being critical readers of them, more alert to the means of persuasion and identification that they use.

For scholars, this essay suggests many fruitful lines of inquiry. The framework of the iconic, immersive narrative offers one clear approach to reading at once the sacred/profane, visual/verbal texts that are religious comics. In other words, this understanding encourages a more holistic view of their hybrid nature, recognizing that they constitute more than the sum of their parts. They are not *just* comics that happen to be about the religious, nor religious expressions that *just* happen to be in comics format. Theoretically minded researchers might also tease out and explain the implicit questions of how time might alternatively be understood or represented, and whether there abides a more fundamental reason that comics and religion persist as the sole necessary challengers of typical human representations of time.

Creators will hopefully feel challenged and empowered to experiment ever more with the interesting mix of comics and religion. Powerful synergies lie therein, waiting for creators to take advantage of them and craft new techniques by which to present alternative perspectives on the world. Scholarly reflection at its best leads back to practice, and, in the case of comics scholarship, ideally impacts both co-creators: readers and artists. The power of these iconic, immersive narratives awaits the interpretation of pen and brush.

Notes

1 Association of Jewish Libraries, "Bibliography Bank," 2007, *Association of Jewish Libraries*, http://www.jewishlibraries.org/ajlweb/resources/bib_bank.htm (accessed October 29, 2009).

2 Anant Pai, "Magic in Words and Pictures," *India Perspectives* (September–October 2008), 26.

3 Clifford Geertz, "Religion as a Cultural System," *Anthropological Approaches to the Study of Religion*, ed. Michael Banton (New York: Praeger, 1966), 4.

4 Scott McCloud, *Understanding Comics* (Northampton, MA: Kitchen Sink Press, 1993), 44.

5 McCloud, *Understanding Comics*, 36.

6 Michael Welch, *Flag Burning: Moral Panic and the Criminalization of Protest* (New York: Aldine de Gruyter, 2000), 31.

7 Welch, 43.

8 Jack Kugelmass, "Jewish Icons: Envisioning the Self in Images of the Other," in *Jews and Other Differences: The New Jewish Cultural Studies*, ed. Jonathan Boyarin and Daniel Boyarin (Minneapolis: University of Minnesota Press, 1997), 50.

9 David Morgan, "Imaging Protestant Piety: The Icons of Warner Sallman," *Religion and American Culture* 3.11 (Winter), 44.

10 Will Eisner, *Comics & Sequential Art* (Tamarac, FL: Poorhouse Press, 2005), 5.

11 McCloud, *Understanding Comics*, 9.

12 Scott McCloud, "Five Card Nancy," *ScottMcCloud.com*, http://scottmccloud.com/4-inventions/nancy/index.html (accessed October 29, 2009).

13 Durwin S. Talon, *Panel Discussions: Design in Sequential Art Storytelling* (Raleigh, NC: TwoMorrows, 2003), 12.

14 Marshall McLuhan and W. Terrence Gordon, *Understanding Media: The Extensions of Man* (Corte Madera, CA: Gingko Press, 2003), 225.

15 McLuhan, 227.

16 Vito Evola, "Cognitive Semiotics and On-line Reading of Religious Texts: A Hermeneutic Model of Sacred Literature and Everyday Revelation," *Cogprints.org*, http://cogprints.org/4863/1/Cognitive_Semiotics_and_On-Line_Reading_of_Religious_Texts.pdf (accessed October 29, 2009).

17 Evola, 3.

18 Mircea Eliade, *The Myth of the Eternal Return: Cosmos and History* (Princeton, NJ: Princeton University Press, 2005), 34.

19 McCloud, *Understanding Comics*, 43.

20 Jack T. Chick, "Trust Me!," Chick Publications, 1994, http://www.chick.com/reading/tracts/0025/0025_01.asp (accessed April 30, 2009), 1.

21 Chick, 18.

22 Chick, 19–21.

23 James Sturm, *James Sturm's America: God, Gold, and Golems* (New York: Drawn & Quarterly, 2007), 29.

24 Sturm, 30.

25 Sturm, 3.

26 James Sturm, "Comics: Finding My Religion," *Graven Images: Religion in Comic Books & Graphic Novels* conference, Boston University, April 11, 2008.

27 Deepak Chopra, Saurav Mohapatra, Satish Tayade, Abhishek Singh, and M. Subramanian, *Deepak Chopra Presents India Authentic* (New York: Virgin, 2007), 10.

28   Gerda Smets, "Time Expression of Red and Blue," *Perceptual and Motors Skills* 29 (1969), 511–14.

29   While the series has just begun as of the time of this writing, Mike Carey and Peter Gross's *The Unwritten* (DC/Vertigo) appears to be addressing these very ideas.

Killing the Graven God:
Visual Representations of the Divine
in Comics

ANDREW TRIPP

GOD IS PROBLEMATIC IN GRAPHIC narratives. Images shape the narrative flow of comics and graphic novels, but these graphic narratives require images to represent a monotheistic God. To varying degrees, the Abrahamic faiths oppose the potential idolatry of having physical representations of divinity. The fifth- and sixth-century Christian theologian Pseudo-Dionysius wrote a spiritual practice and developed an apophatic theology of unknowing (apophasis being the attempt to know what God is *not*). He sought to move past the idolatry of words[1] to direct contemplation of God by means of theophany, the manifestation of the divine to a human or humans. This form of theology argues that God is unknowable in completeness; all words fail to describe the completeness of God. God can only be understood through God's self-revelation to humanity. Thomas Aquinas incorporated Pseudo-Dionysius' apophatic theology in the *Summa*, where Aquinas claims that the only useful name of God is "Who is," since any other name limits God by attributing something to God.

> Our mind cannot be led by sense so far as to see the essence of God; because the sensible effects of God do not equal the power of God as their

> cause. Hence from the knowledge of sensible things the whole power of
> God cannot be known; nor therefore can His essence be seen.[2]

Though God, in this understanding, is beyond sensible imagination and
limitless, authors and artists of graphic narratives depict God directly
and metaphorically. Depictions appear in venues from the Vertigo
imprint, to mainstream superhero comics, to independent presses.
Treatment of God's image displays the implicit theology of the authors
and artists, but brings up the trouble of displaying an image for something that is beyond/more than an image.

Images of God define God as much as words name God. By assigning
an image to God or the Divine Reality, the graphic representation displays the assumptions of the artist or the author about God's unnamed
attributes and what the artist or author believes the audience under-
stands about God. When God is depicted in a graphic narrative, normally
unstated or undefined elements of God are forced into expression, since
the artist has the necessary task of imaging God. The essence of the
Abrahamic God is unutterable and nameless,[3] however, so it is impossible to have an unequivocal depiction of the Divine Reality. Images for
the Divine must be metaphorical and point beyond the depiction to the
larger reality of God's nature.

In several graphic narratives, images of God go through changes and
death-rebirth cycles that connote something larger than the individual
depiction. These images for God act as symbols with multivalent meanings, which speak to communal experience and understanding without
in-depth explanation. The radiant being of life in an anthropomorphic form is not the whole of God, or even the singular depiction of
God's essence, but it hints at a broader reality and understanding. This
mutable treatment of divine imagery puts forth a definition of what it
means to be God. While there is no standard for divine imagery in comics and graphic narratives, themes emerge from the internal dialogue
within narratives when they wrestle with what it means to be God — the
metanarrative shows how elements of Western pop culture perceive the
Divine. A form of absurdist understanding appears in the metanarrative, where the irrational exercise of defining the indefinable forces
a humanly impossible possibility. Examples of this include depictions
of God with suicidal ideation in *Fallen Angel*, or God the masturbatory
lunatic in *Chronicles of Wormwood*. Impossibly absurd depictions point to
the failure of images to adequately portray God.

Treatment of Divine Images in Graphic Narratives

The treatment of God's image varies in the graphic narrative medium. *Lucifer* shows an evolution of God through multiple persons. *Strange Girl* shows God's evacuation from reality, but questions whether this means God is no longer present. *Spawn* shows a violent struggle between YHWH and Satan where the truth of absolute divinity transcends both of them. *Proposition Player* updates the idea of God and the heavenly sphere through a capitalistic understanding of souls and divine power. *Swamp Thing* shows a grand union between primordial darkness and absolute light. *Preacher* imagines the death of God at the hands of vengeance. *Chronicles of Wormwood* displays God as an insane bearded and robed figure who becomes strangely linked to Satan. *Warlock* displays the relationship between God and Jesus in the roles of High Evolutionary and Adam Warlock and plays out the troubled relationship between remote divine and worldly do-gooder.

Divine images evolve in the *Lucifer* narrative. The comic book series portrays Lucifer, the fallen angel, and his interactions with the world after he gives up control of Hell. The first time God is depicted chronologically in the narrative, God is an anthropomorphic being of light. As the narrative progresses, the next chronological depiction of God is of the stereotypical old man with white hair. For a time, Lucifer is the Divine over a world of his own creation, and as the narrative unfolds, Elaine, the daughter of the angel Michael and granddaughter of God, also becomes God of her own world. Elaine is a demi-human/demi-angel who finds apotheosis (the state of becoming divine) at the death of her father, the angel Michael. When the traditionally depicted radiant being of light/old bearded white man God decides to leave the holy throne, Elaine becomes the new Divine Reality. In her final apotheosis, Elaine merges the realities of God's world, Lucifer's world, and her own world into a single universe. Elaine then joins with creation because, due to the painful experiences she had while relating with her own world, she has no desire to remain active as a personal God. With the merger of the three creations, the essence of the world becomes one with the Divine. The transformation of images for the Divine fulfills Pseudo-Dionysius' *exitus-reditus*, where God is unnamed as father, as man, as good, as evil, as woman, and as person. The reader is left with God who is the ground of being.[4] This God is with and behind existence, and allows existence through divine presence.

Strange Girl follows this trend of God vacating reality. Bethany Black, the daughter of devout Christian fundamentalists, is the only member of her family who does not ascend to Heaven during the Rapture. Bethany eventually dies in the post-Rapture dystopia and ascends to Heaven, where she meets the normative "old white man" God among the clouds. God asks Bethany what she wants for her Heaven, and Bethany convinces God to vacate existence so she may live in a world with no Heaven, no Hell, no angels, and no demons. She asks for a world where choice matters because of nontheistic ethics instead of religious imperatives. When God gives her this Heaven, Bethany returns to an Earth where there are still churches and believers despite the absence of God. Issue 18 ends with the line from Voltaire, "If God did not exist, it would be necessary to invent him."[5] The narrative includes God's departure, but the reader is left to question whether, in Bethany's new world, if there is truly an absence of God. Any answer is left to the reader, forcing her to place herself in the narrative and answer her own question.

Spawn follows a much more violent track in the destruction of divine images. In the narrative, Spawn is a human imbued with demonic skin that provides him with supernatural powers, which he uses for good. In the course of the narrative, YHWH and Satan are placed in the bodies of children because their creator (who is at once the Man of Miracles, the Keeper of the Greenworld, Jesus, and Kali) wished for his/her children to know what it was like to become human and find love. YHWH is not the absolute divinity in this narrative, and YHWH and Satan are siblings. The Man of Miracles hopes that the two antagonistic divine powers will find humanity through the love of family. This hope fails, however, since the true nature of both YHWH and Satan overtakes the pair of children, and the two begin to fight each other once again. This battle between the two starts Armageddon and kills all of humankind. In the process, Spawn becomes imbued with divine power and creates a new world without a link to Heaven or Hell so that humankind itself can be free. After the creation of a new world for humans, he gives up his godhood and returns to his previous state as Spawn, since he still cannot forgive himself for his previous sins. God shifts from a traditional Western God, to the God behind the God in the Man of Miracles, to the apotheosis of a superhero in a world without divine presence.[6]

Reflecting both contemporary seeker sensitivity and consumer culture where religion becomes commoditized, Bill Willingham's *Proposition Player* spins a tale reimaging and reimagining the Divine Reality. Joey Martin, a poker player at an off-the-strip Vegas casino, purchases the souls of his coworkers for a beer. Now possessing these souls, he gains the attention of the Divine Reality. An angel arrives and threatens Joey for the souls, while a demon helps the man become a new player in the cosmic pantheon. The angel leads Joey to Asgard's decaying ruins and Odin's dilapidated mead hall, whose ruin was caused by Christianity's conquest of souls. Joey balks at the angel's threats, and the host of minor gods and forgotten deities back his plan to form a new religious order. In the course of the narrative, the Divine Reality reimages itself from a Heaven with angels and alabaster to a casino and its proprietor — Joey Martin the Proposition Player. The epilogue finishes with the narration,

> This is the story of Joey Martin, a proposition player who only ever wanted to play in the big games, and who, eventually, played in the biggest game of all. Along the way, he sort of, accidentally, became God. Yes, that's God with the big 'G,' as he controlled more souls than any other deity, trinity, or pantheon in the history of the universe.[7]

God becomes the master of the house in the world of chance instead of YHWH, a sky god in the clouds. God moves from order and justice to a figure of chance, odds, and swagger.

Continuing in this Vertigo tradition is Alan Moore's reimaging of God in *Swamp Thing*. Moore leads Swamp Thing to discover evil in the "American Gothic" plot arc and exposes the creature to American culture's worst flaws. Moore also injects a naturalistic understanding of the cycle of life into Swamp Thing's encounter with the Parliament of Trees. Following Swamp Thing's confrontation with the nature of evil, the black of primordial chaos reemerges from its slumber. Heroes venture forth to battle with the ancient dark, and each hero is defeated in turn. Swamp Thing approaches the darkness and enters into the cosmic force's being. Unlike the heroes who battled the entity, Swamp Thing communicates with the ancient dark without malice and explains the cycle of life as a metaphor for its existence. Swamp Thing explains to the entity that the brilliance of virtue only springs from fertile dark loam. Light cannot exist without dark defining what is not light. This communication enables the ancient dark to reach up and accept the hand of God, instantly joining with God. Moore has Phantom Stranger, an intentionally mysterious cosmic interloper, act as the voice of the narrator at the conclusion of the story. The Stranger informs Swamp

Thing that light and shade still exist, but their conflict has been altered. Both everything and nothing change as light and dark hold hands in union.[8] Both hands are the hands of God. The completeness of divinity includes both brilliance and darkness.

Other examples of God's destruction or fluctuation appear in darker narratives. Garth Ennis destroys images of the Divine in two separate narratives. In Ennis' more famous narrative *Preacher*, God originally is depicted as an anthropomorphic being of light. Prior to the start of the narrative, God vacates the holy throne due to the entity Genesis, the threatening offspring of an angel and a demon's copulation. After working out the means to destroy Genesis, God returns to Heaven. When God returns to the heavenly throne room, the Saint of Killers stands between God and the throne. The Saint of Killers, an old-West gunslinger turned natural force, desires vengeance for the horrors God inflicted both on him and on the world. As God stands before the Saint, God's image shifts from glowing and benevolent to wrathful and dark. God's visual transformation fails to impress the Saint of Killers, who murders God with his Colt revolver, crafted from the sword of the original angel of death. After this deicide, the Saint of Killers sits on the holy throne himself. The Saint of Killers is the only being in Heaven, and the dead bodies of God and the angels lie at his feet. The Saint of Killers pushes his Stetson down and sleeps:[9] death becomes God, and the God-Death slumbers. Visual metaphor describes a passive God, a sleeping power of all-pervasive death. The all-powerful and active but all-too-human God gives way to this intractable image.

In *Chronicles of Wormwood*, Ennis portrays God in a slightly different fashion from *Preacher*. Instead of the anthropomorphic being of light, God is a white-robed, white-bearded white man. Still, Ennis does his best to disrupt this divine image in a similarly violent fashion. Ennis begins the narrative with God as a masturbatory lunatic. The main character of the narrative, the Antichrist, uses the Spear of Longinus to pierce both God and Satan, shish kebabing them together. The spear creates a union of God and Satan similar to the duality of good and evil in *Swamp Thing*. The perpetual union, much to Satan's dismay, still leaves God in a "top" position with all of his masturbatory tendencies.[10] Cosmic good and evil are impaled in an unhappy union, kept apart from the rest of reality.

Independent comics and Vertigo series display bleak and mutable images of God. The content of these comics is much more mature in nature because these books are not marketed to children or sold in grocery store magazine aisles. Evil can be seductive or qualified instead of absolute, as with the traditional comic book villain. God can be flawed or deranged, which *Preacher, Chronicles of Wormwood* and *Spawn* directly show and *Proposition Player* infers. *Lucifer* and *Swamp Thing* embrace the dark as being equally divine as the light, and as sympathetic as more traditional depictions of God.

Mainstream DC and Marvel comics are forced to represent God through the pantheon of superheroes and villains instead of the obviously religious representations shown in the imprints or independents. Marvel treats the retelling of the Christian myth directly in the *Warlock* narrative. The High Evolutionary, an artificially advanced human, creates a Counter-Earth in seven score hours from a rock of the original Earth. The High Evolutionary makes a world where humanity never learns evil and lives in the paradise it deserves.[11] The comic series depicts High Evolutionary as a human clad in armor, and his paradise is perverted by the interference of Man-Beast, an anthropomorphic feral monster. Similar to the serpent tempting and corrupting creation in the book of Genesis, Man-Beast is the allegorical adversary to High Evolutionary's role as God. High Evolutionary despairs at the fate of the fallen world, and he plans to destroy creation in a fashion analogous to the flood myth in the book of Genesis. Adam Warlock, an artificial *ubermensch* designed on the original Earth, intercedes to prevent the destruction of Counter-Earth.[12] During his mission on Counter-Earth, Warlock periodically is summoned to the presence of High Evolutionary. Unlike the High Evolutionary's original appearance as a metallic anthromorph, as the story progresses his depiction becomes a disembodied head. At Warlock's eventual crucifixion, the High Evolutionary is not shown, as in the Mark and Matthew passion narratives where God forsakes Christ on the cross. When Warlock returns from his resurrection, he conquers the evil of Man-Beast without the visual depiction of High Evolutionary's presence. In many ways, this parallels the Christian narrative of Jesus becoming coequal with YHWH and the ultimate victory of Jesus over evil. The creator God becomes ever more transcendent while the incarnational God grows in significance and temporal importance.

Marvel created narratives with a more univocal image of God with *Marvel Premiere*. Dr. Strange appears underneath the heading of Sise-Neg, a sorcerer from the future, on the first page of issue 14 of the Silver Age comic *Marvel Premiere* (1974). To make the wordplay obvious, under the heading of Sise-Neg is a subheading of "Genesis," and between

Dr. Strange's legs are the words "Book of Revelations appears amongst shimmering light."[13] The story begins with a monologue from Sise-Neg, who is in the process of journeying backward in time to control all magic in the universe until he reaches the time of creation. Controlling the magical power of all of time, Sise-Neg becomes God. At first, Sise-Neg appears as a glowing anthropomorphic male. As he journeys backwards through time, gaining control of ever more power, his appearance becomes that of a disembodied glowing head with lighning radiating from his eyes and mouth. The story retells the tale of Sodom and Gomorrah, with Sise-Neg being the one responsible for their destruction after telling the residents that they have angered God.[14] Moving further back in time, Sise-Neg's visage becomes less distinct, and he is shown forming Eden for the first two proto-humans.[15] Sise-Neg travels to the time before creation and completes his apotheosis. The image for his true Godhood is eyes, a nose, and a mouth placed over the Big Bang. He finishes with the monologue, "When you remember this, think not of the Man called Sise-Neg — but the God called Genesis."[16] The world exists as before, unchanged despite Sise-Neg becoming God, because along the way to achieving ultimate power, he learned everything is as it should be. This image puts forth a deterministic understanding of God, where absolute power is impotent to effect true change. The universe follows the Leibniz ideal of present reality being the best of all possible creations.

These mainstream lines show the comic superhero as the symbolic divine. Sise-Neg and High Evolutionary are unimaged as their apotheosis becomes more complete and transcendent. When the analogy is direct, as with Warlock acting as Christ, mainstream comics speak with already existing images that the reader can project to divine proportions in the context of the narrative. Comic book death and rebirth is a known cycle,[17] so it serves well as an analogy for the fluctuating image of God in narratives that include God. The analogical images point to what God might be, and the fluctuations of the images allow for multiple understandings of God instead of a limited single depiction.

A separate trend in depictions of God occurs when the author writes himself into the story as the creator. While less impressive than depictions of massive beings with supernatural powers, the uncanny feeling of the creator as God still reflects an understanding of ultimate reality. In *Animal Man*, author Grant Morrison enters the story in his final issue as writer of the series. Morrison explains to Animal Man how he controls

Animal Man's emotions, destiny, and powers, and he criticizes our reading of comics. Morrison breaks the "fourth wall" when he articulates to Animal Man,

> We'll stop at nothing, you see. All the suffering and the death and the pain in your world is entertainment for us. Why does blood and torture and anguish still excite us? We thought that by making your world more violent, we would make it more "realistic," more "adult." God help us if that's what it means.[18]

In showing off his power to manipulate and control Animal Man's life, Morrison demonstrates the capriciousness of a creator who takes pleasure from the pain of its creation. We see a flawed, petty, powerful, omnipotent, weak, and all-too-human Divine who is looking for meaning in the midst of its creation. Interestingly, Morrison claims that comic characters are much more real than himself.[19] Morrison's creation is more tangible and real for him than reality.

God the author and creator also appears in *Fantastic Four*. After Ben Grimm (aka the monstrous, superheroic Thing) dies, his teammate Mr. Fantastic creates a machine that will send the rest of their Fantastic Four team into the afterlife. Making their way into Heaven, the Fantastic Four come upon God imaged as Jack Kirby, their creator at Marvel Comics. Sue Storm, Mr. Fantastic's wife, responds incredulously, asking why she is taller than the Almighty. God responds to this outburst by telling the Fantastic Four that creation finds "the humanity in God."[20] God offers advice and humility in his dealings with the Fantastic Four. God erases the wounds on Mr. Fantastic and draws the rock hide back on Ben Grimm before sending the team back to Earth. God leaves them with a parting gift, a drawing of them in advanced years, together in a happy ending.[21]

Symbolic Hermeneutics and Divine Images

This trip through the destruction and eventual restoration of images for divinity asks the question, "What is God?" Hero, monster, man, woman, angel, devil, light, dark, death, good, evil, duality, insanity, the ground of being, a construct of human need, the anthropomorphic representation of an idea — all were answers to that question from graphic narratives. No single answer provides for the fullness of God, and it follows apophatic theology that each is destroyed, altered, or refined so that new, fuller depictions of the divine can live in our imaginations. We see the return to God in fuller or deeper images where God is metanamed by our words. God beyond God, God beyond existence, God beyond life, and God who conquers Godself all emerge from these graphic narratives. God is all of these images and beyond all of these images, living in our minds and our imaginations as something that cannot be fully named or described except through metaphor and analogy, since no single image adequately defines God.

Beyond this apophatic theology, there exists a power in creating images of the Divine. God as the androgynous being of light; or God as the white-robed, white-bearded white man; or God the luminous hand coming from the heavens is instantly recognizable without words to label the images as God. In these symbols, we project our reality and form an understanding of what it means to be the Divine.

The symbols of God point to a greater understanding of what God is, a form of graphic shorthand whose alteration through the course of the narrative tells the reader not only about his or her understanding of God, but about the self-identity of the producing culture.[22] The empirical examination of divine images is important, but the symbolic understanding of the imagery and the methods we use to understand symbols for God in the context of narratives requires some discussion. Why can we implicitly understand that a robed, bearded white male in the clouds is automatically God, or the radiant anthropomorphic being who consists of tangible light is the image of God? What about these symbols points to divinity instead of idolatry? Conversely, some explanation must exist for the sense of surprise when God's image does not keep to accepted norms. Grant Morrison and Jack Kirby, at first reading, are absurd images for God. How could a pop culture artist represent divinity? Possibly the most absurd image is the most important, however, because we can break through the symbol to see the meaning and significance instead of coming to accept the symbol in itself as God.

Symbols act as objects on which we can project ideas and with which we can form relationships as we construct a reality from the images found on the page of the graphic narrative. The nature of the image pointing beyond itself allows the reader to see more in the story than what is immediately extant. Comics use motion lines and dynamic poses to demonstrate motion or action.[23] Similarly, images of God have the capacity to suggest more than just the static image on the page.

However, a problem exists with any symbolic representation, especially when the symbol points to something inherently unknowable. As twentieth-century philosopher Paul Ricoeur claims, symbols give rise to thought. How do symbols at the same time provide a framework for understanding while not limiting conception, which would narrow the symbol to just a sign?[24] Symbols point beyond themselves and force the viewer to engage at a deeper level, while signs act only to display a singular meaning.

The multivalent capacity of symbols allows for shifting understandings and world-construction by the readership, whose own cultural context will vary with time. Each encounter with a symbol allows the reader to construct a mental reality based on his or her own identity and awareness, since humans project themselves into symbols.[25] Examining the symbolic representation in the midst of its context through the narrative while recognizing our cultural presuppositions about the norms of symbols lends us a hermeneutic, a method for discovering meaning. According to Ricoeur, this heremeneutic enables a "second naiveté." The reader has the ability to read the symbolic representation in his or her own context, as well as the capacity to see the symbolic representation in the context of the author, or the symbolic representation in relationship within the created world of the narrative. This second naiveté in symbolic hermeneutics gives rise to diverse understandings inside the context of the narrative instead of a singular understanding. Symbols themselves fight idolatry, which allows only a singular hermeneutic that binds and constrains reality.[26] Narratives of space journeys, mythical heroes, and fourth-wall-defying metafictions speak to our existence even though cosmic quests or superpowers are not part of our everyday lives. Readers can experience a narrative more deeply by projecting themselves into its symbols, however. The endurance of the symbols allow readers to understand their reality in light of the reality of the narrative, as well as for the reader to understand the reality of the narrative in light of his or her personal reality.

Is our own cultural uncertainty about God so great that even when our narratives tell of God's changing depictions and changing symbols, we still doubt the direct effect of God's presence? These mutating symbols for God only have meaning in their symbolic system. Such systems are grounded in a cultural context, since it is from cultural norms that we understand what these images represent.[27] Narrative flow functions as a mimetic form that plays out the relationship between individuals, synthesizing difference to form concordance.[28] All of these disparate images, symbols, and understandings of God in narrative relationship form an organized, cohesive thought. Yet it is impossible to say anything sensible about God apart from personal experience.

Ceaselessly, symbolic understandings of God in graphic narratives undergo transitions, death, and rebirth. This never-ending transition says much about our cultural projections and understanding of divinity when our symbols, our guards against idolatry, must change, morph, die, and be reborn. When God returns — or is reborn — does any functional difference occur in the overall world of the graphic narratives? In the narratives referenced above, no large-scale change in reality and experience happens due to the changes in God. After Spawn separates the world from Heaven and Hell, the world still has demons. *Strange Girl* has a world with churches, and Bethany's father still is a preacher even though God has left creation. After Animal Man's encounter with the creator, he returns ignorant of the grand reality of his existence, and the only noticeable change is the transition of authors away from Grant Morrison. As Phantom Stranger narrates in *Swamp Thing*, everything and nothing changes with the understanding that God is both the glowing hand of creation and the abyssal hand of chaos.

In comic books, God can be seen as ineffectual because radical shifts in God's nature make no functional changes in the lives of those who come into direct contact with God. God's complete reality is unknowable and undefinable, but the relationship individuals have with what is often a very personal God in these narratives should have some effect. Yet there is no consequence to God's existence, changes in God's relationship to the world, or changes in those who have relationships with God. The cultural value of God is so insignificant that God becomes the butt of a visual gag, skewered on a spear with Satan. Some may see the value of God's existence as called into question for our culture when the narrative we use to describe God is one of continual change and impermanence.

These arguments have some weight, but they fail unless one only performs a cynical, first-order reading of the stories. When describing the Eternal, Complete All in All with temporal images, one is undertaking an irrational pursuit. Rational displays of God are absurd, so the only logical means of displaying God is through the irrational and ever-changing. Through the absurd, we undertake a hermeneutic of suspicion that lets the reader engage the symbols in a higher-order reading.

Such a reading can discern how this personal relationship and engagement with God affects the individual, the world of the narrative, and the greater world in which the narrative is placed. The absurdity of the metanarative of God's imagery is the only metanarative that transcends simplistic definitions to allow for critical engagement with meaning. God in narrative images must be an unknown and unknowable God, or the images cannot depict the divine nature.

Notes

1   Pseudo-Dionysius, *On the Divine Names and the Mystical Theology*, trans. C. E. Rolt (Montana: Kessinger Publishing Company, 1997).
2   Thomas Aquinas, *Summa Theologica*, trans. Fathers of the English Dominican Province, Second and Revised Edition (1920; online edition 2008), Chapter 12, Article 11, http://newadvent.org/summa/1012.htm#article11.
3   Pseudo-Dionysius, *On the Divine Names and the Mystical Theology*, trans. C. E. Rolt (Montana: Kessinger Publishing Company, 1997).
4   Mike Carey, *Lucifer: Morningstar*, Vol. 10 (New York City: DC Comics, 2006).
5   Rick Remender, *Strange Girl: Golden Lights*, Vol. 4 (Berkeley, CA: Image Comics, Inc, 2007), 88.
6   David Hine, *Spawn: Armegeddon* (Berkeley, CA: Image Comics, 2007).
7   Bill Willingham, *Proposition Player* (New York City: DC Comics, 2003), 138.
8   Alan Moore, *Swamp Thing: A Murder of Crows* (New York City: DC Comics).
9   Garth Ennis, *Preacher: Alamo* (New York City: DC Comics).
10 Garth Ennis, *Chronicles of Wormwood* (Rantoul, IL: Avatar Press, 2007).
11 Thomas et al., 11–17.
12 Thomas et al., 20.
13 Steve Englehart, "Dr. Strange Master of the Mystic Arts," *Marvel Premiere* Vol. 1, #14 (New York City: Marvel Comics Group, March 1974), 1.
14 Englehart, 15–16.
15 Englehart, 23.
16 Englehart, 31.
17 A David Lewis, ed., "A Symposuim, Ever-Ending Battle," *International Journal of Comic Art* 8, no. 1 (2006): 163–282.
18 Grant Morrison, *Animal Man: Deus Ex Machina* (New York: DC Comics, 2003), 222.
19 Grant Morrison, *Grant Morrison Q and A at the New York Comic Con*, (April 19, 2008).
20 Mark Waid, *Fantastic Four: Hereafter* (New York City: Marvel Comics, 2004), 60.
21 Waid, 62.
22 Stewart Hoover, *Religion in the Media Age* (New York: Routledge, 2006), 11–12.
23 Scott McCloud, *Understanding Comics* (New York: HarperPerennial, 1993), 110–15.
24 Paul Ricoeur, *The Symbolism of Evil*, trans. Emerson Buchanan (Boston: Beacon Press, 1969), 349–50.
25 McCloud, 36.
26 McCloud, 350–4.

27 Paul Ricoeur, *Time and Narrative*, trans. Kathleen McLaughlin and David Pellauer, Vol. 1 (Chicago: University of Chicago Press, 1984), 58.

28 Ricoeur, *Time*, 66.

Echoes of Eternity: Hindu Reincarnation Motifs in Superhero Comic Books

SAURAV MOHAPATRA

Vasamsi jirnani yatha vihaya navani grhnati naro'parani
tatha sarirani vihaya jirnany anyani samyati navani dehi
As a person gives up old and worn out garments,
Thus does the eternal soul give up old shells and is born anew.

— Chapter 2, Verse 22, Srimad Bhagvad Gita[1]

I F I MAY BE SO bold as to say so, in my view Indian philosophy is fatalistic to a fault. The concept of reincarnation is ingrained into its basic belief system. Hinduism is based on the core concepts of fate (karma) and soul (atma). The universe is viewed as a giant engine whose operating principle is karma, and the souls are but cogs in this machine. It is a self-sustaining, renewable system where, depending on their diligence and adherence to rules of righteousness (dharma), the souls are reincarnated into other bodies in subsequent births. Though the newly born souls perform different functions than their previous ones, they somehow maintain a beautiful continuity in their form. There is room for a supreme being (param-atma, the uber-soul) in this scheme, yet its role is that of an observer and a gold standard of existence that any other soul can strive for and attain based on a life or lives well-lived (according to the tenets of dharma). The most ancient of the Vedic philosophical schools subscribed to this view of universe as an engine, constantly rearranging its constituent components based on a system of equations. Each cog strives to attain perfection in the purest of forms by performing its current assigned function to the fullest possible extent. But as the philosophy was formalized into a theosophy (and eventually a religion), it gave birth to more rigid views of this karmic cycle and degenerated into what would later become the abominable practice of the caste system. A punitive view arose of what happens — or does not happen — when one goes though one's life adhering to the now-formalized tenets of dharma.[2]

But this philosophy in its purest form, for me at least, manifests itself quite pristinely in an unlikely arena — comic book superheroes. Think of it: a whole universe where larger-than-life figures lead their lives as ordained by the principles of "good triumphs over evil" and "with great power comes great responsibility." From time to time, heroes die, but the almost karmic pull of their legacy is far too strong for them to remain dead. Just like the concept of the immortal and eternal atma, the superhero is reborn into a new body (in some ways reminiscent of the old body, but different in others). In some cases, the universe that contains the hero(es) itself is reborn and bound by the illusion (maya) of the parameters of their existence.

Crisis on Infinite Earths (DC Comics) illustrates this theme well.[3] The almost karmic pressure of the co-existence of multiple versions of their iconic heroes forced DC Comics to create a story line where entire universes were wiped out — heroes erased from existence and then brought back (reborn) into newer versions of themselves. This narrative move was a logical continuation of the phenomenon that gave rise to the more science-hero-oriented Silver Age, which contrasted with the more mythic and fantasy-oriented Golden Age. A prime example is the transfiguration of the Green Lantern from the possessor of a magical item to a more science-fiction-inspired Galactic Cop in possession of an alien device. The core of Green Lantern mythos (the atma) remains the same, however: a honest and courageous man who has the power to craft constructs out of his own imagination. Yet his physical milieu underwent a major transformation.

By taking the concept even further, another resonance with the Vedic philosophy arises — the concept of param-atma. Together with the creative team that crafts the stories, we the readers become the analogues of the Supreme Being that observes the universe. Sometimes we play a part (the creators playing a more active part, of course) as with the call-in vote for the death of Jason Todd, the second Robin in the Batman stories.[4] Sometimes we play a more passive role, just watching the stories unfold with an awareness of what came before, and savoring or abhoring the changes. Superheroes live, die, and rise again based on whether we buy the comics and continue to read. Our judgment concerning the karma from a superhero's previous reincarnation affects how he or she is reborn, and the whole cycle repeats itself at the next such occurrence, where the current incarnation is judged again based on its "actions" and "deeds."

Since one of the more mainstream examples of this type of storyline, the death and return of Superman,[5] has been discussed elsewhere in this collection, I shall focus on others. These are based on personal preference and a strong belief on my part that the creators involved have had access at both a conscious and meta-conscious level to the paradigms and philosophies of Vedic Hinduism. They are also chosen because of my love for slightly more esoteric comics universes, where the creators and readers are less bound by rigid tenets of market-pleasing supply and demand (reminiscent of the formalized rigidity that later suffused Hindu theosophical evolution).[6] First of these is Alan Moore's run of *Supreme* (Awesome Comics),[7] especially his concepts of "Revision" and "Rebirth" as envisioned in the "Supremacy" storyline. Secondly, I will focus on Grant Morrison's work in *Animal Man* (DC/Vertigo),[8] particularly the elevation of the protagonist's consciousness and his subsequent meeting with his "creator" (a fictional version of Morrison himself).

Given the complex nature of the scriptures of Vedic philosophy and Hindu religion, and since I am focusing on the motif of karmic reincarnation of the soul, I will be using verses quoted from Srimad Bhagvad Gita and concentrating on the second chapter (titled "Sankhya Yoga: The Eternal Reality of the Souls Immortality"), which deals specifically with the concepts of the soul and reincarnation based on a karmic scheme. The Bhagvad Gita (literally "The Song of God") is a revered scripture in Hindu religion. Composed of seven hundred verses, the Gita features a conversation between the warrior-prince Arjuna and Krishna (his friend and mentor and the ninth incarnation of the god Vishnu) on the battlefield before the start of the Kurukshetra war. Responding to Arjuna's moral dilemma about fighting against his own family, Krishna explains to Arjuna his duties as a warrior and prince and elaborates on different Yogic and Vedantic philosophies with examples and analogies. In essence, the Gita is a concise and condensed guide to Hindu philosophy and to the much larger Vedantic body of knowledge, expertly narrowed down to its most practical essence. As Mahrshi Mahesh Yogi describes it, the Gita "is a lighthouse of eternal wisdom that has the ability to inspire any man or woman to supreme accomplishment and enlightenment."

The Gita is also refered to as the Gitopanishad, implying that it has the status of a Upanishad, a Vedantic scripture second only in importance to the four Vedas themselves. Since the Gita is drawn from the epic Mahabharata, it is classified as a Smriti text (a scripture created by an author from memory or from prior sources). However, those branches of Hinduism that give it the status of an Upanishad also consider it a Sruti or "revealed" text, placing it on par in terms of origin and source with the ancient Vedic body of knowledge.

Alan Moore's Supreme

> *Dehino'smin yatha deha kaumaram yauvanam jara*
> *tatha dehantara praptir dhiras tatra na muhyati*
> Just as in the physical body of the embodied being is
> the process of childhood, youth, old age,
> Similarly in the transmigration from one body to another
> the wise are never deluded.
>
> — Chapter 2, Verse 13, Srimad Bhagvad Gita

Alan Moore's run of *Supreme* redefined the boundaries of comic book storytelling, while at the same time celebrating the naïve joy that was nearly lost due to the influence of Moore's own work in the darker storylines of *Watchmen* (DC) and *Swamp Thing* (DC/Vertigo). Perhaps the single greatest moment for me in reading *Supreme*, a thinly veiled Silver Age Superman pastiche, came in the very first story (now collected in *Supreme* Vol. 1, *The Story of the Year*). The superhero Supreme returns to Earth, only to find that it is not quite as he remembers; in fact, Supreme's memory is full of gaps. Suddenly, several alternate versions of himself arrive and drag him into a strange place dubbed the Supremacy. Here, Supreme encounters myriad versions of himself and is introduced to what I find most interesting as a concept, "Revision." The name and capitalization are supplied by Moore via the voice of one of the characters. Moore posits that the meta-verse in which Supreme exists periodically revises itself and reincarnates the protagonist in a different avatar: almost, but not quite the same character. The residents of the Supremacy, versions of Supreme who existed prior to the most recent one, are a nice touch and a nifty storytelling device. At a macro-level, though, I could not help but wonder if Moore was consciously blending meta-fiction elements with the ancient Hindu concept of reincarnation. Given the mystic leanings in his body of work and his self-confessed fondness for "magick," it is not only highly probable, but almost a certainty that Moore channeled the Vedic concept of rebirth into his narrative for Supreme, if not directly, then via the slightly diluted version available via Tibetan Buddhism.

Regarding "Revision," one theory presented in the voice of one of the "alternate" Supremes is consistent with the "observer effect" from quantum physics. The very existence of Supreme affects the texture and fabric of reality, which rearranges itself periodically to maintain its balance. Interesting as this theory is, however, it pales in grandeur before the second. The alternate view of "Revision" as proposed by the same character is that "Reality has always modified itself at intervals and we, the Supreme Ones, are merely advanced enough to notice."[9] This echoes the sentiment in the verse quoted above. The essence of Supreme transmigrates from one incarnation to the other, as does the entire fictional meta-verse containing him. The Supremes, since they possess an advanced/evolved intellect, are able to sense this transmigration beyond the boundaries of their own existence, and gradually they have learned not only to survive the "Revision," but also to carve their own niche — the Supremacy, in the interstitial limbo of this meta-verse.

Across the revisions, the core of what Supreme is (his "atma" if you will) remains consistent, yet his outer form (the "deha" or corporeal body) changes in appearance and form. Though each of the previous Supremes maintains some degree of sapient autonomy, at a more subconscious level, they share a unified consciousness and are able to sense and bond with each other. At some level, each of the Supremes is aware of the cyclic nature of this constant reincarnation. As Supreme interacts with some version himself that never quite "existed" (e.g., Sister Supreme, the Gold and White Supremes), it becomes clear that this cycle is not limited by time and space. An avatar may exist outside of what we would perceive as linear time, in the realm of "possibility"

Figure 1

or in the amorphous lattice of the Creator's imagination. To quote the Gold Supreme, "it doesn't make it any less real."[10]

As Supreme bids adieu to the Supremacy and prepares himself for what is to be his time on Earth, his thoughts are poetically rendered by Moore, echoing the basic tenets of Hindu karmic philosophy.

> If what they say is true, I've barely existed before this incredible moment! My real past hasn't been filled in yet and my future awaits in whatever new world that exists beyond that dimensional doorway!

May the gods of the galaxies grant me the courage to take this fearful step wherever it may lead.[11]

This is the Vedic philosophy of karma at its purest. The path that Supreme chooses is simply an acceptance of his dharma to fulfill his karmic destiny. This birth/incarnation of his atma is one that every Vedic tenet encourages in those that accept it. We can only be in harmony with the universe and, ultimately, the param-atma by focusing on our current life and fulfilling the purpose that we, by existing in this particular juncture of space-time, have created for ourselves.

In many ways, Supreme (and by extension, his original inspiration, Superman) represents an ideal of human existence. Even though superheroes are powerful and, one might say, evolved beyond the norms of day-to-day existence, they still choose to live their lives by a code and try to fulfill a purpose in the larger scheme of things. During the period of the writing of *Story of the Year*, Moore made a conscious decision to veer away from the then in-vogue trend of "dark and gritty" superheroes to present a tale of a hero who exists bound by the dharma of his existence and works to fulfill his greater karmic destiny. Though layered with complex symbolism and meta-fictional elements, at heart Moore's run of *Supreme* remains a celebration of the core karmic principles of the Vedic school of thought.

Figure 2

Grant Morrison's Animal Man

> *Na jayate mriyate va kadacin nayam bhutva bhavita va na bhuyah*
> *ajo nityah sasvato yam purano na hanyate hanyamane*
> The soul never takes birth and never dies at any time
> nor does it come into being again when the body is created.
> The soul is birthless, eternal, imperishable and timeless
> and is never terminated when the body is terminated.
>
> — Chapter 2, Verse 20, Srimad Bhagvad Gita

Along with Moore, Grant Morrison is another skilled writer of graphic fiction whose work is steeped in metaphysical and meta-fictional elements. Morrison typically deals in ideas and archetypes and favors a constant stream of conscious and unconscious symbolism in the narrative. For me, Morrison's seminal work is his run of DC Comics' *Animal Man*. Morrison took over an existing character and brought his own brand of storytelling to it, revamping the series and taking it on a journey that mirrors the protagonist's quest to be elevated to a higher plane of consciousness. Buddy Baker, the titular character, is blessed with the ability to temporarily channel and acquire the power of any animal on earth (and in some cases even beyond). But Morrison's Animal Man becomes increasingly self-aware of his fictional existence. His consciousness becomes so elevated that he finally meets his "Creator," a version of Grant Morrison himself.

At the most basic level, the nature and source of Buddy Baker's power is a clever reworking of the all-pervading atma that exists within each of us. Morrison's Animal Man experiences a brief resonance with a particular soul, thus acquiring the power it bestows on his shell, albeit temporarily. Hindu philosophy does not limit the existence of the soul to just the human or animal bodies. The atma exists within all, irrespective of sapience or even sentience. The rocks, the trees, and the earth itself are blessed with souls. In ancient India, the rishis ("sages") retreated to sylvan solitude to commune with the universe and experienced a oneness with nature and all beings. For them, the path to true enlightenment originated from the act of renouncing the physical trappings of the body and its baser needs. Instead, they focused on the all-pervading sameness with which the atma endows each and every entity of the giant karmic engine that is our universe.

In the course of the narrative, Buddy gradually overcomes the physical obstacles in his way. His quest becomes more metaphysical as his consciousness is elevated. Here, again, the narrative is soaked in motifs gleaned, perhaps, from the ancient Vedic corpus of knowledge — Animal Man traverses an illusory landscape reminiscent of maya, which the truly wise must pass through to reach a state of enlightenment.[12] He finally realizes his existence as a comic book character and even manages to breach the final frontier: the panel border. Animal Man is then able to step forth into a new world and meet his Creator face to face. His quest finally ends as he meets Morrison himself, who explains to Buddy about his existing in a comic book, "a reality shaped by committee."[13]

Buddy asks the inevitable question: "Am I real or what?" Morrison's answer (both as a character and the writer) is a poetic discourse on the nature of "Reality": "Of course you're real! We wouldn't be here talking if you weren't real. You existed long before I wrote about you and [. . .] you'll still be young when I'm old or dead."[14] This sentiment resonates with the concept of the soul as eternal, going through cycles of birth, death and rebirth, yet remaining in essence the same timeless entity. Though Morrison's take on Animal Man remains one of the most thought-provoking attempts at telling the tale of Buddy Baker, there were other iterations that came before it and several that followed. Among all these iterations, the core of what Buddy/Animal Man is remains essentially the same, yet each writer brings their own unique perspective to the mix. The details change from one incarnation to the next, yet the soul of the character remains the same.

Morrison then takes the motif a step further and places the creation above the Creator: "You're more real than I am."[15] Or, as the Gita says,

> *Acchedyo'yam adahyo'yam akledya'sosya eva ca*
> *Nityah sarva-gatah sthanur acalo'yam sanatanah*
> The soul is indestructible; the soul is
> incombustible, insoluble and invulnerable.
> The soul is eternal, all pervasive, immutable,
> immovable and primordial.
>
> — Chapter 2, Verse 24, Srimad Bhagvad Gita

The Gita holds the soul as the only invariant in the cosmos, which is in constant flux. Morrison's statement underlines this and serves to further highlight an undercurrent of karmic philosophy in the narrative of *Animal Man*.

Figure 3

Conclusion

> When all you have is a hammer, everything looks like a nail!
>
> — Anonymous

Rich and insightful as Vedic literature is, I have also found wisdom in the most mundane of sources. I do not claim to be a scholar of the scriptures, nor do I proclaim myself an avid student of the comic books. I have been lucky enough to be professionally involved with a bit of both, and that coupled with my own personal interest has given me a window onto a unique synergy between two seemingly disparate worlds. In examining the comic book stories for reincarnation motifs, perhaps I have found patterns where none exist.

As a reader of comic books and someone who enjoys a yarn well told, however, I find it fascinating that writers such as Moore and Morrison have either consciously or unconsciously taken the grammar and language of what began its life as a juvenile entertainment and infused it with imagery and philosophy that echoes one of the most erudite and ancient bodies of knowledge known to humanity. Both Moore and Morrison, by dint of their own philosophical leanings, maintain a literary connection with Eastern mysticism and philosophy and are perhaps among those most open to its influences. Both are known for the overt and implicit symbolism and for the multi-layered themes that add a tangible depth to their works. I, for one, do not consider these resonances a mere coincidence. Moore set out to tell the ultimate superhero story and in doing so, probably reached out to a philosophy that provides an instant synergy with the norms and form of superhero mythos. Morrison, on the other hand, set out to explore and explode the boundaries of meta-fiction, with a strong emphasis on the cyclical nature of the existence of both fictional and real characters. As is his wont, he also underlined the amorphous nature of reality by markedly blurring the line between Creator and creation.

Whatever their intentions, I (as I am sure countless other readers have as well) have been fortunate enough to read this symphony of symbolism as highlighting basic truths of our existence. These works also demonstrate the continuing power of knowledge that has been handed down in India from ancient times. I leave you with one of my most favorite verses from the Bhagvad Gita, one that I believe sums up my approach to the stories I love:

Jatasya hi dhruvo mrtyur dhruvam janma mrtasya ca,
tasmad apariharye'rthe na tvam socitum arhasi
For one who has taken birth, death is certain
and for one who has died, birth is certain.
Therefore in an inevitable situation
understanding should prevail.

— Chapter 2, Verse 27, Srimad Bhagvad Gita

Notes

1   All quotations from the Bhagvad Gita are taken from A. C. Bhaktivedanta Swami Prabhupada, *Bhagvad-Gita As It Is* (London: Bhaktivedanta Book Trust, 1997).
2   A basic introductory text to comprehend more about the Vedic scriptures and other texts of the Hindu religion is Dominic Goodall, ed., *Hindu Scriptures* (Berkeley: University of California Press, 1996).
3   Marv Wolfman, George Perez et al., *Crisis on Infinite Earths* (New York: DC Comics, 2001).
4   Jim Starlin et al., *Batman: A Death in the Family* (New York: DC Comics, 1988).
5   Dan Jurgens et al., *The Death of Superman* (New York: DC Comics, 1993).
6   Even with these parameters, there are several excellent illustrations of the principles being discussed in this essay that I could not include given the constraints of time and space. I would definitely recommend the reader follow up on them if they believe the thesis of this piece or find it in the least entertaining. The rebirth of Jenny Sparks as Jenny Quantum and the concept of a long lineage of shamanistic heroes in tune with the Earth (whose latest incarnation is The Doctor) form one such instance in Warren Ellis's *The Authority* (Wildstorm). Reincarnation as an explicit theme is touched upon in *Hawkman* (DC Comics) and *Moon Knight* (Marvel). Even *Spider-Man* in J. Michael Straczynski's hands (*Amazing Spider-Man Vol. 9: Skin Deep*, Marvel) becomes an examination of totemic spider powers that might have existed in many incarnations before.
7   Alan Moore et al., *Supreme: Story of the Year* (West Carrollton, OH: Checker Book Publishing Group, 2002).
8   Grant Morrison et al., *Animal Man Vol 3: Deus Ex Machina* (New York: DC Comics, 2003).
9   Moore et al.
10   Moore et al.
11   Moore et al.
12   The concept of an illusory shroud that must be pierced is an oft-repeated theme in Morrison's body of work, further expounded upon in *The Invisibles* (DC/Vertigo). However, that particular concept is not unique to Hinduism or Vedic philosophy, and so we will focus on the resonances with our chosen topic, karmic reincarnation.
13   Morrison et al.
14   Morrison et al.
15   Morrison et al.

The Christianizing of Animism in Manga and Anime: American Translations of Hayao Miyazaki's *Nausicaä of the Valley of the Wind*

ERIKO OGIHARA-SCHUCK

N JAPANESE DIRECTOR HAYAO MIYAZAKI'S 1984 anime *Nausicaä of the Valley of the Wind,* the story climaxes when Nausicaä, the Princess of the Valley, throws herself into the path of the dashing herd of giant Ohmu insects. The outraged insects are about to race into and destroy her valley; the only solution to their anger is to calm them by returning an injured baby Ohmu. Yet their panic is so intense that they cannot stop even then — only after they throw Nausicaä skyward is calmness achieved. Shortly thereafter, they gather around the lifeless Nausicaä and resurrect her with their miraculous powers. The story concludes with a celebration of her return to the Valley.

This scene of Nausicaä's encountering the Ohmu has invited both Christian and animistic readings. On one hand, it has promoted an interpretation of Nausicaä around the Christian themes of salvation and resurrection. Due to her self-sacrifice and resurrection, Japanese scholars Takashi Sasaki and Masashi Shimizu consider her as a Christ-like savior,[1] and American scholar Susan Napier considers her as an active female messiah figure.[2] On the other hand, the scene has triggered animistic interpretations, reflecting Miyazaki's own advocacy of a belief in the existence of gods and spirits everywhere, a point that Christianity refutes.[3] For instance, Hiroshi Aoi argues that Nausicaä's self-sacrifice to propitiate the "anger of the earth" is grounded on an animistic recognition of omnipresent spirits.[4] Miyazaki himself stated that an animistic motivation is the intent of the scene. According to him, Nausicaä throws herself before the rushing insects not because she wants to protect her people as their savior but because she desperately wants to return the injured baby Ohmu.[5] He claims that it is her respect for nature which drives her to sacrifice herself, as she is "dominated by animism."[6]

How did American audiences with their Judeo-Christian background respond to the conglomerate of religious traditions represented in the anime film and manga comics versions of *Nausicaä*? Completed ten years after the release of the anime, the manga *Nausicaä* departs from the anime in several ways, particularly by expanding the animistic themes. In general, animism interacts differently with Christianity in the two versions. The two religious traditions are conflated in the anime, but in the manga they oppose each other, with animism surviving at the end. Differences between the anime and the manga are also apparent in the English translations. Although attempts to remain faithful to the Japanese texts are evident in both the anime and manga translations, a much lesser degree of revision of the animistic elements is found in the manga translation. Yet I would argue that the difficulty of representing animism in English is nonetheless evident in both media, to the extent that the translations can even be interpreted as a "Christianizing" of the original texts.

From Anime to Manga

Nausicaä is best known in its anime version, but it actually began and ended as a manga. Miyazaki launched the story as a serial comic in the magazine *Animage* in 1982. After turning it into an anime in 1984, he returned to the manga form due to dissatisfaction with the anime. He said there was something nagging him about the film's content, and he did not feel that the story had ended.[7] Consequently, until 1994, he continued working on the manga *Nausicaä* while producing other animated films. He recalls that the manga was his "heaviest work" and that he was relieved each time he had to suspend work on the manga to produce a new anime film. He admits the manga allowed him to produce more anime films by restraining him from trying to make them heavy and thus a source of struggle.[8]

The anime *Nausicaä* is based on the first two volumes of the manga and inherits their animistic themes, such as a belief in the god of the wind and a humble attitude toward nature. The anime differs significantly, however. One major point of difference, as mentioned earlier, is the establishment of Nausicaä as a messiah figure through her death and resurrection. Although this scene is an important climax in the anime, it does not exist at all in the manga. Further, in the anime, Nausicaä's Christlike quality is illustrated by several scenes in which she holds her arms outstretched, like a cross (see Figure 1). Such a pose is completely absent in the Japanese manga version (see Figure 2).[9]

The manga that followed the anime's completion carries on the story, in which Nausicaä questions what was narrated in the anime. In the anime, the Ohmu, the giant insects dwelling in the poisonous forest called the Sea of Corruption, smash into Nausicaä and cause her death. The Ohmu attack in response to the baby Ohmu's deliberate injury by other humans. In the manga, instead of being killed and resurrected by Ohmu, Nausicaä asks if the humans can indeed search for the baby in the Sea of Corruption, because it is an extremely dangerous action. She then learns that the injured baby Ohmu had not been stolen but was artificially raised by the Dorok, a religious group not found in the anime. The Dorok in the manga are responsible for creating the Sea of Corruption in order to control the ecosystem for mankind's survival. In

Figure 1. **Miyazaki, *Nausicaä of the Valley of the Wind*, still, 1984.**

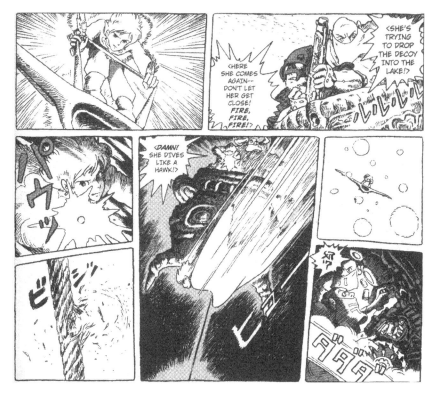

Figure 2.   **Miyazaki, *Nausicaä of the Valley of the Wind*, 1995.**

contrast, in the anime the forest is introduced as a product of pollution resulting from the Seven Days of Fire. In the manga, Nausicaä attempts to reach the capital of the Dorok empire to close the crypt where all the knowledge about manipulating the ecosystem is stored. Nausicaä's decision is motivated by her belief that humans should no longer self-ishly attempt to control the natural world.

On a more abstract level, however, Nausicaä is against the dualistic worldview that lies at the heart of the Dorok's manipulation of nature. According to Nausicaä, the Dorok's creation of the Sea of Corruption to destroy the world and then purify the Earth was driven by a dualistic thinking that divides the world into purity and corruption. This world-view takes for granted that one of the opposing elements has to be simply eliminated in order for the other to endure. In the course of the story, Nausicaä states, "We blind ourselves by looking at the world simply in terms of 'purity' and 'corruption,'"[10] and she eventually pronounces her stark opposition to this idea of "one or the other." Referring to the people of a thousand years ago who had created the Sea of Corruption, she laments, "Why didn't those men and women realize that both purity and corruption are the very stuff of life? Suffering and tragedy and folly will not disappear in a purified world. They are a part of humanity."[11] Likewise, Nausicaä challenges the Dorok's god — who divides the world into light and darkness — by claiming that they cannot be separated: "Life is the light that shines in darkness."[12] Her dispute with the god ends as she asserts her belief of god dwelling in nature: "We can know the beauty and cruelty of the world without the help of a giant tomb and its servants. Because our god inhabits even a single leaf and the smallest insects."[13]

Nausicaä's advocacy of animism and her opposition to dualistic thinking reflect Miyazaki's own worldview. During an interview after the completion of the anime in 1984, he stated, "I like animism. I am convinced by the idea that stones and wind have personality."[14] After the completion of the manga in 1994, he articulated his opposition to a dualistic worldview, especially one that divides the world into good and evil. "I can say at least that it is a lie that we can defeat our enemy because we are just, and then obtain peace. We will make mistakes with a variety of judgements if we don't understand that humans who have done good can do something bad in the next moment."[15] This view about each human's disposition to do both right and wrong directly parallels his understanding of animistic gods' ambivalent quality of being both good and evil, as he states in regard to Japanese gods: "It's not that Japanese gods consist of bad and good gods, but it's like the same one god becomes a rough god at one time and at another a calm god who brings green."[16] In the meantime, the Dorok's desire for the destruction of the world, followed by the birth of a purified land and their God's justification of the process, recalls the book of Revelation, where the Second Coming of Christ follows an apocalypse ending the "sinful" world.

From the perspective of religion, the anime and manga versions of *Nausicaä* differ substantially. In the anime, animistic and Christian themes remain conflated through the representation of Nausicaä; her attempt to sacrifice herself can be interpreted as stemming from her animistic respect for nature coupled to a Christ-like desire to protect her community. On the contrary, in the manga, animism and Christianity are put into tension, as seen in her confrontation with the Dorok's dualistic worldview that parallels Christian apocalypticism. How then did American translators, with the task of making the texts accessible to American audiences with a Judeo-Christian background, engage the two versions of *Nausicaä* that have two different religious approaches?

The American Anime Translation

Disney Studio's English translation of the anime *Nausicaä of the Valley of the Wind* by Cindy David Hewitt and Donald H. Hewitt was meant to be faithful to the original version, in stark contrast to New World Pictures' earlier English translation under the title *Warriors of the Wind.*[17] Disney's translation nonetheless made significant changes to the original text and especially to the expressions of animistic beliefs that Miyazaki had deliberately made part of the story. *Nausicaä*'s anime translation thoroughly erases animistic elements found in the original Japanese text to conform to the Judeo-Christian worldview shared by the majority of American audiences.[18] One notable instance of this "Christianization" is the translation of "the god of the wind" (*kaze no kami-sama*).[19] Nausicaä and the other residents of the Valley of the Wind understand that they are protected by the wind, as it carries poisonous spores disseminated from the Sea of Corruption away from their land. Hence, the wind is addressed as their deity. However, the English translation effaces this animistic belief by either transforming it into the Judeo-Christian "God" or by reducing it to just ordinary "wind."

The transformation of the god of the wind into God takes place in the translation of Nausicaä's Japanese prayer "the god, god of the wind, please protect all of us" (*kami-sama, kaze no kami-sama, dōka minna o mamotte*). Its English translation changes "the god of the wind" into the monotheistic God: "Please dear God, please hear this prayer, you must protect the people of the valley." This Christianization is again noticeable in the translation of the old woman Obaba's mention of "Mr. (Ms.) Wind": "This area is protected by Mr. (Ms.) Wind who blows from the sea" (*koko wa, umi kara fuku kaze-sama ni mamorarete oru kara no*) becomes: "We have the wind from the sea to protect us from the jungle of poison."

This depersonification or desanctification of "Mr. (Ms.) Wind" (*kaze-sama*) into "the wind" also reverses the supremacy of nature over humans that is implied by the Japanese word *sama*, a respectful form of the titles Mr. and Ms. By addressing the wind with *sama*, the old woman establishes a hierarchical relationship between humans and nature, with nature having dominance. However, the English version inverts this relationship and instead posits human supremacy over nature: "We have the wind from the sea to protect us from the jungle of poison." Here, the depersonalized wind is reduced to a property over which humans have control. This resonates with the human-centered hierarchical relationship between humanity and nature in the common Christian worldview.

Likewise, the translation of Nausicaä's reference to two injured insects from "a good child" into "a good boy" also suggests humanity's supremacy over nature. When Nausicaä calls the insect "a child" to calm it down, she means to be intimate, treating it as her own kind. At first glance, the English translation into "a boy" does not seem to differ much from "a child," except that its gender is now specified as male, which better matches the insects' violent and aggressive traits. However, reference to the insect as "a boy" promotes the human supremacy over nature by putting insects into the service of humans: unlike the word "child," "boy" is frequently used for domestic animals (such as dogs) that are trained to work for their human keepers; in the past, it was used as a derogatory term for African-American slaves.[20] All in all, "boy" places an insect almost in a position of servitude, whereas "child" humanizes it.

The translation of Nausicaä's conversation with one of the injured insects, a baby Ohmu, continues the reversal of the human-nature relationship suggested in the original Japanese version. When encountering the baby Ohmu deliberately injured by humans, Nausicaä sobs and apologizes in Japanese, "Don't get angry. You don't need to be afraid. I am not your enemy. I'm sorry, I'm sorry. I can't say 'please forgive us,' can I? This is too terrible, isn't it?" (*Okoranai de. Kowagaranakute ii no. Watashi wa teki ja nai wa. Gomen. Gomen ne. Yurushite nante ienai yo ne. Hidosugiru yo ne*). Nausicaä recognizes the insect as the subject of power, almost suggesting the image of the angry God of the Old Testament who is in the position of forgiving or punishing people. However, the English translation shifts the subject of power from the insect to Nausicaä: "I am not going to hurt you. Don't be frightened. I am not your enemy. I am sorry. Is there any way you can forgive us? How we've treated you so badly!" The agency of action here is Nausicaä, a human who claims not to harm the insect, whereas in the Japanese version the insect has the agency.

The translation further elevates the status of humans when it suggests the possibility of forgiveness through, "Is there any way you can forgive us?" instead of the Japanese, "I can't say 'please forgive us,' can I?" In both the Japanese and English sentences, the insect is the agent of forgiveness for humans and so retains power over humans. Yet while Nausicaä in the Japanese line does not consider forgiveness to be a possibility, in the English line she asks for it, although admitting that it must be hard. Here, Nausicaä's concern is mainly directed toward humans, while in the Japanese version she completely surrenders herself to the Ohmu.

The wind's animistic personification is eliminated in the English translation, and humans' supremacy over nature is implemented, directly contributing to a Christian gloss on the story's climax, which involves Nausicaä's death and resurrection. As mentioned earlier, this scene has already invited an interpretation of Nausicaä as a Christ figure among Japanese viewers due to her status as the savior of her people. The English translation increases this interpretation's plausibility by eliminating the animistic reading of the same scene, in which Nausicaä's self-sacrifice is for nature rather than for her people (an interpretation proposed by Miyazaki himself). By stripping out the film's animistic elements, the English translation turns the *Nausicaä* anime into a Christian eco-fable.

The American Manga Translation

Contrary to the anime translation, the English translation of the manga *Nausicaä of the Valley of the Wind* by David Lewis and Toren Smith retains the animistic elements and does not introduce any conspicuous Christianization. "The god of the wind" is translated word for word, and there is no inversion of nature's supremacy over humans.[21] The only subtle change made to the story's animistic element is seen in the translation of the climax; Nausicaä's plausibly animistic claim is rendered instead as a pantheistic one, when *kami* in her phrase, a word for both God and god(s), is translated into the singular "god." Pantheism is further suggested by the possibility that the "god" is actually meant to be the "God" in the following phrase that, conforming to the tradition of English-language comics, uses only capital letters: "OUR GOD INHABITS EVEN A SINGLE LEAF AND THE SMALLEST INSECT."[22] Yet, the translation generally emphasizes animistic beliefs even more than the Japanese version; for example, a passage about the discovery of a girl from the Valley of the Wind — "I go now, it is incredible that you are alive!" (*Ima iku, yoku mā buji de!*)[23] — is translated as "We're coming! Thank the gods you're all right."[24] Overall, the translation retains many of the Japanese text's religious elements by carefully following the manga's expansion of animistic themes.

Nonetheless, the difficulty of translating animism manifests in the manga at an abstract level, as it struggles to express the idea that there are neither absolute good nor absolute bad beings, be they gods or humans. The manga translation counters Miyazaki's intention of blurring the boundary between good and evil in his characters. This is accomplished by the literal translation of *oni* as "demon," as well as the insertions of the words "evil" and "devil" throughout the story.

In the manga, the term *oni* is associated with the Dorok, Kushana (the princess of their enemy) and also Nausicaä. The Japanese name for the Dorok is *doruku*, which is composed of the two characters, *do* for the earth and a character for *oni*, which is now pronounced *ruku*. The Dorok addresses Kushana as *oni*[25] and Nausicaä as *kishin*,[26] or "demon god." The Dorok's calling the two princesses either *oni* or *kishin* implies recognition of the two women as dangerous, violent, and harmful; the Chinese character *oni* in the Dorok's Japanese name "Doroku" communicates to the reader the same aggressive traits. Hence, it is reasonable that *oni* and *kishin* for Kushana and Nausicaä are equally translated into "demon,"[27] while *ruku* in the Dorok's Japanese name is not semantically translated into English.

Moreover, the English word "demon" does not capture the full complexity of *oni*. Using a character imported from China, *oni* has evolved within Japanese cultural tradition into a complex term with many variants.[28] One is its possible overlap with Japanese animism. *Oni* is interchangeable with *kami*, the term used for the Japanese god(s), as is suggested by the Dorok's reference to Nausicaä as *kishin*. Based on his study of various *oni* in Japan, Atsuhiko Yoshida argues that the boundary between *oni* and *kami* is extremely ambiguous, and Tōji Kamata makes a similar argument by examining violent qualities in some well-known Japanese gods.[29] For both scholars, the overlap between *kami* and *oni* is closely related to the fact that Japanese gods are not understood to be good at all times; Japanese gods oscillate between good and evil, depending on how humans approach them, and when evil is aroused, the gods may be calmed, but not eliminated and suppressed. Miyazaki also emphasizes the oscillatory quality of *kami*: "Gods also become rough gods, and hence they need to be calmed down, but once they are calmed down, they are gentle and peaceful gods with a smile."[30] *Oni* are also good and evil and hence ambivalent, and *oni* in violent and harmful states can be tranquilized and made beneficent to humans.[31]

This ambivalent character of *oni* and *kishin* is not communicated fully by their English counterpart "demon." Unlike an *oni*, which is violent and harmful but can be calmed down, a "demon" necessitates violent confrontation because it is evil by nature; it must be expelled, exorcised, and exterminated.[32] Hence, the Dorok's calling Kushana and Nausicaä "demon" in the English version implies that violence is the only result of their confrontations. This is not so in the Japanese version, where the Dorok's perception of the princesses as *oni* or *kishin* more or less suggests their awareness of a non-violent solution to their conflicts and the possibility of coming to good terms with their enemies. All in all, the English word "demon" solidifies the Dorok's worldview of absolute good and total evil, while its Japanese counterparts *oni* or *kishin* leaves such a worldview open for question. Interestingly, the English translation "demon" reinforces Miyazaki's intention more than his Japanese version because he saw the Dorok retain and promote dualism, but the Japanese words that they use to refer to their enemies embrace oscillatory meanings and hence challenge their dualistic worldview.

By presenting the Dorok as evil in the eyes of the two princesses, the English translation further enhances the aggressive nature of their confrontations. For example, when Nausicaä — who at one point claims, "you end up destroying everything if you divide the world into just friends and enemies"[33] — senses the presence of the spirit of the Dorok emperor, she says "He . . . He is evil,"[34] and Kushana states, "Those Dorok lands have truly fallen under an evil cloud."[35] In the Japanese version, however, these lines are written without terms that literally mean "evil"; Nausicaä calls the emperor "dangerous" (*abunai*) instead,[36] and Kushana's original Japanese for "an evil cloud" is "an ominous shadow" (*fukitsu na kage*).[37] Transformation of the negative expressions "dangerous" and "ominous" into "evil" amplifies the Dorok's villainous nature and a dualistic worldview.

The English translation also uses idiomatic phrases containing "God(s)" and "devil," which are totally absent in the Japanese version. Phrases like "She was lost in combat, by God!"[38] for "She was lost in combat!" (*Sentō chū ni yukue fumei ni nattan da zo!*)[39] on one hand, and the Dorok's "Who the devil is she?"[40] for "What a fellow" (*nan te yatsu da*)[41] on the other hand, are both idiomatic and hence do not literally address the God or a devil. Nonetheless, these usages of "God" and "devil" establish a dualistic worldview where good and evil are in conflict; the reiteration of "devil," as in "Where the devil are they going?," "What the devil is this?," and "Those devils have thick armor,"[42] emphasizes a militant attitude toward the enemy and a perception of the enemy's vile nature. Moreover, "She was lost in combat, by God" and "By the gods, I'd survive!"[43] suggest a belief in the existence of a protective, benevolent power.

Such delineations of good and evil are a strand of Christianization. It is true that the manga translation substantially retained animistic elements while the anime translation did not. Nor did the English manga translation purposefully reform the text to the Christian worldview. The translation of *oni* into "demon" might simply stem from the limitations of the English language, whereas the insertion of idioms with "devil" and "God(s)" conversely reflects the opposite, as such idiomatic expressions do not exist in Japanese. Further, the translation of various negative words with the word "evil" may generally conform to the tradition of magical fantasy literature that has often divided the world into good and evil, light and darkness.[44] Nonetheless, dualistic logical thought is at the heart of many forms of Christianity. Neither the English language nor Western fantasy conventions can be severed from Christian traditions, as renowned Christian apologist C. S. Lewis states, "Christianity agrees with Dualism that this universe is at war."[45]

Conclusion

After the completion of the manga *Nausicaä of the Valley of the Wind*, Miyazaki continued pursuing animistic themes in animated films centered on Japanese gods, such as *Princess Mononoke* (1997) and the Oscar-winning *Spirited Away* (2001). His ongoing criticism of the dualistic worldview is evident in these films, as their characters are presented to be a mixture of good and bad, with some oscillating between the two. In these films, Miyazaki's belief in an animistic, non-dualistic worldview is much more explicit than the anime *Nausicaä*. Yet in *Nausicaä*'s manga version, by putting the two worldviews in tension and making the animistic worldview superior through Nausicaä's victory, Miyazaki expresses his belief very directly compared to his other works.

Ironically, however, as the manga was translated into English, the same contestation between animism and dualism emerged at an intertextual level. The American translation confronts the original version and specifically the animistic messages by enveloping the text in a dualistic worldview. This confrontation does not alter the storyline, which climaxes in Nausicaä's claim of animism, or pantheism according to the translation. Nor does it significantly nullify animistic motifs throughout the story, in contrast to the anime translation, which erases them completely. Yet, the confrontation effaces animism at an implicit level, since animism, according to Miyazaki, negates the presence of absolute good and absolute bad.

The delineation of dualism is presumably an important strategy to make the manga accessible to the American audience. The same strategy is also seen in the Disney translations of Miyazaki's other films. The visibility of the strategy in this dense, complex manga for adults reveals that clarification of good versus evil is foremost a cultural issue, more or less stemming from the audience's Judeo-Christian tradition.[46]

Notes

1 Takashi Sasaki, *"Miyazaki Anime" Himerareta messeiji: Kaze no tani no naushika kara hauru no ugoku shiro made* ("Miyazaki Anime" Hidden Messages: From Nausicaä of the Valley of the Wind to Howl's Moving Castle) (Tokyo: KK Bestsellers, 2005), 205–9; Masashi Shimizu, *Miyazaki Hayao o yomu: bosei to kaosu no fantazii* (Reading Miyazaki Hayao: Fantasy of Maternity and Chaos) (Tokyo: Chōeisha, 2001), 161.

2 Susan Napier, *Anime from Akira to Howl's Moving Castle: Experiencing Contemporary Japanese Animation* (2001; New York: Palgrave Macmillian, 2005), 259–60.

3 Animism is by nature a controversial term. After E. B. Tylor brought it forth in *Primitive Culture* in 1871, scholars in various fields have approached and defined the term in different ways. In this essay, I use the term broadly, corresponding to Miyazaki's usage of it.

4 Hiroshi Aoi, *Miyazaki anime no angō* (Codes in Miyazaki Anime), (2004; Tokyo: Shinchōsha, 2006), 64.

5 Hayao Miyazaki, *Shuppatsuten 1979–1996* (The Starting Point) (Tokyo: Studio Ghibli, 1996), 472.

6 Miyazaki, *Shuppatsuten*, 341. Hereafter, all the English translations of Miyazaki's statements and Japanese lines in the anime and manga versions of *Nauiscaä* are mine.

7 Miyazaki, *Shuppatsuten*, 522.

8 Miyazaki, *Shuppatsuten*, 534.

9 Nausicaä, however, also carries a messiah-like role in the manga, although she never dies and resurrects. See Marc Hairston, "The Reluctant Messiah: Hayao Miyazaki's *Nausicaä of the Valley of the Wind* Manga," *Manga: An Anthology of Global and Cultural Perspectives*, ed. Toni Johnson-Woods (London: Continuum, 2009); Hiroshi Yamanaka, "Mangabunka no naka no shūkyō" (Religion in Manga Culture), *Shōhi sareru shūkyō* (Consumed Religions), ed. Susumu Shimazono and Kenji Ishii (Tokyo: Shunjūsha, 1996), 175–81.

10 Hayao Miyazaki, *Nausicaä of the Valley of the Wind*, trans. David Lewis and Toren Smith (1995; San Francisco: VIZ Media, 2008), 7:130.

11 Miyazaki, *Nausicaä*, 7:200.
12 Miyazaki, *Nausicaä*, 7:201.
13 Miyazaki, *Nausicaä*, 7:208.
14 Miyazaki, *Shuppatsuten*, 472.
15 Miyazaki, *Shuppatsuten*, 528.
16 Miyazaki, *Orikaeshiten 1997–2008* (The Returning Point) (Tokyo: Studio Ghibli, 2008), 40. Miyazaki calls traditional Japanese *kami* worship animism, but he strictly differentiates it from "religion": "I have a feeling that there is animism in me rather than a religion." *Shuppatsuten*, 341. Probably because of his strong repulsion to "religion," he never uses the term Shinto to refer to animistic themes that he praises and inserts in his works.
17 This version extensively altered the original version by editing out about twenty minutes of footage and changing the main character's name to Princess Zandra. For a detailed discussion about New World Pictures' *Warriors of the Wind*, see Ryoko Toyama, "Nausicaä of the Valley of the Wind: Frequently Asked Questions," Team Ghiblink, http://www.nausicaa.net/miyazaki/nausicaa/faq.html.
18 In 2007, 78.2 percent of the American population claimed Christianity as their religion. The US Census Bureau, "Religious Composition of U.S. Population: 2007," *The 2009 Statistical Abstract* (Washington, DC: US Department of Commerce, 2009), http://www.census.gov/compendia/statab/tables/09s0074.pdf.
19 *Nausicaä aus dem Tal der Wind* (Nausicaä of the Valley of the Wind), DVD, directed by Hayao Miyazaki (1984; Munich: Universum Film, 2007).
20 The tenth definition of "boy" according to *Collins Cobuild English Language Dictionary* is: "Boy is used to address a male animal such as a dog or horse."
21 Hayao Miyazaki, *Kaze no tani no naushika* (Nausicaä of the Valley of the Wind), 7 Volumes (Tokyo: Tokuma Shoten, 2008).
22 Miyazaki, *Nausicaä*, 7:208.
23 Miyazaki, *Kaze*, 6:112.
24 Miyazaki, *Nausicaä*, 6:106.
25 Miyazaki, *Kaze*, 5:124.
26 Miyazaki, *Kaze*, 3:135.
27 Miyazaki, *Nausicaä*, 5:118, 3:129.
28 Noriko T Reider, "Transformation of the Oni: From the Frightening and Diabolical to the Cute and Sexy," *Asian Folklore Studies* 62:1 (2003): 133–57.
29 Atsuhiko Yoshida, *Oni to akuma no shinwagaku* (Mythology of Oni and Demons) (Tokyo: Seidosha, 2006), 28. Tōji Kamata, "Nihon shinwa no oni to kami no isō" (A Phase of Oni and Kami in Japanese Mythology), presented at "Symposium: Oni and Demons," Nagoya, Japan, Sept. 30, 2001, http://homepage2.nifty.com/moon21/ronbun08.html.
30 Miyazaki, *The Starting Point*, 501.
31 Brian Bocking, *A Popular Dictionary of Shinto* (Great Britain: Curzon Press, 1996), 140.
32 The first definition of "demon" in *Collins Cobuild English Language Dictionary* is "an evil spirit."
33 Miyazaki, *Nausicaä*, 7:32.
34 Miyazaki, *Nausicaä*, 2:127.
35 Miyazaki, *Nausicaä*, 3:45.
36 Miyazaki, *Kaze*, 2:133.
37 Miyazaki, *Kaze*, 3:51.

38 Miyazaki, *Nausicaä*, 2:13.
39 Miyazaki, *Kaze*, 2:19.
40 Miyazaki, *Nausicaä*, 2:40.
41 Miyazaki, *Kaze*, 2:46.
42 Miyazaki, *Nausicaä*, 2:55, 2:106, 5:41.
43 Miyazaki, *Nausicaä*, 3:16.
44 Akiko Waki, *Mahōfantazii no sekai* (The World of Magical Fantasy) (Tokyo: Iwanami Shoten, 2006), 34.
45 CS Lewis, *Mere Christianity* (London: HarperCollins, 1952), 45.
46 For a translation analysis of *Spirited Away*, see Ogihara, "'Estranged Religion' in Anime: American and German Translations of Hayao Miyazaki's *Spirited Away*," *2007 Conference Volume of the German Association for American Studies*, ed. Jeanne Cortiel, Kornelia Freitag, Christine Gerhardt and Michael Wall (Heidelberg: WINTER, 2009).

RESPONSE AND REBELLION

On *Preacher*
(Or, the Death of God in Pictures)

MIKE GRIMSHAW

"WE PHILOSOPHISE ON THE END of lots of things, but it is here that they actually come to an end."[1] In his episodic "postcard" treatise on hyperreal America, Jean Baudrillard posits a vision of the US as simultaneously a paradoxical "realised utopia"[2] and "the *only remaining primitive society*"[3] — a dystopian utopia, a society best understood from the sacrificial expanse of the desert horizon. Baudrillard's aphorism on America as the land of "last things" signifies the spiritual context of postmodern Generation Xers — a melange of tradition, pop culture, gnostic occultism, and our newly mediatized religious sensibility.[4] Ryan Gilbey has labeled it "The Doom Generation," noting a turn to images of gothic distress and horror in music, fashion, and entertainment. This is a generation seeking answers to questions that may not have acceptable answers, a generation feeling disenfranchised from "the old ideologies or beliefs or 'traditional politics' whose relevance has withered as the decade has worn on."[5] For Gen X exists in a para-world [in the twin senses of *para* as prefix; both "beside" and "beyond"][6] in relation to their baby-boomer parents: a world of multiple narratives of re-enchantment expressing an eclectic, largely anti-establishment attitude, one highly suspicious of religious orthodoxy yet receptive to the fantastical, the occult, and the gnostic. This dystopic milieu finds pop culture realization in the pages of Garth Ennis' *Preacher*, a 66-issue graphic novel. For, if Nietzsche proclaimed the death of God in the 1880s, and the "Death of God" theologians debated the merits of this claim throughout the twentieth century, and *Time* famously asked the question, "Is God dead?" to the public in 1966, then readers of the *Preacher* comic actually see it happen. God dies. God is shot. God is killed. And the readers understand why.

In January 1995, DC Comics (under its adult Vertigo[7] imprint) published the first of what would become a long-running series that finally concluded in October 2000. Over the course of sixty-six issues, the reader is taken on a roller-coaster ride through contemporary America with side trips to the Vietnam War, through the Dublin 1916 uprising, across the Western frontier in the 1880s, along the south of France, up into Heaven, and down into Hell itself. Ostensibly the story of Jesse Custer, a fallen preacher literally hunting for God, this labyrinthine plot involves vampirism, frontier revisionism, graphic sex and violence, Kurt Cobain's suicide, small-town American gothic, serial killers, secret societies, Grail legends, fallen angels, an indestructible Saint of Killers, the ghost of John Wayne, a God who abandons his creation, and the course of true love. Created by Garth Ennis,[8] an expatriate northern Irishman, and largely drawn by Steve Dillon, *Preacher* is an important example of the gnostic lure of both intentionally blasphemous and esoteric religion in what could be termed the underground of contemporary religiosity and popular culture. For while *Preacher* may be relatively unknown to scholars inside the academy, it is big news to those outside. Myriad spin-off websites and discussion pages explore the series at length, and continued rumours of a movie version in various stages of early production continue to circulate.

The Outline

Preacher is a Byzantine interlocking of stories that slowly unfold and at last coalesce into a final showdown where God is killed. The lead character is Jesse Custer, a typical hero: tall, dark, rugged, and good-looking. Raised in a Southern gothic house of horrors, he briefly escapes and embarks on a life of grand theft auto before being dragged back and forced to become a hellfire Texas preacher "for some obscure little Presbyterian-Baptist sect no-one's ever heard of."[9] This phase ends when personal and communal tragedy strikes and the wandering preacher is reborn into worldly temptation. Possessed by Genesis, the offspring of an angel and a demon, Jesse is literally the possessor of the voice of God, able to command all who hear him speak.

The central focus of *Preacher* is Jesse's hunt for God, whom he pursues through the underworld of contemporary America to find out why God has abandoned Heaven.[10] Accompanying Jesse in his quest are Tulip O'Hare and Cassidy. Tulip, on one level, is a typical adolescent female fantasy figure: overtly sexualized, often flimsily dressed or naked, yet also a "tough talkin', pistol packin' mama" — the "best friend with breasts" of so many pop-culture dreams.[11] Tulip is both lover and sidekick to Jesse, Bonnie to his Clyde. Also accompanying them is Cassidy, an alcoholic Irish vampire.[12] Once human, Cassidy was bitten by a vampire while fleeing the Dublin 1916 uprising. Having befriended Jesse, he is also in love with Tulip, which adds tension to the trio's relationship.

If Jesse is hunting God, he is turn is hunted by the Saint of Killers, a bounty hunter made immortal by his hatred for God. Following personal disaster on the Western frontier in the 1880s and a resultant delight in gratuitous violence, the Saint was sent to Hell. His cold heart snuffs out Hell's flames, however, and his hatred for God makes him immortal. He replaces the Angel of Death, murders the Devil, and sets out in pursuit of both Jesse and God. The plot is therefore a classic quest narrative: will the hero succeed, or die trying? Death stalks the world, and our hero seeks to locate and overcome the absent father (God).

Starr, the increasingly mutilated senior agent of the Grail and protector of the sacred bloodline of Jesus, is also hunting Jesse. From its headquarters in the south of France, the Grail has kept the messianic bloodline pure for 2,000 years by only allowing familial inbreeding. Unfortunately, such genetic limitation has resulted in an imbecilic faeces-throwing messiah. Seeking to take over the Grail, Starr kills its leader the Allfather and pursues Jesse in order to make him the new messiah.

Preacher also includes a cast of supporting players, notably "Arseface" (whose deformed features are the result of a bungled Kurt Cobain copycat suicide attempt) and the redneck Jody, a good-ol' boy and the muscular factotum of Jesse's evil grandmother.[13] There are also Louisiana vampire-wannabes, San Francisco sexual deviants, New York serial killers, repressed Midwestern psychotics, and mysterious Grail functionaries. Readers learn about the love story of Jesse's parents, the tragedy of Tulip's father, and Cassidy's participation in the Irish uprising and his life in Depression-era New York; they encounter various angels and demons in Heaven and Hell and a revisionist reading of the American frontier. If Gen X inhabits a para-world to their Boomer parents, then *Preacher*'s is a para-world to the American dream.

The graphic novel is well suited to such a number of characters and story lines for two main reasons. First, within the realm of the comic anything is possible; alternate universes are almost prerequisites (at least within superhero comics, which have dominated the medium in twentieth-century America). Secondly, the serial form enables the unfolding and interlinking of a variety of stories that can be told at a leisurely pace.[14] Graphic novels are thus meta-fiction in graphic form: they combine multiple story lines in a way familiar to a generation raised on television dramas and soap operas. Incorporating cinematic cut-aways, storyboarding, and framing, graphic novels are narratively transgressive in context and content. This quality makes them ideally suited to romanticized expressions of composite mythologies in a culture whereby, in the words of underground pop group favorites The Clean: "Anything could happen and it could be right now. The choice is yours, to make it worthwhile."[15] As such, *Preacher* is a series of interlocking narratives that circle around the central quest for God. We gain background on all the characters and are granted access to elements that initially seem unrelated, but that *Preacher* synthesizes into a sprawling saga of pop-culture religiosity: the search for meaning and purpose in a hypothetical contemporary America. This is an America that appears to be in terminal decay. Whether in a small town or a large city, deviance, disaster, crime, and brutality are never far below the surface of a society that may call on religion as a justification but is, in fact, abandoned by God.

Preacher's undercurrent of frontier violence in the form of the Saint of Killers acts as a sub-narrative and explanatory device. The blood spilled in the American West and the murderous acts committed have stained the land and its inhabitants, and a land founded on violence can never be pure or peaceful. The link is made with the ideology of blood sacrifice in the 1916 Dublin uprising. Ennis critiques the neo-romantic ideology of a sacrificial outpouring of blood that would, it was hoped, change history. Cassidy, at this time just a normal Irish youth, flees from the slaughter and in the process is attacked by a vampire: he becomes a blood sacrifice. Yet his blood sacrifice is one that symbolically stands for Ireland itself, which continuously feasts on the blood of her own people. Cassidy, driven abroad by both types of blood sacrifice (national and personal), arrives in America where a new form of national blood sacrifice will occur in the 1960s and early 1970s with the Vietnam War. Here the State acts as vampire, sucking the life out of its own combatants.

The religious core of *Preacher* is the theme of humanity abandoned by God. Whether the situation is incipient Irish nationalism, a bloodthirsty Western frontier, the Vietnam War, or contemporary America's social decline, God is either absent or neglectful and needs to be called to account. God is even absent from the messianic line so faithfully kept by the Grail, for what should be purity becomes imbecility and corruption — in a sense, God even abandons his earlier effort at self-representation. Here, Ennis' Northern Irish Protestantism (even if latent) comes to the fore. Ennis expresses himself as an outraged Puritan, implying that it is better to destroy than to allow contamination (whether societal or religious) to continue. In this, Ennis is closer to Brett Easton Ellis than Douglas Coupland in his particular version of a Gen X sensibility. Ellis's *American Psycho* is likewise a puritan howl of disgust that seeks transgressive redemption in a world seemingly corrupted by nihilism, a brutal contrast to Coupland's ineffective philosophizing in *Life after God*.[16] Ennis's vision as expressed in *Preacher* is that life after God is the aim, not the lament; the death of God is the creation of hope and new possibility, not the end of meaning.

Throughout, Jesse is the confused existential hero whose only reliable source of guidance is the ghost of John Wayne, the embodiment of a mythological frontier virility and virtue. Ennis suggests that only our own contemporary mythologies — those derived from pop culture — can guide us. Central to Ennis' work is the emphasis on contemporary mythologies and the way they enable a generation raised on mass media to make some moral sense of life in an increasingly traumatized world. It is important to note, however, that it is never one coherent mythology at work, but rather a series of composite mythologies and traditions that allow people to meaningfully navigate contemporary existence. In its suspicion and rejection of singular meta-narratives, postmodern spirituality turns towards a salvific, redemptive use of pop culture — often against traditional religion and its claims and institutions. Spirituality is therefore a commodity of possibilities for individuals to make use of as they can.

In the end, the Grail collapses, God is killed, and Jesse and Tulip ride off into the sunset in a world without God. Yet this world seems more at peace. Ennis's underlying theme is that religion and God are ultimately harmful and destructive, as they ultimately seek to control, separate, and enslave.

The Themes

1. Frontier revisionism and sub-kenotic adoptionism

For Garth Ennis, a product of mass media culture, the frontier has two sources: the old Westerns he watched on television as a child in Ireland, and later the "spaghetti Westerns" of Sergio Leone and the European ultra-violent school of cowboy existential apocalypse.[17] In a foreword to the series, he also notes the major influence of Clint Eastwood's *Unforgiven* upon the character of the Saint of Killers, the cold-blooded cowboy who takes on the mantle of the Angel of Death.[18] Yet the Saint's indestructibility also links into recent pop-culture vigilantes *Robocop* and *Terminator*. The difference here is that the Saint is a spiritual "alien cyborg" (a mix of human and non/inhuman) from the past now acting in the present, not a piece of rampant "man-made technology"[19] from some machine-controlled future. This is an interesting point, for often these indestructible vigilantes speak of our fear of technology, a fear that can be traced back to the romantic gothic horror of Mary Shelley's *Frankenstein* (1816).

In *Preacher*, however, the point is more theological. If future mechanical cyborg killers are the result of humanity's interference with the created order, then the Saint of Killers is a reminder of the destructiveness that lurks within human beings, a destructiveness unleashed by God's interference and then abandonment. The killing machine we have to fear is not some imagined future event created by Promethean humanity, but rather a potential within all divinely created humanity. The Saint implies that we all possess the vengeance, destructiveness, and cold-hearted detachment of a wrathful God. As such, this reality raises ontological issues. For if the wrathful God of our violent, destructive *imago dei* is no more — has been killed — does this offer humanity the potential for a new beginning? The fact that Jesse and Tulip ride off into the clichéd new life of the Western sunset could suggest so — but only if God is truly dead.

As part of an imagined mythology (the Death of God as an event rendered in, and rendered possible by, America), *Preacher* makes great use of Western mythology and motifs, fulfilling Jim Kitses' definition of the postmodern Western as "blending mythology and demythology, revisionism and nostalgia."[20] Ennis undertakes a form of frontier revisionism heavily influenced by Clint Eastwood's *Unforgiven* and the paradoxically moralistic amorality of two Western archetypes: the Revenger and the Gunfighter. The Revenger acts alone in an act of personal redemption to overcome a world that has created his state of despair. He is the site of a moral panic within the self, seeking to overcome that which threatens to destroy him. Often this can only be achieved in an act of redemptive violence. By imposing physical death on another, he frees himself from the death of his own soul. The Revenger has links to the Gunfighter, who acts as the defining symbol of a society in chaos.

Both types of characters act as moral agents — the Revenger on a personal level, the Gunfighter on a public one. Yet these moral agents are unable to separate morality from violence and exhibit a puritanical delight in chastisement, suffering, and cleansing pain. As Richard Slotkin notes, "in the world of the gunfighter . . . moral suasion without violent force to back it is incompetent to achieve its civilizing ends; it is foolish at best, at worst a species of complicity with evil."[21] *Preacher* also references another Eastwood film, *Pale Rider*, where the Angel of Death exacts God's vengeance on a frontier community. Yet in *Preacher*, vengeance is wrought not by, but rather against, God. God is the cause of evil, not its answer: it is God who stands against civilization; God who acts as a force of disruptive chaos; God who has to be tamed, broken, and exterminated because of his outlaw actions. In effect, this is the residue of the ancient Gnostics' rejection of the creator God Jehovah, who has to be overcome if true existence is to be attained. Only here, there is no transcendent "good God" or divine spark to be released; rather, in an anti-gnostic turn, it is embodiment — and our engagement with the embodiment of others — that truly saves and redeems us.

To be read both underneath (as supporting text) and against this position (as text of challenge) is the act of ultimate blood sacrifice: the Christian typology of redemption through violence initiated by the sacrificial death of Jesus. Bataille sees this typology as reflecting the central principle of theology that "the world is complete" and "is maintained at every time and in all places, including the night of Golgotha."[22] This leads him to posit a form of Hegelian dialectic of completion and incompletion. God has to be killed, claims Bataille, so "to see the world in the weakness of incompletion."[23] Yet the sacrifice of the crucifixion, the act of salvific solidarity, can have meaning only if the incompletion is overcome. Christianity's message is that the act of completion is actually incomplete, yet will be made complete by God joining in our incomplete state and holding out the promise of completion for all those who believe in the act of divine dialectic.

Preacher responds to this notion in two ways. On the one hand, it claims that if Jesus' bloodline did survive, it is now incomplete, having been corrupted by those seeking to protect it. The incarnation is a one-off — the surviving human bloodline needs divine intervention to be completed, but the theme of this story is the abandonment of humanity by God. On the other hand, *Preacher* moves past Bataille's dialectic to claim that the act of completion for humanity is to ensure that the world's permanent state will be the weakness of incompletion. God has to die to save the world, yet it is only by the abandonment of God in death that the world will be set free. To live in a world that is theologically complete is to fail to hold God to account.

The underlying claim of *Preacher* is that God is an irresponsible father,[24] the one who abandoned his son and now abandons his responsibilities. In this sense Jesse, orphaned by his human parents, is now also orphaned by his divine father. In this reading, Jesse actually becomes a type of Christ figure. Starr, in his desire to remake Jesse as the new messiah, is actually closer to the mark than he realizes. The divine possesses Jesse: in this case Genesis, the new beginning. Jesse, as recipient of this power and knowledge (being like God and so referencing Genesis 3.5), is the new Adam, the partial kenotically-inflected being who is to overturn the old law of God and call the irresponsible father to account. In this pursuit, Tulip then becomes a new Eve, partial temptress but also embodying the independence of the midrashic Lilith. Cassidy is the serpent, the voice of temptation and in- (or non-)humanity. Yet in this new creation, even the non-human still exhibits more humanity than the creator does.

2. The Grail

The second theme of *Preacher* is pop culture in general, ranging from the influence of musician Kurt Cobain and the effects of his suicide upon his fans (*pace* "Arseface"), to Anne Rice's New Orleans vampire gothic lore, to the ethos and sensibility of the American road movie. In many ways, *Preacher* is a road movie in graphic form.

The road movie is a cinematic expression of the existential search of both society and the individual. *Preacher* moves its characters through dystopic America, an America that has become radically secularized by the abandonment of God. Now it is not just the city that is secular, but also heartland America, whether the Deep South, the Midwest, or the western desert. As noted, *Preacher* also exhibits an underlying mythology of the frontier, for in its violence the frontier is a permanent

state of experience in a world abandoned by God. Yet the road movie
thesis is one that works well within the cultural logic of *Preacher* because
as Bennett Schaber remarks, its underlying rhetoric has always been
strongly biblical — whether that of Exodus for those of the pre-World
War II period or apocalypse for those post-war.[25] The road movie is typically a dual journey involving both a physical and spiritual search, where
neither replaces the other but the two instead operate as interdependent.[26] On one hand, *Preacher* follows in the template of *Easy Rider* and
its utopian search for peace of self through a dystopian America, yet in
its fetishization of violence and beauty, it also references *Bonnie and Clyde*
and *Natural Born Killers*. The road in *Preacher* is the road to God, and
Preacher here also references the ultimate American existential quest of
The Wizard of Oz. In Oz, the wizard is revealed to be a small man hiding
behind an artificial persona. In *Preacher*, God is similarly unmasked by
a collection of outcasts who are symbolically reborn and remade on the
journey.

The quest narrative is therefore central to pop culture as the attempt
to narrate and mythologize meaning amidst the collapse of meta-
narratives that characterizes postmodernity. The sense of hidden
knowledge, the pursuit of a quest of and for "real" meaning, exposes
the central rejection of both the secular modern world and relativistic
nihilism. Pop culture is propelled by a romantic core that, religiously,
posits Schleiermacher over and against Kant — and in fact over all
the "cultured despisers" of low and popular culture — by claiming the
central value of intuitive feeling and emotion in the pursuit of hidden
and unrecognized truth.

The Grail mystery is a continuing theme in pop culture, as evidenced
recently by the eager embrace of Dan Brown's *The Da Vinci Code* (2003).
Preacher posits an alternative use of the Grail mystery, and it has an obvious debt to the pop culture phenomenon of *The Holy Blood and the Holy
Grail*.[27] As the authors note in their introduction to the revised edition in
1996, "material from *The Holy Blood and the Holy Grail* found its way into a
multitude of . . . fictional narratives, from tacky thrillers and pot-boilers
to very serious literature indeed."[28] In outline, the book concerns the
mystery of Rennes-le-Château in the South of France and the sudden
wealth experienced by the local priest Bérenger Saunière at the end of
the nineteenth century. A New Age detective thriller that predates *The
Celestine Prophecy*, it offers up a mixture of esoterica, divine bloodlines,
hidden conspiracies, the Templars, the Cathars, and a still-operating

secret society. In the book, the secret society is dedicated to promoting the claims and interests of the Merogovian bloodline as rightful heirs of the throne of France and as possessors of the Holy Bloodline. The Cathars and the Templars are involved in the protection of both the bloodline and various esoteric secrets.

Holy Blood promotes what it claims are "key facts," all of which are to be found either implicitly or explicitly in *Preacher*. It claims the existence of a secret order acting behind Western history, one seeking the legitimate and justifiable restoration of the Merogovian dynasty and bloodline to the thrones of France and other European nations.[29] *Preacher* differs, however, in that while *Holy Blood* claims the bloodline is diffused throughout European nobility, in *Preacher* the bloodline is undiluted, if inbred and moronic.

Re-reading *Preacher* after *The Da Vinci Code* demonstrates how powerful mythologies find themselves expressed in diverse ways, both as mainstream "airport novel" (*Da Vinci Code*) and as counter-cultural graphic novel. If *The Da Vinci Code* is a sanitized quest, then *Preacher* expresses the quest as a onto-theological rupture of both beliefs and bodies that makes use of the motif of horror in two distinct ways. First, it reflects the excesses of cinematic horror and splatter movies: death and violence occur in close-up, slow frame detail. Linked into the Western motif, these cartoonish representations recall the ballet of death and violence in Peckinpah's *The Wild Bunch*, where "the mix of slow and regular motion allows the audience to experience the subjective distortion of time experienced by those engaged in violent action."[30] *Preacher* posits a dystopic America where violence and degradation exist just under the symbolic realized utopia of existence.[31] Horror, blood, leakage, and penetration seek to destroy both the personal body and the body politic.

While Bataille may claim that the crucifixion "is a wound by which believers communicate with God,"[32] the wounds experienced in *Preacher* are a worldly crucifixion that signals the abandonment of this world by God. The world is a site of Kristevan abjection, where "the corpse, seen without God and outside of science . . . is death infecting life."[33] The reanimated, immortal corpse of the Saint of Killers, stalking heaven and earth in pursuit of his divine prey, is an instance of this leakage of death into life. Yet this corpse cannot be excluded from God's territory, precisely because it is "accursed of God" (Deut. 21.23);[34] it is God's abandonment of his territory that has resulted in a corpse-stained land.

Yet while it is the absence of God that has allowed horror to flourish, it is also the continued existence of the absent God that perpetuates the horror of life. For horror is a body language, a language born of the crisis of identity in a world suffering ontological disrupture.[35] This language seeks to re-experience and remake the limits of the body and existence, to articulate the liminal fear that containment (of the self, the fear, the threat, or the inside of the body) will fail.

In *Preacher*, Ennis suggests that horror, leakage, disruption, and suffering occur because God has abandoned his responsibilities. The horror occurs not because of God's existence (or otherwise), but rather because of the wilful inaction of God. Yet while acts of horror do occur because of divine inaction, *Preacher* also claims that God seeks to inspire terror (and so force humanity to seek refuge in him). Therefore, God must be called to account for his abandonment of the world (abandonment being one of the traditional motifs of horror and terror), yet with an awareness that acts of terror and horror will continue. With God dead, however, humanity will finally take responsibility for this world and its existence — and that includes its potential and possibility for horror and terror. The death of God will not end terror or horror, but it will return such events to the orbit of humanity's control. In a radically secularized existence, horror and terror continue to exist and continue to be random and disruptive, but the solutions to them are now within humanity's sphere of action.

Preacher's Aesthetic

It would be easy to dismiss *Preacher* because of its form of presentation. The comic book is often seen to reside on the low-culture end of the cultural spectrum: a form of entertainment as opposed to literature, a repository of adolescent views and attitudes, and a type of text for those unable to cope with narratives without pictures. Here they fall under Adolf Loos' designation as *ornamentation*, the signifier of either a criminal tendency or a degenerate mind in an unornamented modern world.[36]

Yet the history of the cartoon as societal comment has roots in the anonymous woodcuts illustrating seventeenth-century broadsheets that commented on religious and foreign affairs in Britain. One of the earliest series telling a story in sequential pictures was Hogarth's *A Rake's Progress* (1755). While the comic became a mainstay of a mass public during the 1930s with the rise of the American superhero, there was also the parallel rise of the countercultural comic: both the anti-rational horror comic and comics of Rabelaisian excess, as in the work of Robert Crumb. Heavily influential upon the ethos of *Preacher* was the British comic *2000 AD*, which appeared in the middle of the punk explosion in 1977. Ennis wrote for *2000 AD* before shifting to Vertigo, and he seems never to forgotten its raison d'être as propounded by Roger Sabin:

> At its core it stood for a distrust of any kind of authority; a romanti-
> cised belief in working-class culture (street credibility); the worth of
> rebellion for its own sake; and the fetishisation of violence (real or
> imaginary).[37]

This nihilistic punk aesthetic is an important undercurrent to *Preacher*, not only in Jesse's a/theology, but also in its critique of Kurt Cobain and the nihilistic music of grunge as sub narrative. Ennis suggests that to believe in the salvific, redemptive example of suicidal rock stars (whether Sid Vicious or Kurt Cobain) is as self-defeating as believing in a God who professes love but displays indifference. Here "Arseface" stands in for all damaged humanity, briefly succeeding himself as punk-rock celebrity because of his hideous appearance, but then just as quickly discarded. Ennis states that it is the lack of paternal affection that drives adolescents into the worship of these nihilistic, narcissistic stars. Here the inauthentic punk star is an analogy for the inauthentic God who likewise feeds off his fans, fans who damage themselves in attempting various forms of salvific imitation. *Preacher* is therefore a moralistic narra-tive represented in perhaps the supreme narrative form of pop culture, the comic book. The comic book (or graphic novel) occupies a unique place in narrative presentation because it operates in a manner similar to the Christian icon. An icon is "a window to the divine" where the image presented is not there as a concrete one-dimensional presence or presentation, but rather exists as an opening to an encounter: the observer looks through the presented image to the reality behind it. That which is represented is only an approximation of the non-visual truth that is posited as existing behind and beyond the image. Comics (especially graphic novels) exist in a similar fashion. As one critic has noted of the comic genre, "The illustrations are not really illustrations of what's going on. The narration isn't really describing what's going on. There is a gap there, and somewhere in that gap is reality."[38]

To read a comic is to engage in looking beyond what is being presented to the fuller picture behind the panels. This acknowledgment of the artificiality of presentation paradoxically allows the presentation of the fantastical as "real." The other important link is that *Preacher* is making use of a mythology and history that, from the viewpoint of late modern post-enlightenment society, appears fantastical and "artificial." As was noted in an interview with Garth Ennis,

> Of course, being the comic world allows you to throw in casually, "We have this reanimating serum that can bring fish back to life." Which would be out of place in a more realistic book. Like in *Preacher*, there's a lot of supernatural things going on, but if you accept Christian mythology, that's the only jump you have to make. In DC you have Christian mythology and radioactive superheroes and space aliens . . . [39]

The comic can present what is, in a modernist, secular world, often viewed as unpresentable. Yet in its mixing of genres and mythologies, *Preacher* is perhaps the ultimate form of a postmodern, eclectic, religious pastiche. It aims not only to implement such a cosmology on the world of its readers, but also must at some level already reflect their eclectic cosmology for it to garner acclaim both critically and in the realm of consumer appreciation. While a movie can approximate this experience, only a comic book series can enable a drawn-out engagement over a period of five years to create of a sub-world — or perhaps a para-world — for the reader to engage with and within.

Conclusion

One could dismiss *Preacher* as low culture, juvenile, adolescent, sophomoric, ill-informed and the like. But that would be to miss the point of both the series and of the comic book itself. *Preacher* provides important insight into the religious sensibility of postmodern culture: it is predominantly visual and tribal in its affiliations and interests; violence and sex are nearly ubiquitous inclusions in narrative structures; the body is celebrated, transfigured, mutated, and transgressed, but not denied; and the individual can overcome any opposition, whether human or divine. As such, *Preacher* represents Gen X in search of itself, a generation reading of a loss (the death of God) heard of in their parents' generation, but now experienced in *graphic* detail. *Preacher* reflects the sensibility of a generation willing to suspend disbelief in anything as long it is *not* traditional, orthodox Christianity, a generation existing in Baudrillard's dystopian critique of New York: "completely rotten with wealth, power, senility, indifference, puritanism and mental hygiene, poverty and waste, technological futility and aimless violence."[40] *Preacher* is the universe of those who identify more with Bret Easton Ellis' outraged morality tales of fragmented, postmodern society than with Douglas Coupland's rival inactive, ironic "Gen X" of hypermodernity.[41] Coupland might seek "life after God," but Ennis (and Ellis) are attempting to come to terms with the full implications of a life *with* God. For in a radically secularized world, there would have been no point or meaning in *Preacher*. In *Preacher*, Gen X confronts its greatest demon — that their parents did not, and could not, kill off God.

Notes

1   Jean Baudrillard, *America*, trans. C Turner (London/New York: Verso, 1988/1993), 98.
2   Baudrillard, 77.
3   Baudrillard, 5.
4   There have been many recent texts that build upon this current state of Western society (particularly that of America — and by implication the "global America" of the commodified, mediatized world). See Tom Beaudoin, *Virtual Faith: The Irreverent Spiritual Quest of Generation X* (San Francisco: Jossey-Bass, 1998); Harold Bloom, *The American Religion: The Emergence of the Post-Christian Nation* (New York: Simon & Schuster, 1992); Douglas Coupland, *Life After God* (New York: Pocket Books, 1994); Erik Davis, *Techgnosis: Myth, Magic + Mysticism in the Age of Information* (New York: Three River Press, 1998); Bruce David Forbes & Jeffrey H Mahan (eds.), *Religion and Popular Culture in America* (Berkeley: University of California Press, 2000); Eric Michael Mazur and Kate McCarthy (eds.), *God in the Details: American Religion in Popular Culture* (New York: Routledge, 2001); and Mark C Taylor, *About Religion: Economies of Faith in Virtual Culture* (Chicago: University of Chicago Press, 1999).
5   Ryan Gilbey, "Doom Generation: New Tales from the Dark Side," *The Face* 4 (May 1997): 122.
6   The use of "para" raises interesting issues for our contemporary preference for using "post" when we often seem to really mean "para." In particular, the much-vaunted "post-modernity" and "post-secular" could be argued to really express, in many instances, a "para-modernity" and a "para-secular." See Victor E Taylor, *Para/inquiry: Postmodern Religion and Culture* (London & New York: Routledge, 2000). The notion of para-world comes out of my reading between Taylor's work and the world of graphic novels and the increasing use of "post-secular" to describe the return of religion, especially in its political forms. It is interesting that most discussion on the "post-secular" does not mention popular culture, which is arguably the most prevalent site for para-religion and para-mythologies.
7   DC Comics launched Vertigo as "mature comics" in 1993.
8   Ennis, from Belfast, worked previously on the seminal British comic *2000 AD*

and then for Vertigo on the very anti-establishment (both religiously and politically) *Hellblazer*. He was also behind the titles *Hitman, Unknown Soldier,* and *The Darkness.* In 1991, the publisher Robert Maxwell (under pressure from the UK's Evangelical Alliance) withdrew an early graphic novel by Ennis called *True Faith* from publication. The Evangelical Alliance was offended by, among other things, a description of God as "a blockage in the world's toilet." See James Tweed, "True Faith," *New Statesman* February 15, 1991: 15. The discussion on "True Faith" was within a wider section in *New Statesman* centered around "Rushdie and Fatwa" (16–19) discussing the various responses to religious censorship. In the article, Ennis is quoted as stating in a Radio Four interview: "I don't like evangelicals, I don't like Church, I don't like Christianity, I don't like any of that stuff . . ." (16).

9   Garth Ennis et al, *Preacher* #43, November 1998, 19.

10 God is masculine, closer in form to a Greek God — all flowing hair and beard and rugged musculature.

11 Tulip draws on a pulp tradition of sexualized action-women, from Wonder Woman to Charlie's Angels and Tankgirl on to the virtual Lara Croft of *Tomb Raider.*

12 Laurence Rickels in *The Vampire Lectures* (Minneapolis/London: University of Minneapolis Press, 1999) notes that it is often the alcoholic who is a prime candidate for becoming a vampire (2), as well as the suicide (23). Here Cassidy escapes from the mass suicide, becomes a vampire and copes with it by becoming an alcoholic. Ennis is prone to twist established lore.

13 Ennis' take on Southern society is strongly influenced by movies such *Deliverance* and *Southern Comfort*, where crazed, inbred hillbillies mix twisted fundamentalist Christianity, sexual deviance, and extreme violence.

14 For an introduction to graphic novels in all their variety, see Paul Gravett, *Graphic Novels: Stories to Change your Life* (London: Arum Press, 2005).

15 Arising out the gothic gloom of late 1970s Dunedin, New Zealand, The Clean combined the influences of the Velvet Underground, Dylan and punk to become favorites of the alt-music world from college radio in the USA to John Peel in England. Evidencing their debt to popular culture and the world of comic books, not only was the cover of the 4-track recording *Boodle Boodle Boodle* EP (Flying Nun, 1981) a cartoon of the band by band member Hamish Kilgour, the original EP was accompanied by a comic book hand-drawn by the band and their friends. This link of a punk ethos to comics is also represented in New Zealand by the multi-talented punk doyen Chris Knox, who has for many years combined music (The Enemy, Toy Love, Tall Dwarfs, solo career) and comics, including the magazine *Jesus on a Stick*. See Grant Smithies (ed.), *Soundtracks: 118 Great New Zealand Albums* (Nelson, NZ: Craig Potton Publishing, 2007).

16 Douglas Coupland, *Life after God* (New York: Pocket Books, 1994); Bret Easton Ellis, *American Psycho* (New York: Vintage, 1991). For a detailed critique of both Bret Easton Ellis and Douglas Coupland, see Mike Grimshaw, "Cultural Pessimism and Rock Criticism: Bret Easton Ellis' Writing (as) Hell," *Ctheory*, Article: a112, September 25, 2002, http://www.ctheory.net/articles. aspx?id=346.

17 The best source available in English is Christopher Frayling, *Spaghetti Westerns: Cowboys and Europeans from Karl May to Sergio Leone* (London/New York: I.B. Taurus, 1981, 1998). Frayling notes the mix of types that underwrote the spaghetti hero as "a mixture of James Bond, Che Guevara, Hercules and

Judas" (xii). Possible influences for *Preacher* include the anti-clerical *Django* films, the bandit-priest of *A Bullet for the General* (1961), the sex-maniac priest of *Find a Place to Die* (1968), and the bounty-hunting preachers of *No Room to Die* (1969) and *Reverend Colt* (1971) (Frayling, 79).

18 Garth Ennis, "Foreword," *Preacher: Ancient History* (New York: DC Comics, 1998), 2.

19 The use of the term "man" here is deliberate, for in science fiction the post-human cyborg is nearly always created by a man.

20 Jim Kitses, "Introduction: Post-modernism and the Western," *The Western Reader*, eds. J. Kitses and G. Richman (New York: Limelight editions, 1998), 16.

21 Richard Slotkin, *Gunfighter Nation: The Myth of the Frontier in Twentieth Century America* (New York: Athaneum, 1992), 402. Slotkin states that the frontier myth ". . . represented the redemption of the American spirit or fortune as something to be achieved by playing through a scenario of separation, temporary regression to a more primitive or 'natural' state, and regeneration through violence" (12).

22 Georges Bataille, *Guilty*, trans. B. Boone (Venice/San Francisco: The Lapis Press, 1988), 27.

23 Bataille, 27.

24 The Saint of Killers returns to his vigilante ways when his family is brutally murdered in his absence.

25 B Schaber, "'Hitler Can't Keep 'Em That Long': The Road, the People," *The Road Movie Book*, eds. S. Cohan and I. R. Hark (London & New York: Routledge, 1997), 20.

26 S Roberts, "Western Meets Eastwood. Genre and Gender on the Road," *The Road Movie Book*, 53–4.

27 M Baigent, R Leigh, and H Lincoln, *The Holy Blood and the Holy Grail* (London: Arrow Books, revised edition, 1996).

28 Baigent et al., 18.

29 Baigent et al., 106–7.

30 Richard Slotkin, *Gunfighter Nation*, 593.

31 Tracing lineage from de Tocqueville, Baudrillard states "America is powerful and original; America is violent and abominable. We should not seek to deny either of these aspects, nor reconcile them" (*America*, 88).

32 Bataille, *Guilty*, 31.

33 Julia Kristeva, *Powers of Horror: An Essay on Abjection*, trans. L. S. Roudiez (New York: Columbia University Press, 1982), 4.

34 Kristeva, 109.

35 Linda Badley, *Film, Horror and the Body Fantastic* (Westport, Conn./London, 1995), 7.

36 A Loos, "Ornament and Crime," *Adolf Loos: Pioneer of Modern Architecture*, ed. L. Munz & G. Kunstler (London; Thames & Hudson, 1966), 226–31 (original essay 1908). Loos' essay became a theoretical underpinning of the modernist movement, influencing Mies van der Rohe and his famous dictum: "Less is more" — perhaps the pre-eminent "touchstone" of modernity.

37 Roger Sabin, *Comics, Comix and Graphic Novels: A History of Graphic Art* (London: Phaidon, 1996), 133.

38 Frank Miller, *Amazing Heroes* (July 1986), 37–8, quoted in R. Sabin, *Comics, Comix and Graphic Novels*, 9.

39 Steve Johnson, "Garth Ennis Writes Heroes without Costumes," Interview with

Garth Ennis, *Mania* April 18, 1997, http://www.fortunecity.com/tattooine/sputnik/53/scifi/g_ennis.htm.

40 Jean Baudrillard, *America*, 23.

41 Bret Easton Ellis has written a series of novels (*Less than Zero, The Rules of Attraction, American Psycho, The Informers, Glamorama, Lunar Park*) expressing a puritan outrage at postmodern society and its commodification of existence. Douglas Coupland (*Generation X, Shampoo Planet, Microserfs, Life After God*) takes a more mannered approach of switching between ironic inertia and utopian celebration.

Superman Graveside:
Superhero Salvation beyond Jesus

A. DAVID LEWIS

It would be easy to see the many incarnations of Superman
[. . .] simply as a product marketed in different fashions,
but the creators of Superman know that it carries meanings
beyond its status as a commodity. For instance, Jenette
Kahn, president of DC Comics, described Superman
in 1983 as "the first god of a new mythology."[1]

— Ian Gordon

Superman, then, must remain "inconsumable" and at the same
time be "consumed" according to the ways of everyday life. He
possesses the characteristics of timeless myth, but is accepted
only because his activities take place in our human and
everyday world of time. The narrative paradox that Superman's
scriptwriters must resolve somehow, even without being aware
of it, demands a paradoxical solution with regard to time.[2]

— Umberto Eco

For at least the third time, Superman is attending Batman's funeral. In
Adventure Comics #462 (April 1979), Superman stands at the front
of the mourners paying their respects to Bruce Wayne, the revealed
alter ego of Batman. "The eulogies have been said," states the narrative

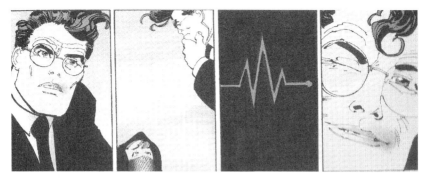

Figure 1. **Superman, attending the funeral of Bruce Wayne, gives a silent acknowledgment to his "deceased" ally's return (Miller, 4.46).**

caption, so one can only guess what words one half of the World's Finest Team had to offer about the other.[3] This scene, however, takes place on Earth-2, a parallel dimension to the central Earth-1, so this Batman's death, while final, is not transversal; on many other separate Earths, Batman lives on. This is only *a* death of Batman, not *the* death of Batman. In a similar fashion, on yet another version of Earth — one set nearly a cynical score into the future — Superman again attends Batman's burial. The two men and their two ideologies had battled in the streets of Gotham, and the hardened, darker Batman was the victor, but he was quickly felled by all-too-human heart failure. Superman, in his mild-mannered guise of Clark Kent, is still black-and-blue from their fight and, again, says nothing. Only a surreptitious wink communicates his silent acknowledgment of the quiet pulse emerging from the grave (see Figure 1); this tell-tale heart relieves Superman of any guilt, with Batman having intentionally drugged himself into a death-like coma to escape the authorities. His compatriot Robin will free him, and they will go further underground (literally) to conclude the landmark series *Batman: The Dark Knight Returns* (1986). Superman, witness to it all, will remain mum, while his erstwhile ally has another "death" along with another life.[4]

Whether Batman can have an ultimate end is the subject of Neil Gaiman and Andy Kubert's 2009 "Whatever Happened to the Caped Crusader?" two-part story. There, for a third time, Superman attends his teammate's funeral, but now he shares some of his thoughts (see Figure 2).

SUPERMAN: I told him, "Our job is to *inspire* them. To be *better* than they are so that *they* can be better than they are. And look at *you*.

Figure 2.   **Regardless of who, exactly, will kill Batman — villains or readers —
Superman does not seem prepared to face such an end himself nor let his ally face
a final end (Gaiman, 7).**

You're *frightening* them. You're as bad as the worst of them." He said,
"*No . . .*"

BATMAN (flashback): No, Clark. *I'm* what stands between the worst
of them and the city.

SUPERMAN (flashback): They've made a treaty. *All* of them. If I take
you back to Gotham, they'll *kill* you. They won't stop until you're
dead.

SUPERMAN: He smiled that scary smile. He said, "And while they're
trying to kill me, they aren't killing innocents. Now take me home."
So I did. That was the last time I saw him.[5]

Superman's eulogy follows those of megalomaniac Ra's al Ghul, of Robin the Boy Wonder, of arch-nemesis the Joker, of Bat-Girl Betty Kane, among others — and each account contradicts the others. There is no one death for the legend of the Batman. In some cases, he perishes "*hugely*, bravely, *saving* the city from something that would destroy it. Sometimes it's a *small*, ironic, unnoticed death."[6]

In short, Batman, the thin blue-and-gray line between moral society and immoral chaos, will never stop in his mission until he is dead, and the circumstances of the death are irrelevant. "They've made a treaty," said Superman, who will forever attempt to save the day once again. "They won't stop until you're *dead*," he warned, likely referring to Batman's rogues gallery, but just as applicably to Batman's readership. Neither will ever let him rest, and Superman, despite his mandate to safeguard life, will always be there to witness this demise. Batman may hold the line against Evil and Chaos, but Superman holds the line against Death and Inexistence.

I.

The converse is not entirely equal; Batman is rarely called upon to stand at a funeral of Superman, the rare exception being Superman's own death defending the city of Metropolis from the monstrous Doomsday creature in 1992.[7] Batman served as a pallbearer in the superheroes' private service following the public memorial. In *Superman: Day of Doom*, produced by DC Comics ten years after that day, Clark Kent's boss, *Daily Planet* Editor-in-Chief Perry White, recalls the event:

> It was incredible . . . The type of thing normally reserved for the most respected heads of state. I think *every* single person in Metropolis turned out that day. People were lined scores-deep along the funeral route. The entire J.L.A. [superhero team] came and, in a very private moment for them, away from the crowds, the world's greatest heroes carried Superman to his final resting place. Later, the President himself delivered a very moving eulogy. In short, the city was paralyzed for *days*. Superman made Metropolis synonymous with vitality and life. Suddenly we were synonymous with *death*.[8]

Was this *the* death of *the* Superman? This was the central Earth-1 Superman, the main Superman, not a clone nor a robot nor an impersonator. This was not one of DC Comics' "imaginary stories," those non-canonical tales removed from the burden of publication consistency and continuity. DC Comics editors declared him dead in the press, and the scientists within the comic concurred. In fiction and in fact, Superman had been slain.

Superman was dead — briefly. Fiction mirrored fact again as characters and readers wore black armbands bearing his S-chevron[9] (included with special editions of his comic book for real-life fans). Derivative Supermen arose, either claiming or honoring his legend. Loved ones, including fiancée Lois Lane and adoptive parents Jonathan and Martha Kent, grieved. His loss was experienced by all except, perhaps, DC Comics, which made a killing in sales during that time.[10] The pseudo-science involved in explanations of his return, a freak result of his alien Kryptonian physiology, matter far less than the experience, albeit temporary, of his passing. As Superman later tells his wife, "When Doomsday hit me for that final time . . . I was . . . gone. I don't even know how to describe it . . . but in every practical sense, I was *dead*."[11]

How "present" Superman was at his "funeral" is a matter of speculation, but his return is not. Since 1993, Superman's adventures have continued,[12] so Perry White's evaluation of the funeral means one of two things. Either Perry was incorrect and Superman was never truly deposited in his "final resting place" (i.e., he never died), or, more intriguingly, Perry was strangely accurate and Superman's "final resting place" is back on Earth, fighting the never-ending battle. To say it another way, either Superman never died — because to die means not to be alive, which he is[13] — or he did die, but death had little to no effect on his vitality. The result of either line of thought is the same: Superman overrides death. He is antithetical to it.

This resurrection (or overcoming of death) spurred the latest wave of comparisons between Superman and Jesus. Never mind that Superman's own creators, writer Jerry Siegel and artist Joe Shuster, plainly cite biblical Samson, Greco-Roman heroes like Hercules,[14] the pulp hero Doc Savage, and the works of Edgar Rice Burroughs as their inspirations.[15] Superman was taken out of their hands long ago. Comics scholar and writer Danny Fingeroth says that the "main metaphor systems at war for credit" over Superman "are Moses and Jesus,"[16] with each having its proponents. Rabbi Simcha Weinstein, perhaps predictably, reads Superman's escape as baby Kal-El from the doomed planet Krypton as highly Mosaic, right down to his hidden heritage and Hebraic name.[17] "[I]t can be argued that the Mosaic take has the more resonant, long-term credibility," says Fingeroth in his book on Jewish immigrants' impact on the burgeoning comics industry. "On the other hand, Superman isn't a leader like Moses, but a one-at-a-time savior like Jesus."[18] Moreover, unlike Moses, Superman spread himself across both of his heritages, both as an extraterrestrial and as an American Midwesterner.[19] Greg Garrett reads this as a far closer parallel to Jesus, with history's "continuous wrangling over the nature of Christ, about how human he was or how God-like."[20] In his own survey of the Superman/Jesus linkage, Ken Schenck reads the fluctuating portrayals of Superman and his powers as reminiscent of Christianity's struggles with "balancing Christ's divinity with his humanness."[21]

Ironically, it is this shared strain between the Human and Other that ultimately separates Superman from Jesus, no matter how tempting the comparison may be. Had Superman never evolved or developed as a character since Siegel and Shuster's conception of him as a strange visitor from another planet, then perhaps reading Superman as a spandex Christ figure might be less problematic. "Similarities between the old Superman of the monomythic tradition and the Jesus Christ of Christian tradition are easy to find," says George Aichele in his essay "Rewriting Superman."[22] But note Aichele's use of the word "old." The Campbellian Superman, the Siegel and Shuster Superman, may have overlapped more cleanly with Jesus, but the character and all his modern difficulties now align with the American monomyth decribed by John Shelton Lawrence and Robert Jewett.[23,24] Diverging from Campbell's, their monomyth includes the character's sexual prohibitions, isolation, and refusal of temptation.[25] Any superheroes, says *Our Gods Wear Spandex* author Christopher Knowles, can be considered "'essentially savior figures' [. . .] not so much a fulfillment of a wish for power as they are an optimistic statement about the future and an act of defiance in the face of adversity."[26] But Superman, as the superhero *par excellence* and figurative flag-bearer for the genre, exhibits such a masterful control over his power,[27] an unbelievable morality,[28] and, most importantly, a full dual life as human and more-than-human, all of which put Superman into a unique category of "savior."

II.

At the funeral for the heroic Metamorpho, Superman is one of the only attendees — as if any other mourners were needed! The priest

Figure 3.   **Superman, in his temporary electric costume, must speed off to save more lives, with the story Metamorpho (aka Rex Mason) now his as well, however temporarily (Morrison and Porter, 3).**

conducting the prayers explains his lack of surprise to Superman (see Figure 3): "Well, the sad fact is, normal people aren't very interested in metahuman funerals anymore, Superman. Everyone knows you people come *back* all the time."[29] This is a surprisingly prescient, self-aware comment from a character within the fiction. In fact, of the memorial statues shown surrounding Metamorpho's grave, the late Green Arrow, Green Lantern, Flash, and Tomorrow Woman all return within the next dozen years, as well as Metamorpho himself. Each of their respective passings seemed so permanent and was treated with reverence, and Superman attended each sorrowfully. Yet, like Superman, in time they all return.

This is not to suggest that Superman is some sort of literal ressurector or that all of his allies play the role of Lazarus to his Jesus. As if to complicate the easy comparison of Superman to Jesus, the next issue of the series pits him and his teammates against errant angels of Heaven,[30] making the superheroes simultaneously equivalent to and distinct from the divine beings. The author of these adventures, Glaswegian writer Grant Morrison, deliberately makes the borders between life/death and mortal/divine porous — as they have always been for the superhero genre, if in a far less acknowledged manner. Morrison also scripts

Superman's later eulogy for his fallen ally J'onn J'onzz the Martian Manhunter (see Figure 4), where the mix of grief over loss and hope for return are given a more blended expression: "J'onn J'onzz was my *friend*. Always there, always *strong*, always reliable [. . .] We'll all miss him. And pray for resurrection."[31]

Superman will not be doing the resurrecting, just as he cannot bring back his late Kryptonian parents, his human family members, his allies, or their loved ones. Like Batman and the Martian Manhunter, Superman bears a further hallmark of the superhero, that of lost family.[32] [33] Depending on which version of Superman's origin one consults, he could be considered — like Marvel Comics' Spider-Man — doubly orphaned after the deaths of the Kents; both of these heroes have lost their biological parents and, in many storylines, their adoptive ones as well.[34] If there was one thing neither Jesus nor Moses were, it was orphans; though their respective lives were atypical in having layers of immediate guardians in addition to that of remote sires, each had an over-abundance of parents in their lives. This is not so for superheroes,[35] who find both freedom and a thirst for justice from their losses.[36]

But if Superman is not attending funerals to acknowledge either his allies' finitude or his own closure, what purpose do these rites and his presence serve? These superheroes have seen Heaven,[37] confronted Hell,[38] dwelled in Sheol,[39] visited Purgatory,[40] and experienced almost every sort of afterlife existence. None have proven to be *the* answer to eternal being, only a *potential* answer, only as providential as one of those alternate dimensions like Earth-2 or the future in *Dark Knight Returns*. The funeral for slain Wonder Girl Donna Troy — at which Superman is, of course, in attendance — takes the reader from the site of her memorial directly to her awakening in an unknown plane of existence, ready to do battle.[41] None of these (non-)resolutions have proven to be the exclusive path to salvation following the end of bodily life. They are continuances, new planes, or mystical states, but not unquestionably divine, nor final.

If viewed less as certain ends than as memorials, then one can view the focus of these funerals as memory instead of mortality. As real-life people sometimes do with the departed, these deceased characters can be remembered truly as characters — roles in a suspended story. It may sound sentimental to remember the fallen through tales and yarns, but this lens better explains the function of Superman at these memorials.

Superman is a savior, but in a manner decoupled from Christology. Superman's own alien origin detracts from the faith necessary in viewing

Figure 4. **Superman leads prayer for the Martian Manhunter's return. Until then, the alien's story remains Superman's to safeguard (Morrison and Jones, 12).**

Jesus as Christ. Readers know Superman to be Kryptonian, to be Kansan, to be Metropolitan, and to be American all at once; each label has merit, and one does not invalidate the other. For over 20 years, the approach to the character has been to portray Clark Kent as less of a disguise for Superman and more an aspect of his genuine self.[42] As Susie Paulik Babka in the *Irish Theological Quarterly* comments, "many of the stories revolve around his quest for belonging, the desire to assimilate into ordinary society and marry Lois Lane, his longing for the life he might have had on Krypton, what he must do to fulfill Jor-El's expectations."[43] All of these aspects of his personality are a matter of record, not speculation. To say the same of Jesus, however, enters into false Christology, says Babka:

> In other words, while popular culture has gleefully connected Superman and Jesus, as far as Christian doctrine goes, Superman provides a foil that uncovers why Christologies of the *tertium quid* have ultimately failed in doctrinal development: if the Savior is an alien, either to humanity or God or to both, then he does not bring human beings into the fullness of intimacy with God. An alien savior reinforces human alienation from God, as well as God's remoteness from human beings.[44]
>
> Jesus Christ can no more be an alien to human beings than to God the Father. If the humanity of Christ is substantially different from that of the rest of us, if he can do something of which no other human being is capable, or has the potential to fulfill, whether it be to heal, to raise the dead, or to live a sinless life, then Christ is not human. [. . .] More importantly, if Christ's divinity is somehow alien to God's, then the suffering of Christ on the cross is peripheral to God, a matter more for pity or sympathy from God than solidarity with those who cry out to God in the midst of catastrophe.[45]

Superman is, no question, an alien, an E.T. attempting also to be a human. He lives as *tertium quid*, a "third thing," an option that that would disallow Jesus as a savior, but paradoxically enables Superman as one.

III.

Supergirl, Superman's cousin Kara Zor-El, dies during the landmark 1986 *Crisis on Infinite Earths* series. *The Daily Planet* front-page story notes that Bat-Girl will give the eulogy at Supergirl's televised memorial service, while Superman will be conducting a private burial. He clearly is in attendance at the public ceremony, and newscaster Lana Lang's comments practically make him the focus, not his fallen cousin: "It has been said that a true hero stands for truth and justice. Well, those words certainly pertain to Supergirl, cousin of Superman. Supergirl, who, today, sacrificed her life not only to save Superman but to save our world and countless others."[46] While a picture of smiling Kara fills a huge JumboTron screen at the memorial, the last clear view readers have of her face is on the third of the eleven panels filling the page. One additional blurry glimpse is given in panel six, then she is even further removed from the reader with only pieces of her uniform — notably, the Superman/El family chevron — still visible. Superman's private burial consists of Kara being wrapped head to toe in a cape-like, chevroned shroud and of his committing her body to the infinity of space (see Figure 5). Kara is never seen in this sequence, only a wrapped cadaver bearing the family mark and being carried in Superman's arms. Superman soliloquizes, saying that her death prevents him from forgetting "how mortal we really are,"[47] the "we" encompassing either empowered survivors of Krypton or superheroes in general, Kara included either way. However, that "we" later adopts the same distance from Supergirl that the previous page did with the JumboTron; Superman ends his private service, saying, "We live on remembering and honoring the past, but always looking toward the future."

Supergirl is no longer part of this "we," no longer part of her own story. She has already been committed, already absorbed, into Superman's mythos, become part of his identity rather than having her own. The gradual obscuring of her image and the shift of pronouns is epitomized by the seventh panel of that page: a full-body shot of Superman[48] displays him holding the chevron-branded remains with the cloth-embroidered S-shield overlaying his own chest-emblem. "And now, Kara, you are gone," says Superman, "and I grieve,"[49] suggesting that her absence has become part of his presence.

Superman saves stories. His form of salvation is more akin to that of a metanarrative computer hard drive than a spiritual messiah. When characters' ability to further their own stories either ends or is indefinitely suspended, they become part of his story, marked by his attendance at their funerals. Each character becomes Enkidu to Superman's greater Gilgamesh. Consider the extended depiction of the Martian

Figure 5. **Supergirl, reduced to a chevroned shroud in death, is dismissed into space, her cousin Superman maintaining her memory (Wolfman, 216).**

Manhunter's funeral, where Superman is one of six heroes who tele-pathically received the history of J'onn and his extinct planet upon his death. Each of them was mentally beamed this knowledge as J'onn's last living act. Of the half-dozen, though, Superman seems the only one who can easily put it into words. "We're not just *caretakers* of J'onn's personal history, we're also now the caretakers for a lost race – a lost planet. And it's a responsibility that I humbly accept, as obviously you all do . . ."[50] Yet Superman was already host to this sort of responsibility, the living memory of Krypton, of his cousin, and of his fallen allies. Better than any character, he knows, "We were J'onn, and he was us."[51]

Superman is a *figurative* ressurector, a fictional savior in both senses of the word *fictional*. To revisit an earlier statement, this is how the mono-mythically American character is designed to cope with his *post*modern difficulties. "Umberto Eco described Superman in a 1972 article as a mythological virtuous archetype," says Ian Gordon in *Comics & Ideology*, "locked in a timeless state and thereby never fully consumed by his audi-ence."[52] Superman, says Eco, cannot be a dynamic character but must appear so; for him to effect real change or alter the status quo begins to unravel the character, leaving him acutely vulnerable to questions of cosmic responsibility and human independence. In order to maintain the Superman who co-exists as Clark Kent[53] and lives to help — rather than rule, ignore, or abandon — humanity, a timeless Superman must be preserved, one who exists in what Eco calls an "oneiric climate."[54] In this dream-like, atemporal environment, Superman conducts acts that seem to mark the passage of time but, in terms of their impact to his state as a character, do not. Funerals are one of the more perfect illusions in which he can participate to this end.

Implicitly, Superman's attendance at a funeral communicates to the reader two things: (1) that Superman acknowledges the deceased character as a person of importance in his own endless narrative, and (2) that the passage of time that has led to this character's death seems to apply to Superman as well. Achilles dies, but Odysseus continues. This maneuver, not conscious to the Superman character and perhaps not entirely intended by his writers and editors, allows Eco's concept of consumption to be engaged by another hero, a stand-in for Superman's own. This is a further dividing point between him and Jesus: *Others* die so that he may live.[55]

Of course, this is not some vampiric or parasitic existence Superman leads. These characters are not dying *so that* he endures; rather, he endures so that they may die. Since 1938, Superman has created the heroic mold that allows superheroes' exploits and sacrifices to be recognized, honored, and remembered. When the metropolis of Coast City was wiped off the map by a massive, malevolent machine, Superman established an eternal flame spire there, saying, "Let this spire, built from the very engine that once stood here, serve as a tribute to their memory – and as a reminder to us that our kind shall *always* be needed. I swear, as long as I'm alive, there will be no more *Coast Cities!*"[56] More often for characters rather than ruins, Superman is that flame. They have been saved; their light remains kindled either until they return or for all of Superman's days.[57]

IV.

At the funeral for the Green Lantern (aka Hal Jordan), Superman proclaims, "The best way we can honor Hal is to remember him."[58] And, following the service for Green Arrow (secretly millionaire Oliver Queen), Superman secures any photos of the occasion from seeing print in the media and jeopardizing Queen's loved ones.[59] It might seem ironic that Superman, who by day works for the *Daily Planet*, would push for keeping such stories out of the news and solely in the minds of the heroes' closest,[60] but that potential contradiction never seems to create friction for readers. Vanessa Russell extrapolates on a point suggested by Rocco Versaci in his book *Graphic Language*, suggesting that Clark's role as a reporter has surpassed Superman's; sequential art's potential has shifted, with the era of status-maintaining derring-do abdicating its primacy in comics to the real-world chronicling power of such creators as Art Spiegelman, Marjane Satrapi, Joe Sacco, and Harvey Pekar.[61] Yet, there appears to be no conflict in Superman collecting and storing characters' tales, an action presumably more suited to Clark and the comics medium in general, according to Russell.

This contradiction becomes disentangled by Superman's function as a chronicle himself. Attention to formatting is important here: the *Superman* comics and movies certainly qualify as stories, but Superman, the character, is himself a collective. Said another way, Superman is less a character than a container. Despite Siegel and Shuster's own words to the contrary,[62] many writers have speculated on the serendipitous Hebrew equivalencies for his Kryptonian name, Kal-El.[63][64] If one must acquiesce to the pervading view that his Kryptonian name links

Superman to God and his angels, then one could also take advantage of the Hebrew meaning for *kal*, namely "vessel."[65] With or without this etymological maneuver, though, the sharp division emphasized by Russell between Clark the Reporter and Superman the Hero can be overcome by reading the latter as the repository for characters' biographies and essences. In a manner of speaking, deceased characters become typographical characters in the book, the album, that is Superman.

Rather than hinging upon Hebrew coincidences, Superman-as-vessel can be better related to an angelic or divine function through Eco's characterization of his oneiric existence: "*To act*, then, for Superman, as for any other character (or for each of us), means to 'consume' himself[, but] a myth is 'inconsumable.'"[66] Superman is left in a middle existence comparable to literary critic Frank Kermode's explanation of *aevum*, the middle existence of angels. If one embraces — rather than dodges — the idea of Superman as *tertium quid*, then he aligns far better with an angel than Christ, with *aevum* than eternity:

> The angels could not be pure being, since then they would be indistinguishable from God [. . .] They are therefore neither eternal nor of time. So out of this argument, which is ultimately an argument about origins, there develops a third durations, between that of time and eternity. [. . .] St. Thomas calls this third order *aevum*.[67]

Superman must operate in this half-eternal/half-temporal existence of angels, *aevum*. It is here that he becomes his own Fortress of Solitude, the timeless, untouchable space where characters' stories may be saved.

Morrison's work on Superman should be taken as a meditation on this function of the myth, of Superman as the metanarrative, non-Christological savior. Numerous commentators have examined the multiplicity of Superman, both in print and in other media. In film, television, radio, and animation, Superman has been played by Kirk Alyn, George Reeves, Christopher Reeve, John Haymes Newton, Gerard Christopher, Ron Ely, Dean Cain, Tom Welling, Brandon Routh, Bob Holliday, David Wilson, Bud Collyer, George Newbern, Patrick Warburton, Tim Daly, Christopher McDonald, Yuri Lowenthal, Bob Hastings, Danny Dark, Jeff Kramer, Crispin Freeman, and Christopher Corey Smith. This is not nearly a complete list, nor does it include mention of the writers, artists, and editors who have shaped — or been guided through — the adventures of the Man of Steel since 1938 in comic strips, comic books, and graphic novels. Television and comic book writer Mark Evanier says, "Today, we have a version that is a rough amalgam of about a dozen guys who've drawn the book in the last decade or so. I personally think this is a very well-drawn (and usually, well-written) Superman."[68] And, of course, there are the Super*men* who populate each world of the multiverse, including Overman, "the guilt-ridden champion of *Earth 10*, where Nazis *won* the Second World War [. . . a]nd Air Force Captain Allen Adam, the 'Quantum Superman' of *Earth 4*, in a condensed universe where the laws of physics are *different*," and so forth.[69] When Superman speaks at the funeral of a Batman whose attendees include alternate-dimension Bat-Girls and Robins, one has to ask: which Superman is this?

Morrison suggests through his stories that there is only one Superman, a unified concept that all the others reflect and expand.[70] Before working on the character himself, Morrison lauded the very concept of Superman as a "forward thinking, utopian idea[, a . . .] new world testament."[71] Superman is the ultimate story, defying the linearity of Judaism, Christianity, and Islam; instead, he is always "to be continued,"[72] the supreme open text. In *Final Crisis: Superman Beyond 3D*, Morrison has Superman do battle with Mandrakk, the embodiment of story's end and a creature who feeds off universes' finalities. Moreover, Mandrakk corrupts one of Superman's dimensional counterparts, the immoral Ultraman, turning him into that Vampire Superman who *does* prey on others. Extradimensional beings known as the Monitors fear that Mandrakk, their kin, will be successful in inevitably consuming reality — don't all stories end? But Monitor Weeja Dell knows Superman to be their champion against the "self-assembling hyper story"[73] of Mandrakk: "Deep within the Germ-Worlds, I found a better story, one created to be *unstoppable, indestructible!* The story of a *child* rocketed to *Earth* from a doomed planet . . ."[74] Superman is the answer against finality; he is the story that, never-ending, can sustain all stories.

"If reality is measured in part by the effect something has on the world," affirms Schenck in *The Gospel According to Superheroes*, "then Superman is real. He has inspired and impacted countless lives and continues to do so. He calls us to follow his example and fight for truth and justice in the world."[75] Though earlier it was noted that Superman is only alive or dead fictionally — a standing some might be tempted to reduced down to the same null status — his survival legitimately impacts the reality of his creators, of DC Comics, of his writers and editors, and of his readers. Real-world people have become beholden to the potency and importance of the character.

V.

In Act 5, Scene 1 of *Hamlet,* the titular Prince encounters the exhumed skull of the late court jester Yorick and makes the deceased entertainer forever part of the Shakespearean experience. Though Yorick has not spun off into the intertextual and multimedial successes of Rosencrantz and Guildenstern, Romeo and Juliet, or Edgar's Childe Roland, the posthumous spotlight put upon him by Hamlet has kept the character metaphorically alive. One only knows of his infinite jest because of the epic protagonist's attention to his passing.

Superman has attended a myriad of funerals, including those of minor characters Larry Lance, Sue Dibny, and his own father Jonathan Kent. In the muted depiction of the Kent funeral, Clark's wife Lois speaks one of the few lines of dialog. When Superman says, "There's nothing I can do," she responds, "Yes there is. Never forget what he taught you."[76] His anguish is visible, and he falls to the floor, holds his scalp in his hands, and lets his glasses fall to the floor beside the lucky horseshoe he had made for Jonathan. The difficulty of absorbing the end of his human father's story, both emotionally and metatextually, is immense, but he suffers through it in honor of some of Jonathan's final words: "Don't let *anyone* or *anything* get in your way."[77] Like Yorick, Jonathan will be preserved by the hero he raised. So, too, will Lance, Dibny, and others be saved.

These characters not only fuel Superman to endure, but they also shape him. Factual or fictional, Alvin Schwartz's account of a tulpa visiting him to explain the presence of Superman in his life includes the insight that the "fragmented beings that were his villains shared a certain archetypal reality with the one you call the Man of Steel."[78] That is, much of Kal-El's identity is built by those most intimate to him, whether romantic or sparring partners.

Comics studies scholar Peter Coogan writes:

> Lester Roebuck in "The Good, the Bad, and the Oedipal" proposes that Superman's foes, particularly Lex Luthor, represented twisted father figures, and Superman's struggles against them are therefore Oedipal. Kal and Jor-El and his father look identical. Lois looks just

like Lara. Lara LorVan, Kal-El's mother's maiden name, reproduces the "LL" motif of Superman's primary romantic involvements (Lois Lane, Lana Lang, Lori Lemaris, and Lyla Ler-Rol). So does her married name, Lara Jor-El (i.e. Lara El). Kal-El, in his life as Clark Kent, therefore attempts to reproduce the relationship of his parents in his own life by finding the woman most like his mother.

Superman's chief supervillain, Lex Luthor, stands out as a twisted version of Jor-El. Luthor is a leading scientist on Earth, but unlike Jor-El he has turned his gifts to selfish pursuits.[79]

Coogan stops short of overtly relating the "LL" — or "El El" — of Lex Luthor to Superman's "romantic involvements," but the arch-villain certainly is part of Superman's passion for justice, if not directly a part of his passion for love.[80] All this emphasizes that, like his parents, Superman has always been a soteriological being, one who saves by internalizing the memories and drives of others.

There is nothing in Max Weber's theory of salvation, at least by Kevin Surin's assessment, that precludes this manner of salvation from religious consideration. Given the urgency with which others have attempted to yoke Superman to Jewish or Christian lore, associating him with untethered "religion" should be reasonable. Surin writes, "The fundamental aspiration of the various doctrines of salvation is to provide a solution to the 'problem' of the world,"[81] and Superman has become, as he was for Jerry Siegel, one such solution. His publication and narrative history has become "a comparative mythology of salvation,"[82] one of Weber's categories for the fundamentals of a faith.

Without necessitating the trappings of Judaism or Christianity, Superman is a worldview, "a commitment, a fundamental orientation of the heart, that can be expressed as a story or in a set of presuppositions."[83] The character offers a cornerstone for an evolving worldview: Superman as a symbol of life, of hope, of a battle for the never-ending. On the comics pages, on television, on the radio, in film, online, and in everyday American cultural experience, Superman continues to hold that line against the void. While individuals may not endure, he will — as a character, inspiration, savior, and vessel. He exceeds one category and has become a force of unity, spandex existentialism on a flight path toward metanarrative monism.

Notes

1   Ian Gordon, "Nostalgia, Myth, and Ideology: Visions of Superman at the End of the 'American Century,'" *Comics & Ideology*, ed. Matthew P McAllister, Edward H Sewell, Jr., and Ian Gordon (New York: Peter Lang, 2001), 177.

2   Umberto Eco, "The Myth of Superman," *Arguing Comics*, ed. Jeet Heer and Kent Worcester (Jackson, MS: University Press of Mississippi, 2004), 150–1.

3   Paul Levitz (w) and Joe Staton (a), "Only Legends Live Forever," *Adventure Comics* #462, April 1979, 12.

4   Frank Miller (w, a), *Batman: The Dark Knight Returns* (New York: DC Comics, 1986), 4.45–7.

5   Neil Gaiman (w), Andy Kubert (p), and Scott Williams (i), *Detective Comics* #853, April 2009, 7.

6   Gaiman et al, *Detective Comics* #853, 13.

7   Dan Jurgens (w, p), Jerry Ordway (w), Louise Simonson (w), Roger Stern (w), et al., *The Death of Superman* (New York: DC Comics, 1993).

8   Dan Jurgens (w) and Bill Sienkiewicz (a), *Superman: Day of Doom* (New York: DC Comics, 2003), 53–4.

9   Peter Coogan suggests the use of this word as "a more concise term than chest symbol, chest shield, insignia, icon, or any of the various terms used to indicate the iconic symbols that indicate superhero identities" in *Superheroes: The Secret Origin of a Genre* (Austin, TX: MonkeyBrain Books, 2006), 254.

10 David Landis, "Superman Sells Faster Than . . .," *USA Today*, November 20, 1992, Final Edition, News Section, 1A.

11 Jurgens and Sienkiewicz, 77.

12 In attempting to find the presumed-dead Aquaman in 2003, Superman and his JLA teammates died yet again, only to have their lost bones be mystically resurrected. See Joe Kelly (w) and Doug Mahnke (a), *JLA: The Obsidian Age, Books One and Two* (New York: DC Comics, 2003).

13 True, Superman is fictional, but one's status of being alive or dead within that fiction is not irrelevant. He is as alive as anything is within his reality, and, as will be addressed later, he does impact non-fictional reality, as does his (im)mortality.

14 Danny Fingeroth, *Disguised as Clark Kent* (New York: Continuum, 2007), 32.

15 Julius Schwartz and Brian M Thomsen, *Man of Two Worlds* (New York: HarperEntertainment, 2000), 142–3.

16 Fingeroth, 44.

17 Simcha Weinstein, *Up, Up, and Oy Vey!* (Baltimore: Leviathan, 2006), 26–7.

18 Fingeroth, 44.

19 To his credit, Fingeroth also says, "The character is a mixed metaphor and works fine that way. Those looking for a one-to-one correspondence between Superman and a specific biblical figure are destined for frustration unless they willfully ignore certain elements of the character" (44).

20 Greg Garrett, *Holy Superheroes! Revised and Expanded Edition* (Louisville: WJK, 2008), 23.

21 Ken Schenck, "Superman: A Popular Culture Messiah," *The Gospel According to Superheroes*, ed. B.J. Oropeza (New York: Peter Lang, 2005), 34.

22 George Aichele, "Rewriting Superman," *The Monstrous and Unspeakable*, ed. George Aichele and Tina Pippin (Sheffield, England: Sheffield, 1997), 92.

23 See John Shelton Lawrence and Robert Jewett, *The Myth of the American Superhero* (Grand Rapids, MI: William B. Eerdmans, 2002).

24 Garrett states, "John Shelton Lawrence and Robert Jewett argue that the

American monomyth is actually an ongoing retelling of the Judeo-Christian story of redemption" (7), but this seems to be a misreading of their concept based more on Eden and Adam than, transitively, a 'second Adam' Jesus.

25 Randy Duncan and Matthew J Smith, *The Power of Comics* (New York: Continuum, 2009), 228.

26 Duncan and Smith, 238–9.

27 Duncan and Smith, 227.

28 Schenck, 39.

29 Grant Morrison (w), Howard Porter (p), and John Dell (i), *JLA* #5, May 1997, 3.

30 Grant Morrison (w), Howard Porter (p), and John Dell (i), *JLA* #6, June 1997.

31 Grant Morrison (w) and J.G. Jones (a), *Final Crisis* #2, August 2008, 12.

32 Richard Reynolds, *Superheroes: A Modern Mythology* (Jackson, MS: University Press of Mississippi, 1996), 12.

33 Coogan suggests that, in addition to being a motivating source of tragedy, this fulfills superheroes as "metaphors for freedom [. . .] the freedom from the restrictions of gravity, the law, families, and romantic relationships. Perhaps this is why so many superheroes are free of their families as unmarried adult orphans" (14).

34 Danny Fingeroth, *Superman on the Couch* (New York: Continuum, 2004), 72–3.

35 Fingeroth holds the opposite position to this in *Superman on the Couch*, 71–2.

36 The origin of this trope may lay in the real-life murder of Siegel's own father, killed by robbers at their family clothing store in Cleveland. There was no bringing him back. See Fingeroth, *Disguised*, 41.

37 Mark Millar (w) and Ariel Olivetti (a), *JLA: Paradise Lost* #1–3, January–March 1998.

38 Mark Waid (w), Scott Peterson (w), Howard Porter (p), Phil Jimenez (p), et al., *Underworld Unleashed* (New York: DC Comics, 1998).

39 Geoff Johns (w), Matt Smith (p), and Steve Mitchell (i), *Day of Judgment* #1–5, November 1999.

40 Keith Giffen (w) and Tom Denerick (a), *Reign in Hell* (New York: DC Comics, 2009).

41 Judd Winick (w) and Alé Garza (p), *Titans/Young Justice: Graduation Day* (New York: DC Comics, 2003), 61–7.

42 Aichele, 82.

43 Susie Paulik Babka, "Arius, Superman, and the *Tertium Quid*: When Popular Culture Meets Christology," *Irish Theological Quarterly* 73 (2008): 122.

44 Babka, 116.

45 Babka, 129.

46 Marv Wolfman (w) and George Perez (p), *Crisis on Infinite Earths* (New York: DC Comics, 2001), 215.

47 Wolfman and Perez, 216.

48 Only his feet and his cape are in any way masked, one by the snow and the other by the panel border. Said another way, on what Superman stands and how far his presence reaches are obscured.

49 Wolfman and Perez, 216.

50 Peter J Tomasi (w) and Doug Mahnke (p), *Final Crisis: Requiem* #1, September 2008, 29.

51 Tomasi and Mahnke, 2.

52   Gordon, 180.

53   Aichele, 82.

54   Eco, 153.

55   Superman addresses his survivor's guilt and the consequences of such an existence in JM DeMatteis and Liam McCormack-Sharp's *Superman: Where Is Thy Sting?* (New York: DC Comics, 2001).

56   Dan Jurgens (w, p) and Joe Rubinstein (i), *Superman* (v. 2) #83, November 1993, 24.

57   Again, it bears emphasizing: Superman does not operate simply as a metaphorical savior. He is also a metanarrative savior, the *terium quid* that belongs neither fully to humanity nor divinity but to the reality of fiction.

58   Ron Marz (w), Darryl Banks (p), and Romeo Tanghal (i), *Green Lantern* (v. 3) #81, December 1996, 11.

59   Brad Meltzer (w), Phil Hester (p), and Ande Parks (i), *Green Arrow* (v. 2) #16, October 2002, 3.

60   One of Clark's final acts in the non-canonical *All-Star Superman* series is to write the last account of Superman. See Grant Morrison (w) and Frank Quitely (a), *All-Star Superman* #11, July 2008.

61   Vanessa Russell, "The Mild-Mannered Reporter: How Clark Kent Surpassed Superman," *The Contemporary Comic Book Superhero*, ed. Angela Ndalianis (New York: Routledge, 2009), 239.

62   Schwartz, 143.

63   Weinstein, 27.

64   Garrett, 19.

65   Weinstein, 27.

66   Eco, 150.

67   Frank Kermode, *The Sense of an Ending* (New York: Oxford University Press, 2000), 70.

68   Mark Evanier, *Wertham Was Right!* (Raleigh, NC: TwoMorrows Publishing, 2003), 15.

69   Grant Morrison (w), Doug Mahnke (p), and Christian Alamy (i), *Final Crisis: Superman Beyond 3D* #1, October 2008, 18.

70   While it is not addressed here, readers should also consult Morrison's other multi-series event focused on Superman, *DC Comics One-Million* from 1998, exactly ten years prior to *Final Crisis*. Superman as enduring and proliferating — pro-life-rating — plays a central role to the main plot.

71   Garrett, 70.

72   Grant Morrison (w), Doug Mahnke (p), and Christian Alamy (i), *Final Crisis: Superman Beyond 3D* #2, March 2009, 32.

73   Morrison et al, *Final Crisis: Superman Beyond 3D* #2, 19.

74   Morrison et al, *Final Crisis: Superman Beyond 3D* #2, 21.

75   Schenck, 44.

76   Geoff Johns (w), Gary Frank (a), et al, *Superman: New Krypton Special* #1, December 2008, 6.

77   Johns et al, *Superman: New Krypton Special* #1, 8–9.

78   Alvin Schwartz, *An Unlikely Prophet* (Rochester, VT: Destiny Books, 2006), 75.

79   Coogan, 102.

80   Schenck relates the observation of Neil Bailey, who observes that "fans read the comics as much or more for Lex Luthor, Superman's archenemy, than for Superman *per se*" (39), suggesting Lex as an essential component of Superman's story, along with Jor-El, Lana, Lois et al.

81 Kevin Surin, "Liberation," *Critical Terms for Religious Studies*, ed. Mark C. Taylor (Chicago: University of Chicago Press, 1998), 177.

82 Surin, 177.

83 James W Sire, *The Universe Next Door* (Downers Grove, IL: InterVarsity Press, 2004), 17.

"The Apocalypse of Adolescence": Use of the *Bildungsroman* and Superheroic Tropes in Mark Millar and Peter Gross's *Chosen*

JULIA ROUND

"**D**OGS WORK IN MYSTERIOUS WAYS,"[1] and *Chosen* (Dark Horse, 2004) is a comic as strange and inverted as this quotation implies. This twist story about Satan and the end of the world leads the reader to believe that the 12-year-old protagonist, Jodie Christianson, is the reincarnated Jesus Christ. However, tricks throughout the narrative build to a surprise ending that reveals that Jodie is, in fact, the son of Satan and will be leading this side in Armageddon. To tell this story, *Chosen* uses traditional narrative and superheroic conventions to re-present religious dogma as subjective rather than objective and leverages a variety of paradoxical and contrasting methods.

Writer Mark Millar said his Scottish Catholic upbringing meant he "wanted to do a book about faith that *wasn't* about child-molesting priests or all the usual shit you get when we liberals write stories about the Church. I wanted to write something about the Church without taking the piss out of it, and write something about Jesus that wasn't judgmental or mocking."[2] Instead, *Chosen* offers a postmodern religious allegory that acknowledges its contradictions and plays on audience expectations. Rather than using a grandiose narrative of belief and allegory (of the type more usually associated with religious texts), *Chosen*'s narrative style is established as teenage from the very first scene, in which Jodie and his friends are searching for a torn-up "stroke mag."[3] Throughout the comic, Jodie's reactions to the religious events taking over his life are couched exclusively in teenage terms: typically, one of the first miracles he attempts is turning water into wine. ("By the time we got home, of course, the story was that I'd also multiplied the loaves and conjured up a thousand little Snickers bars."[4]) Similarly, his response to religious adulation is a typically understated: "All the *bowing* and stuff's pretty damn cool."[5] The teenage motivation extends to the widest level of the text, whose events are redefined in contemporary terms: "Okay, you got to think of the Old Testament as *Star Wars,*" continuing, "Everybody likes it, the characters were great, and its huge success was always gonna change the world forever."[6] Jodie draws similar parallels between the New Testament and *The Empire Strikes Back* and between his own life and *Return of the Jedi,* again with reference to their popularity and fandom.

This redefinition doesn't just rely on the use of teenage language and movie genres but is also closely focused on the superheroic. When he starts to realize his new powers, Jodie initially concludes that he must be "a friggin' *mutant*" rather than a deity, commenting, "Obviously I'd been reading my *X-Men* with a little more fervor than I'd been reading the *good book.*"[7] His perceptions of taking on his role are also heavily colored by superhero myths. When he learns he must leave his hometown of Peoria, he states: "[T]hey want me to go live in New York for a while and then they're gonna send me 'round the world to learn philosophy and karate and all *that* kinda shit, I guess."[8] Here, the mysterious training in the Far East directly references *Batman.* This characterisation of religion as superheroic is key to the text and is also present in Simon Pegg's introduction, which likens Advent, the birth of Jesus, to the superhero origin story. He says that Advent is the most memorable part of this "famous hero legend,"[9] just as Spider-Man's bite or the murder of Batman's parents are the best-known parts of their respective stories.

In addition to these overt references to superheroics, the overall structure of *Chosen* supports a reading of the comic as superhero narrative. For example, the parallels that are drawn between Jodie and Jesus recall a common strategy in comics: the mirroring of hero and villain. The similarities between hero and villain have been explored many other times in comics history: for example, Doctor Doom was introduced to the *Fantastic Four* comics in a story voiced by superteam leader Reed Richards (Mr. Fantastic) as a rival scientist whose genius matched his own.[10] They have also been referenced in comics such as *The Killing Joke* by Alan Moore and Brian Bolland, both metaphorically, as in the opening line, "There were these two guys in a lunatic asylum,"[11] and explicitly, as when the Joker states the similarities between himself and Batman: "All it takes is one bad day to reduce the sanest man alive to lunacy. [. . .] You had a bad day once, am I right?" and "[S]omething like that, I bet. Something like that . . . something like that happened to me, you know."[12] The Joker's argument here is that both he and Batman have been reduced to criminal activities by traumas in their lives (i.e., the death of the Joker's wife and the death of Batman's parents). The parallel between hero and villain has also been noted by comics creator Frank Miller, who states that "the Batman folklore is full of Doppelgängers for Batman. The Joker is one of them [. . .] Two-Face is identical to Batman."[13] As such, in the superhero world, multiple similarities can be drawn between the allegedly opposing forces of hero and villain. This strategy is used to create the misleading narrative of *Chosen*, and Jodie even concludes in the penultimate panel that he has "a lot more in common than most people would imagine"[14] with Jesus.

As well as relying on teenage tropes and superheroic references, *Chosen* can also be defined as a *Bildungsroman* tale. This term, which in German means "novel of education," was coined by Johann Morgenstern in the early 1820s. It is generally used to describe a story that tells of the maturation and moral, social, or psychological development of a young protagonist. Although it traditionally refers to a historically limited genre of German literature, the story structure can, of course, appear within other texts outside that time period.

Traditionally, theorists such as Roy Pascal have defined the genre by its themes and content, focusing on the hero's naïveté, his development through mistakes, and the good guidance he receives from his companions.[15] However, this thematic definition has recently given way to new interpretation and current criticism that instead considers the *Bildungsroman*'s structural and narrative features. In so doing, it defines the plot events in terms of self-understanding rather than personal growth; emphasizes the dual position of the protagonist (as both reflective narrator and developing subject); and notes a circular (rather than linear) narrative structure. These later critics also agree that the genre model can also be applied to more recent works and can be used as a "heuristic tool" to compare texts.[16]

Critics such as Martin Swales comment that "the problem of *Bildung*, of personal growth, is enacted in the narrator's discursive self-understanding rather than in the events which the hero experiences."[17] Therefore, even a story such as *Chosen* can still qualify as a *Bildungsroman* since Jodie's arrival at self-understanding is the significant factor rather than the expected happy ending. Swales continues, "Even the nonfulfillment of consistently intimated expectation can, paradoxically, represent a validation of the genre by means of its controlled critique."[18] In this light, *Chosen's* twist ending (which contradicts the "consistently intimated expectation" that Jodie is Christ) also evidences the *Bildungsroman* as it critiques our one-sided assumptions about the story. Swales concludes that the *Bildungsroman* "is written for the sake of the journey, and not for the sake of the happy ending toward which that journey points."[19] So, although it might seem that the nature of Jodie's story (as a moral descent rather than a moral maturation) means it cannot be a *Bildungsroman*, using this aesthetic definition of the term means it can nonetheless be viewed as one.

Michael Beddow also rejects thematic definitions of the *Bildungsroman*, instead arguing that the genre's ultimate aim is to use the hero's *fictional* experiences to provide insights into human nature that could not be adequately conveyed by argument or non-fiction.[20] This perspective is echoed by Michael Minden, who focuses his study upon the dual subject position of the protagonist (as both narrator and subject) that underpins such a narrative, saying, "It is precisely this *double* determination that is reflected in the *Bildungsroman*: the (secret) alliance between an assured narrative voice, equipped with general maxims [. . .] and the 'poor dog' of an empirical subject who has to make his way amid the vicissitudes of concrete circumstances."[21] In so doing, Minden distinguishes between *Bildungsroman* and autobiography, explaining how the gap between naïve subject and knowing narrator makes the tale universal by "disowning" personal experience.[22]

This process is also apparent in *Chosen*. The text uses the first-person retrospective narration of the 33-year-old Jodie telling his story; rather than simply recounting what happened, however, comments and scenes relating to this present time are intercut throughout. For example, the adult Jodie's comment — "It's really quite *charming* in retrospect"[23] — evaluates the whole tale from his knowing perspective. His narrative also contains direct address to the reader, from the opening line: "Close your eyes. [. . .] Can you remember what it was like to be twelve years old again?"[24] Through the paradoxical linguistic structure of sentences like these (which combine words like "remember" and "again"), the narrative is suspended beyond time, set in a moment of reflection on all our childhoods. Here we can see both the "universalizing" process that Beddow identifies and also the dual temporal position (of narrator versus subject) noted by Minden.

This duality is continued throughout *Chosen*, and, in fact, the comic is able to emphasize this contradiction even further by presenting both voices (of the child and adult Jodie) in dialogue as well as in narration rather than making the adult voice the only narrator. Childhood and adulthood are thereby compared throughout, for example in comments such as "We're all the heroes in our own life's stories, you see. It doesn't matter if you're *twelve years old* or a *hundred* and twelve."[25] Similarly, the penultimate panel, which reveals the adult Jodie to be the President of the United States (an adult position of great responsibility), also simultaneously positions him as a child through the dialogue, in which he defines himself and Jesus as "two boys with overbearing fathers."[26] In this way, *Chosen*'s narrative proceeds from a paradoxical position that uses the contradictions of the *Bildungsroman* (a story that is simultaneously about both child and adult) to indicate that its religious content will also run contrary to our expectations.

A *Bildungsroman* aesthetic can be seen in *Chosen*'s use of a dual subject position, its circular narrative structure, and the arrival at "self-understanding" apparent in the ending. As such, the twist ending is also key to the narrative structure of this comic. Jodie is an unreliable narrator who deliberately manipulates his story, as is shown through his knowing comments and retrospective evaluation of events. This technique has a precedent in both prose (such as Agatha Christie's *The Murder of Roger Ackroyd*) and visual culture (films such as Bryan Singer's *The Usual Suspects*).

As a literary tradition, the "twist" ending takes various forms (including *peripeteia* and *agnarosis*, defined below) and can be traced back to classic literature such as the story of Oedipus.[27] This story (along with *Chosen*) uses *agnarosis* (discovery), best defined as a character's sudden recognition of their own or another's true identity/nature. Jodie's discovery of his real identity and destiny certainly falls into this category, but the text also relies on other forms of the twist ending to maximize its shock impact. *Chosen*'s narrative twist can also be defined as an example of *peripeteia*, the sudden reversal of the protagonist's fortune that emerges naturally from the character's circumstances. For this tactic to succeed, it must be logical within the timeframe of the story (otherwise it, instead, becomes an example of *deus ex machina*: "the god from the machine," when an unexpected or previously unindicated event is used to resolve the narrative). *Chosen* takes great pains to enforce the use of *peripeteia* over *deus ex machina* by carefully including clues about Jodie's real nature alongside "evidence" of his divinity.

Throughout the comic, we are led to believe that Jodie Christianson is the reincarnated Jesus Christ through devices such as his name, initials, and even the cover of the book, which depicts him crucified on a telegraph pole. His parents' sexless marriage and his group of "teenage apostles" (including Maggie representing Mary Magdalene) also support this interpretation.[28] However, as Millar and Gross point out in an interview included in the book, clues to Jodie's real identity are also scattered throughout the comic. He is addressed as "little prince" by the nurse Lilly (Lillith) and pictured with a horned shadow on the same page.[29] Later in the text, Jodie's shadow appears reversed,[30] and a blackboard shows the partially obscured Latin text ". . . sunt quae videntur,"[31] meaning "things are not what they seem." At a wider level, the *Star Wars* analogy (where the villain Darth Vader is revealed to be Luke's father) gives another clue to the reality of Jodie's parentage.

The serialized nature of the comics medium reinforces this narrative construction as mini-cliffhangers are positioned at the end of issues. For example, Jodie first arrives at the idea that he is the son of God on the final page of *Chosen* #1, after reading Revelation, and the final page of *Chosen* #2 introduces the potential for Armageddon.[32] Tension points are also frequently placed in the final panels of pages. For example, the very last panel on page 64 reveals that Jodie is about to meet "your *father*." We, the readers, are forced to pause to turn this page before the climax is revealed by Lilly during the next page, concluding with, "Why, *Satan*, of course. We're going to meet *Satan*" (see Figure 1).[33]

The repetition, stress, and curt phrasing all combine to emphasize the impact of this sentence, as do the visual elements of these panels, whose initial close-up shots of Jodie's and Lilly's eyes ensure our attention is focused on the words of this important conversation. The final panel perhaps also visually conveys Jodie's "fall" as their car speeds away from the readers' perspective, partially obscured already as it descends

over the brow of a hill. Peter Gross's composition puts the car exhaust fumes in the foreground of this panel, perhaps representing the clouds of a heaven Jodie is leaving behind, while Jeanne McGee's coloring paints the horizon he is speeding towards an ominous red that might be either a sunset or metaphor for Hell.

The denouement on the following page, set in the present (where the adult Jodie is telling his story), provides the perfect counterpoint to this revelation. The subdued coloring contrasts with the pastel tones used on the previous (facing) page, again emphasizing the difference between Jodie's past innocence and his present position. However, this scene, too, contains further twists, including the surprise that Jodie is the President of the United States. It also relies on similar shock tactics to those noted on the previous page, as in Jodie's blunt and ironic summary of his first meeting with his father (see Figure 2).

The visual content of this panel is surprisingly blank, showing only the shadowed face of our narrator in mid-shot and ensuring that our attention is focused on the words (again, a similar strategy to that noted

Figure 2. **Millar and Gross, *Chosen*, 66.** Jodie reflects on his first meeting with his father.

previously). All the impact comes from the language: the repetition ("laughed and laughed and laughed") and sarcasm ("ten thousand of his nearest and dearest") combine with excess to give this statement its shock value. Rather than using visual emphasis or even emotive language, the long sentence conveys its horror in a factual and additive manner. It begins by establishing the rape simply and bluntly ("he raped me") and then stating that this lasted for "close to seven full years," with multiple assailants ("his friends too"), all prefigured by his mother's similar abuse ("just like they'd fucked my mother frigid"), before finally concluding by reminding us that Jodie was just twelve at this time ("thirteen years before").

In this regard, it is interesting to note that Minden says that incest and inheritance are used in *Bildungsroman* as thematic motifs to express development. He defines incest, not simply literally, but as "a motif expressing the quintessence of desire, with its logical end in the collapse of all differences"[34] and notes that these two motifs (of incest and inheritance)

> also have their expression on the level of narrative technique. The *Bildungsroman*, as we have said, relies upon the co-operation of these two principles. The hero, hesitant about his creativity, relies upon the confident offices of one in no such doubt: the narrator. To that extent, this is the configuration of autobiography, in which a mature and accomplished voice recounts the vicissitudes of the less complete person he once was.[35]

We can certainly see this technique being used in the narrator's description of his meeting with his father, as the adult Jodie's bitterness and blunt truths are juxtaposed with the naïveté and dreams of the child Jodie. Motifs of incest and inheritance combine to give the relationship between the adult and child protagonist the sense of inevitability that Minden also identifies as key to the *Bildungsroman*. After all, Jodie has always been Satan's son (despite being unaware of it), and in this sense, *Chosen*'s narrative is not linear but circular, as Jodie's journey of discovery leads him "home."[36]

As such, we can see that *Chosen* uses superheroic tropes and a *Bildungsroman* aesthetic to present its religious content by juxtaposing revelatory narrative content with traditional religious language and events. For example, much of Millar's phrasing is intentionally evocative of the biblical: Jodie's initial survival of the accident with Jess Caldwell's truck is described as a "*miracle*"[37] by Father Tom O'Higgins, and subsequent scenes are linked obviously with their biblical equivalents. The scene where Jodie answers questions in the school staff room is followed directly by his mother's summary of the story of Jesus in the temple, which she concludes by stating that watching him in the staff room "was my temple moment, Jodie."[38] In this way, the two scenes are overtly linked.

Similarly, Jodie's resurrection of Angel the dog openly references the Lazarus miracle, as Jodie's narration cynically notes:

> Why I put so much time and effort into this one, insignificant dog

is something that I still can't figure out. Was I just trying to make a believer of doubting Tom O'Higgins? Or was I just keen to top the *Lazarus* trick with *showbiz pyrotechnics?*[39]

Both of these scenes are not only explicitly tied to their biblical counterparts but also defined as moments of evidence. As Jodie's mother explains, "Up until that point [seeing Jesus in the temple] they just couldn't be *certain.*"[40] Similarly, Jodie's summary of the Lazarus scene defines its purpose as convincing the faithless. These events are also noted in Simon Pegg's introduction as "occurrences that convince even the town's most faithless that this boy is destined for greatness in the biblical sense."[41]

Presenting these events in this way enables Millar to explore and reflect upon the notion of faith. As Jodie's unreliable narration informs readers, "Ironically, it was only the *non-believers* who still huddled in their pews and prayed to God via their balding, cheese-breathed *middleman,*" while, outside the church, Christianity was "happy and thriving."[42] However, deconstructing this scenario instantly shows that describing those in church as "non-believers" is dubious — since, for those outside the church, faith has become fact. This is reinforced at many points in the text. For example, the cancer-ridden Mrs. Freemont's fears of dying vanish once she is assured of Jodie's divinity; as she says, "that was before I knew he [God] was *real.*"[43] The text's narration does the same thing, for example, as Jodie states, "My existence meant that God was as real as McDonald's and Burger King."[44] The nature of these similes, while typically consumerist, also suggests that faith become fact is cheapened (due to the fast food industry's quick-fix nature and sacrifice of quality in favor of convenience and cheapness).

The one person who remains unconvinced of Jodie's divinity is Father Tom O'Higgins. He explains this in conversation with Jodie's teacher Ben Freemont, in response to Ben's question:

"You're starting to *believe* in him, aren't you?"

"Actually, I'm not. I've never been more sure this kid is a *fake.* Trouble is — I look around and I see Mona McKenzie standing up without her crutches and Jess Caldwell learning to drive again and a little part of me really starts to wonder, Benny."

"About what?"

"Whether I'm the goddamn problem here. [. . .] Maybe the reason
I can't see what everyone else sees in this kid is because my *faith* is
gone."[45]

On the surface, it is therefore easy for readers to believe in Jodie and
dismiss Father O'Higgins's doubts as those of a faithless priest. But
Millar takes pains to emphasize that the priest's dislike of Jodie is innate:
"There was just something about this bratty little would-be Christ that
happened to make his *skin crawl.*"[46] This allows Millar to reverse faith
and fact: Jodie's existence "proves" the reality of God, whereas Father
O'Higgins's dislike of Jodie goes against the physical facts (such as the
miracles he has performed) and in this sense is based solely on belief. In
this way, Millar reverses the traditional positions of religious conviction
and physical fact to question the idea that faith can be proved.

This reversal plays expertly with the tenets of comics narratology. The
narrative of comics relies on three main tenets: the depiction of time as
space, the involvement of the reader (to decipher panel contents and
fill in the "gutters"), and the creation and sustenance of the hyperreal.
This is defined by Jean Baudrillard as the replacement of reality with
simulation, as images, signs, and signals stand for events and objects.[47]
Consider, for example, "reality" TV shows: not only do the viewers
experience a narrativized and selective version of events, but these are
filtered through the medium of television so what they actually receive
is no more than a virtual representation. In comics, the hyperreal is
most frequently achieved through the use of stylized art and through
the mobility of visual and verbal perspectives that can be juxtaposed
and contradictory.[48]

Chosen exploits all of these tenets. The time-as-space narratology is
undermined by a narrator whose evaluative comments are interjected
into the story at various points and whose narrative opens with the
contradictory request to "Close your eyes."[49] The narrator addresses
the readers directly at many points throughout the text, and so he also
controls our interpretation of the text's events. The unreliable narrator
misdirects us towards signs that reinforce an interpretation of Jodie as
divine, rather than satanic.

The role of the interpretive reader is also played with in other ways.
Critics such as Mark Currie have addressed the question of view and

vision in postmodern narratives and commented on the "tension between seeing and writing [. . .] in contemporary narratology,"[50] since seeing overrules the authority of verbal narrative. Comics often exploit this tension for dramatic or humorous purposes, and *Chosen* is no exception. For example, in the opening scenario, Jodie's narration defines childhood security as "knowing Mom and Dad and God would always be there when you *needed* them," while simultaneously the reader is shown the truck that is about to fall on him.[51] Forcing the reader to weigh the visual against the verbal thereby becomes another tool to emphasize the unreliable narration. This is further emphasized by the following double splash page, whose perspective places the reader directly behind Jodie, also about to be crushed by the truck.

In terms of artistry, *Chosen*'s artwork (drawn by Peter Gross) connotes the natural and realistic, while containing enough background detail to provide the visual clues discussed earlier. The watercoloring (by Jeanne McGee) also allows for similar clues. Jodie's childhood is predominantly painted in pastel colors, although some key scenes, such as his resurrection of Angel the dog, are colored an ominous red.[52] (Gross's depiction of Jodie in this panel is equally demonic, as only the whites of his eyes are showing and his hair is raised to resemble horns.) The pastel watercolors that dominate the comic contrast with the scenes featuring the adult Jodie, which are painted in muted, darker tones. However, allowing the ethereal coloring to dominate also reinforces the narrative misdirection towards the pastoral, leading us to interpret the book as a simple parable. As Mark Millar puts it, the coloring gives the book "a quiet tone and a realistic atmosphere that made everything very fairytale, but also very natural [. . .] there was a beautiful verisimilitude brought to Jodie's world."[53] This stands in contrast to the mass perception of comics artwork as brightly colored pop art. As such, *Chosen* offers a hyperrealist comics universe where seeing is quite literally believing, and the artistic style strives to create realism. This also informs the above discussion of visual versus verbal narrative, as the visual elements of the comic are given a realistic presentation in contrast to the unbelievable narrative content.

In this way, both the medium and content of *Chosen* align to subvert the traditional presentation of religious argument. This is supported by contradictions in the text such as the omniscient yet unreliable narrative voice, the inversion of religious faith and physical fact, and the juxtaposition of *Bildungsroman* and superheroic tropes with religious content. These paradoxes are achieved by subverting comics narratology and indicated by both visual and verbal markers. For example, even the reversal (of god/dog) apparent in the sentence "dogs work in mysterious ways"[54] can be read as a hint that the story we are reading is inverted, both in terms of its creation (as Millar worked backwards from his twist ending) and subverted content.

Chosen has much in common with religious texts. Its content is faithful to that promised by Revelation, and its message is evangelical — not as a representation of the Christ tale but as a modern allegory that encourages individual thought and, in the final analysis, emphasizes the dominance of faith over certainty. Even the supporting appendices — not one, but two Afterwords (from Brother John Hanson and Brother Richard Hendrick, respectively) — can be seen as encouraging diversity and interpretation. It even extends its evangelical thread to comics: "Did you ever read any of that stuff? Frank Miller's *Daredevil?* Byrne's *Fantastic Four?* Chris Claremont's seminal and kinky run on *X-Men?* It's all so much better than you might expect."[55] In this sense, the narrative aligns religious and superheroic myth. As Mark Millar says, "[S]uperhero comics in particular are essentially just modern-day tellings of the same old myth stories, except God didn't wear Clark Kent's glasses as he moved among mortal men." Along similar lines, Peter Gross comments that biblical "stories are important but nobody really knows if they're real. [. . .] I can't help but wonder why it isn't enough for people to take their religion as powerful stories."[56]

Chosen redefines religious content as subjective rather than objective by emphasizing the need for personal interpretation through misdirection and inversion. It aligns religious stories with tales of the superheroic in terms of structure and content, using various symbols and overt references. In so doing, it uses a *Bildungsroman* structure where Jodie arrives at moral maturity as he reaches his satanic destiny, and it presents this journey in non-Manichaean terms. (Manichaeism, an antiquated religion that originated in Persia, focuses on the struggle between a good, spiritual world of light and an evil, material world of darkness. The term is most often used to describe a black-and-white/good-or-evil perception of morality or the world.) This step toward social commentary is also demonstrated by the final revelation that Jodie has become President of the United States, which can perhaps be read as a comment on global politics or the dangers of nuclear weaponry.[57]

In *Chosen*, Mark Millar breaks down the clear-cut Manichaean morality that often underpins religious texts. He rejects absolutes and fixed morals by leading the reader to misinterpret events and presumed signs. By tricking us into having sympathy for the devil, the narrative's sudden ending forces us to question every step of what had seemed either an obvious parable or an expected church-bashing. Instead, *Chosen* reveals it has been telling us an entirely different story, one that calls attention to the assumptions and inconsistencies in our treatment of religious content. As social commentary, the comic reflects contemporary concerns about belief within today's culture of religious diversity, evangelical atheism,[58] and widespread agnosticism. By debunking our expectations, *Chosen*'s apocalyptic ending forces us to examine our assumptions and beliefs: putting faith into practice.

Notes

1 Mark Millar (w) and Peter Gross (a), *Chosen* (Milwaukie, OR: Dark Horse, 2005), 7.
2 Mark Millar and Peter Gross, 'The Gospel According to Millar and Gross," *Chosen*, 68.
3 Millar, Gross, *Chosen*, 2.
4 Millar, Gross, *Chosen*, 30.
5 Millar, Gross, *Chosen*, 48.
6 Millar, Gross, *Chosen*, 31.
7 Millar, Gross, *Chosen*, 20.
8 Millar, Gross, *Chosen*, 57.
9 Simon Pegg, "Introduction," *Chosen*, npag.
10 Stan Lee (w) and Jack Kirby (a), *Fantastic Four* #5, 1962.
11 Alan Moore (w) and Brian Bolland (a), *The Killing Joke* (London: Titan Books, 1988), 3.
12 Moore, Bolland, *The Killing Joke*, 38–9.
13 Roberta Pearson and William Uricchio, (eds.), *The Many Lives of the Batman* (New York: Routledge, 1991), 36.
14 Millar, Gross, *Chosen*, 66.
15 Roy Pascal, *The German Novel* (Manchester: Manchester University Press, 1956), 60.
16 Martin Swales, *The German Bildungsroman from Wieland to Hesse* (Princeton, NJ: Princeton University Press, 1978), 161.
17 Swales, 4.
18 Swales, 12.
19 Swales, 34.
20 Michael Beddow, *The Fiction of Humanity* (Cambridge: Cambridge University Press, 1982), 5.
21 Michael Minden, *The German Bildungsroman* (Cambridge: Cambridge University Press, 1997), 7.
22 Minden, 5.
23 Millar, Gross, *Chosen*, 65. The "present day" is also represented on pages 20–1 and 66–7.
24 Millar, Gross, *Chosen*, 1.

25 Millar, Gross, *Chosen*, 66.
26 Millar, Gross, *Chosen*, 66.
27 It is interesting to note that Minden comments that "the successful negotiation of the Oedipal stage is nevertheless a sort of *Bildungsroman*" (13), proposing that, if the titular protagonist had been able to reconcile himself with the shock discovery of his true identity, the aesthetic structure of this text would fall into this category.
28 Millar, Gross, "The Gospel According to Millar and Gross," 68.
29 Millar, Gross, *Chosen*, 10
30 Millar, Gross, *Chosen*, 34.
31 Millar, Gross, *Chosen*, 13.
32 Millar, Gross, *Chosen*, 22, 44.
33 Millar, Gross, *Chosen*, 65.
34 Minden, 1.
35 Minden, 4.
36 Minden, 1.
37 Millar, Gross, *Chosen*, 8.
38 Millar, Gross, *Chosen*, 17–19.
39 Millar, Gross, *Chosen*, 62.
40 Millar, Gross, *Chosen*, 19.
41 Pegg, "Introduction."
42 Millar, Gross, *Chosen*, 46.
43 Millar, Gross, *Chosen*, 47.
44 Millar, Gross, *Chosen*, 43.
45 Millar, Gross, *Chosen*, 52–3.
46 Millar, Gross, *Chosen*, 46.
47 See Jean Baudrillard, *Simulacra and Simulation* (Ann Arbor, MI: University of Michigan Press, 1994) for a full discussion.
48 For further discussion of this point, see Julia Round, "Visual Perspective and Narrative Voice in Comics: Redefining Literary Terminology," *International Journal of Comic Art* 9:2 (Fall 2007), 316–29.
49 Millar, Gross, *Chosen*, 1.
50 Mark Currie, *Postmodern Narrative Theory* (Basingstoke, Hampshire: Macmillan, 1988), 127.
51 Millar, Gross, *Chosen*, 4.
52 Millar, Gross, *Chosen*, 61.
53 Millar, Gross, "The Gospel According to Millar and Gross," 68.
54 Millar, Gross, *Chosen*, 7.
55 Millar, Gross, *Chosen*, 35.
56 Millar, Gross, "The Gospel According to Millar and Gross," 74.
57 My thanks to Craig Spence for this observation.
58 For example, as evidenced by the publication of Richard Dawkins's *The God Delusion*. Dawkins also contributed towards an advertising campaign that ran in London, England during 2009, which placed advertising billboards on buses stating: "[T]here's probably no God. Now stop worrying and enjoy your life." The campaign sits alongside the advertisements of various Christian groups. Further details available at http://richarddawkins.net.

From *God Nose* to *God's Bosom,* Or How God (and Jack Jackson) Began Underground Comics

CLAY KINCHEN SMITH

IVEN THEIR GRAPHIC DEPICTIONS OF sexuality, violence, and substance abuse, underground comics would seem to have little — if anything — in common with traditional Christian theology. More frequently, theology has served as one of the Establishment punching bags pummeled by undergrounds. Their reputation for being antagonistic to religion was earned with numerous derogatory portrayals of churches and religious people: everything from men voyeuristically peeping at nuns to *Tales from the Leather Nun*'s graphic explorations of sexuality.[1] On closer examination, however, underground comics share a deep and abiding relationship with Christian theology. In fact, undergrounds originated from a series of theological explorations in the early 1960s and returned to those origins when they self-resurrected in the latter half of the 1960s. As suggested here, the relationship between undergrounds and Christian theology is much more complex than it initially seems.

This relationship between undergrounds and Christianity began rather furtively with a shadowy group of alternative artists using a campus copier.[2] At the University of Texas at Austin in the early 1960s, a group known as the Texas Mafia — chief among whom were Jack Jackson, Gilbert Shelton, and Frank Stack — worked for the *Texas*

Ranger, a monthly college-humor magazine published by the University. Because the *Ranger* was a state-supported publication, the group faced increasing difficulties in publishing the countercultural material that they felt needed distribution. After going underground to avoid retribution, the three assumed pseudonyms (Jackson's was "Jaxon" because of his accounting job — a play on "taxes" by Shelton).[3]

This trio openly collaborated and inspired each other. During this period, Jackson, Shelton, and Stack created icons of the underground world. By 1962, Shelton had already created his seminally infamous underground character Wonder Wart Hog, but he had found no venue for publishing those stories because of their extreme nature. Theology did not enter into Shelton's work, which promoted virtually every form of excess. On the other hand, Stack had begun a series specifically focused on religion. As he explains, he chose to create his *New Adventures of Jesus* comics as a medium of social protest against the escalating war in Vietnam and the global Cold War, as well as a personal rejection of Christian belief: "My little religious jokes were a kind of abstract argument against blind acceptance of potentially fatal assumptions. That they couldn't have been published at the time only supported the notion that there was a pretty strong cutting edge to them."[4]

But Stack faced another, larger obstacle: fear of reprisal, first from his Army superiors, then from the University. Consequently, he "chose the easy way out, continued to draw the cartoons, mean as ever, and used a pseudonym that sounded like 'Gilbert Shelton' [Foolbert Sturgeon] till the heat finally blew over about 20 years later."[5] Shelton published Stack's first *The Adventures of Jesus by F. S.* "(no Foolbert Sturgeon yet)" in 1962 using the university's copier.[6] However, Stack's Jesus stories had a limited distribution (about 50 copies handed out, not sold, to University students).

Stack's initial explorations of theological issues focused almost exclusively on Jesus and used a minimalist, black-and-white pen drawing style. Most of Stack's stories combine illustrations of popular jokes (like the one about Jesus casting the first stone) with theological issues, as in his exploration of the *Pericope Adultarae* found in John 7.53–8.11. In one of his "Stories from the Good Book" series, Stack has Jesus's audience wonder why he is writing in the dirt rather than telling them why they should not stone the woman, as they cannot read. The group member who threw a stone then excuses his action based on his confusion of "sin" and "cent" ("I thought you said 'without cent' Excuse me."), after

which one member of the group offers Jesus a stone ("Gosh! Sorry we
started without you, Jesus! We didn't know you went in for stuff like
this! Here! Bop her a good one!").[7] In answer to this series of miscom-
munications, Jesus disgustedly walks away saying, "The Problem isn't sin.
It's stupidity!" His judgment earns him both verbal condemnation from
the crowd and a rock to the head.[8] As his conflation of popular joke and
pericope indicates, Stack was pointedly indicting the crowd's rejection
of Jesus's message of love and acceptance. It also illustrates Stack's larger
agenda of foregrounding such rejections of Jesus and his teachings in a
format targeted to a popular audience.[9] Several undergrounds repeated
this formula in the late 1960s, but Jackson broke with this qualified
exploration of biblical themes to engage deeper issues directly.

From Stack's *Jesus* to *God Nose*

As he has explained in numerous interviews, Jackson initially drew on
Stack's work to produce his own alternative examination of Christian
theology with *God Nose*. However, Jackson differs from Stack on several
key points. Like Stack, Jackson uses a minimalist, black-and-white style
both for aesthetic and practical reasons. Jackson includes earlier artists
such as Jack Davis, who used a similar style, among his influences; in
addition, he would have had access to copiers that could only reproduce
black-and-white work. Unlike Stack, Jackson focuses almost exclusively
on God rather than on Jesus; this paradigmatic shift enabled him to
explore broader theological issues than Stack had.[10]

While the title character of Jackson's *God Nose* stories is *the* deity in his
comic's universe, God Nose is not the white-bearded, Jehovah-like figure
popularized in religious art and Christian iconography. Instead, he is a
parody of that iconographic figure — a robed, bespectacled, bearded
older man who wears a crown with three balls on top (reminiscent of a
pawnbroker's sign) and high-top tennis shoes, and he sports an overly
large nose, his signature appendage. Jackson extends this distinction
by representing God in a variety of mundane situations and scenes.
In Jackson's stories, God Nose is as likely to play basketball with the
Earth or pretend with his toys (like a Golgotha playset complete with a
crucified Jesus and Roman soldiers) as he is to spout divine injunctions
— perhaps more likely. By creating such a parodic figure, Jackson is
able to explore theological issues that he could not have, had he directly
attacked an iconographic God.

To further telegraph this distinction between God Nose and traditional icons, Jackson utilizes a simple, open line drawing style that is the antithesis of the elaborate paintings that depict God iconographically. Instead of tightly controlled panels, Jackson uses a panel-less format, one which further emphasizes his difference from other comic artists' work and the nonconformity of his subject matter and arguments (though he modestly claims that he had not yet developed his artistic abilities at that time).[11] Working in tandem with his open-dialogue approach, his page layouts reflect the same openness as the arguments in them. Conventional panels will not contain what he has to say and draw; moreover, the dialogue contained in those words and images are meant to open conversations literally and figuratively.

One of the main places that this agenda manifests itself is in the name *God Nose*. Jackson's intentional conflation of *nose* with *knows* telegraphs his agenda to invite dialogue about the nature of God and promote deconstructive perspectives relative to this particular deity (and by extension, the Christian God). Moreover, he compounds this agenda with the further conflation of *God Nose* with *God Knows* — physicality is conflated with omniscience. Parody, Jackson proclaims, will lead to a greater degree of clarity.

With these tools in hand, Jackson launched an intense agenda to encourage dialogue about theology. One of his most obvious targets is religious hypocrisy, as illustrated by his story, "God Nose there's vice in high places" (1964).[12] In the story's opening panel, Jesus confronts an unlikely situation occurring in God Nose's heaven: rape. When Jesus confronts God Nose, asking why St. Peter must "ravish every maiden that comes to heaven," God Nose replies matter-of-factly, "It's the third law of entropy, son . . . [*sic*] everything that comes up must go down."[13] To cue his readers to the story's parodic mode, Jackson peppers this incident with visual puns, like the musical notes and the words "Rock, rock" coming from the rocking chair in which God Nose is seated.

Jackson further signals his intent through his characters' dialogue. When Jackson has Peter explain that he is compelled by law to "ravish maidens," Jesus interjects, "That's out of context fellow!! You're juxtaposing things that juxt oughtin' to be! [*sic*]" God Nose then proposes a revision of "our induction procedure" that would prevent Peter from being "in a convenient position to cast them down." Jackson concludes this story with Jesus' affirmation, "Yes .. it's juxtaposition of things .. [*sic*]" and the words "The End He He (Get it?)."[14] Here Jackson intentionally foregrounds the drive toward definitive positions: on the one hand, he argues, this story is *just a position of things* — one of many possible positions that could be taken; on the other hand, he argues that such relativity precludes any absolutes on the subjects that he has presented in this story: everything from literal (over)interpretation of biblical passages, to the sexuality of angels, to the very nature of God and God's relation to God's law. As this "juxtaposition" of visual and verbal puns with intentional misinterpretation indicates, Jackson openly encourages readers to deconstruct the texts he presents at several levels, from the hermeneutical to the exegetical; by extension, he invites readers to employ similar techniques for theological and biblical issues.

Perhaps one of the most illustrative examples of this strategy occurs in Jackson's story "An Analysis of the Philosophical & Ethical Implications of Contraception — Theory & Application or: Something Always Comes Between Us" (1964). There, Jackson explores the role of divinity in conception by dramatizing it as a musical set on the wedding night of a Protestant husband and a Catholic wife, in which God Nose and a chorus of seamen (an intentional pun by Jackson) perform their numbers. As with his other work in *God Nose,* Jackson features loose, open-style black-and-white pen drawings: no panels confine his text and drawings.

During this production, the Catholic wife and God Nose openly debate the legitimacy of contraception as well as various aspects of its application (illustrating the title). The following exchange occurs after God Nose has demonstrated the inherent weakness of condoms by placing one over his nose and rupturing it with a sneeze:

Wife: But I said symbolic refusal of your admission. The Church and I see coitus as so unified and sacred that any improvisation upon it attacks the very relationship between you and us.

God Nose: Symbolism, schymbolism!! Enough of that crap! I'm there whether you want me or not. I see you make screwing meaningful, and I see you make it senseless, but I still see it, and there's no way, artificial or otherwise, that you can root me out. Especially since my participation is in tee-niny osmophoric form.

Wife: Tee-niny osmophoric form?

God Nose: Yes, with a mere wave of my magic — er, sinus wand, I can transform into a wee little thing, and that's how I so enjoy all the different fun & games methods of birth control.[15]

God Nose demonstrates his enjoyment in "all the different fun & games" by alternately slipping-and-sliding in spermicidal cream, using a diaphragm as a trampoline, and wearing two six-guns so he can "head off gondatrophic hormones at the pass" with the Pill. Jackson ends this dialectic with God Nose's musical solo, which extols the virtues of guilt-free sexuality. The husband and wife embrace the value of that philosophy (and with it, each other), and the chorus of seaman encourages readers to do likewise.

However, Jackson is not simply satisfied with deconstructive wordplay; he is equally intent on indicting the ways that human beings live out their theological (mis)understandings. In those cases, he is much more direct in his criticism, though he does not abandon his paratextual exercises and punning. We can see this shift in his story "God Nose Goes to Sunday School, or Pew, What a Smell" (1964). While this story's subtitle indicates a parodic intent, the story itself is a blistering indictment of those who hypocritically misinterpret Christian tenets of unequivocal love. He portrays the effects of such hypocrisy verbally and visually through a series of panels that depict the excess such positions can bring their holders. The story climaxes with the teacher (whose facial features Jackson has exaggerated) waving a cross and an American flag as he qualifies that day's lesson of "love one another" by reducing the Golden Rule to what he calls the Golden Text: "So the Golden Text — like Jesus would have said it if he were here now — is: 'Love one white, protestant, right-wing, free-enterprising, blond, blue-eyed, red-necked another!'"[16]

The story ends with a nonchalant God Nose sitting on the words *Dat's All Folks* — a conflation of Porky Pig's famous ending phrase for Warner Brothers cartoons with an affected African-American pronunciation. The combination indicates God Nose's (and Jackson's) literal and figurative position on the bigotry so openly expressed in this Sunday School classroom. While this ending might not satisfy those who wanted to see the misled teacher and students learn a better way or even receive some divine justice, it underscores Jackson's intent in presenting such a scenario as a means of exposing religious hypocrisy. The God in this universe is neither impotent nor uninterested, Jackson argues through this *non-answer*; instead, this God encourages readers to act morally and to be aware of how hypocrisy pervades religious institutions. As Jackson demonstrates here and in much of his other work, he is less concerned with making moral indictments than he is with inviting his readers to right the wrongs represented in such stories.[17] Moreover, Jackson's work encourages readers to ask questions about a range of theological issues. As illustrated literally and figuratively in scenes where humans directly petition God Nose with questions perennial or universal, God openly invites humans to question.

Not Strictly Drug-Induced: The Resurrection of *God Nose* and the Undergrounds

The complexity of Jackson's theological explorations counters any claims that his God Nose stories were simply the results of taking peyote — a claim that Jackson has even made. For example, Jackson has claimed that these stories were "strictly drug-induced" and "an attempt to render some of the ridiculous absurdities that had come through from those peyote sessions."[18] However, Jackson also qualified this position in other interviews, as when he defined the influences on his work as primarily Jack Davis, then countered, "Mostly it was just dope."[19] Jackson even dismissed his God Nose stories as the product of youth. Yet he maintained a consistent focus on theological issues throughout his career and returned to God Nose in his late work. In interviews, Jackson holds an indeterminate position about his God Nose stories; clearly, however, Jackson's work contains subtle and profound theological arguments, none of which is simply the byproduct of drugs. Much of his work has an exegetical — if not homiletic or catechetical — agenda.

After his initial foray into underground comics with *God Nose*, Jackson retreated to the much more conventional existence of accounting until 1966, when he moved to the San Francisco area and became the art director for the dance poster session of the Family Dog. While in California, he participated in the area's flourishing counterculture movement with expatriate members of the Texas Mafia. Together, this group co-founded Rip-Off Press in 1968, a publishing house which would become one of the primary venues for publishing underground comics.

Recounting that period in his work, Jackson explains that his "only claim to fame was 'God Nose,' and everybody was asking 'Oh, you gonna' do some 'God Nose' stuff?'"[20] In trying to find his voice in this new milieu, Jackson revived God Nose in *Hydrogen Bomb Funnies* (1970) and continued it in a series of strips for the *Express Times*, a San Francisco underground paper. Subsequently, he released a reprint of *God Nose* in 1971 through Rip Off Press. But Jackson was dissatisfied with these revivals: as he classified it, the attempt to revive *God Nose* "was real strained. I'd quit taking peyote after I left Texas, and it just didn't click anymore. It was a matter of working the character out of my system, and once I'd done it, I was ready to push ahead."[21]

And push ahead he did, exploring a different drawing style and a greater variety of venues. In his stories for series like the EC-based *Skull* and *Slow Death*, he developed the style that would distinguish his later historical works. While he composed no more God Nose stories during this time, he incorporated and foregrounded themes of moral responsibility in all of his work. As his later work makes explicit, Jackson remained focused on the theme of exploitation — particularly in the name of God.

Before turning to the ways that Jackson continued and refined that theme in his later work, we should pause briefly to note the coalescence of factors at this point in Jackson's career and in the development of underground comics. While the undergrounds had begun with explicit explorations of God by Stack and Jackson, they had soon turned to extreme scenarios — the sorts of "copious amounts of thrillingly explicit sex and nauseatingly gruesome violence — or, not infrequently, vice versa" that have become synonymous with the genre.[22]

In the late 1960s, many underground artists engaged aspects of Christian theology through their stories. Some did so benignly: in one story, a misbehaving youth turns into an angel, then flies away to prove that he can be a good boy; in another, dinosaurs confuse the asteroid that will end their lives with God.[23] Others indicted the capitalist appropriation and adulteration of Christian theology, much as Jackson had done.[24] Still other artists at this time eschewed diatribe and parody for sophisticated examinations of religion, as did Justin Green and Art Spiegelman in their autobiographical works — explorations that will distinguish them as undergrounds wane.[25] Such explorations are traceable back to the work by Jackson and Stack from the beginning of this decade.

We can also see the ripple effect produced by Jackson and Stack in other undergrounds' exploration of theology. One of the most prominent examples occurs in Crumb's famous *Despair* (1970), which features the rejection of a messianic, pacific Jesus by corporate and individual interests. Jesus' proclamation of "Peace, My Brother!" earns a brutal physical and verbal assault by a range of white males. Above this panel, Crumb explicitly states his thesis: "Saints have come to show us 'The Way,' only to have their asses stomped into the dirt!!"[26] Crumb's message here is clear: when he comes again, Jesus will endure the same sorts of rejection he experienced during his first time on Earth. The corollary, of course, is that followers of pacifistic countercultures face the same sorts of rejection. Equally clear is the continuity of Crumb's work with that of Stack and Jackson.

However, other undergrounds vitriolically attack Christianity as yet another institution of the Establishment to be abolished. For example, the *SuperJesus* comic (1972) profiles a bumbling combination of Superman and Jesus (aptly named SuperJesus) who cannot save anyone,[27] while *Up From the Deep* (1971) features a similar character meting out physical punishment to hippies and other "undesirables" as part of a divine judgment.[28] This shift from benign savior to malevolent superhero also marks the general shift toward extremism that characterized undergrounds at this time.

Tellingly, we can also see this shift in Stack's work. In a revival of his earlier work, Stack has Jesus turn increasingly violent at his rejection by humanity: for example, Jesus turns his fingers into a gun to shoot a bad guy dead and turns police who have arrested him into swine.[29] Stack continues this trend in stories like "Jesus, Saviour of the World" (1970):[30] there, God plays a practical joke on Jesus by making him think that the world was destroyed in a nuclear holocaust, then threatens to really destroy the earth if Jesus "press[es him] for answers!"[31] By dramatizing this situation, Stack casts God as an arbitrary creator — an indictment consistent with his own views, but not voiced in his original Jesus-oriented stories. There, Stack presented a benign, humble Jesus who was most often the victim of humanity's stupidity; here, he is a vindictive savior and the victim of a vindictive God.

The shift in Stack's Jesus is indicative of the larger current against religion promoted by undergrounds published at the end of the 1960s. As they did with other subjects, underground artists pushed the boundaries of Christian theology to (and perhaps past) their limits by incorporating extremes of sexual and violent imagery.[32] *Tales of the Leather Nun* (1973) and Jim Gardner's graphic depiction of St. Peter in *Yellow Dog Comic* #18

(1970) illustrate the extent of such graphic material. At the end of "The Leather Nun 'Gets Hers,'" Spain Rodriguez's contribution to the anthology, the Leather Nun approaches a life-sized crucifixion in a church, then sexually excites the statue before mounting its erect penis. As she does so, the nun reassures readers, "It's OK. We're married."[33] Similarly, Gardner graphically depicts St. Paul masturbating with the help of a clown holding a paper bag.[34]

An Undying Theme

Jackson was not immune to such currents, as illustrated by his contribution to the *Leather Nun* anthology, "Tales of the Leather Nun's Grandmother." This story revolves around an Egyptian priestess's dilemma when her vagina becomes a portal that could allow evil, transdimensional forces to take over the universe.[35] As the tale graphically portrays, sex is the only way to prevent this cosmic disaster. In keeping with his contemporaries, Jackson uses plenty of sexual imagery and ends with a final panel featuring a demon eating ejaculate. Significantly, this story departs from Jackson's usual tone.

More often, Jackson chose to focus on didactic stories. While many of these resemble EC-type horror stories, they all have a cautionary moral against treating others — be they genetic mutants, intergalactic beings, or human neighbors — inhumanely.[36] Notably, Jackson brought those themes into his later work; there, he shifted his focus to more historical settings, but continued to argue for humane treatment of others. Jackson's last story for the undergrounds, "White Man's Burden" (1973), combines all of these factors into a moral lesson against the usurpation of power in the name of freedom.

As these stories demonstrate, Jackson maintained a sense of moral integrity in the vast majority of his stories of the late 1960s. Recalling his work from this period, Jackson comments on the idea that trying to destroy the oppressor destroys the redeemer:

> It's kind of an undying theme with me because I see it constantly going on in our society. We have the revolutionaries that have this militant stance and keep saying, "We won't cop out. We won't become reactionary." Then as soon as somebody offers them enough loot they take the easy way out. Pretty soon you can't tell them from the people they've been raving about all the time.[37]

While Jackson maintains this theme throughout his work, he also continues his explicit and implicit references to Christian theology. Notably, the charge leveled against the last, living white male is that "[y]ou have even debased God to your own image and contrived an agonizing death for his only son."[38] Despite his assertions otherwise, such examples illustrate that Jackson never abandoned religious themes in his later work.

By retaining this moral sensibility, Jackson opposed the hyperbole dominating undergrounds. In large part, that domination limited the potential for undergrounds to affect the change that they claimed to champion. The hyperbolic satire defining the undergrounds inscribed any social reform that they promoted within a space that enabled "free speech" but simultaneously silenced that speech's potential to effect substantial social change. The voices of the underground remained underground, echoing within that space. Instead of a breeding ground for countercultural ideas, the comics became their burial ground, because their voices were too easily dismissed as so much rant.

When undergrounds succumbed to the consequences of decreased venues for distribution, increased anti-obscenity legislation, and co-optation by mainstream publishing in the mid-1970s, Jackson pursued his own agenda and created a body of work defined by its historical revisionism. In this work, he retains his trademark black-and-white style, but he uses it to depict historical atrocities and histories otherwise erased by dominant power structures. As he noted in several interviews, doing so was economically punishing but morally rewarding.[39]

Jackson's first work from this period targeted Anglo-American injustice towards Native Americans in a series of comics that were anthologized into his highly acclaimed *Comanche Moon* (1979); subsequently, he expanded this subject by featuring injustices perpetrated by Hispano-Americans against Native Americans in *God's Bosom* (1989–90), then explored injustices by Anglo-Americans against Hispano-Americans in *Los Tejanos* (1982). In works like *Indian Lover* (1999), he indicted the prejudice experienced by those who are non-racists.[40] In keeping with his revisionary impulse, Jackson also maintained an almost exclusive focus on the nineteenth century, when (as he says) folks "turned genocide into a fine art."[41] By doing so, Jackson tried "to tell the story of 'the neglected historical others'" as part of his larger agenda to foreground injustice.[42] Jackson's turning from *God Nose* to historical work like *God's Bosom* did not abandon his indictment of established religion and its attendant power structures, or even abandon sophisticated theological exploration; rather, it refocused his lens from the face of God to faith in God, and toward how people seek to appropriate God's authority as justification for their immoral actions against others.

Perhaps that message is best summed up by the ending of one of his later works and his last revival of God Nose, "Oat Willie's Mid Life Crisis" (1987). There, Jackson alternates between closed and no panels, and he blends his original loose, open style with the detailed style that characterizes his later historical work. This alternation highlights both his dialogic play within the storyline and the intellectual openness of his original work. When the protagonist, Oat Willie, phones God Nose to resolve his dilemma over mortality, God Nose replies that he is "not going to give away the plot now."[43] Instead, he counsels Willie, "Do your part, man! That's all anyone expects. Just do your part!" When Willie counters that he is "just a character in a comic book," God Nose exclaims, "You got it, babe! In your very own comic book, right?!" Willie then realizes that he is in charge of his own life — that he can "write the storyline [him]self." God Nose concludes: "It sure does, Willie. You can be any ol' thing your heart desires. After all, this is your life we're talking about!" The agenda that God Nose promotes here for Oat Willie is the same as that promoted by Jackson for his readers: open engagement with deep theological issues, promotion of such engagement for popular audiences, and an emphasis on moral responsibility in dialogue with a divine authority, who lovingly and intentionally encourages all of us to "write the storyline yourself."

Notes

1   The references here are to the cover of *Yellow Dog* #1 (1968), which shows a diminutive male voyeur peeking under the habit of gargantuan nun, or any of the *Tales From the Leather Nun* series, which graphically depict the sexual exploits of a jack-booted, barely clothed nun.
2   Frank Stack, *The New Adventures of Jesus: The Second Coming* (Seattle, WA: Fantagraphics, 2006), 15.
3   Bill Sherman, "Tejano Cartoonist: An Interview with Jack Jackson," *The Comics Journal* 61 (Winter 1981): 101.
4   Stack, 157.
5   Stack, 16.
6   Stack, 15.
7   Stack, 27–8.
8   Stack, 27–8.
9   In the afterword to his collection *The New Adventures of Jesus*, Stack confirms this position with the following elaboration on the origin and purpose of his stories: "The basic idea of *Jesus* came from a chapter in *The Brothers Karamazov* called 'Dimitri's Dream.'"

10   While Jackson uses Jesus in a few of his stories, these exceptions focus almost
     exclusively on Jesus, like "King of Serfdom with incidental music for banjo
     and harmonica, B flat major, opus 32 or My Son, The Folksinger," which has
     God Nose send Jesus to Earth to avoid falling under the spell of televangelists.
     To convince him to go, God Nose tells Jesus to be a folksinger. While on Earth,
     Jesus has the usual series of encounters with nonbelievers, misbelievers, and
     the law that we have seen in Stack's work, including turning the police about
     to arrest him into bullfrogs; however, here Jesus becomes King of Serfdom
     by learning to surf, and he never resorts to violence. See Jack Jackson,
     Underground Classics: Jaxon Volume 1: God Nose (Auburn, CA: Rip Off Press,
     1988), 7–14.
11   Sherman, 101.
12   In his *God Nose* stories, Jackson frequently leaves parts of his story titles in
     lower case. In this article, I have retained those original formulations in my
     references to those stories.
13   Jackson, *God Nose*, 5.
14   Jackson, *God Nose*, 6.
15   Jackson, *God Nose*, 18–19.
16   Jackson, *God Nose*, 24. Jackson pointedly uses the term *nigger* in this story to
     foreground this Sunday School's racism.
17   In the final two panels of "Black Masses," Jackson invites a similar revisionary
     impulse from readers when he leaves God Nose's speech balloon empty.
     This balloon would have contained the answer to racial unrest; instead of
     supplying it, however, Jackson devotes the entire last panel to an explicit
     invitation for readers to "solve the race problem and win valuable prizes"
     (Jackson, *God Nose*, 4). The parodic nature of this *solution* foregrounds the
     impossibility of easy solutions to such issues. Again, Jackson places the moral
     responsibility on readers rather than supplying them with a ready answer.
18   Stanley Wiater and Stephen R Bissette, *Comic Book Rebels: Conversations with the
     Creators of the New Comics* (New York: Donald I. Fine, Inc, 1993), 32–6.
19   Sherman, 101. Reducing *God Nose* to a side effect of drug experiences has
     led critics like Robert C Harvey to misinterpretations like "these comix were
     likely to be funny only to those readers who were stoned at the time." See
     Harvey, *The Art of the Comic Book: An Aesthetic History* (Oxford, MS: University
     of Mississippi Press, 1996), 204.
20   Sherman, 102.
21   Sherman, 101. Estren summarizes Jackson's relation to *God Nose* this way:
     "Jaxon feels his art has grown enormously since 1963, and he now disowns
     most of his work in *God Nose*— indeed, he feels his cartoon *starts* with his work
     for *Skull Comics*, which was first published in 1970." See Mark James Estren,
     A History of Underground Comics (Berkeley, CA: Ronin Publishing, 1992), 83.
22   Kim Thompson and Gary Groth, "Devoured by His Own Fantasies,"
     Introduction to *Optimism of Youth: The Underground Work of Jack Jackson* (Seattle,
     WA: Fantagraphics Books, 1991), 6.
23   The first example occurs in Don Dohler's Pro Junior one-page "In His Child
     Hood" (1971); Estren reproduces a single panel from Dohler's story on
     page 47 of his survey, *A History of Underground Comics*. The second example
     occurs in Pete Poplaski's *Quagmire* #1 (1970), also reproduced in Estren.
     Notably, R Crumb's one-page joke "The Last Supper" (1986) continues such
     explorations long after undergrounds were gone. In this one-page story, the
     protagonist reports to his coworkers that his father had died during supper

the previous evening and that he had upset his family by asking if he could finish his father's pudding. Witek reproduces this story in its entirety. See Joseph Witek, *Comic Books as History: The Narrative Art of Jack Jackson, Art Spiegelman, and Harvey Pekar* (Oxford, MS: University of Mississippi P, 1989), 136.

24   Joel Beck's "The Profit" (1966) tellingly conflates prophecy and product in its title and storyline, and John Thompson's provocatively titled series "Spiritual Stag Film" (1968) promotes a New Age alternative. Interestingly, Thompson's work resembles Jackson's in style and substance. See Joel Beck, *The Profit* (Berkeley, CA: Go Broke Press, 1966) and John Thompson, "The Spiritual Stag Film," *Yellow Dog Comics* vol. 1, #1–5 (Berkeley, CA: Yellow Dog, 1968).

25   Rosenkranz reproduces the several panels from Green's work seminal work *Binky Brown Meets the Holy Virgin Mary* (1972) on page 170 of his survey *Rebel Visions*. See Patrick Rosenkranz, *Rebel Visions: The Underground Comix Revolution: 1963–1975* (Seattle, WA: Fantagraphics Books, 2002), 170. Drawing on Green's work, Spiegelman published the first installment of *Maus* as part of an underground comic in 1972.

26   Estren reproduces a single panel from this story on page 166 of his survey, *A History of Underground Comics*. This panel profiles the conversation that I have included in this text.

27   While it might seem far-fetched at first, critics like Burton Mack argue that American culture draws heavily on Christian iconography, and particularly on Jesus, as the model for pop culture superheroes (a point also made by Greg Garrett). See Burton L Mack, *Who Wrote the New Testament?: The Making of the Christian Myth* (New York: HarperOne, 1996) and Greg Garrett, *Holy Superheroes! Revised and Expanded Edition: Exploring the Sacred in Comics, Graphic Novels, and Film* (Westminster: John Knox Press, 2008), 11.

28   Estren reproduces a single panel from the *Up From the Deep* story on page 168 of his survey *A History of Underground Comics*. While this panel only hints at this character's actions, it provides a useful summary of that character. As those who have access to the full story can see, this Jesus is far from a loving Savior. Readers can see an equally violent SuperJesus character in Renaud Façade's "Overman vs. God!!" in *Yellow Dog Comics* #15 (1969).

29   Stack, 45, 39.

30   This story originally appeared in *Hydrogen Bomb and Biochemical Warfare Funnies* #1. This comic also printed Jackson's "The Return of E^2."

31   Stack, 104–6.

32   Yet another example occurs in Jim Osborne's "Kid Kill" (1971), which features a man who is reciting the opening to the Lord's Prayer and masturbating while a speed demon breaks forth from his chest and hacks a woman to pieces.

33   Pilcher, et al. reproduce the climax of this story on page 151 of their survey, *Erotic Comics*. See Tim Pilcher, Gene Jr. Kannenberg, and Aline Kominsky-Crumb, *Erotic Comics: A Graphic History from Tijuana Bibles to Underground Comix* (New York: Harry N. Abrams, Inc. 2008), 151.

34   Rosenkranz reproduces the opening panel from this story on page 168 of his survey, *Rebel Visions*.

35   Jackson, *Optimism*, 87–93.

36   EC Comics were also known as Entertaining Comics, the house that brought such memorable horror titles as *Tales of the Crypt* and then produced *Mad* as a consequence of the censorship of comics in the 1950s.

Jackson's work at this time falls into two broad categories. The first consists of EC-horror-type stories like "The Intruder" (13–20), "Pussy Whipped" (21–31), "The Secret" (32–9), "The Black Saint and the Sinner Lady" (53–60), "The Hound" (78–86), and "Death Rattle" (92–101). While engaging humor and horror, these stories also include general caveats against treating others inhumanely. The second category, while similar in tone, foregrounds how perspective determines value, like "The Light in the Distance" (45–52), "Gene Shuffle" (61–9), and "Homesick" (70–7). Each of these stories profiles how inhumanity towards others will merit repentance from the victimizers. Page references here are to Jackson's *Optimism*.

37   Sherman, 102.
38   Jackson, *Optimism*, 106.
39   For example, see Gary Groth, "Critique Revisited: An interview with Jack Jackson," *The Comics Journal*, http://www.tcj.com/237/i_jackson.html. Originally printed in *The Comics Journal* #213 (June 1999).
40   Jack Jackson, *God's Bosom and Other Stories: The Historical Strips of Jack Jackson* (Seattle, WA: Fantagraphics Books, 1995), *Indian Lover: Sam Houston & the Cherokees* (Austin, TX: Mojo Press, 1999), and *Los Tejanos: The True Story of Juan N. Seguin and the Texas-Mexicans During the Rising of the Lone Star* (Seattle, WA: Fantagraphics Books, 1982).
41   Jack Jackson, *God's Bosom and Other Stories: The Historical Strips of Jack Jackson* (Seattle, WA: Fantagraphics Books, 1995), 84.
42   Groth, "Critique," 2.
43   Jackson, *God's Bosom*, 135.

A Hesitant Embrace: Comic Books and Evangelicals

KATE NETZLER

"**I**RRESISTIBLE ACTION. UNDENIABLE TRUTH." Z Graphic Novels offers it all — eighth-grade ninjas, time-traveling insects, a bumbling strongman, and ethnically diverse, environmentally friendly superheroes. The animated mini-trailer on the Z Graphic Novels website both proclaims that "amazing adventures await!" and showcases epic battles and heroic feats in glossy graphic form. In August 2007, Z Graphic Novels, an imprint of Zondervan Publishing, launched the first two issues of six different Christian comic book series, with the remaining issues prepared for release in the next few years. But even more than its spiffy new take on a popular art form, Z Graphic Novels is eager to promote its biblically-based stories and "God-honoring alternatives." These comic books are presented to appeal to both the savvy cultural consumer and the serious Christian. The eighth-grade ninja is, in fact, looking for her divinely given purpose between study hall and saving the world; the superheroes are in the employ of a mysterious and ambiguously benevolent being known as the Morningstar; and the strongman is the son of Samson, searching for the source of his strength while ducking flying tree limbs and the wiles of Delilah's beautiful daughter.[1] The world of Christian comic books is expanding rapidly, taking new visual and artistic cues from mainstream "secular" comics while remaining committed to their religious purpose.

Christian comic books are growing up, but they are coming of age within an increasingly ambivalent religious tradition that is simultaneously appreciative of and skeptical toward popular culture. The examination of explicitly labeled Christian media reveals a two-tiered concern: (1) the ambivalent relationship between evangelical Christianity and pop culture in general and (2) the more specific problem of using form and content by artists within the media itself along with the role of Christian comic books in the larger media as a whole. Examining the cultural roots and contemporary religious influences of Christian comic books provides direction for a conversation on the cultural divide between the ideas of secular and sacred in American Christianity. It is this constant struggle between the Christian content and the comic book form that defines both the appearance and marketing of Christian comic books today and points to an ambiguous future for Christian popular culture.

However, to begin with, there are two subtle but absolutely essential points that must be clarified. First, Christian comic books are not the same as comic books about religion or about Christianity. They are developed, marketed, advertised, and explicitly labeled as "Christian," which consequently implies certain assumptions about the content, message, and conclusions of the comic books. They are centered on themes of faith in God and espouse Christian values and morals with the express purpose of spiritual edification or evangelism. Violence, sex, profanity, and other mature themes are kept at a minimum, and the conclusions are hopeful and redemptive. The label "Christian comic book" is also ecumenical, as denominational lines are often blurred for the sake of evangelism. Second, Christian comic books are not correlative to comic books from other religions; "Jewish comics" or "Muslim comics" do not necessarily carry the same intrinsic assumptions. Christian comic books are less interested in commenting on or questioning Christianity than they are interested in presenting a religious worldview for the sake of evangelism.[2] In fact, this focus on evangelism colors every religious, cultural, or artistic effort that falls under the designation of Christian media and drastically influences the acceptable content of Christian comic books.

Evangelicals have long had an ambivalent relationship with popular media and culture. The backbone of the evangelical tradition is the belief that Jesus Christ is the personal and communal savior of all humankind and that Christians are bound by a biblical charge to spread this message far and wide.[3] In order to evangelize more effectively, evangelical Christians throughout the twentieth century have looked to the methods and tools of the "secular" world, often successfully expanding the use of mediums such as film, advertising, music, radio, television, print, and illustration to serve a religious purpose and to reach new audiences. As media scholar Quentin Schultze comments, "From its beginning, the Christian church was a communicating church, and evangelicals were that church's naively hopeful pilgrims who repeatedly entered new media lands."[4] Evangelicals are often quick to embrace new media, but they are similarly quick to criticize and remain skeptical of its possible abuses by the secular world. While evangelical Christians are called to spread the Gospel, they also believe they are called to be set apart from the temptations and unchristian influences of the world[5] (i.e., popular culture and media), and this directive remains central to the evangelical cultural agenda.

Schultze, in his article "Evangelicals' Uneasy Alliance with the Media," outlines this ambiguous relationship in three points: (1) evangelicals consider evangelism to be the primary use for any media, (2) evangelicals see mainstream media as a threat to their values and beliefs, and (3) evangelicals have a "highly personalistic approach to morality" that colors their critique of media and the understanding of their role in popular culture.[6] Schultze's third point highlights the prominence of the individual in evangelicalism, a trait that is also conspicuous in the world of comic books. Reading and experiencing a comic book is a personal endeavor and highly individualistic. Acceptance into a group of comic book aficionados is dependent on one's personal effort to acquire accurate and extensive comic book knowledge, and the community is formed by individuals with similar personal experiences. Many comic books also focus on stories of the individual who challenges or saves society and who often goes through a personal crisis or rebirth. This emphasis on personal moral and ethical development is easily transferred to the evangelical value of personal faith, and the majority of Christian comic books rely on this well-established character motif. However, it is Schultze's first two points that express the key conflict and provide a helpful lens through which to view the development of Christian comic books.

Christian comic books have existed since the earliest days of comics and cartoons. In the late nineteenth century, cartoons and comics illustrating biblical themes began appearing in small denominational publications. By the mid-twentieth century, these cartoons and single-page comics gave way to Christian comics in booklet form. David C. Cook Communications, Standard Publishing Company, and other national and international missionary organizations began including comic-book-style stories in Sunday School curricula and packets of evangelistic material. The earliest Christian comic books were primarily illustrated versions of Bible stories and the life of Jesus, with much of their text coming directly from scripture. Billy Graham and Oral Roberts both sponsored short-lived comic book series in the 1950s that showcased "True Life Tales" of hope and salvation, and Al Hartley produced Christian versions of the Archie comics in the 1970s.[7] The early generations of Christian comic books were far more interested in the evangelistic possibilities of juxtaposing pictures with words than with exploring the artistic nuances of a new medium. However, in the last two decades there has been a move toward the creation of unique stories and visual reinterpretations of the Christian message for a new generation. Christian comic books have developed into a solid niche market and, with large Christian publishing companies like Zondervan and PowerMark Comics replicating the marketing strategies of mainstream comic book companies, the Christian comic is moving out of the Sunday school classroom and onto bookstore shelves.

This is happening in large part because of the growth of independent communities and groups dedicated to the creation and production of Christian comics. A group of five independent artists, known collectively as Community Comics, has formed a comics studio dedicated to publishing products that are "professional, high quality, entertaining comic books with a Christian focus."[8] The Christian Comics Art Society (CCAS) Internet forum, based on the West Coast, has hundreds of online members,[9] and Christian Comics International just concluded its Second Annual International Christian Comics Competition with contributors from twenty-four countries.[10] The amount of and demand for Christian comics may still be small compared to other forms of Christian media, but the world of Christian comics is growing steadily, forming a solid community, and finding expression in a variety of forms and styles.

The widening scope of the Christian comic book is indicative of the creative ability of evangelicals to find prospects for evangelism in the most unlikely of places, but this creativity is still subject to the concerns and suspicions of the evangelical sensibility. As Schultze points out, while evangelism is the primary goal for Christian media, there is still a notable skepticism for new mediums in general. This uneasiness is especially conspicuous in the presentation and marketing of Christian comics as alternatives to mainstream "secular" comics. There is a preoccupation with reassuring the consumer that is echoed throughout independent and corporate Christian comics alike. Whether focusing on the positive message of Christian comics or emphasizing the negative influence of mainstream comics, the vast majority of Christian comics are forced to engage the question of sacred content and secular form. Zondervan's Z Graphic Novels and PowerMark Comics offer examples of the two approaches to this question.

Z Graphic Novels whole-heartedly embrace the strengths of ultra-modern media in transforming ancient truths into a more relevant form. The website's FAQ section explains that: "[i]n an increasingly visual culture, Z Graphic Novels serve as gateways for readers to experience biblical messages in a current cultural context. [. . .] Intricate plotlines and colorful characters deliver the newest way to connect to some of the oldest messages."[11] They emphasize the translation of biblical values into a "language" that is attractive to contemporary readers. Z Graphic Novels use comic books as a tool for communication, emphasizing the positive aspects of the books and focusing on the message over the medium.

Z Graphic Novels also explicitly markets their comic books as alternatives to mainstream comic books. The first piece of information presented on the Z Graphic Novels website is the phrase "God-honoring alternative" that booms across the animated mini-trailer. Even before seeing the comic books themselves, the consumer is informed that these comic books honor God, implying that the medium will not detract from the message. The use of the word "alternative" is central here, as it suggests not only a negative judgment of mainstream or "secular" comics but also an assumption of the need for a Christianized version. This is a typical marketing device that persuades the consumer to stop purchasing one kind of product and to begin purchasing another similar but supposedly improved version. However, this is also a significant theological statement, claiming that for Christians, there is a right and wrong choice in cultural consumption and that this choice is based on religious content. In addition, the concept of an alternative also implies that there is a degree of visual similarity between two versions of the same medium and that the only significant difference is the content. Thus, in three words, audiences understand that Z Graphic Novels is committed to both biblical truth and artistic sophistication, but the latter only as it is useful to the former.

PowerMark Comics also exemplifies the evangelical suspicion of contemporary media and explicitly presents itself as a praiseworthy alternative, but it focuses primarily on the negative aspects of mainstream comics to make this point. Published for over ten years by Light for the Lost (an Assemblies of God ministry), the PowerMark Adventure series follow the exploits of a diverse group of superheroes as they attempt to save the world. A letter posted prominently on the website from the series creator, Steve Benintendi, explains the motivation for PowerMark Comics. He writes,

> There was a day when you could feel good about kids reading comics. Now you have to look long and hard to find a comic book that doesn't present a value system and moral code that are at odds with the Christian lifestyle. The truth is, many comics today are just plain nasty. At Powermark, we strive to be entertaining, yet minimize violence and what could be considered mature themes. Our mission is simple. We are determined to present the Holy Scriptures to our youth and children in an entertaining fashion while remaining true to the message contained therein.[12]

Benintendi uses the language of alternatives, but he also exploits the fear of secular media as a dangerous role model. PowerMark Comics are offered as a direct way to combat the distorted nature of modern media and are seen as an entertaining way to communicate a specific message. For PowerMark, the comic book is not just a tool but a defensive weapon.

Community Comics, on the other hand, emphasizes both the Christian message and the unique potential of the comic book, expressing a commitment to both the content and the form. The statement of purpose on their website promises that they are "committed to using [their] talents, experiences, and passions in service to Christ in this dynamic and virtually unlimited art form."[13] Community Comics looks to accomplish this through service to Christ, their readers, the Christian comics community, and the independent comics creator. Because of their wide experience in many aspects of the comic book industry, the artists of Community Comics have a more open approach to Christian comics and are willing to deal with more complicated themes. Their comics range from medieval clashes between knights and dragons to reinterpretations of the life of King David, but they also offer such collaborative works as *Tempest*, a one-shot that deals with helplessness and theological ambiguity in the wake of Hurricane Katrina. Though the creators understand service to Christ as their ultimate goal, they also have a sense for the medium itself and are willing to explore both religious and artistic possibilities.

However, even the artists of Community Comics show signs of unease. One collaborative comic, *Paro-Dee*, is explained as "featuring work by people who have worked for Marvel, DC, and many other independent publishers, [but] the most important thread connecting these artists and writers is not their abilities with the pen (which is great), but their love for Christ (which is greater)."[14] They have a certain understandable pride in their artistic credentials, but it is inevitably followed by a reassurance that these credentials are not the primary evaluative criteria. There is a sense of self-consciousness and an impulse to justify their religious position that reflects the ambivalence echoed in the larger evangelical culture.

Another independent Christian comic book, *Megazeen*, presents an interesting case study for the relationship between Christian and comic book. Their twelfth issue, the *Megazeen of Horror*, follows in the footsteps of campy EC horror comics of the 1940s and 1950s, it and includes such short stories as "I was a Teenage Street Preacher," "Psalm 23 and the Vampire Death Squad," "Gideon's Army: The Quick and the Undead," and the "Bone-Chilling Saga of Frank Gun," American protector against the Nazi Vampire Menace. The introduction warns the reader, "These are not tales for the squeamish and weak of heart, and certainly not for those foolish mortals who think they know how a Christian comic should be."[15] The creators are optimistic about the possibilities of the relationship of comic books and evangelical Christianity and celebrate the unconventionality of this particular pairing. The issue acknowledges and reinterprets the genre through two different approaches: creating situations of horror based on traditional Christian themes and reinterpreting classic horror motifs to present an evangelistic message.

As an example of the former, "Psalm 23 and the Vampire Death Squad" writer and artist Dean Rankine illustrates the words of Psalm 23 with a storyline about a small girl overcoming the Vampire Death Squad (VDS). In one panel the words "and your rod and your staff, they comfort me" float above the image of the girl gleefully brandishing a cross and a wooden stake at the VDS. The word "rod" is written in the illustration, with an arrow pointing at the cross, and the word "staff" is pointing to the wooden stake. The VDS looks terrified, and in following panels the girl stabs them with the stake ("You prepare a table before me in the presence of my enemies") and burns them to a crisp with holy water ("You anoint my head with oil; my cup overflows").[16] Rankine reinterprets the words of the psalmist to apply to the conventions of the vampire narrative.

The latter approach is exemplified by the story "Frank Gun" (see Figure 1). The story, written by Tom Hall and Joe Endres and drawn by Dan Barlow, follows Frank Gun, "an unstoppable military force" created in 1941 by US scientists from the remains of unidentified soldiers. In order to save a God-fearing America from the clutches of the evil Hitler, Frank Gun thrashes a werewolf and then prevents a group of vampires from launching a swastika-covered missile toward the United States. The story is a parody, with a clear-cut good vs. evil plot line and overly dramatized ethnic stereotypes. However, the story is framed as a conflict between the faith of the good God-fearing Americans (represented by Frank Gun) and the atheistic Nazi vampires. Before the final attack, the vampires mock Frank Gun for praying and believing in a weak God, but Frank Gun replies, "No, my God is mighty . . . and so is my .45 revolver!" and then closes the missile bay doors so the bomb explodes with the vampires.[17] The story uses conventional horror characters and plot devices but replaces the content with explicitly Christian dialogue and frames the conflict in explicitly Christian terms. In this case, it places Christian content into the horror genre form.

The Christian comic book is undergoing, whether consciously or not, an identity crisis. A heavy responsibility is placed on the shoulders of Christian comic book writers and artists. Not only must they produce a comic book with unique characters, intriguing plotlines, and stunning graphics, but the stories must reflect a personal transition that is — either subtly or blatantly — toward salvation in Christ. A Christian comic book cannot be merely a Sunday School lesson or merely a comic book; it must bridge the gap between evangelism and entertainment and between glorifying God and contributing to the comic book medium.

Quentin Schultze maintains that evangelicalism has a distinct disinterest in tradition that both leads it to a cheerful faith in the future and "makes it increasingly susceptible to commercial exploitation."[18] This disinterest in tradition may lead to an admirable use of cutting-edge

Figure 1.   Frank Gun combats the Nazi vampire menace with brute force and a
personal connection to God. The independent comic *Megazeen of Horror* plays
with the conventions of evangelistic rhetoric and the horror comic genre to create
a Christian horror comic that challenges the relationship between evangelicalism
and modern media. Dan Barlow, (a), Tom Hall and Joe Endres (w). "Frank Gun."
Megazeen of Horror #12: 34.

technology and marketing, but it also causes a distinct absence of any sense of self or identity. With most Christian comics being marketed as alternatives, the focus is often on the content over the form. At the same time, as Douglas Wolk comments in his book *Reading Comics,*

> Comics' content and their social context are inextricably linked. Reading comics, or not reading them, often presents itself as taking some kind of stand; in picking up something with words and pictures to read, you become the sort of person who reads comics, and that can be a badge of pride or shame or both.[19]

Christian comics operate in a similar way because, not only are readers making a statement by reading a comic book, but they are making a statement about what kind of comic books they will read.

The label "Christian" has quickly become a brand name that informs the consumer of the identity of the product being offered. Since this label is also a set of religious beliefs, it draws even bolder boundaries. It quickly communicates that this product is different from other products not only in a commercial way but in a moral and ethical way as well. It reveals not only the quality of the product but the quality of the world-view behind it, making a value judgment on the appropriateness of the worldview. Constantly referring to Christian media as an "alternative" is indicative of the way that evangelical Christians view their place in society: as a group set apart. This naturally leads to the belief that Christian media is also set apart and is not subject to the criticism or standards of secular media.

By labeling these books "Christian," publishing houses, critics, and consumers are effectively removing Christian comic books from a place in the medium as a whole. As a separate "Christian" medium, these comic books are no longer required to participate in or interact with the demands and criticisms of the medium. The niche market moves to being the only market. Christian comic books are forced to respond to and engage with the limits of their own subculture before engaging the larger world of media, if they do so at all. This label makes Christian comic books generally exempt from any outside criticism, either social or artistic. The standards are so dramatically different that comparing a Christian comic with a mainstream comic becomes futile. Thus, Christian media plays a trump card and continues to perpetually isolate itself, while simultaneously claiming to be utilizing a new medium just like everyone else. Christian comic books are caught in a tug of war between their "Christian-ness" and their "comic book-ness." Evangelicals fully grasp the power available in modern media, but they are afraid and suspicious of the negative ways that a secular world has used this media. Their answer has been to co-opt the many forms of mainstream media for evangelistic purposes. While understandable, this ambivalence is increasingly problematic when applied to an inherently dynamic medium like comic books. Comic books are a complex, self-critical, and self-perpetuating medium where the form and content are inextricably linked. Telling a story through a comic book necessitates the manipulation of the form itself, so it is important that these two aspects of comic books are considered equally. However, in many Christian comic books, the content is merely funneled into a form. While comic books like the *Megazeen of Horror* do this in order to comment on both the stereotypical black-and-white evangelistic message and the conventions of comic books, there is a serious concern as to uncritically channeling content into a certain form. Much of Christian media operates in this way and consequently continues to perpetuate a false dichotomy between faith and art.

While there has been great progress toward a more holistic view of the interaction of faith and art, this topic must continue to be addressed. Can evangelicals maintain the essential Christian message of their religious tradition while still experimenting visually with a medium that has a distinctive tradition of its own? Or does having an unshakable message force artists to maintain an artistic status quo? A religious tradition that prides itself on relevancy in a changing world should be continually reinterpreting the ways that message is communicated and not merely transplanting the same content into different forms. Until evangelical Christians can move away from this either/or mentality, they will never fully attain either their evangelistic or artistic potential. Both evangelical Christianity and the comic book medium can benefit from a greater understanding of the role of religion in popular culture and the influences and effects this relationship has in the lives and ideas of readers and artists. At this point, however, even though there is movement towards understanding, the relationship between Christian and comic book is still only a hesitant embrace.

Notes

1   "Graphic Novels," Zondervan, http://www.zgraphicnovels.com.
2   Two notable exceptions include Steve Ross's *Marked* (New York: Seabury Books,

   2005) and Doug TenNapel's *Creature Tech* (Canada: Top Shelf Productions, 2002).

3 Matt. 28:16–20 NIV.

4 Quentin Schultze, "Keeping the Faith: American Evangelicals and the Media," *American Evangelicals and the Mass Media,* ed. Quentin J. Schultze (Grand Rapids, MI: Academie Books), 26.

5 Rom. 12:2 NIV.

6 Quentin Schultze, "Evangelicals' Uneasy Alliance with the Media," *Religion and Mass Media: Audiences and Adaptations,* ed. Daniel A. Stout and Judith M. Buddenbaum (Thousand Oaks, CA: Sage Publications), 67.

7 "Notable Christian Comics," Christian Comics International, http://www.christiancomicsinternational.org.

8 "What is Community Comics," Community Comics http://www.community comics.com/news13.html.

9 "A Network of Christian Fellowship for Comics Fans, Pros, and Amateurs," Christian Comic Arts Society, http://christiancomicart.ning.com/.

10 "Notable Christian Comics."

11 "Graphic Novels," Zondervan.

12 Steve Benintendi, "Powermark Parents: Letter from Powermark creator, Steve Benintendi," *PowerMark Comics,* http://www.powermarkcomics.com.

13 "What is Community Comics," Community Comics, http://www.community comics.com/news13.html.

14 "Paro-Dee," Community Comics, http://www.communitycomics.com/cc_partners_parodee.html.

15 Uncredited, *Megazeen of Horror* #12, 2006.

16 Dean Rankine, "Psalm 23 and the Vampire Death Squad," *Megazeen of Horror* #12, 20.

17 Dan Barlow (a), Tom Hall, and Joe Endres (w), "Frank Gun," *Megazeen of Horror* #12, 34.

18 Quentin Schultze, "Keeping the Faith," 29.

19 Douglas Wolk, *Reading Comics: How Graphic Novels Work and What They Mean* (Cambridge: De Capo Press, 2007), 60.

Narrative and Pictorial Dualism in *Persepolis* and the Emergence of Complexity

KERR HOUSTON

O N PAGE 284 OF *The Complete Persepolis*, a teenaged Marjane Satrapi is in real trouble. Forced to submit to an ideological test at the hands of an Iranian mullah, she stands nervous and contrite, fully aware that both her lifestyle and her idiosyncratic beliefs are far from conventionally pious. For much of her life, religious and political conformity have seemed to involve absolutes and simplifications. Is it possible that a mullah, a religious authority, could see value in her respect for a more nuanced and less systematic set of values?

At the same moment, an adult Marjane Satrapi is also facing a challenge. Over most of the first 280 pages of her graphic novel, Satrapi has depicted religion and politics as spheres characterized by dogmatic claims and extreme dualisms — as a world, in other words, of blacks and whites. But, Satrapi wonders, can a graphic novel suggest a more complex and varied set of values? Can black and white images communicate her teenaged character's evolving moral individualism? And, if so, how?

Originally published in four French-language volumes between 2000 and 2003, *Persepolis* recounts Satrapi's experiences as a girl in Tehran during the late 1970s and early 1980s, then as a teenaged student at a private school in Vienna. Throughout, the relationship between private and public spheres is complex. As a maturing Marjane abandons her childhood image of God, she watches her native country publicly embrace a fundamentalist religiosity. At the same time, Marjane also struggles to reconcile the liberal secularism of her parents with the religious propaganda of a country embroiled in war with Iraq. Amid the strictures of the Islamic regime and the vocal skepticism of her parents, young Marjane grows up in an environment sharply defined by a range of religious assumptions and expectations.

Even as it describes a nuanced ideological landscape, however, *Persepolis* also involves a series of exaggerations and drastic contrasts. This process of simplification is clearest in Satrapi's treatment of institutionalized religion, which she repeatedly presents as extreme and inflexible. Throughout the book, figures of religious authority — Islamic and Christian — issue a stream of absolute decrees, irrational pronouncements, and violent threats. In turn, through narrative and compositional juxtapositions that construe public religious life as static and architectural, and secular life as loose and flexible, Satrapi also develops forceful contrasts between institutionalized religion and liberal Western secularism. Moreover, the book's visual style, heavy brushed lines in black ink on white paper, yields a series of stark coloristic contrasts. Satrapi's use of profile and frontal poses acts at times like a binary code, allowing potent oppositions between characters and ideas. Ultimately, these contrasts are so stark, so binary, and so central to the book's basic logic that *Persepolis* seems to propose an essentially dualistic philosophy, with the young Marjane attempting to navigate a course between the extreme poles of reactionary religiosity and Western liberalism (or capitalist temptation).

Ultimately, however, Satrapi does not seem content with such a simple either/or schema. She finally urges the reader towards a third possibility, an educated spirituality with room for complexity and fluidity. The initial image of religion and of history as merely dualist eventually seems a product of Marjane's childish simplifications, and Satrapi nudges her readers towards a more sophisticated and adult understanding of deeply complicated issues.

Satrapi's initial reliance upon — and her final jettisoning of — a relatively simple dualism may help to explain some of the emotional appeal of the massively popular *Persepolis* (which was subsequently made into a motion picture). Over the course of reading the book, a reader experiences something like Marjane's own coming of age: an initially simplistic worldview finally opens on to a more complex landscape. We grow with

Marjane as we read the book, and thus we relate to its protagonist as we contemplate the evolution of both Satrapi's native country, Iran, and of her native medium, comics.

Institutionalized Religion and an Implicit Dualism

For much of *Persepolis*, public religiosity is associated with absolutism and inflexibility. On the second page of the book, a mullah flatly decrees in the wake of the Islamic Revolution that "all bilingual schools must be closed down." His phrasing is rigid, accommodating no exceptions and allowing no debate. Subsequently, his tone is echoed in the public criticism of Marjane by an aggressive guardian of the revolution on a Tehran street several years later. Charged with upholding and explaining the duties of Muslim women, the guardian jabs a finger at the teenaged Marjane's shiny Nike shoes and Michael Jackson pin and abruptly announces that Marjane's sneakers are "punk" and thus immoral (see Figure 1). In a caption set just below the guardian's pointing finger, the narrator flatly dismisses such a charge as ridiculous: "It was obvious that she had no idea what punk is."[1] But the guardian has no interest in learning. The tone of her charge precludes discussion, and in fact she soon tells the frightened Marjane to shut up. The guardian thus seems little more than an incurious bully, and she is typical of most religious authorities in *Persepolis*, who present an unyielding façade of stark confidence and power.

These episodes also suggest the potential irrationality and anti-intellectualism of an institutionalized religion, a theme thrown into high relief in a third episode. Shortly after the regime closes the universities, it also decrees that all women are to wear the veil when in public. A spokesman on television explains the reasons behind the new policy: "Women's hair emanates rays that excite men. That's why women should cover their hair!" The spokesman's explanation does not form part of a mutual conversation; instead, emanating from a television set, it is a decree, intended to be accepted rather than publicly discussed. The only discussion that occurs is private, domestic, and generally ineffective: in their living room, Marjane's parents cannot believe their ears. "Incredible!" cries her father. "They think all men are perverts!"[2] This response is placed beneath the original decree in the panel, like Satrapi's criticism of the guard of the revolution. Similarly, it forms a marginal and disenfranchised commentary that strives to both undermine the

Figure 1. **Marjane is publicly criticized by guardians of the revolution.** Excerpt from ***Persepolis: The Story of a Childhood*** by Marjane Satrapi, translated by Mattias Ripa and Blake Ferris, translation copyright © 2003 by L'Association, Paris, France. Used by permission of Pantheon Books, a division of Random House, Inc.

claim of the spokesman and accent the fundamental irrationality of the government's position, but it can never do so directly.

As Satrapi casts the moralizing codes of the Islamic regime as undemocratic and uninformed, she also associates religious conformity with hypocrisy and even violence. Shortly after the institution of the veil, Marjane's mother watches disapprovingly through a window as a neighbor dressed conservatively in a full chador passes on the sidewalk. "Look at her!" complains Marjane's mother. "Last year she was wearing a miniskirt, showing off her beefy thighs to the whole neighborhood. And now madame is wearing a chador."[3] The pious symbolism of the chador is thus merely a façade and cannot erase a liberal past. But the neighbor's self-serving embrace of the chador is ultimately a mild example of hypocrisy when compared to the verbal violence of other figures supposedly acting in the name of Islam. Shortly before seeing her covered neighbor, for example, Marjane's mother is publicly insulted by a pair of fundamentalists for not wearing the veil; in her words, "They said that women like me should be pushed up against a wall and fucked. And thrown in the garbage."[4] The raw violence of the language is disturbing, and its effect is only intensified by the fact that it is being used by allegedly pious men. But such a conflation of violence and religiosity is hardly unique. Later in the book, Marjane's family is driving home from a party when they are stopped by gun-bearing officials. Smelling wine on Marjane's father's breath, one of the officials derides him as a "piece of westernized trash" and, after nearly beating him, flatly informs him that if it weren't for his wife's pleas, "You'd already be in hell!"[5] Public representatives of Muslim piety are repeatedly presented as hypocritically decadent, vulgar, or vicious.

Importantly, however, Satrapi also suggests that hypocrisy, absolutism, and irrationality are not unique to Iran or to Islam. Instead, in her book such traits typify extreme religiosity in general; indeed, as Marjane notes at one point, "In every religion, you find the same extremists."[6] It is hardly surprising, then, that the nuns who oversee her Viennese boarding house neatly resemble Tehran's zealous guardians of the revolution in their aggressively critical behavior. When one of the nuns sees Marjane eating pasta from a pot, she points rudely at Marjane and declares, "It's true what they say about Iranians. They have no education." When Marjane responds in kind, she is summoned to see the assistant of the mother superior, who promptly tells her, "Shut up, you insolent girl."[7] The unexpected, uncharitable language recalls the earlier rebukes of Marjane and her father in Tehran, and it allows Satrapi to posit a broad tonal equivalence between institutional Islam and institutional Christianity. The two systems may differ in many ways, but Satrapi proposes a shared tendency towards violence and towards a common set of superficial forms — commonalities that later allow Marjane, in a remarkable moment, to appropriate Michelangelo's *Pietà* in drawing an Iranian war martyr for an art school admissions exam.[8] Her use of a Christian icon in the service of an Islamic republic is telling, for it implies that, much as members of the two religions issue similarly violent insults, they can both evidently find meaning in the same violent image.

As Satrapi associates institutionalized religion with specific tendencies, however, she also relies upon a contrast between traditional

Figure 2.   **Supporters and opponents of the veil face confront each other. Excerpt from *Persepolis: The Story of a Childhood* by Marjane Satrapi, translated by Mattias Ripa and Blake Ferris, translation copyright © 2003 by L'Association, Paris, France. Used by permission of Pantheon Books, a division of Random House, Inc.**

religions and modern, secular values. This contrast is established in the first chapter of the book as groups of veiled and unveiled women shout at each other in a public confrontation (see Figure 2). The tension between their philosophies is neatly communicated by the diametrically opposed faces and the binary color palette, but it is also implicit in the related caption: "There were demonstrations for and against the veil."[9] The conflict is reduced to a simple either/or equation: one is either for the veil or for freedom. Similarly, a page later, Marjane-as-narrator tells readers, "Deep down I was very religious but as a family we were very modern and avant-garde."[10] The use of the word *but* is revealing, as it implies a tension or opposition: religion is fundamentally incompatible with modernity. Again, the point is also made in pictorial terms: below the caption, symbols of the realms of religion (a black arabesque on a white ground) and science (white gears on a black ground) are placed over her two shoulders, as though they were competing alternatives. Importantly, though, Satrapi once more suggests that these dualisms are not merely Iranian. In the second half of the book, two exceptional oversized panels separated by no more than a few pages depict the interior of an Austrian church — staid, architectonic, and static — and an anarchist party — buoyant, kinetic, and energetic.[11] Through contrasts such as these, *Persepolis* advances a central dualism that construes public religious life as confining (or even oppressive) and conventional, while secular life is portrayed as loose and flexible.

But a dualistic view of the world, Satrapi reminds us, is not her own invention. Instead, she gestures towards other dualistic philosophies and relates her own narrative mode to established systems of thought. At several points, *Persepolis* refers to Marxist principles and to what the narrator calls "the dialectical materialism of my comic strips"; indeed, as a little girl Marjane is fond of Marxism and its accent upon large opposed historical forces.[12] But the young Marjane is also an enthusiastic reader of Zarathustra (or Zoroaster), the ancient Persian prophet. The first three rules of her childhood creed were rooted in his teachings, and she "wanted . . . to celebrate the traditional Zarathustran holidays."[13] It is therefore worth remembering that Zoroastrianism (also sometimes called Mazdaism), a Persian religious tradition rooted in the teachings of Zarathustra, is also dualistic. Zarathustra posited a single god, Ahura Mazda, but he also held that Mazda was actively opposed by Ahriman, an agent of chaos and falsehood. The resulting struggle between these two irreconcilable forces, argued Zoroaster, shaped world history.[14] By openly referring to the ideas of Marx and Zarathustra at the beginning of her book, Satrapi not only indicates her childhood heroes, but she also relates the tensions of 1970s Iran to broader philosophical contexts. Mazda and Ahriman, bourgeoisie and proletariat, fundamentalism and liberalism: the structure of *Persepolis* is rooted in established, relevant philosophies of conflict.

Artistic Strategies in *Persepolis*

But is *Persepolis*'s interest in dualism unusual in its genre? A comparison with a relevant moment in a graphic memoir published two years before *Persepolis* can help to clarify this issue. At one point in *Persepolis*, the narrator tells us that, shortly after the revolution, "The way people dressed became an ideological sign. There were two kinds of women. There were also two sorts of men."[15] The assertion, like the related images of fundamentalist and "modern" women and men, is curtly binary; it leaves no room for nuance or compromise, but instead offers an analysis organized around two poles — a point made concrete by the hard lines that separate the fundamentalists from their modern counterparts. The two panels are typical of *Persepolis*'s dualistic analysis, but they differ considerably from a comparable passage in Joe Sacco's *Palestine*, a 2001 graphic memoir in which Sacco travels through the Occupied Territories to record the views of Palestinians in the early 1990s. At one point, Sacco interviews a number of Muslim women about current

Figure 3. **Palestinian women offer opinions regarding the veil.** Excerpt from *Palestine* by Joe Sacco, © 2002 by Fantagraphics Books.

attitudes towards the veil — which, it is rumored, Hamas is attempting to require. The women, in answering, offer a range of reasons for wearing the veil (see Figure 3), and the variety of their explanations suggests a broad complexity that is simply repressed by Satrapi's insistence upon two types of women.[16]

This contrast between *Persepolis* and *Palestine* can be meaningfully extended, for the two works are also very different in visual terms. Throughout his book, Sacco's irregular (and often trapezoidal) frames, powerful diagonals, rapid changes in viewing angle and scale, and reliance upon images that exceed their frames or bleed off the page all create a nervous energy that communicates the narrator's uneasiness and trepidation as he travels into unfamiliar and potentially dangerous areas. His nuanced rendering of material details and specific textures and his wide variety of shading techniques precisely convey the physical squalor of Palestinian dwellings and refugee camps. Satrapi's drawings, on the other hand, are consistently and conventionally framed, suggesting an implicit distance between the depicted events and the world of the reader.[17] The physical environments in *Persepolis* are generally indicated only cursorily, as the author seems more interested in archetypal conflicts than in specific settings. *Persepolis* also eschews complex shading, as Satrapi uses a brush and India ink to depict a world that is both figuratively and literally composed of black and white — as in the image, discussed above, of the groups of women chanting for and against the veil. Such artistic decisions allow Satrapi to create a world in which there are only two types of women and in which the dichotomy between institutionalized religion and secular modernism is distinct.

If her palette helps Satrapi in evoking a dualistic world, so too does her judicious use of frontal and profile figures. For the most part, she renders her figures in variations on a three-quarters view: readers see them at an angle. Occasionally, though, she departs from this norm and offers strict frontal or profile views that carry a resulting intensity and a specific set of visual associations. To put it differently, the infrequency of strict frontal and profile figures in *Persepolis* only intensifies the significance of those examples, as the absoluteness of the poses often implies a character's extreme emotional state or the drama of a particularly important narrative moment. In a handful of cases, for example, Satrapi uses the frontal view to imply the unusual vulnerability of the figure represented: in one especially stirring moment, Marjane and her deeply emotional parents are shown frontally as they listen, crying, to the forbidden Iranian national anthem.[18] At several other points, frontality denotes resoluteness: figures making proclamations, for instance, are depicted frontally in a way that accents the unwavering confidence of the speaker.[19] Finally, Satrapi sometimes uses frontality to indicate sanctity: Marjane's beloved uncle Anoosh is first introduced to us in a frontal view.[20] Along with the disk of radiating light that glows behind him like a halo, the frontal pose suggests his virtuosity in a young Marji's eyes. Frontality can imply a range of associations in *Persepolis*, but it commonly indicates extremity: extreme emotion, extreme public confidence, or extreme virtue.

Satrapi also repeatedly uses strict profile views to convey ominous authority and negative power, or (in combination) to suggest either overt conflict or confrontation. On the first page of the book, a teacher is shown in profile as she commands her students to don the veil, and the Islamic Revolution is condensed into a crowd of gesturing figures in profile. Later, the guardians of the revolution who loom over Marjane as they examine her button and her sneakers are depicted in profile (again, see Figure 1). So, too, are a heartless Iranian hospital director who refuses to authorize care for an ill patient, and the Austrian nun who infuriates Marjane by insulting Iranians.[21] Profile views in *Persepolis* often indicate blunt, ungenerous power, conflict, or even violence. But Satrapi also occasionally opposes profile views in a single panel to generate a sharp sense of conflict between two positions. Again, the public debate regarding the veil (see Figure 2) offers a good example, as does a subsequent pair of panels in which demonstrators and soldiers are depicted in profile facing one another.[22] The opposed profile views imply strict opposition; such images offer no sense of mediation or compromise.[23]

Satrapi employs what might be called a rudimentary semiotics of pose, as strict frontal and profile views are used to suggest distinct qualities. Such a strategy is hardly unique to *Persepolis*, however. In his *Words and Pictures*, published in 1973, the art historian Meyer Schapiro collects an array of examples of frontal and profile depictions in the history of art and seeks standard associations or meanings for these poses. Frontal depictions, Schapiro argues, have often been used by artists to suggest holiness or transcendence, while profile views commonly connote evil. Satrapi's decisions to depict her revered uncle Anoosh frontally or to show the sneering guardians of the revolution in profile are therefore grounded in ancient precedent. So, too, is her occasional opposition of profile views to generate conflict. As Schapiro observes, "One could also achieve a powerful expression of polar meanings in opposing to each other two profiles."[24] Indeed, in his deeply enjoyable *Making Comics*, Scott McCloud thoughtfully illustrated the theme of conflict with two opposed profiles.[25]

But perhaps one could go further still. If *Persepolis*'s use of profile and frontal depictions draws on well-established artistic traditions, it could also be seen as having a specifically local relevance. Satrapi's judicious use of these poses links the visual style of her narrative to both Persian artistic traditions and to the ancestors of the modern comic book. Consider the Persian aspect first: the most common figural pose in classical Persian painting is the three-quarters view, the vast majority of figures in traditional Iranian paintings being rendered at this angle. Earlier Persian artists occasionally employed absolute frontal or profile views to indicate status and spirituality or conflict, however. For instance, a famous fourteenth-century copy of the *Shahnama*, or Book of Kings (the Iranian national epic composed in roughly 1,000), includes an exceptionally rare frontal image of an angel hovering above flames.[26] The pose communicates the figure's sanctity and neatly anticipates Satrapi's treatment of Anoosh. Similarly, fifteenth-century Persian paintings occasionally include intense battle scenes in which opposed animals or figures are shown in contrasting profiles.[27] These opposed camels, horses, and soldiers express the intensity of their fight through their pose and are the direct ancestors of Satrapi's demonstrators — or, perhaps, the Iranians who protest in profile in *Persepolis* are the descendants of a much earlier generation of warriors, a theme implicit in Marjane's father's claim that "[a]fter a long sleep of 2,500 years, the revolution has finally awakened the people."[28]

If Satrapi's characters evoke Persian ancestors, her visual style can also be related to some of the ancestors of modern graphic novels. One of the earliest images reproduced in David Kunzle's celebrated *History of the Early Comic* is an English woodcut, likely executed shortly after 1500, that depicts the *Pietà* framed by a series of figures and details related to the Passion (see Figure 4).[29] Granted, this early, overtly religious image had a very different intended purpose and audience than *Persepolis*, and as David Carrier reminds readers, "Comparing such inherently different visual art forms as comics and old-master paintings without hidden bias is tricky."[30] Nonetheless, a series of formal similarities between *Persepolis* and the English woodcut can still be seen as reinforcing comparable

Figure 4. Lamentation, with surrounding details, from a fifteenth-century woodcut. Oxford, Bodleian Library, MS Rawl.D.403, f. 1 (Courtesy Bodleian Library, Oxford).

goals. Beyond their shared interest in the *Pietà*— the subject, again, that Marjane renders in her art school exam — the two works both use heavy outlines and simplified compositions. In a brief discussion of Satrapi's style, moreover, Paul Gravett once referred to "the bold simplicity of her woodcut-style drawings."[31] Furthermore, both works use a combination of images and text and a set of simplified symbols to make a complex narrative easily legible: in the woodcut, central narrative objects such as the chalice from which Jesus served wine at the Last Supper, and in *Persepolis*, overdetermined chapter headings such as "The Wine." The woodcut even uses a semiotics of pose that is comparable to Satrapi's; while most of the figures in the image are depicted in three-quarters view, a fully frontal image of Jesus's face, imprinted on the Veronica cloth, occupies the center of the upper register. There are also two figures depicted in profile: a Jew in the top register spits towards Christ and, at the bottom of the image, Judas betrays Jesus by kissing him. As in *Persepolis*, then, frontality indicates sanctity, and profile views suggest violence. In a range of ways, *Persepolis* draws on visual traditions native to the earliest ancestors of the modern comic book.

Satrapi may or may not have known the English woodcut, and she may or may not have seen reproductions of the Berlin *Shahnama* before drawing *Persepolis*. Ultimately, however, the visual style of *Persepolis* is rooted in a series of artistic decisions that not only accent the importance of contrast and dualism (through a dichotomous palette and opposed profile views), but also clearly relate to established traditions— including Iranian and graphic traditions.[32] As a result, *Persepolis* is firmly rooted in an art historical past that is relevant to its narrative and its medium. Its visual style recalls the earlier history of a region and of an art form, and the book describes longstanding cultural dualisms or divisions. This is especially meaningful in a book that presents Iranian history as constantly present and oppressive: "2,500 years of tyranny and submission," as Marjane's father phrases it at another point.[33] The final task, then, is to consider how Satrapi describes the dissolution of this oppressive period and the resolution of the dualisms that she has established.

Resolution: Complexity and Evolution

Although much of *Persepolis*— the evocations of Marx and Zarathustra, the stark oppositions of black and white and of profile views — seems concerned with creating a world of stark dualisms, there are also some important ways in which the book urges the reader beyond a simply dichotomous worldview. Even as the fundamentalism of the regime and the secular liberalism of Marjane's teenaged friends are contrasted, Satrapi quietly indicates that the distance between these two poles may in fact not be that great. Typically, the point is made graphically: on one remarkable and jarring page, readers see the bodies of teenaged soldiers ("young kids," the caption says) hurled upwards by the force of exploding mines and, just below, the kinetic twists of Marjane and her teenaged friends at a dance party.[34] One scene depicts gruesome violence and the other aerobic joy, but the comparable poses of the figures in the two scenes emphasize a basic similarity: the actors in each are mere teenagers. Furthermore, the teenagers in each scene pursue cheap jewelry: the soldiers cling to the painted plastic keys that will supposedly allow them into Paradise while the teenaged Marjane prides herself on her necklace of "chains and nails." Both martyrs and partygoers, in other words, are youngsters chasing trinkets.

The apparently stark choice between death and life, or between fundamentalism and amoralism, is cast as a false one — as a creation of Marjane's young mind and of an immature Iranian Republic. Much as Marxism and Zoroastrianism posit an initial clash between opposed forces but ultimately argue for a synthesis or a resolution, *Persepolis* finally seems to do the same. Late in the book, in a scene set in 1991, Marjane's narrative voice notes, "My friends and I had evolved. I had tempered my Western vision of life and they, for their part, had moved away from tradition."[35] The absolute dichotomies that characterize much of *Persepolis* begin to break down on both a narrative and a visual level. They further erode at a critical point later in the book, when a deeply nervous Marjane appears before the mullah for her ideological test.[36] Intriguingly, the mullah is depicted differently than most of the other figures of religious authority in *Persepolis*. Instead of being shown frontally or in profile, he is initially drawn in an unusual over-the-shoulder three-quarters view. The reason for this exceptional pose soon becomes clear; he is an unusually open-minded man — or, as the caption tells readers, "a true religious man."

What does that phrase mean, exactly? In its immediate context, it seems to imply Marjane's relieved gratitude for the mullah's willingness to look past the rigid terms of dogma and to accept her idiosyncratic form of piety; he passes her despite her unorthodox views. In a larger context, however, it also implies a transcendence of the rote dichotomy inherent in earlier portions of the book. The mullah does not merely see in terms of whites and blacks, and he does not instinctively condemn all variations from a norm. Instead, he seems willing to weigh cases on an individual basis, recognizing local complexities and partial virtues. He sees, in other words, in the same less-than-absolute manner in which he is depicted. In this sense, he parallels the adult Satrapi, who observed in an interview, "It would be so much easier to say [all mullahs] are shit. My life would be easier. But everything is so much more complex. There is so much good in bad, and so much bad in good."[37]

With such an assertion in mind, the larger logic of *Persepolis* suddenly snaps into focus. True religion, for Satrapi, is not the totalizing, absolutizing world view of Islamic fundamentalism, Catholic dogma, or amoral liberalism. Indeed, by the end of *Persepolis*, each of these is seen as a potentially oppressive system that yields conformity more often than thoughtful self-awareness. True religion, by contrast, seems to involve an ultimately individual combination of faith and a rational acceptance of complexity. Similarly, a rich understanding of history, Satrapi suggests, depends not upon simple dualisms, but rather upon the recognition that dichotomies are illusory products of childhood and ignorance that must be replaced with complexity.

But how to acquire such a sense? In the penultimate chapter, the narrator tells readers (while the adult Marjane, shown in three-quarters view, reads), "I arrived at my usual conclusion. One must educate oneself."[38] Education, for Satrapi, lies not in the total acceptance (or knee-jerk rejection) of any extant system of thought; instead, it lies in a selective, measured, and finally individual response to a wide range of systems. It thus represents a sort of synthesis, involving familiarization with traditional ideas, but also the willingness to criticize and reject those ideas. It means moving beyond unquestioning faith and blacks and whites and turning towards a moderated realm of less stark truths. Education is a tempering of extreme positions.

Persepolis is meant to be a part of such an education, and as we read it we parallel Marjane herself in acquiring an increasingly complex understanding of her world. But that world is not merely personal. Instead, Satrapi's eventual emphasis upon ambiguity rather than simple dichotomies can also be seen as a confident statement regarding the historical place of both the comic and the Iran that it depicts. In initially proposing a relatively absolute dualism, *Persepolis* recalls not only the titanic battles between superheroes and arch-villains that were a staple of early comics, but also the coarse propaganda of the Iranian regime in the years immediately following the revolution of 1979. Such a dualistic scheme, we learn, is endemic to nation and medium; it has its ancestors in opposed fighting camels and in profile images of Judas below frontal icons of Jesus. In emphasizing complexity, however, Satrapi seems to suggest that not only she, but also her native country and her chosen medium, can now deal with difficult and sophisticated themes, transcending the relatively simplistic dualisms that characterized their earlier history and arriving at a richer and a more diverse spectrum of perspectives.

Notes

1 Marjane Satrapi, *The Complete Persepolis* (New York: Pantheon, 2004), 133, panels 1–6.
2 Satrapi, 74, panel 7.
3 Satrapi, 75, panel 4.
4 Satrapi, 74, panel 4.
5 Satrapi, 109, panel 2.
6 Satrapi, 178, panel 7.
7 Satrapi, 177, panel 5, and 178, panel 5.
8 Satrapi, 281, panel 3.
9 Satrapi, 5, panel 1.
10 Satrapi, 6, panel 1.
11 Satrapi, 171, panel 3, and 185.
12 Satrapi, 12, panel 6, and 53, panel 9.
13 Satrapi, 7, panel 3.
14 Gherardo Gnoli, "Zoroastrianism," *The Encyclopedia of Religion*, ed. Mircea Eliade (New York: MacMillan, 1987), 15:579–91.
15 Satrapi, 75, panels 1–2.
16 Joe Sacco, *Palestine* (Seattle: Fantagraphics Books, 2002), 139–40.
17 As Debbie Notkin has noted, Satrapi's "panels vary in size, but not in shape, and each is contained within a box; the form is conventional and simple." Debbie Notkin, "Growing Up Graphic," *The Women's Review of Books* 16/9 (June 2003): 8.
18 Satrapi, 83, panel 4. Other relevant examples appear on pages 53 and 64.
19 See, for example, Satrapi, 40, panel 3.
20 Satrapi, 54, panel 3.
21 Satrapi, 133, panels 3–6, 121, panel 7, and 177, panel 4.
22 Satrapi, 18, panels 2–3.
23 Admittedly, some of Satrapi's profile views are less charged than others: she sometimes uses opposed profile views to denote conversation, for example, or to indicate emotional intimacy.
24 Meyer Schapiro, *Words and Pictures: On the Literal and the Symbolic in the Illustration of a Text* (The Hague: Mouton, 1973), 45. For assertions regarding the particular values of frontal and profile forms, see 32 and 44.
25 Scott McCloud, *Making Comics: Storytelling Secrets of Comics, Manga, and Graphic Novels* (New York: Harper, 2006), 150.
26 Berlin, Staatsbibliothek Preussischer Kulturbesitz, Diez album, f. 71, page 28v.

27 In a fifteenth-century Iranian drawing of fighting camels, for example (Berlin, Staatsbibliothek Preussischer Kulturbesitz, Diez album f. 73, page 67, n. 6), the two animals are depicted in absolute profile, underlining their violent opposition. Similarly, in a Persian painting of a battle scene in a *Shahnama* now in the Bodleian Library in Oxford, enemy horses are shown in profile as they charge towards one another (ff. 6r-7v).

28 Satrapi, 11, panel 1.

29 David Kunzle, *The Early Comic Strip: Narrative Strips and Picture Stories in the European Broadsheet from c.1450 to 1825* (*History of the Early Comic*, vol. 1) (Berkeley: University of California Press, 1973).

30 David Carrier, *The Aesthetics of Comics* (University Park: Penn State University Press, 2000), 93.

31 Paul Gravett, *Graphic Novels: Stories to Change Your Life* (New York: Collins Design, 2005), 71.

32 To play the contrarian, one might ask: couldn't the same be said of many contemporary comics? Might not simplified compositions, consistent frames, and a black and white palette simply be features typical of comics, rather than strategies meaningfully derived from an earlier visual tradition? Well, not quite: a quick survey of relevant examples implies that such a view is reductive or oversimplistic. Even works close in style to Satrapi's ultimately fail to offer completely satisfying analogies, which suggests the singularity of her visual vocabulary. Ted Rall's engrossing *To Afghanistan and Back: A Graphic Travelogue* (ComicsLit, 2002), for example, also sets black-and-white images into a series of standardizing frames, but the predominance of text and the many strongly patterned grounds in his work represent a marked difference from Satrapi's style.

33 Satrapi, 11, panel 2.

34 Satrapi, 102.

35 Satrapi, 312, panel 2.

36 Satrapi, 284, panels 2–4.

37 Annie Tully, "An Interview with Marjane Satrapi," *Bookslut*, October 2004, http://www.bookslut.com/features/2004_10_003261.php.

38 Satrapi, 327, panel 6.

POSTMODERN RELIGIOSITY

Machina Ex Deus:
Perennialism in Comics

G. WILLOW WILSON

READER ONCE ASKED ME IF I think knowledge is a human process. Though discussions about comics are often engaging and intelligent, I was surprised to get such an explicitly academic question. Like all pop culture, comics deal primarily in Zeitgeist: the images of here, the philosophy of now. The origin of knowledge, on the other hand, is a question scholars have been debating for millennia. The discussion has not changed much, not even to make itself more accessible to ordinary people. At first glance, such abstractions seem to have little to do with comics. But beneath the glossy exterior of the monthly pamphlet, in which Spider-Man's hair never grays and Mary Jane passes breezily from bell-bottoms to stilettos, there is an undercurrent of intellectual traditionalism. I was glad a perceptive reader had caught on to it. With a few caveats, I told him no, I don't think knowledge is a human process. "Are we calling this 'machina ex deus,' then?" another reader asked. If God — or knowledge — does not arise from the machine, the machine must arise from God. The idea seems anti-modern, but in the ultra-modern medium of sequential art, it is arguably the norm.

Some of the most popular and respected authors in comics — Neil Gaiman, Alejandro Jodorowsky, Peter Milligan — focus on those symbols and philosophical insights that occur over and over in human history, seemingly independent of culture, time, and geography. In the worlds they create, these symbols live lives unhinged from the meanings humanity ascribes to them; they are drawn not from our imaginations, but from the supernatural architecture that supports reality. In Gaiman's masterpiece *The Sandman*, Dream wanders the earth as a man, here called Morpheus, there Kai'Ckul, his essential nature unchanging. Jodorowsky's genre-defining *Incal* graphic novels use ancient symbolism and sacred geometry to tell a sci-fi epic. Shade the Changing Man, Milligan's brilliant re-imagining of a 60s-era Steve Ditko character, is sent to Earth from the aptly named planet Meta, and has the power to communicate with and manipulate the simulacra of our world. For each of these authors, myths, symbols, and traditions of sacred knowledge are real in the truest sense of the word. Sacred knowledge is not generated by human attempts to understand the world; rather, knowledge itself generates that understanding.

When I spoke to Milligan at a recent comics convention, he was hard at work on a new series personifying Greek myths. We got into a conversation about "primitive" myth traditions, some of the darkest of which — Oedipus, Saturn, Beowulf — seem increasingly relevant in today's war and disaster-ridden world. "They were tapped into something," Milligan said of ancient peoples. "Today we are obsessed with the individual — controlling our destinies, asserting our identities, that sort of thing. Then when we encounter unexpected tragedy, we're at a loss. It's alien to our vision of the way reality functions. But it wasn't to them. They saw into that darkness and loss of control and they came back with something."

That something, according to twentieth-century perennialist philosopher René Guénon, is a "higher order": pure knowledge, derived not from modern experimental science but from its original, supernatural source.[1] Of special significance to comics, Guénon posits that "symbolism is the means best adapted to the teaching of truths of a superior order, both religious and metaphysical."[2] Comics combine two potent forms of Guénon's higher-order symbolism: the ideographic (words) and the synthetic (pictures). Used together, these two varieties of symbolism can recreate the spiritual experience once central to the transmission of higher knowledge.

In that vein, writer-magician Grant Morrison once posited that comics are "hypersigils" — syncretic symbol-sets that influence the very reality on which they are modeled.[3] In other words, comics function like spells or prayers: they are built out of pictures and words with perennial, transcendent significance, and the reader, like a spiritual initiate, actualizes them. When Morrison first made this suggestion in the early 1990s, it was considered revolutionary. But taken in a perennialist context, his position is profoundly orthodox. As Guénon argues, "there are symbols that are common to the most diverse and widespread traditional forms, not as a result of 'borrowing,' which would in many cases be quite impossible, but because they really belong to the primordial tradition whence, directly or indirectly, all these forms have issued."[4] These symbols retain their spiritual potency regardless of the medium in which they appear.

Gathering What Is Scattered

Comics and graphic novels with an obvious perennialist message — often categorized as magical realism, but perhaps more correctly identified as real magic — usually begin with a ritual Guénon calls "gathering what is scattered." In the beginning, according to Guénon, there was unity of both knowledge and form, but in the process of creation, unity was shattered and became multiplicity.[5] To obtain higher knowledge is to recreate unity out of multiplicity. This act of gathering what is scattered is represented symbolically in countless sacrifice-and-resurrection myths: Isis gathering the dismembered body parts of Osiris, the retrieval and entombment of the crucified Christ, the sacrifice and reconstitution of Purusha in the Rig Vedas. Implicit in the gathering of what is scattered is the theme of second birth: the rebirth — usually into greater power, occultation, or enlightenment — of the re-membered.

Both *The Sandman* and *Shade: The Changing Man* begin and end with second births. In the opening issues of *Sandman*, Morpheus is captured, divested of his objects of power, and imprisoned. His unified reign over the Dreaming is shattered, resulting in worldwide outbreaks of nightmares, insomnia, and deathlike comas. Once he frees himself, he embarks on a quest to gather his scattered objects of power: a helmet, a ruby, and a bag of sand. Having regained them, his self-knowledge and influence are greater than they were before his imprisonment.

In *Shade*, the eponymous main character vanishes from his home planet Meta and is reborn into the electrocuted body of a serial killer on Earth. In this new body, powered by "the M Vest," Shade has the power to affect reality with his mind. Nearly the entire seventy-issue series is devoted, in some way or another, to gathering what is scattered: Shade's memories, his identity, and the unified reality that was shattered by his aberrant entrance into our world.

Both *Sandman* and *Shade* conclude with second births as well. In *The Kindly Ones*, Morpheus sacrifices himself to the Furies, and Daniel takes his place as lord of the Dreaming.[6] Shade resets Earth's timeline in order to save the woman he loves, and in doing so sacrifices his powers. He is reborn as an ordinary human being.[7] There is a suggestion in both these series that the search for knowledge is cyclical. Neither *Sandman* nor *Shade* "ends" in the traditional sense of the word; the authors simply draw the curtain closed as their newly reborn protagonists set out once more to gather what is scattered. It is this non-ending that separates these stories from secular literature most decisively. Like all perennial heroes, Morpheus and Shade do not — indeed cannot — truly die. Rather, they are resurrected in new forms, and in experiencing their resurrection we as readers are forced to look at the world from a wider angle. We gain a little inkling of Guénon's "pure" knowledge: the idea that truth is permanent, transcending death.

The Center of the World

"The Center is before all else the origin, the point of departure of all things," says Guénon. "It is the principal point, without form, without dimension, therefore indivisible, and consequently the only image that can be given to primordial Unity."[8] As discussed in the previous section, Unity is a perennialist term for the state before creation. There is, claims Guénon, a "real analogical relation" between Unity and its symbolic representation in sacred literature.[9] In Chilean polymath Alejandro Jodorowsky's *The Incal: The Epic Conspiracy*, the Center (also called the interior sun) is represented quite literally: it is a featureless fortress at the earth's core.[10] This is where the fates of all the characters are set in motion, and where they must return to resolve their crises. In *Shade*, the Center is the Area of Madness, a formless non-space where all things are possible.[11] In both stories, the Center is a point of incredible power.

Because the Center is the origin of all things — good as well as evil, death as well as birth — reaching it, and making the right decisions once it is attained, are matters of great anxiety. Neither the motley band of heroes in *The Incal* nor Shade reach the Center by choice; in both cases the protagonists are driven there by their enemies. The Center, so difficult for the mortal mind to encompass, is a refuge of last resort. The authors emphasize the risk of catastrophic failure. If the protagonists of *The Incal* err while inside "the interior sun," the world will be dominated by the autocratic forces of the Technopope and a grotesque overlord known as the Prezident, who clones himself to stay perpetually youthful. They corrupt the primordial tradition, attempting to gain power and immortality through artificial replication rather than gnosis. If Shade fails to relocate his disembodied self inside the Area of Madness, the "American Scream," a literal manifestation of the nation's insanity and paranoia, will continue its chilling rampage across the United States. The great potential for creation and change inherent in the Center leaves no room for error.

In both stories, the protagonists' journeys to the Center are successful. In *The Incal*, the main characters achieve unity through a hermetic ritual to rebalance the outside world.[12] Inside the Area of Madness, Shade is successfully reunified with himself. He recovers his memories and his identity, and because of this, he is able to remake the human body he inhabits in his own image.[13] Since they are successful, our heroes are able to leave the Center — rather than be consumed within it — through what Guénon calls "the Narrow Door." Represented in *The Incal* by a literal narrow door, and by a slender outline of Shade's own body in *Shade the Changing Man*, the Narrow Door is only open to those who have attained an advanced level of pure knowledge.[14] Symbolically, the characters emerge into a world they are now better able to understand and master.

The Heart and the Guardians of the Center

Closely associated with the Center is the Heart, the physical manifestation of its essence.[15] Archetypally symbolized by an inverted triangle,[16] it appears in global myth traditions as the Holy Grail, the World Egg of Nordic creation stories, and the Brahmanda of the Hindu Vedas. In *The Incal*, the heart is represented by the Incal itself: a tiny, radiant pyramid, a portable fragment of the interior sun, retaining some of the interior sun's formidable capacity to create and destroy. In *Shade*, the heart is the M-Vest, a portable manifestation of the Area of Madness adorned with an inverted triangle. Though both the Incal and the M-Vest are as burdensome as they are powerful, they maintain an important connection between the abstract unity of the Center and the physical, multiplex world. As the bearer of the M-Vest, Shade is what Guénon calls a "guardian of the Center," a living ambassador of primordial unity.[17] In *The Incal*, protagonist John Difool plays a similar role — with equal reluctance.

He acquires the Incal seemingly by accident, and spends a great deal of time resisting the destiny it reveals to him. Both Shade and John Difool are self-consciously cast as everymen; neither is famous, rich, unusually attractive, or free of mundane personality issues. They must be ordinary, since they represent the near-incomprehensible completeness of the Center to ordinary people.

Like Arthur and Excalibur or Frodo and the One Ring, when Shade and Difool accept the Heart — the manifestation of the Center and proxy source of its power — they are thrust into greater destinies. It is not a coincidence that Jesus, another guardian of the Center by perennialist reckoning, is referred to as having a "sacred heart." To be a guardian — or, as we variously call it, a once and future king, a ring-bearer, or a prophet — is to be both blessed and burdened. Unlike a philosopher, a guardian cannot retreat from the world to meditate in isolation. He or she must live in the world, fight in the world, and lead the world. Shade engages in pitched battles against the American Scream, putting his own life in danger to save Earth. Difool is constantly on the run from the forces of the Prezident and the Technopope. Their powers are derived from the Heart — the M-Vest and the Incal — but their tenacity is distinctly, imperfectly human. Guardianship is attended by violence and ostracism. But it is also the most potent reminder to humankind of the origin of all things, and the connection, through the primordial tradition, of the seen to the unseen.

Conclusions

Is there really only one single transcendent intellectual tradition, or is this just an amusing thought experiment based on a series of coincidences? If you make your criteria broad enough and abstract enough, you can prove — or seem to prove — almost anything. Biographers tell us that in life, Rene Guénon was a strange, erratic, and paranoid individual.[18] The school of thought he developed would indirectly influence the Aryan cult theology of the Nazis. Guénon had himself been inducted into half a dozen secret societies and initiatic orders, including several sects of Freemasonry and a Sufi brotherhood.[19] By any measure, it would be unwise to consider such a person a reliable intellectual guide. Yet Guénon's philosophy touches an intriguing nerve. There do seem to be symbols and philosophical insights that cross cultural and temporal boundaries, occurring over and over among peoples who often had no contact with one another. The concepts Guénon unpacks are too intellectual and precise to attribute to a psychological commonality of the Jungian variety. The Center and the resurrection of the sacrificed do not follow logically from universal human instincts to eat, sleep, reproduce, and run away from things with sharp teeth. Guénon's recurrent symbols speak not to a collective soul, but to a collective *mind*.

What's more, it seems as though many of these symbols are intuitive. While authors Grant Morrison, Alejandro Jodorowsky, and Neil Gaiman consciously incorporated comparative symbology into their works, it is not clear that Milligan did so in *Shade*. Was the design of the M-Vest, which perfectly embodies Guénon's "heart" sigil, intentional? And why is it that the average comic book reader need not be a scholar of metaphysics to understand the spiritual importance — and the intended meaning — of these recurring symbols? Could it be that Guénon, unstable though he was, stumbled close to the truth?

It is just possible. Guénon makes one logical error, which, had he avoided it, would have helped him prove his point. If all intellectual and spiritual traditions descend from a single "primordial" tradition, it would not be necessary to believe in that tradition in order to participate in it. Guénon pointedly refers to the sacred as a science, in other words, the study of evidence that exists independently of the observer and that does not change depending on who observes it. Thus, evidence of the "primordial tradition" should be observable to anyone. But Guénon was a committed anti-populist, and believed you had to be initiated into an established gnostic brotherhood (the more secretive, the better) in order to observe and understand the primordial tradition. He scoffed at the idea of "popular" symbols and mythology, saying "their origin, far from being popular, is not even human. What may be popular is uniquely the fact of their survival."[20]

But it is precisely the prevalence of archetypal symbol-sets in pop culture that suggests a primordial tradition. If all authors and artists are drawing on the same source, it should be impossible to avoid the tropes of this *sophia perennis*, this permanent wisdom. Far from diluting and bastardizing the primordial tradition, pop culture would thus represent its continued survival.

Grant Morrison agrees. "The point is not to believe," he says in his seminal essay "Pop Magic," "the point is to do."[21] If there is a primordial tradition, it doesn't need the protection of an elite vanguard in order to continue, just as DNA doesn't need the protection of trained scientists in order to replicate. The perennial tradition continues in pop culture as it continues in high culture, because like all immutable facts of nature, it does not require belief.

To me this is only logical, but I could not find a single Guénonian scholar who agreed with me. Professor Seyyed Hossein Nasr, arguably the most respected living perennialist, told me I was mistaken. "There is no arena of modern life where original meaning [of sacred symbology] is preserved," he said. "It's clear that there is interest — take the popularity of Tolkien, for example. The yearning to rediscover the sacred is still there. But there is no reference to transcendence." However, if there is any popular medium through which the primordial tradition *could* be communicated, Dr. Nasr thinks sequential art is a good bet. "In theory it's a possibility — you could take a series of images based on traditional methods of painting and drawing, and combine them with words that convey profound meaning. We would meditate on that, and the next frame would carry us from the previous theme to a new theme. This is possible."

I think it is not simply possible — I think it is already happening. Parallel to the traditionalist symbology in comics is a deep anti-clerical bias, suggesting that — consciously or unconsciously — writers of comics are out to steal the primordial tradition from the spiritual elite. In *Shade*, the Metan priests who send Shade to Earth are corrupt schemers bent on enforcing their own dogma and increasing their own power. In *The Incal*, the Technopope is a fanatical madman who insinuates himself into temporal politics. These books, along with Gaiman's *Sandman*, Morrison's *The Invisibles*, and many others, show us that transcendence *is* a popular phenomenon. Tradition does not belong solely to Guénon's elite. It is carried forward by many hands, both in comics and in the larger world of pop culture: our collective spiritual past made richer and more relevant as it moves into the future.

Notes

1 Rene Guénon, *Symbols of Sacred Science*, trans. Henry D. Fohr (Hillsdale, NY: Sophia Perennis, 2001), 1.
2 Guénon, 5.
3 Grant Morrison, *Book of Lies: The Disinformation Guide to Magick and the Occult*, ed. Richard Metzger (New York: Disinformation Company, 2003), 21.
4 Guénon, 26.
5 Guénon, 288.
6 Neil Gaiman et al., *The Sandman: The Kindly Ones* (New York: DC Comics/ Vertigo, 1996), 340–51.

7 Peter Milligan et al., *Shade: The Changing Man* #69 (New York: DC Comics/ Vertigo, 1996), 6–12.
8 Guénon, 57.
9 Guénon, 58.
10 Alejandro Jodorowsky and Moebius, *The Incal: The Epic Conspiracy* (Los Angeles: Humanoids/DC Comics, 2005), 114.
11 Peter Milligan et al., *Shade The Changing Man: The American Scream* (New York: DC Comics, 2006), 73.
12 Jodorowsky and Moebius, 138–43.
13 Milligan et al., 73–91.
14 Guénon, 259.
15 Guénon, 401.
16 Guénon, 208.
17 Guénon, 86.
18 Mark Sedgwick, *Against the Modern World: Traditionalism and the Secret Intellectual History of the Twentieth Century* (Oxford: Oxford University Press, 2004), 53, 73–5.
19 Sedgwick, 60, 82–3.
20 Guénon, 24.
21 Morrison, 19.

Conversion to Narrative:[1] Magic as Religious Language in Grant Morrison's *Invisibles*

MEGAN GOODWIN

> Truth speaks best in the language of poetry and symbolism.
>
> — Grant Morrison, *Say You Want a Revolution*

> Nothing is true; everything is permitted. Don't believe anything you read in this paper.[2]

THE INVISIBLES IS A MAGICAL piece of serial art. To be sure, the books are *about* magic: the protagonists are occult terrorists who work spells, shift realities, and invoke god-forms to disrupt alien attempts at controlling human consciousness. But what sets this series apart is that the books themselves *are* an act of magic. Author Grant Morrison wasn't just spinning yarns about postmodern spells and tragically hip sorcerers — he created the books as both tools for his own magical workings and as a large-scale introduction to magic itself.

By presenting magic prominently (though not exclusively) as a kind of religious language, Morrison used *The Invisibles* to illustrate chaos magic[3] as a pragmatic system of religious practice.[4] I use "religious language" in keeping with Webb Keane's theorization:[5] that is, religious language should be understood as linguistic practices that practitioners take as "marked or unusual."[6] These ways of using language suggest "entities or modes of agency" (god/dess/es, spirits, or simply the ability to act in ways) beyond quotidian experience, ontologically distinct from

258

the "everyday here and now."[7] In the context of *The Invisibles*, I suggest that magic often works for its practitioners — that is, both for Morrison and his characters — as a system of linguistic practices marked by a radical and extra-ordinary (i.e., heroic) degree of human agency.[8]

The Invisibles suggests heroic agency in its emphasis on the materiality of magical language. For both Morrison and for his characters, magic as religious language supersedes the performativity of speech acts.[9] The magician's words do not simply *do* things: they *are* things. In and through *The Invisibles*, language — understood in the context of these graphic novels as alphabet-based systems of written communication[10] — makes things happen, matter, become real.[11]

Morrison's Use of Magic

Grant Morrison's *The Invisibles* spanned six years (1994–2000) and seven collected volumes of graphic novels. What begins as a tale of postmodern magical freedom fighters pitted against the dark forces of constraint and conformity is quickly complicated: the good guys resort to savage acts of violence; the evil henchmen become humanized, pitiable. Every character is motivated by lofty intentions to morally questionable (often reprehensible) actions; and no one seems quite clear on which side he or she is on.

The challengingly non-linear narrative primarily follows the activities of one Invisibles' cell, comprised of King Mob, a bald chaos magician bearing a striking resemblance to Morrison himself; Ragged Robin, a red-headed psychic witch from the future; Boy, a former New York cop bent on revenging her brother's untimely (and uncanny) end; Lord Fanny, a transgender Brazilian *bruja*; Lady Edith Manning, a tantrically trained nonagenarian; Jim Crow, a trip-hop rock star who horses for the Vodou *lwa* Papa Ghede; and Jack Frost, a foul-mouthed Liverpool street urchin turned bodhisattva.[12] In the course of fifty-nine issues, this cell travels through time to rescue a fellow Invisible (the Marquis de Sade), steals an AIDS vaccine from a secret military base, defends an urban neighborhood from the assault of corporate-created crack zombies, and foils a plot to have a shoggoth ascend the British throne and doom the world to mental slavery. All these acts are made possible through the use of many different kinds of magic. Indeed, *The Invisibles* suggests that magic is more than a match for men with guns, the weather, the space-time continuum, hostile alien intelligence, and whatever else the universe can conjure.

More than simply narrating the utility of magic, Morrison embodied and performed his role as magician through the graphic novels. From 1994 to mid-2000, the series attempted to shift readers' ways of thinking, to expand their consciousnesses beyond binary modes of thought, and to demonstrate to those readers that they are capable of more than they ever imagined possible. As Morrison himself has said, *The Invisibles* is a spell for creating Invisibles.[13]

Grant Morrison's performance of magic in and through *The Invisibles* draws heavily from the work of Phil Hine, Peter J. Carroll, and other chaos magicians. Hine, author of the influential *Condensed Chaos: An Introduction to Chaos Magic*, presents chaos magic as both philosophy and system of practice.[14] Like Carroll before him, Hine suggests that nothing is impossible and that everything a practitioner thinks she knows is wrong. Chaos magic, Hine argues, makes it possible for an individual's will to effect change in the world — that is, if the would-be magician wants something enough and directs the energy of that wanting in the proper ways, she can change things. A magician can stand outside the system and direct her will toward changing herself and the world. This act of change through will is magic — a manifestation of radical and extra-ordinary (that is, again, heroic) agency.

Magic use is, of course, not limited to chaos magicians or even to broader traditions of Western esotericism. What sets this system of magic apart is the extent to which it has been influenced by chaos theory. As Hine explains, "Chaos Theory [. . .] points out the obvious: that one event can change those that follow in a way that can have a tremendous impact upon us."[15] In chaos magic, using a sigil (the artistic rendering of a written statement of desire or intent as a focal point for directing energy) or temporarily espousing a new belief system can have broad-reaching impact both on the self and on the world beyond.

An understanding of religions as systems of belief and practice — as tools, rather than as identities — is another key feature of chaos magic. Discussing chaos magic in a religious context requires some qualification, however. One cannot strictly call chaos magic a belief system, though it is a system of beliefs. Chaos magic rather treats religions — with all the complexity of their dogmas, rituals, sacred texts, and habits — as tools for helping the magician achieve her desires. It would be inaccurate to say that a chaos magician does not "believe in" the religious system she uses. But neither should religion be understood as a static part of the magician's identity. Beliefs and practices are multiple and mutable, changed at will and according to need. Chaos magic, then, might best be understood as a guide to working *with* religious beliefs and practices.

Magic as Religious Language

Morrison employed many aspects of chaos magic in writing *The Invisibles*. I am most interested, however, in the use of magic as religious language: the alphabetic-based communication that materializes the magician's will. In "Language and Religion," Webb Keane suggests that features of religious language "help make available to experience and thought the very ontological divides to which they offer themselves as a response."[16] Chaos magic's utilization of religious beliefs and practices likewise helps make certain aspects of reality and/or imagination available to the magician's experience and thought.

For Keane, the beliefs and actions comprising religion are both linguistically mediated; practitioners express beliefs through language, setting what is religious apart from "ordinary" experience or the everyday "here and now."[17] Language is also religious practice: religious linguistic practices (both formal, as in ritual, and mundane) construct forms of agency that are "expanded, displaced, distributed or otherwise different from — but clearly related to — what are otherwise available."[18] Keane suggests that religious language makes meaning of practitioners' lives through both practice and belief. Practitioners use religious language to acknowledge and invoke "entities" ("divine or spirit participants" in ritual) or modes of agency that would otherwise be unavailable.[19]

Following Keane's terms, Morrison narrates chaos magic in *The Invisibles* as a kind of religious language. The language of magic makes visible and reifies the series' ontological divide — conformist surrender versus heroic agency and independent thought. Throughout these books, chaos magic provides a linguistic structure for working *with* religious traditions. The Invisibles use language to express beliefs (King Mob declares his allegiance to the Hindu deity Ganesh), acknowledge and invoke "divine or spirit participants" (Jim Crow's invocation of Vodoun Papa Ghede), and realize heroic agency (the group's successful assault on the Dulce military base using a Native American rain dance, a Wiccan pentacle, and masturbation to focus intent). Magic as religious language makes possible extra-ordinary forms of voluntaristic action.[20] Keane's concept of religious language, like Morrison's portrayal of chaos magic, is not strictly belief-based; rather, chaos magic as religious language makes belief and practice meaningful.[21]

Throughout *The Invisibles*, magic as religious language represents imaginative restraint and creative potentiality. Words allow the Invisibles to magically trick, disable, and ultimately kill their opponents. Naming, and the knowing of names, figures prominently. Most importantly, the expanded alphabet of the alien intelligence, Barbelith, reveals the true nature of the universe and allows the characters to transcend language altogether. For Morrison's characters, language is a magical tool, a magical weapon, and ultimately the key to their salvation/enlightenment.

Names are the earliest and clearest use of magic as religious language throughout the series. Each member assumes a code name upon joining the Invisibles; these code names act as emotional aggregates.[22] In Dane/Jack Frost's case, his code name invokes the childhood bogeyman who emerged when his father left the family. The code names of both prominent African-American characters, Jim Crow and Boy, invoke racial stereotypes and transform them into identity-specific archetypes. Crow specifically works within a Haitian Vodou magical paradigm. Boy, formerly Lucille Butler, problematizes both racial and gender stereotypes with her code name and identity. The knowledge of someone's true name confers power to the knower: Satan refuses to give his name throughout the series, while Dane/Jack Frost defeats of the King of All Tears just by knowing the King's true name.[23] Names do not simply describe — they create identities and define the limits of each character.

Magic words in *The Invisibles* further demonstrate the materiality of religious language. Dane creates a magic word (TOTEP, plucked from the television screen) to kill the men chasing him.[24] During her first initiation, Fanny "learns the secret common language of shamans — that language whose words do not describe things but *are* things" from a flower in the garden of life and death.[25] Mr. Skat uses the language of the Nommo, "the *true* tongue; the one *we* hear in our *dreams*, the words that make *things* happen" in skatting away Edith's gun.[26] Sir Miles describes the English alphabet itself as a magic word, saying to the captured King Mob:

> Have you ever wondered why we talk of "spelling?" There *is* a spell word, an "abracadabra," implanted in the brain of every English-speaking child, the root mantra of restriction, the secret name of

a mighty hidden *demon.* Eybeesee-dee ee-eff-geeaitcheye Jaykayell-
emenn-ohpeequeue-are-ess-tee-youveedouble-you-ex-wyezed . . . that
name and all the names it generates were designed to set limits upon
humanity's ability to express abstract thought.[27]

Sir Miles suggests that language itself determines what it is possible to
think — if the mind cannot grasp something linguistically, it cannot
grasp the concept at all.[28] Language is necessary to make things real;
language itself is a kind of magic in the series. Thus magic words, even
the alphabet itself, work to materialize language in *The Invisibles.*
Morrison plays with the ambivalence of language, its ability to create
and constrain. Language-as-constraint is made particularly grotesque.
Sir Miles tortures King Mob using the supernatural chemical Key 17,
which makes written words seem real — thus the word "finger" on
several note cards appears to King Mob as his own severed fingers. Sir
Miles insists, "what you see depends entirely on the words you have to
describe what you see. Nothing exists unless *we say* it does."[29] Likewise,
Coyote triggers horrific false memories in Boy by exposing her to the
"real" 64-letter alphabet (see Figure 1). The same alien language knocks
King Mob's cell out with a "viral" word and stops their assault on the
hidden base by inducing auto-critique: King Mob stops shooting and
begins talking about the impotence of revolutionary hero characters,
and Fanny laments drag's failure to disrupt essentialized gender roles.[30]
Coyote explains, "We're able to *do* these things to your mind because
we have the keys to a *wider* world which you have not been *educated*
to comprehend. There *are . . . things* all around. Things you never *see*

Figure 1. **Coyote explains the alien metalanguage, ubersprech, to Boy. The letter
"triple-you" is visible to the far left of the panel.**
Grant Morrison, *The Invisibles: Counting to None* (New York: DC Comics, 1999), 163.

because you don't have the *words*, you don't have the *names*."[31] Helga, the Invisibles' "logonaut," creates Key 64/logoplasm, which makes words real, from "the twisted language of the angels."[32] King Mob finally kills the King-of-All-Tears, the would-be global tyrant, with a word. After dosing the Archon with logoplasm, King Mob shoots the shoggoth with a gun that fires, not bullets, but a flag that says "pop"[33] (see Figure 2). The materiality of magical language often functions as a tool of cruel restraint and destruction throughout these graphic novels.

Magic as religious language also represents the potential for radical creativity, however. Using technology that allows her to float in an "ocean of living words," Robin literally writes herself into the story of the Invisibles[34] (see Figure 3). As King Mob later explains to Mason, "Robin read a story called '*The Invisibles*' and wrote herself a *part* in it until she realized it *was* all *real*. That's how *magic* happens."[35] When Robin stumbles across the oracular head of John the Baptist, she discovers that it speaks an "eternal language . . . the language of ecstasy and dreams. The primal tongue of fire." Satan explains that the head speaks with "the original voice of the unconscious mind and everyone who hears it interprets it differently. Everyone hears what they need to hear."[36] He asks her to imagine "what kind of world might we make where such a language would be the common tongue," foreshadowing the infinite possibility realized in the Barbelith's metalanguage.[37]

Magic as religious language also functions as a tool to transcend consensus reality in *The Invisibles*. The eternal language of John the Baptist's oracular head, the "ubersprech" Helga strives to decipher, the language

Figure 2. **King Mob kills the King of All Tears with a word. "A bullet in the right place . . . is no substitute for the real thing."**
Grant Morrison, *The Invisibles: The Invisible Kingdom* (New York: DC Comics, 2002), 280–1.

of the Nommo, Fanny's shamanic language, the alien language Mason learns during his abduction — all these employ "emotional aggregates," in which "one word, one sound, represents a whole complex of ideas and associations and feelings."[38] The intelligent satellite Barbelith uses the 64-letter alphabet of ubersprech to "wake up" the Invisibles. "Waking up" entails the recognition that humans *created* Barbelith to save themselves, to teach them that humanity had linguistically constructed the constraints of consensus reality. Ultimately, Barbelith self-destructs to create the supercontext, in which everyone communicates through the meta-language of emotional aggregates. In the Invisibles' utopian future, humanity transcends language. Words no longer have to signify things or even materialize — all communication happens through the direct transmission of emotion and intent.

Figure 3. **Robin in the Ganzfeldt Tank, "a warm ocean of living words," writing herself into Sir Miles' story, The Invisibles.**

Grant Morrison, *The Invisibles: Kissing Mister Quimper* (New York: DC Comics, 2000), 155, 173.

The supercontext collapses opposition. "You identify with everything in the universe that is *not-self* and dissolve the existential alienation dilemma in *unity*. All is one and several is none."[39] Information from the supercontext, such as Barbelith provided through ubersprech, initially manifests as "not-self" — the body rejects it as something literally alien, which is why Helga vomits while trying to learn the language.[40] The creation of the supercontext dissolves this boundary between self and not-self. This is, at last, the message of *The Invisibles*. It isn't a story about two opposing sides — the Invisibles and their adversaries are moving toward the same end. The goal of *The Invisibles*, then, is to use language to move the reader beyond linguistic constructs, toward realization of a broader, non-consensus reality. All binaries (good/evil, right/wrong, material/immaterial) are ultimately dissolved into meaninglessness.

The series ends with Dane directly addressing the reader, explaining: "We made gods and jailers because we felt small and ashamed and alone . . . we let them try us and judge us and, like sheep to slaughter,

Figure 4. **Jack's last sentence expands beyond the page, extending *The Invisibles* hypersigil into the world beyond.**
Grant Morrison, *The Invisibles: The Invisible Kingdom* (New York: DC Comics, 2002), 286.

we allowed ourselves to be . . . *sentenced*. SEE! NOW! OUR SENTENCE IS *UP*."[41] (See Figure 4.) Note the multiple valences of "sentence" here. Language, words — sentences — created consensus reality within the universe of *The Invisibles*. That reality, in turn, constrained, sentenced, and imprisoned Morrison's characters. With the collapse of language and the conclusion of the series, the sentence — as both words and a system of constraint — comes to end.

Magic in Dialogue

Of course, Morrison's characters are not only talking among themselves. As I suggested in my introduction, Morrison did not merely write about magic; rather, the series itself was an act of magic. Morrison used *The Invisibles* as both a magical tool and an illustration of his own religiosity. What began as a public forum for the author's philosophical and spiritual ruminations became a program for global paradigm shifts. Morrison finally intended *The Invisibles* to "expand and destroy consensus reality."[42] Similarly, Phil Hine suggests that "the magical revival is powered by . . . the need for escape routes from the perceived tyranny of Paramount Reality."[43] Grant Morrison's work with *The Invisibles* represents several such escape routes, both from the Paramount Reality of what is possible within serial art and from the (perceived) reality of what it is possible to do with serial art.

Morrison pushed the boundaries of graphic novels from the first issue of *The Invisibles*. I have discussed the subject matter at length; however, the artistic renderings of Morrison's story are also of note. The books shift serial art paradigms in their use of a fifth printing color (again evident from issue 1), use of negative space to create the logo, and "artist jams" whose distinct styles are meant to indicate shifting realities in a single issue.[44] Likewise, the art throughout the book makes use of Hindu, Buddhist, Vodou, Brujería, Christian, Native American, and popular culture imagery — an artistic rendering of chaos magic's religious multiplicity. Even the title can be read in multiple ways: the cell strives for anonymity, invisibility; Vodoun spirits (or *lwas*), are also known as Invisibles; and Morrison credits Terrence McKenna's *Invisible Landscape* as the origin of his super-context concept.

The Invisibles began, Morrison reports, as a forum for his personal philosophical inquiries and magical agendas. He wanted to gather a community of like-minded, magically aware individuals in a time when communities were far harder to come by, before internet technologies (and thus internet communities) were more prevalent.[45] Morrison began the comic as a spell, a "hypersigil"[46] meant to create Invisibles, magic-using different-thinkers. He focused his intent in a sigil drawn on his chest and charged the spell with the energy from a bungee jump.[47]

In many ways, *The Invisibles* in general and the King Mob character specifically got their start as Morrison's self-focused spellwork. In addition to mystical community building, Morrison was creating a character with whom he could identify and whom he wanted to emulate. He shaved his head soon after he began writing about the (bald) King Mob character (see Figure 5), did sigil work to bring someone who looked like Ragged Robin into his life, and incorporated many of his own behaviors into storyline and character.[48] King Mob's lung collapsed at the end of volume one during what Morrison calls a viral storyline; Grant Morrison's lung collapsed shortly after, during a bout with near-fatal septicemia.[49] In *The Invisibles*, King Mob attempts "to get over the loss of his girlfriend and the death of his cats by turning himself into a pop god with a gun."[50] Morrison attests that he got over the death of his cat and his personal emotional issues by embodying the King Mob character.

Morrison turned to spellwork again when sales slumped. In the now infamous letters column of Volume 1, #16, Morrison instructed readers on the creation of sigils. Again, a sigil is a stylized representation of the statement of intent that the magician focuses on to manifest her will. After explaining the making and use of sigils, Morrison asked for his readers' help. He instructed them to concentrate on the sigil printed in the column while masturbating during a set day, Thanksgiving 1995 — this column is now known as the "wankathon"[51] (see Figure 6).

Figure 5. **King Mob and Grant Morison.**
Left: Grant Morrison, *The Invisibles: Entropy in the U.K.* (New York: DC Comics, 2001), 131. Right: photo courtesy of http://www.grantmorrison.com (accessed 2 May 2009).

Masturbation was meant to clear the reader's mind and help focus intent[52] — here, the intent to keep Vertigo from dropping the comic. Morrison claims that the spell worked, though he attributes the aforementioned life-threatening septicemia to kickback energy from the wankathon. (Artist Phil Jimenez also claims partial credit for keeping the series going.[53])

Morrison's focus with *The Invisibles* began as primarily personal, but by the end of the series, he had far loftier goals. As I mentioned, *The Invisibles* was ultimately meant to "expand and destroy consensus reality." The final frame of *The Invisibles* ends with an off-panel quotation mark: "OUR SENTENCE IS UP.[54] Morrison intended this panel to extend the spell (that is, the hypersigil intended to create Invisibles and destroy consensus reality) into the world at large.[55]

Grant Morrison has said that there are as many different ways to read *The Invisibles* as there are readers for the comic.[56] I read *The Invisibles* as a work that primarily explores the power of magic as religious language. Morrison's words throughout the series affected both the way he thought and acted as well as the ways his readers continue to think and act in the wider world. The words and images worked on Morrison; they're intended to work on the reader as well.

Does the reading experience work as gnosis? Phil Hine closes his introduction to chaos magic with discussion of gnosis, or deep personal knowledge of spiritual mysteries. "Gnosis," he writes, "is not merely the act of understanding, it is understanding which impels you to act in a certain way. Thus as you work with magic, magic works upon you. Such is the nature of Chaos."[57] Perhaps Grant Morrison's intention for his *Invisibles* is to offer the possibility of such gnosis — this series of graphic novels impels its readers to think and more importantly to *act* in certain ways. Thus as the reader works with these books, the books work upon her.

Figure 6. **Wankathon sigil. Morrison instructed readers to masturbate while concentrating on this symbol. The energy released by their simultaneous orgasms was supposed to prevent the comic from being canceled.**

Grant Morrison, "London," *The Invisibles*, Vol. 1, #16 (Nov. 1995), Vertigo [DC Comics].

As I have shown, Morrison's narrative works upon his readers in specific ways. *The Invisibles* is a spell for creating Invisibles: magic-using free-thinkers, aware of their own heroic agency. The series demonstrates the plural utility for magic use and rewards attention to detail, particularly with regard to the materiality of language. An Invisible is aware of the linguistic terms that structure reality and, more importantly, of how to manipulate and shift those terms to disrupt and remake structure. At the last, Morrison's *Invisibles* illustrates the possibility of shaping the world to fit the magician's desire — as King Mob says, the Invisibles work toward "everyone getting exactly the kind of world they want . . . everyone including the enemy."[58]

This ambivalence is characteristic of Morrison's language, and ultimately of *The Invisibles* itself. In the end, Morrison offers his readers no explicit instructions — the series is a road map, a "door made of words."[59] Language constrains and structures both the characters' experiences and the ways in which the reader engages the story. But Morrison also uses words, letters — language — in unusual and disruptive ways: rendering words as art; using letters in non-word forms; and hinting at a reality that transcends linguistic structure. For Morrison, language is a tool to manifest will, constrained only by the magician's imagination. *The Invisibles* works to shift the reader's perception and signal the radical creative potential of magic as religious language.

Notes

1   The title is a nod to King Mob's narrative defeat of the King of All Tears: "the supercontext absorbs the King effortlessly, welcoming his quaint ferocity, converting it to narrative." Grant Morrison, *The Invisibles: The Invisible Kingdom* (New York: DC Comics, 2002), 281.
2   As the authors of *Anarchy for the Masses* note: "Don't believe anything you read in this book [is] a strange way to open, to be sure, but taking any interpretation of THE INVISIBLES as definitive is to miss the point altogether." Patrick Neighly and Kereth Cowe-Spigai, *Anarchy for the Masses: The Disinformation Guide to* The Invisibles (New York: Disinformation, 2003), 9.
3   Spellings of "magic(k)" vary among authors. Many writers on chaos magic adopt Aleister Crowley's spelling (i.e. magick), meant to distinguish the occult workings of a true magician from those of stage magicians. Regarding the spelling of magic with a "k," see Aleister Crowley's *Magick, Book IV* and *Magick in Theory and Practice*. *The Journal for the Academic Study of Magic* prefers "magic," however; my writing reflects that preference.
4   By focusing on language — words — here, I do not intend to minimize the consideration of magic as the material effects of *images*. Imagery, of course, is of equal import for scholarly engagement with serial art. While such an analysis is, unfortunately, beyond the scope of this essay, I suspect Morrison's

work would stand up equally well to a consideration of magic as religious imagery.

5 I'm taking Webb Keane far afield here, as readers familiar with *Christian Moderns* will no doubt recognize. However, the materiality Keane ascribes to semiotic ideologies is — as I shall argue — appropriate and insightful in conversations about graphic novels in general and *The Invisibles* in particular.

6 Webb Keane, "Language and Religion," *A Companion to Linguistic Anthropology*, ed. Alessandro Duranti (Malden: Blackwell Publishing, 2004), 431.

7 Keane, 431.

8 Morrison's use of magic throughout the series is, of course, not limited to linguistic practices. More, the deliberate embodiment of narrative constructs (fictional characters, pop icons) deserves further scrutiny. On this point, see Megan Goodwin, "Liber/Corpus: Grant Morrison's Reflexive Relationship with his *Invisibles*," (paper presented at Graven Images: Religion in Comic Books and Graphic Novels, Boston, MA, 11–13 April 2008).

9 See Austin's *How To Do Things With Words* and Derrida's "Signature, Event, Context." My invocation of speech acts here does not directly refer to Bakhtin, though his theory of dialogism influenced my third section.

10 In discussing language solely in terms of written communication, I am not siding with or against Derrida regarding the primacy of writing or speech (cf. *Of Grammatology*). Rather, I suggest that graphic novels circumvent this debate altogether by rendering all speech (and indeed, most sounds) in writing.

11 See King Mob's killing of the King-of-All-Tears with a word — "pop," printed on a flag shot from a toy gun. Regarding the ontological materiality of signifiers, or "pop" (culture, cola) as the "real thing," see also Zizek's *The Sublime Idea of Ideology*.

12 *Bruja* is Spanish or Portugese for (female) witch.

The *lwa* (or *loa*, also known as *Mystères* or — notably — the Invisibles) are Vodou spirits, intermediaries for Bondye, the Creator. *Lwa* will sometimes possess a Vodoun practitioner, taking over her body to speak and act through her. The possessed practitioner is known as a "horse." For more on American Vodou, see Karen McCarthy Brown's *Mama Lola: A Vodou Priestess in Brooklyn*.

In Buddhism, a bodhisattva is a "heroic-minded one" (Sanskrit: satva) for "enlightenment" (bodhi). The bodhisattva defers nirvana to help all living beings reach enlightenment. In *The Invisibles*, Jack works with Barbelith to bring about the supercontext, a higher form of consciousness.

13 Patrick Neighly and Kereth Cowe-Spigai, *Anarchy for the Masses: The Disinformation Guide to* The Invisibles (New York: Disinformation, 2003), 38, 235; see also Grant Morrison's February 5, 2001 "Digital Ink" column at http://www.grant-morrison.com.

14 Phil Hine and Grant Morrison were both strongly influenced by Peter J Carroll's *Liber Null* (1978) and *Psychonaut* (1981). However, Carroll's work is dense and far less approachable than Hine's — thus my reliance on *Condensed Chaos* in this section.

15 Phil Hine, *Condensed Chaos: An Introduction to Chaos Magic* (Tempe: New Falcon Publishing, 1995), 22.

16 Keane, 431.

17 Keane, 431.

18 Keane, 431.

19   Keane, 431, 441.
20   Keane, 431.
21   Keane, 431.
22   On the construction of identities based on emotional aggregates, see Phil Hine's work on egregores, particularly "On the Magical Egregore," http://www.philhine.org.uk/writings/ess_egregore.html.
23   Grant Morrison, *The Invisibles: Entropy in the U.K.* (New York: DC Comics, 2001), 196.
24   Morrison, *Entropy*, 126.
25   Grant Morrison, *The Invisibles: Apocalipstick* (New York: DC Comics, 2001), 172, 172.
26   Grant Morrison, *The Invisibles: Counting to None* (New York: DC Comics, 1999), 97. The Nommo are the ancestral spirits of Mali's Dogon tribe.
27   Morrison, *Entropy*, 63.
28   On the linguistic limits of human thought, see Wittgenstein's *Philosophical Investigations* and Foucault's "A Preface to Transgression."
29   Morrison, *Entropy*, 63. Emphasis in the original.
30   Morrison, *Counting*, 213.
31   Morrison, *Counting*, 214–15. Emphasis in the original.
32   Morrison, *Invisible Kingdom*, 201. Regarding the "twisted language of the angels" — I read this simply in terms of magic as religious language. It is possible, however, that Morrison is referring to Enochian, an allegedly angelic language recorded in the journals of sixteenth-century occultist John Dee.
33   Morrison, *Invisible Kingdom*, 280–1. See also note 11 on this point.
34   Grant Morrison, *The Invisibles: Kissing Mister Quimper* (New York: DC Comics, 2000), 155.
35   Morrison, *Kissing*, 202. Emphasis in the original.
36   Grant Morrison, *The Invisibles: Say You Want a Revolution* (New York: DC Comics, 1996), 216–17.
37   Morrison, *Say You Want*, 217.
38   Grant Morrison, *The Invisibles: Bloody Hell in America* (New York: DC Comics, 1998), 15.
39   Morrison, *Invisible Kingdom*, 271. Emphasis in the original.
40   Morrison, *Invisible Kingdom*, 277.
41   Morrison, *Invisible Kingdom*, 286. Emphasis in the original.
42   Grant Morrison, "Digital Ink, 5 Feb 2001," February 5, 2001, *Grant Morrison – The Official Website*, http://www.grant-morrison.com/ink_5.htm (accessed October 31, 2009).
43   Hine, *Condensed*, 126.
44   Neighly, Cowe-Spigai, 15, 208.
45   Neighly, Cowe-Spigai, 236.
46   Morrison, "Digital Ink."
47   Tom Coates, "Grant Morrison," *Barbelith Webzine*, June 29, 2001, http://www.barbelith.com/cgi-bin/articles/00000033.shtml (accessed October 31, 2009). The energy (both from the fear and the momentum) of the bungee jump gave force and gravity to Morrison's intentions, expressed linguistically through the sigil on his chest. Morrison activated those intentions through the bungee jump's kinetic energy. For more on activating spellwork, see Hine's *Condensed Chaos*.
48   Morrison, "Digital Ink"; Neighly, Cowe-Spigai, 233.
49   It's worth noting that both King Mob and Grant Morrison sustained word-

related injuries. Under the influence of Key 17, King Mob thought that his face had been infected with flesh-eating bacteria and that his fingers had been cut off; Morrison attributes his near-fatal septicemia to an energy kick-back from the wankathon, a large-scale working focused on a sigil — a magical drawing formed from the combined letters of a statement of intent (Neighly, Cowe-Spigai, 244).

50 Morrison, "Digital Ink."

51 Neighly, Cowe-Spigai, 68–9.

52 The sexual transgression of the act lent the act further energy. On the religious energy of deliberate sexual transgression, see Georges Bataille, *Death and Sensuality: a Study of Eroticism and the Taboo.*

53 Neighly and Cowe-Spigai, 69.

54 Morrison, *Invisible Kingdom*, 286.

55 "THE INVISIBLES actually ends with off-panel quotation marks, signifying the transition from the fictional universe of THE INVISIBLES to our own. Grant Morrison frequently describes the series as a narrative hypersigil — this is the point at which the spell extends into reality, the reader shifting from passive receptor to active participant" (Neighly, Cowe-Spigai, 217, 247).

56 Neighly, Cowe-Spigai, 116; Morrison, "Digital Ink."

57 Hine, *Condensed*, 190.

58 Morrison, *Say You Want*, 204.

59 Morrison, *Say You Want*, 185, 201.

"The Magic Circus of the Mind": Alan Moore's *Promethea* and the Transformation of Consciousness through Comics

CHRISTINE HOFF KRAEMER AND J. LAWTON WINSLADE

N ITS EARLY ISSUES, Alan Moore's 1995–2005 comic book series *Promethea* garnered lavish admiration from readers. Praise for the strong female and queer characters, tight writing, and innovative layouts by artist JH Williams filled the comic's letters column, and feminist comic book artist and writer Trina Robbins gushingly called *Promethea* "what Wonder Woman should be if she hadn't been destroyed by generations of idiots."[1] In a move that upset many readers and caused the comic's circulation to drop, however, Moore put his pedagogical aims first. When speaking of the series, Moore concedes that his intention was to draw readers in with a superhero conceit, then use the increasingly esoteric storyline to expose them to the concepts of Western occultism. "It seemed to make sense that we should start at the shallow end, with inflatable arm-bands, so as not to alienate the readership from the very outset (the plan was to wait about twelve issues and then alienate them)," he quips in a 2002 interview.[2] After the twelfth issue of the series, in which the titular heroine makes a journey into the world of Tarot cards (what Moore describes as "probably the most experimental story I have ever done"[3]), it was too late to turn back. Thereafter, the series abandoned any pretense of being a traditional superhero book and took its heroine

274

on a journey through each of the spheres of the kabbalistic Tree of Life, the Hebrew mystical system appropriated by Western occultists. By this point, *Promethea* had clearly become an outlet for exploring the key concepts of magic and occultism that Moore himself has studied.

Though readers accustomed to Moore's revisionist superhero narratives, such as *Watchmen* and *Batman: The Killing Joke*, may have been turned off by the heavy esoteric content, Moore's occult adventures at the turn of the millennium were by no means a departure for the eccentric Northampton author. Rather, these explorations were a logical development in Moore's intriguing career, emerging from a period in his life in which he was collaborating on live spoken-word performances under the name "The Moon and Serpent Grand Egyptian Theatre of Marvels."[4] Moore often speaks of his fortieth birthday party, where he decided to forego a typical midlife crisis by "going completely mad" and brazenly declaring himself to be a magician.[5] Moore's approach to comics and the creative process has always had an arcane aspect, however. In fact, in an early essay on "how to write comics," published after the success of *Watchmen* (1986) made him a darling of the mainstream comics industry, he describes the weaving of a comic narrative as a kind of hypnosis, with "the transitions between scenes [being] the weak points in the spell that you are attempting to cast over [the readers]."[6] His complex narratives "cast spells" over his audience, whether he is challenging his readers to question the moralism of the superhero genre (*Watchmen*); fascist politics and media (*V for Vendetta*); notions of identity, humanity, and the natural world (*Swamp Thing*); or attitudes and values around fantasy literature, sexuality, and pornography (*Lost Girls*). *Promethea* effectively brings Moore's superhero work together with his ongoing interest in occultism, which has been previously represented in his collaborations with artist Eddie Campbell (for example, the densely researched *From Hell* (1991–8, 1999) and the kabbalistic *Snakes and Ladders* (2001), which was based on one of Moore's spoken word performances).

In *Promethea*, Moore takes the notion of the self-empowered superhuman even further than that of *Watchmen*'s *ubermenschen* Ozymandias and Dr. Manhattan and once again involves a deity-like superhero in a plot to end the world. Here, Moore takes this "end of the world" cliché, a constant threat in the highly dramatic world of superheroes and supervillains, and transforms it into his own idea of the postmodern apocalypse — "the world" that is destroyed is not our physical world, but rather our illusory constructions of reality. This move situates Moore squarely in the Romantic literary tradition and particularly as an heir of William Blake, one of Moore's major influences. For Moore, as for many of the Romantics, imagination is a divine attribute and a way to participate in the ongoing creation of the universe. Like Blake, Wordsworth, and Coleridge, Moore dreams of a utopia achieved not through political revolution, but through a radical change in consciousness produced by art. The conclusion of *Promethea* stages a Romantic apocalypse of the imagination updated with a strong feminist agenda, elements of contemporary politics, and knowledge of the Western occult tradition.

In a further variation on the usual tropes of the superhero genre, where the hero's powers are often invoked through a speech act ("Shazam!" or "Flame on!" being two famous examples), in *Promethea* creative writing is used as a trigger. College student Sophie Bangs's thesis research into the recurring literary character Promethea leads her to Barbara Shelley, the widow of an artist who had drawn the demigoddess into his wife's body with his creative process. With her husband dead, however, Barbara has become disillusioned with heroism and is now able to manifest Promethea only weakly, if at all. The two women are suddenly confronted with threatening forces, and at Barbara's behest, Sophie scribbles a poem — essentially an invocatory hymn — to Promethea as a goddess of imagination. Sophie's act of creation brings Promethea into the manifest world, and Sophie's own body serves as the vessel for the demigoddess's power.[7]

Moore seems to intend *Promethea* as a creative act that, like Sophie with her poem, pulls powerful forces of spiritual transformation into the everyday world of the reader. As he told *Comic Book Artist* (*CBA*) in a June 2003 interview, Moore wrote the kabbalistic issues in a state of ritual meditation. In order to describe each of the states of consciousness that Promethea's alter ego Sophie Bangs would explore, Moore himself sought to achieve them and to produce art as expressions of those states — states that, perhaps, could then be triggered in the reader. "What you were seeing in the comic is not the report of the magical experience," he told *CBA*. "It *was* the magical experience."[8] In a May 2003 interview, Moore spoke of the fascist tendencies he sees arising in the international environment after 9/11, and he suggests that his art provides readers "access to the mental tools to get them beyond this situation [. . .] attitudes, mental tools, ways of looking at things, that could actually be of use in these otherwise turbulent times. That's the plan. With *Promethea*, it is entirely overt."⁹ Yet the tools provided are not simply the occult concepts that Moore hopes his readers will employ. Using the unique artistic advantages of the comics medium, the comic itself becomes a potential tool for creating the positive shift in consciousness portrayed in its conclusion.

If we consider the comics medium as a type of sequential art, as comics theorist Scott McCloud claims, Moore's use of comics for educational purposes has a long and rich history. McCloud's *Understanding Comics* includes renderings of medieval French and ancient Egyptian narrative art, as well as several panels from a 36-foot long pre-Columbian picture manuscript, which narrates the history of the political and military hero "8-Deer Tiger's Claw."¹⁰ Similar examples of sequential art can be found around the world, from figures inscribed on ancient Greek urns to illustrated medieval Japanese scrolls. One illustration in *Understanding Comics* reproduces a series of scenes entitled "The Tortures of Saint Erasmus," a bloody late medieval work portraying the sufferings of a Christian martyr.¹¹ Although this kind of art might be off-putting to contemporary tastes, it served the same religious purpose as the great stained glass windows of European cathedrals, with their scenes of the life of Christ and the acts of apostles and saints. Such works instructed and were thought to inspire devotion in medieval worshippers, many of whom were illiterate.

Some distinction remains in American culture between "low" art and "high" art, so the notion that a comic could effectively serve as a trigger for a spiritual state in the same way a cathedral window can, may seem counterintuitive to some. Art historian David Freedberg's *The Power of Images*, however, explores the history of response to images in Western culture and charts the persistence of viewers' intense emotional, spiritual, and sometimes physical responses to both popular and fine art. If anything, Freedberg asserts, it is *more* acceptable to have strong and varied responses to popular art forms, under which he includes everything from personal religious images sold for home altars to erotic photography (comic books would certainly also fall into this category).¹² Moore seems to be counting on this mysterious power of images — and his audience's openness to being viscerally engaged by a comic book — to make the otherwise didactic *Promethea* issues successful.

Freedberg's history of image response provides a framework for how an interactive comic book reading experience might function. Published in the late 1980s, *The Power of Images* is now somewhat dated, particularly in its assumption that eroticism in both secular and religious art serves a male gaze and does not have an arousing effect on women. The book does, however, present convincing evidence for the persistent Western belief in images' power to affect viewers psychologically and spiritually, as well as to move them to action. For example, in time periods as diverse as ancient Greece and the Renaissance, writers have advised looking at beautiful images of human beings during sexual relations and pregnancy to assure the health of children; undesirable images were felt to contribute to similar characteristics in one's offspring.[13] Freedberg also provides ample evidence of belief that religious images channel the powers of the gods, saints, or spirits that they represent. Images of the Virgin Mary have been especially renowned for their ability to heal, and during the Renaissance, images of Christ were often held before the eyes of condemned criminals as they were led to execution in order to maximize their chances of salvation.[14] More generally, Freedberg gives numerous accounts of viewers' experiences of images having life: portraits' eyes are felt to follow the viewer around the room, sculptures of deities are chained up to keep them from escaping, paintings or wax images are made of enemies or criminals and then punished by ritual hanging or dismemberment, and statues — particularly religious ones — are washed, fed with offerings, caressed, kissed, engaged sexually, and attacked by viewers.

Although Freedberg provides a model for explaining the power of images, he does not deal with the unique characteristics of the comics medium, which provides special advantages for a creator seeking to engage an audience on many levels. Comics theorists have argued that the comics form is an unusually interactive form of media. Drawing on reader-response criticism, critics such as literary scholar Charles Hatfield emphasize that the form's hybridity is unusually adept at creating the sense of incompleteness that invites the reader's act of interpretation.[15] Hatfield writes,

> The fractured surface of the comics page, with its patchwork of different images, shapes, and symbols, presents the reader with a surfeit of interpretive options, creating an experience that is always decentered, unstable, and unfixable. As Robert P. Fletcher observes, this fragmentation urges readers to take a critical role, for comic art "calls attention to its fictionality by displaying its narrative seams" (381).[16] The reader's responsibility for negotiating meaning can never be forgotten, for

the breakdown of comics into discrete visual quanta continually fore-grounds the reader's involvement. The very discontinuity of the page urges readers to do the work of inference, to negotiate over and over the passage from submissive reading to active interpreting.[17]

Hatfield laments that American criticism on comics reading tends to fall into two camps: that comics are a "stepping stone" towards literacy because they are "easy," or that they discourage the development of complete literacy because they are "easy."[18] Yet, the ability to deeply read a comic requires a complex grasp of the many ways comics represent time, interrelate word and text, and use borders and layout to indicate narrative sequence, to name just a few of the "codes of signification" with which Hatfield is concerned. He accuses existing comics scholarship in English of "skimming" rather than "reading" comics by ignoring the increasingly sophisticated forms that an experienced comics-reading audience makes possible.[19] For Hatfield, comics are a potentially "demanding" medium, one that asks a great deal from a reader who engages in the interpretive act of forming a relationship with the text. The tension between formal elements (word and text) that he sees as central to the medium insists on a "different order of literacy," one that is visual as well as textual.[20]

To take advantage of the complexities made possible by the comics medium, Moore and artist JH Williams use, unusual page layouts and juxtapositions between text and images to capture the mood of Sophie/Promethea's psychedelic travels in the Immateria, the realm of the imagination. Panel borders curve, turn wavy, or melt entirely; other panels wrap around occult symbols or are grasped by beasts, angels, or demons. In some cases, there are no panel borders at all, and several progressive scenes stretch across what would normally be a splash page (i.e., a page-sized single panel). This experimentation is taken to an extreme in *Promethea* #12, which is structured as one elaborate, multi-layered 24-page comics panel. Based on the astral advice of one of the previous Prometheas, Sophie attempts to converse with the two snakes of her caduceus, her magical weapon and the classic symbol of both Hermes and the medical profession. She pleads, "I need to understand magic, and I think I've reached a point where just studying it in books isn't enough. I need to understand it from the inside." Perhaps this is also exactly where Moore seeks to take his readers, inside the "magic circus of the mind." This February 2001 issue, in which the snakes guide Promethea on a journey of discovery with the Major Arcana cards of the

Tarot deck as signposts, is a strange reading experience, only exceeded by Promethea's later journey into each sphere of the kabbalistic Tree of Life. Each page combines the snakes' narration, Sophie/Promethea's questions, Tarot cards, and Scrabble letters spelling out anagrams for the word "Promethea" with the text of a joke told by various incarnations of twentieth-century magician Aleister Crowley (see Figure 1). Abandoning any semblance of traditional comic paneling, the issue impressionistically mixes images and dialogue balloons, layering imagery so thickly that it is practically impossible for the reader to absorb everything at first reading. Even Sophie confesses that she is "having trouble keeping the different threads separate." The snakes Mack and Mike (nicknames for "macrocosm" and "microcosm") give her and the reader valuable advice: "It's like a fugue: you have a choice of following a single voice, or letting each strand grow less clear the music of the whole to hear."[21]

In this issue, Moore emphasizes the Tarot's dual aspects as both lexicon and narrative, as Mack and Mike explain each card of the Tarot as a stage in the creation of the Universe and, ultimately, human history. For instance, the Hanged Man card represents the Dark Ages, Art (or Temperance) represents the Renaissance, the Moon represents the Nuclear Age, and the Sun represents the late 1960s, in which the playing children of the traditional Tarot image are Flower Children. In keeping with the theme of macrocosm and microcosm, the comic presents Crowley, perhaps the most influential writer of the early-twentieth-century occult movement, progressing from a fetal stage through childhood, adulthood, old age, and death as he simultaneously tells his joke, which doubles as a meditation on the power of thought and perception. Crowley's text is echoed by the dialogue between Sophie and the snakes through the use of repeated phrases and puns. Like Sophie/Promethea, the reader is invited to actively seek and interpret connections between these narrative threads. As the issue's various titles ("The Magic Theatre," "A Pop Art Happening," "A Poetry and Light Show") indicate, Moore intends the comic to be performative, interactive, and experiential in the same vein as *The Birth Caul* and *Snakes and Ladders*, spoken word pieces that Moore performed just prior to writing the early issues of *Promethea*. In fact, Moore has stated that writing Promethea specifically emerged from these performances and his intention to work on the subconscious minds of audiences through a multimedia sensory overload. He likens this overload to a "fugue state" or a psychedelic drug

Figure 1. **A page from *Promethea* #12, demonstrating a visual fugue.**

trip in which the individual experiences a sequence of events simultaneously. *Promethea* #12 attempts to both capture and communicate this state of mind.[22]

Moore's explorations of the hermetic kabbalah, where the visual is combined with the linguistic in a way that makes abstract occult philosophy satisfyingly concrete, are intended to be equally as experiential as the Tarot issue. Each of ten issues is dedicated to a sephira (a particular emanation or power of the divine) on the cosmic map known as the Tree of Life, and each attempts to capture a different mode of consciousness. Moore's exploration of the emotional sphere of Netzach is given form in oceanic, softly bordered blues and greens, suggesting both salty tears and the characters' helplessness when caught up in currents of love and grief; the harsh severity of Gevurah is rendered entirely in red and black and communicated in heavy lines and deep shadows; the shining sphere of Keter, the source of creation, is printed in gold on white, the words of the characters' dialogue fading in slowly as if they were only just coming into being. As Sophie and Barbara climb the tree, the issues' artistic styles — drawing on artists as diverse as Andy Warhol and Vincent Van Gogh — veer increasingly toward abstraction, as the characters travel away from the concrete material world and toward the limitless ineffability of pure existence. Though occultists have written dozens of books attempting to characterize the states of consciousness that make up the Tree of Life, only Moore and Williams have realized them so vividly, transforming them from dry correspondence tables correlating colors, smells, and personality traits into living environments open to anyone with eyes to see. The dialogue between Sophie/Promethea and Barbara allows the reader textual access to their psychic and emotional states as they verbally describe what they are experiencing.

Because of its focus on language and magic in the intellectual sphere of Hod, *Promethea* #15 is a particularly apt illustration of Moore's methods of audience engagement. In the hermetic kabbalah, which was adapted from the traditional Jewish kabbalah by the Golden Dawn in the late nineteenth and early twentieth centuries, planetary correspondences are given enormous weight, and Hod is heavily marked by the influence of Mercury.[23] The issue is colored in a palette of primarily orange and gold, and the Greco-Roman god Mercury (or Hermes) and the Egyptian god Thoth both figure prominently in the narrative as representations of communication, intellect, mathematics, and scholarship. The style of the issue is heavily influenced by M. C. Escher, whose visual experiments

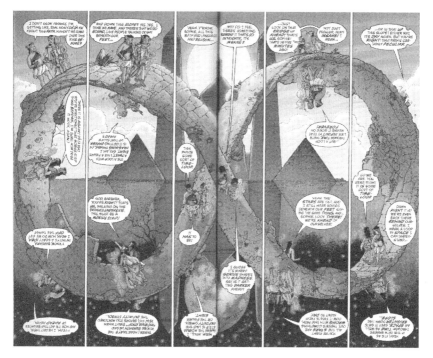

Figure 2. **Sophie and Barbara walk the Möbius strip in** *Promethea* **#15.**

with recursion fit the somewhat obsessive, analytical consciousness that Moore seeks to portray. Particularly striking is the adaptation of a print by Escher, a Möbius strip around which the characters walk as they slowly realize that they are caught in a time loop (see Figure 2). Barbara comments, "Y'know, Sophie, all this math and language and reason . . . why do I feel something behind it that's so intricate, so insane?" Sophie replies as they descend the slope of the strip, shortly to realize the trap they've fallen into: "I guess it's where genius shades into madness."[24] Moore and Williams force the reader to turn the book upside down and sideways to follow the conversation as the viewer's eyes follow the layout's twisting path — an experience of an overabundance of analytic, intellectual energy.[25]

Later, as Sophie and Barbara discuss the nature of language with Hermes, the god asserts that everything is made of language: "Oh, especially me! How could humans perceive gods . . . abstract essences . . . without clothing them in imagery, stories, pictures . . . or picture-stories, for that matter."[26] Startlingly, the god breaks the comic's fourth

Figure 3.　**Hermes acknowledges the reader in *Promethea* #15.**

wall to turn to the audience, and the elegant coloring gives his eyes an eerie glow (see Figure 3).[27] The effect and implication is that because the gods are made of language, they are present in the book the reader is holding. The reader, in turn, is included in a narrative being played out as part of the ongoing development of creation. Sophie's story is not simply entertainment, Moore insists; the forces she is experiencing are part of the reality that shapes the reader's experience. Hermes' breaking of the fourth wall is an invitation to experience the blurring between story and reality, and to see oneself as a story being told in the mind of God, just as Moore tells Sophie's tale.

In addition to its subject matter, the visuality of alchemical literature may be a direct influence on contemporary occult texts like Moore's. Western esotericism scholar Arthur Versluis has argued for what he calls "ahistorical continuity" in various occult traditions that have been passed down through literature and art, rather than through a direct (teacher to student) initiatory lineage.[28] He specifically points to the many diagrams and drawings in these dense alchemical texts, such as those of Robert Fludd and Michael Meier. The purpose of these pervasive illustrations in theosophic, Rosicrucian, and alchemical literature, Versluis maintains,

> is to emphasize and amplify the hieratic nature of these traditions. If a book is to serve an initiatic function, it can better do so if it reveals its subject in words and images both. In this way, the book becomes hieroglyphic — it is not merely an abstract discussion *about* some topic, it actually reveals (*hiera-*) the nature of its subject.[29]

Almost restating Moore's assertion about the comic being the magical experience itself rather than merely a report of it, Versluis describes a sympathy between an esoteric author and his or her reader that prompts a "gnostic shift in consciousness" — an experience of divinely revealed knowledge that cannot be fully captured in words. This imaginative participation allows the reader or audience "to participate in a work and to be transmuted by it, an initiatory process that takes places through words and image, or through what we may also call the induced vision of art."[30]

Moore invites the audience's participation in *Promethea* most explicitly in the final issue of the series — appropriately, the thirty-second issue, conforming to the thirty-two paths of the Tree of Life. Probably the most ambitious of all the issues of the series, #32 has thirty-two pages of non-ordered panels consisting of overlapping line drawings brushed with psychedelic pastels and sprinkled with stars and ankhs. Text balloons describing occult principles, scientific theorems, historical facts, and descriptions of tarot paths and sephirot are tangled together with a monologue in which Promethea directly addresses the reader. According to the supplement in the final trade paperback collection, Moore's script begins with the punning note, "Okay, this is a very strange artefact we're putting together here, but if we all stay calm it should work like a dream."[31] Readers are encouraged to remove the pages from the final issue and juxtapose them in whatever way they choose. However, when put in a certain order, the pages form poster-sized paintings of Promethea's face, which emerges from what otherwise looks like a jumble of random images and text. In the trade paperback, both of these paintings are included as reduced size posters.

The initiation the reader is being invited to experience in this issue is twofold: the issue offers a tactile activity that calls attention to the illusory nature of time and also illustrates the reader's participation in discerning larger patterns in apparent randomness. Promethea's address to the reader implicates the audience in the process of creating this magical "artefact." In her final farewell, she says, "I've enjoyed our dance. You were the perfect partner, and I'm going to miss you. But spacetime is eternal, with everything in it. And you and me are always here, always now. You and me are *forever*."[32] This remark reflects Moore's continuing fascination with quantum theories of time (going back at least as far as *Watchmen*), specifically the notion that it is only our conscious minds that order events into a linear sequence; a perspective is possible in which all events happen at once. In interviews, Moore cites Stephen Hawking's notion of time as a football with the Big Bang and the Big Crunch on either end, what Moore describes as a "gigantic hyper mind in which everything is occurring."[33] In this godlike perspective, all events are connected and nothing is ever truly lost, death being only one point on a timeline. Similarly, the reader of a comic book is able to scan an entire page of sequential panels at once, or flip back to the beginning of the book and re-experience the process of perception. Thus, according to Moore, comics have a unique ability to provide non-linear imagery outside of time; comic fiction occurs in an eternal present in what comics scholar Annalisa Di Liddo calls "a ceaselessly evolving, metamorphic narrative continuum."[34] Further, in assembling the faces of Promethea, the reader is given an object lesson in the nature of reality as Moore sees it. The comic is, in visual form, an analogy for the way consciousness creates meaning. Although the information on the pages appears to be a confused muddle when seen one piece at a time, when the puzzle is completed and the reader stands back, the face of a benevolent goddess — imagination Herself — is revealed. Through the participation of the reader, a larger and more meaningful pattern emerges from apparent chaos.

In this simple cut-and-paste activity, Moore attempts to communicate an experience of a benevolent divine consciousness, one which lovingly embraces all time and space, yet is always necessarily more than the sum of its parts. Indeed, this also seems to be the ultimate message of the apocalypse of the imagination that Moore envisions in *Promethea* #31. Although Promethea does end the world, she does not do it on a physical level; rather, her apocalypse is the paradigm-shattering experience that all of being is interconnected, interdependent, and ultimately one.[35] Speaking directly to the reader, Promethea offers a vision in which all human beings see the divine reflected in themselves, in every other human being, and in everything that is. Having invited the reader to sit with her by a cheery fireplace and hold her hand, she presents a series of mandalas, which are commonly used in Eastern religious art for devotional purposes. In this case, Moore seems to have chosen the circular designs for their connotations of wholeness and unity. "This, then, is revelation," Promethea tells the audience.

> All is one, and all is deity, this beautiful undying fire of being that is everywhere about us, that we are. O man, O woman, know yourself, and know you are divine. Respect yourself, respect the least phenomenon of your existence as if it were the breath of God. [. . .] Know you are everything, forever. Know I love you.[36]

In the aftermath of this experience, which Moore portrays as occurring simultaneously to all people around the world, nothing can be the same; the dualism that fuels agonistic thinking and the resulting conflicts is (at least temporarily) dissolved. When Promethea reaches out her hand to the reader, she offers a glimpse of this interconnected perspective: the reader, whoever he or she may be, is a beloved, full participant in the unfolding of Being. Moore further includes the reader — and himself! — in this experience through the use of a number of self-reflexive scenes: in the moments before the key event, the illustrator and Moore both turn to the reader while working on *Promethea*'s script pages at a computer screen, and Moore mutters, "Uh oh." Elizabeth K. Rosen describes this moment as one "in which both reader and creators acknowledge their imaginative partnership."[37] The very act of reading becomes a collaboration.

From the perspectives of viewer/reader-response, performance theory, and comics theory, there are excellent theoretical reasons for why *Promethea* might trigger meditative, devotional, or religious states in the reader. Yet the question remains: in practice, does the comic *work*? Does it, in fact, provide the "gnostic shift in consciousness" Versluis attributes to successful occult texts? Responses to the comic as it was being released in serial format suggest that not all readers appreciated Moore's effort at occult education; in a December 2002 interview, Moore jovially remarked,

> [W]e have lost several thousand readers over the course of this saga, not as many as I'd expected, and the ones that remain are either dedicated and firm in their resolve, or else have had their cerebral cortex so badly damaged by the last four or five issues that they are no longer capable of formulating a complaint[.][38]

Some readers balked at the didactic nature of the kabbalistic issues, as critic Douglas Wolk acknowledges in his review of the entire series. Wolk notes their "ungainly expository dialogue" and instances of Moore "threaten[ing] to strain an eyelid from winking so hard," even while praising the complex and engaging visuals.[39] While Wolk agrees with readers who felt that Moore was lecturing at them, however, he ultimately defends *Promethea*, claiming, "The idea of it isn't to tell a story so much as to present a gigantic mass of arcane philosophy as entertainingly and memorably as possible."[40]

This purpose has been borne out by the fact that, in trade paperback form, the comic has become known in the occult and Pagan communities as an accessible introduction to hermetic kabbalah. T. Thorn Coyle, occult writer and initiate of the Feri tradition of witchcraft, assigns the Tree of Life issues of *Promethea* to her advanced students as a way to "get [their] feet wet" before moving on to other kabbalistic texts.[41] An October 2007 newsletter produced by a body of the occult order Ordo Templi Orientis in Kentucky reviewed the books as "an ideal teaching tool for new magicians," advertising *Promethea* next to articles on Pagan Pride Day and contemporary Pagans in the military.[42] In March 2009, Pagan news blogger Jason Pitzl-Waters wrote in *The Wild Hunt* that

> Moore is, for all intents and purposes, "one of us." By that I mean he's an occultist/magician who possibly worships the "sock-puppet god" Glycon, and is currently hard at work writing *"a clear and practical grimoire of the occult sciences."* In addition, he also wrote an outstanding 32-issue comic series that doubled as primer in magic entitled "Promethea." [. . .] I think that in retrospect, historians of our wider religious and philisophical [*sic*] movement will pay far more attention to the influence of people like Moore than the dozens of "Wicca 101" niche writers we currently argue and debate over.[43]

While it is unclear whether *Promethea* works as a "conversion" text, anecdotal evidence like the above suggests that within the Pagan and occult movements, *Promethea* is seen as an introductory work meant to draw the new witch or magician more deeply into religious belief and practice. Such evidence suggests that for a prepared reader — one who already has interest in the art of conscious-change, if not much knowledge — *Promethea* can function effectively as a religious text.

Moore himself denies that he has "religious" intentions, but admits that *Promethea* is "a magical rant disguised as a superheroine comic." Here, he matter-of-factly defines "magic" as "simply a new way of seeing the ordinary universe that surrounds us, and ourselves as creatures in that universe."[44] Although Moore acknowledges that the comic may have turned off casual readers, he does note how many readers have been "genuinely appreciative" and read *Promethea* primarily because it *is* instructive in Western occultism. As far as whether he intends to "convert" his readers, Moore ultimately draws a distinction between what he is doing and religion:

All I would be urging people to do in *Promethea* is to explore, in their own way, by whatever means they personally feel comfortable with, using whatever system they happen to feel comfortable with, whether that be Christianity, or paganism, or Hinduism, or anything else, to explore the kind of rich world that I think all of us have inside us. I just want to tell them that that world is there, that there are a variety of ways of exploring it. It doesn't really matter which way you use, or which system you adopt. It's a territory I find very rewarding, very fulfilling, very human. To point out that territory to other people is something I feel happy about doing. To erect a huge church there and officiate over rituals, is not.[45]

Moore is continuing his innovative efforts in occult education with his in-development *Moon and Serpent Bumper Book of Magic,* due out in 2013. Stating his desire to create a book on magic "intended for a mass populace,"[46] Moore is designing the text like a children's activity book, including fact sheets on the history of magic in the style of *Ripley's Believe It or Not* and accompanying board games that illustrate occult principles. With the *Bumper Book,* Moore intends to more fully emphasize the playful nature of magic, and claims, "We want it to be incredibly entertaining, we want it to be a real lot of fun, we want it to have activities that you can play and things that you can do that will be genuinely magically instructive."[47] Clearly, Moore intends for the pedagogical experiment that began with his live performance pieces and developed into *Promethea* to reach an even more mainstream audience.

Promethea remains a challenging work, one that demands a level of engagement from the reader that disallows the ironic distance from one's entertainment that postmodernity encourages. Yet in its potential use for meditation or devotion and its intent to spiritually educate, *Promethea* is solidly within a long tradition of sequential art and Western religious art in general. Further, Moore's work illustrates the unique advantages of the comics medium for religious purposes: the ability to convey substantial amounts of information through text while also presenting the reader with the emotional impact of images makes comics an especially rich medium for reaching out to the spiritual seeker. With Pagans and occult practitioners now enthusiastically embracing Moore as "one of us," *Promethea* has become an important text for those interested in the growth of these new religious movements.

Notes

1   "Imaginary Lines," in Alan Moore (w), JH Williams (p), and Mick Gray (i), *Promethea* #3 (Oct 1999), unpaginated.

2   "Alan Moore Interviewed by Eddie Campbell," *Eddie Campbell's Egomania* (Marietta, GA: Top Shelf Productions, 2002), 22; reprinted in Alan Moore (w) and Eddie Campbell (a), *A Disease of Language* (London: Knockabout, 2005), unpaginated.

3   "The Dark Side of the Moore: An Interview Conducted by Omar Martini," *Alan Moore: Portrait of an Extraordinary Gentleman*, ed. Gary Spencer Millidge (Leigh-On-Sea, UK: Abiogenesis Press, 2003), 116.

4   The comic book versions of *The Birth Caul* (1999) and *Snakes and Ladders* (2001) are collected in Moore and Campbell, *A Disease of Language*. Both pieces are also available as recordings produced with Tim Perkins, as are *The Moon and Serpent Grand Egyptian Theatre of Marvels* (1996), *The Highbury Working* (2000), and Moore's tribute to William Blake, *Angel Passage* (2002).

5   Interview in *The Mindscape of Alan Moore*, dir. DeZ Vylenz (Shadowsnake Films, 2003).

6   Moore, *Alan Moore's Writing for Comics*, Writing for Comics Vol. 1 (Urbana, IL: Avatar, 2003), 17.

7   Alan Moore (w), JH Williams (p), and Mick Gray (i), *Promethea* Book 1 (La Jolla, CA: America's Best Comics, 2000), unpaginated, reprint of *Promethea* #1.

8   Jon B. Cooke and George Khoury, "Alan Moore Interview: The Magic of Comics," *Comic Book Artist* 1:25 (Jun 2003): 41.

9   Jay Babcock, "Magic is Afoot," interview with Alan Moore, *Arthur* 4 (May 2003): 30.

10   Scott McCloud, *Understanding Comics: The Invisible Art* (Northampton: Kitchen Sink Press, 1993), 10–14.

11   McCloud, 16.

12   David Freedberg, *The Power of Images: Studies in the History and Theory of Response* (Chicago: U of Chicago P, 1989), 358–9.

13   Freedberg, 2–3.

14   Freedberg, 5–8.

15   Charles Hatfield, *Alternative Comics* (Jackson: UP of Mississippi, 2005), xiii, referring to Wolfgang Iser, *The Act of Reading: A Theory of Aesthetic Response* (Baltimore: Johns Hopkins, 1978), 166–70.

16   Robert P. Fletcher, "Visual Thinking and the Picture Story in *The History of Henry Esmond*," *PMLA* 113:3 (May 1998): 379–94.

17   Hatfield, xiii–xiv.

18   Hatfield, 36.

19   Hatfield, 66.

20   Hatfield, 67.

21   Alan Moore (w), JH Williams (p), and Mick Gray (i), *Promethea* Book 2 (La Jolla, CA: America's Best Comics, 2000), unpaginated, reprint of *Promethea* #12.

22   "The Dark Side of the Moore," 108.

23   Nevill Drury, *The History of Magic in the Modern Age: A Quest for Personal Transformation* (New York: Carroll and Graf Publishers, Inc, 2000), 54–62.

24   Alan Moore (w), JH Williams (p), and Mick Gray (i), *Promethea* Book 3 (La Jolla, CA: America's Best Comics, 2000), unpaginated, reprint of *Promethea* #15.

25   Moore et al, *Promethea* #15, unpaginated.

26   Moore et al, *Promethea* #15, unpaginated.

27 Moore et al, *Promethea* #15, unpaginated.

28 Arthur Versluis, *Restoring Paradise: Western Esotericism, Literature, Art and Consciousness* (Albany: State University of New York Press, 2004), 142.

29 Versluis, 142.

30 Versluis, 14.

31 Alan Moore (w), JH Williams (p), and Mick Gray (i), "Creating the Dream: The Making of Issue 32," *Promethea* Book 5 (La Jolla, CA: America's Best Comics, 2000), unpaginated.

32 Alan Moore (w), JH Williams (p), and Mick Gray (i), *Promethea* Book 5 (La Jolla, CA: America's Best Comics, 2000), unpaginated, reprint of *Promethea* #32.

33 Interview in *The Mindscape of Alan Moore*.

34 Annalisa Di Liddo, *Alan Moore: Comics as Performance, Fiction as Scalpel* (Jackson: University Press of Mississippi, 2009), 95.

35 Alan Moore (w), JH Williams (p), and Mick Gray (i), *Promethea* Book 5 (La Jolla, CA: America's Best Comics, 2000), unpaginated, reprint of *Promethea* #31.

36 Moore, *Promethea* #31, unpaginated.

37 Elizabeth K. Rosen, *Apocalyptic Transformation: Apocalypse and the Postmodern Imagination* (Lanham, MD: Lexington Books, 2008), 37.

38 "Alan Moore Interviewed by Eddie Campbell," *Eddie Campbell's Egomania* (Marietta, GA: Top Shelf Productions, 2002), 23; reprinted in Moore and Campbell, *A Disease of Language*, unpaginated.

39 Douglas Wolk, "Magic Comic Ride," *Salon.com*, July 1, 2005, par. 10, http://dir.salon.com/books/review/2005/07/01/promethea/index.html.

40 Wolk par. 10.

41 Pers. comm. to Christine Hoff Kraemer, 2009.

42 Soror NCT, "A Comic Book for the New Aeon," *The Fleur de Lis* 1.1 (Oct 2007): 6, http://www.theorteekstasis.org/oto/pdf/newsletter/fleur-1-1.pdf.

43 Jason Pitzl-Waters, "The Importance of Alan Moore," *The Wild Hunt*, March 1, 2009, http://wildhunt.org/blog/2009/03/the-importance-of-alan-moore.html.

44 Tasha Robinson, "Alan Moore," *AV Club, The Onion*, October 24, 2001, par. 12, http://www.avclub.com/articles/alan-moore,13740/.

45 Robinson, par. 13.

46 Robinson, par. 13.

47 Jenny Christopher, "Indie Edge February 2009: Alan Moore," *PreviewsWorld.com*, par. 47, http://www.previewsworld.com/public/default.asp?t=1&m=1&c=6&s=448&ai=79482&ssd=.

Religion and *Artesia* / Religion in *Artesia*

MARK SMYLIE

Offering

AN *APOLOGIA* OF SORTS: I write and draw a fantasy comic book series (or graphic novels, should you prefer a more literary term). It's about a woman, eponymously named Artesia and armed with a sword, who kills a lot of people. She does not wear a chain-mail bikini, which may disappoint some readers. She does, however, get naked every now and then and participate in orgies, so that may mediate their disappointment somewhat.

As a genre, fantasy is *not* — perhaps surprisingly, given how well it is suited to the medium — a common subject for modern comic books or graphic novels, which tend to be dominated by superhero stories[1] or their antithesis, the slice-of-life, portrait-of-the-artist-as-a-young-man, navel-gazing storytelling typical of so-called indie or alternative comics. Fantasy, science fiction, and speculative fiction are still rare in comics, or at least such stories are rare that are not really superhero stories in disguise. Fantasy literature (and its antecedents in mythology, folktale, and legend) is a form of heroic literature, not *superheroic* literature, though I will concede that there has always been an element of the superhuman in fantasy literature, legend, and mythology: the feats of semi-divine Herakles in his *Labours*; the warp spasms of the ancient Celtic hero Cúchulainn in the *Táin Bó Cúailnge*; the ridiculous deadliness of the heroes of the *Song of Roland*; or the Doré illustrations for Ariosto's

Orlando Furioso, with their impossible, almost superhuman tenor.
It has been commonplace in the entertainment industry, at least in my
experience, to claim some kindred resonance in any "heroic" or "superheroic" narrative to the hero-journey as set forth by Joseph Campbell's
monomyth,[2] which might be useful to repeat in some detail:

> The mythological hero, setting from his commonday hut or castle,
> is lured, carried away, or else voluntarily proceeds, to the threshold
> of adventure. There he encounters a shadow presence that guards
> the passage. The hero may defeat or conciliate this power to go alive
> into the kingdom of the dark (brother-battle, dragon-battle; offering,
> charm), or be slain by the opponent and descend in death (dismem-
> berment, crucifixion). Beyond the threshold then, the hero journeys
> through a world of unfamiliar yet strangely intimate forces, some of
> which severely threaten him (tests), some of which give magical aid
> (helpers). When he arrives at the nadir of the mythological round, he
> undergoes a supreme ordeal and gains his reward. The triumph may
> be represented as the hero's sexual union with the goddess-mother
> of the world (sacred marriage), his recognition by the father-creator
> (father atonement), his own divinization (apotheosis), or again — if
> the powers have remained unfriendly to him — his theft of the boon
> he came to gain (bride-theft, fire-theft); intrinsically it is an expansion
> of consciousness and therewith of being (illumination, transfigura-
> tion, freedom). The final work is that of the return. If the powers have
> blessed the hero, he now sets forth under their protection (emissary);
> if not, he flees and is pursued (transformation flight, obstacle flight).
> At the return threshold the transcendental powers must remain
> behind; the hero re-emerges from the kingdom of dread (return,
> resurrection). The boon that he brings restores the world (elixir).[3]

I tend to think that claim of kinship rings false when it comes to the
superhero genre; the hero journey in the superhero narrative usually
seems incomplete or, for lack of a better word, immature in comparison with the full cycle of the monomyth. There is a common theme of
"accidental" power in superhero narratives; with exceptions, the gift of
powers in superhero comics is not predictable, not sought after, and
often only reluctantly accepted. This runs counter to the traditional
heroic narrative, in which the hero journeys expressly for the purpose
of gaining some power, gift, or boon in order to save or transform their

world. Batman may perhaps be held as the closest to the traditional hero in the superhero genre; he deliberately seeks to transform himself through skill and technology into something otherworldly in order to right the wrongs of his city. By contrast, the vast majority of other superhero characters receive their powers by accident of birth or just by plain accident. The superhero narrative *begins* with the boon — the gift of superpowers, by spider bite or alien birthright, by gamma ray or random mutation — and tests the superhero *after they are already super*. This may be a reflection, ultimately, of the superhero's birth as an American archetype, and a manifestation of America's self-image as a reluctant or accidental superpower. The ambivalence that Americans feel towards the exercise of power and world leadership, particularly in the post-Vietnam era, can be felt in the reluctance with which their superheroes take up their mantles.

Further, the superhero begins his journey already more or less immortal, and it is, arguably, the experience of death — the journey into the dark, into the otherworld — that is one of the hallmarks of the heroic narrative and for the generation of hero cult. Indeed, I suppose it could be argued that for the ancient Greeks, for someone to be given hero cult, they *had* to be dead by definition (if a man is alive and receives cult, he's not a hero; he's an emperor or a Pharaoh). Most ancient or mythic heroes die within their epics (as opposed to some unspecified point after their epic is over) — Achilles, Hector, Beowulf, Siegfried, Arthur all come to mind — and often die rather spectacular deaths that help define them *as* heroes. Ask most veterans, or any firefighter who survived 9/11: *the heroes are the guys that didn't make it back*. Most superheroes, in contrast, do not die; their deaths are rare and rarely irreversible.[4]

Other elements are usually missing from a superhero narrative: the passage to a kingdom of the dark or the underworld (for usually in superhero stories there is no *other*world, no sense of any world other than the mundane); the expansion of consciousness that marks the hero's triumph and illumination (for the transformation in superhero comics tends to be a *physical* one, most decidedly not a *spiritual* one); and perhaps most importantly, the notion of the return from the kingdom of dread to restore the world. Heroes in the mold of the classical monomyth journey to save, heal, or transform their world; they often have a fixed goal to which they aspire and against which their success can be measured. The superhero genre, in contrast, is (to me) really a variation of the crime genre. Ultimately, in the world of crime there is a fundamentally cynical world-view: crime never goes away, it's always there, and it is the *natural state of man* (or at least of some men) *to be a criminal.* The policeman, the detective, and the superhero must be ever-vigilant (and ever-present) to fight the doers of evil that plague society. Superheroes are made, created, and called because their societies are incapable of solving the problem of crime. They are anti-democratic — and anti-modern, which I suppose could give them some claim of resonance with the hero of Campbell's (and Rank's and Lord Raglan's) hero narratives, who often come from noble birth. But the superhero stands apart from government, indeed often stands in opposition to it, while in feudal and pre-modern societies, the nobles *are* the government. When a king or a hero journeys to gain a boon to restore their world, they often do so because *it is their duty as those who govern or will govern to undertake the journey.*

Superheroes never go away, they don't die (gloriously or ingloriously) like Achilles, nor do they return home like Odysseus; they're always there, hiding behind their secret identities, ready to emerge to fight the next criminal threat. So just as the superhero is incapable of dying (and thus taking what could be considered just the *first* crucial step in the monomythic hero journey, as well as its inevitable *last*), the superhero is in some ways doomed to fail, as the world of the superhero will always be filled with crime and supervillainy. The superhero genre, like the soap opera, is an unending genre, a serial story that always ends in the same cliffhanger. There is no way for the superhero to achieve some great restoration of a broken world, only gain some small tactical victories in an unending chain of violence and predation. *Gotham will always be Gotham.*

Dismemberment

If science fiction can be defined as speculative fiction that takes a leap in science as its founding difference, then to me fantasy is speculative fiction that looks at the question of what a world would be like if magic, the supernatural, or, more dangerously, religion were *real* and efficacious. As someone who claims to be a fantasy author, therefore, I see my project slightly differently from other authors who may be contributing essays to this book, authors who deal with real, actual religions in real world settings, and who must therefore be concerned with capturing

Figure 1

with some accuracy the rituals and religious sentiments of a living people. Mine is instead an exercise in *false religion* (or perhaps what Campbell called *creative religion*). I offer this label both in the sense that such religion is a make-believe cosmology for a make-believe world, but also that it's an experiment in (re)imagining the religious beliefs of the ancient and medieval worlds. In this fictional setting, some variation of those religions and the gods and goddesses they venerated are, in fact, *real* and *actual*, in contrast to the modern presumption that those gods are *fake* and *imaginary*.

Most characters in comics — whether in superhero comics, so-called fantasy comics, or indie/alt-comics — are irreligious. They practice no particular religion, make no regular ritual observations,[5] contest against the gods that populate their worlds, or disbelieve in them altogether. The divine world, if it exists at all, inspires no awe, no dread, no transcendental ecstasy; it possesses no extra or unusual quality that differentiates it from the mundane world other than being located *over there* instead of *here*. If gods do exist in superhero comics, they tend to be essentially the same as mortals, possessed of the same desires, motives, and fears as humans, but possessed of brute strength and occasionally a supernatural power at the high end of a sliding scale (who can bench press more, the Hulk or Odin?). They are rarely if ever objects of actual worship; if "good," they are reduced to benign observers, or if "evil," reduced to some sort of über-villainy, criminal masterminds who happen to reside on Mount Olympus. In the rare instances in which gods or demi-gods are themselves the main characters in a comic book (Thor, Hercules, Diana/Wonder Woman in some versions), they are most often portrayed as crime fighters, engaged in the same kind of vigilante police work as their mortal compatriots.

I wanted the characters in *Artesia* to instead practice their cult as part of their daily lives, and to view the divine and the supernatural as real motive forces largely beyond their comprehension, if not their control. Artesia's world is a magical universe, a world in which both magic and religion are equally and obviously efficacious, in which hexes and the evil eye, amulets and enchanted swords, faeries and spirit creatures, angels and demons, gods and goddesses all possess a tangible reality and can interact with the characters and influence the success of their actions. Prayers and spells work, the position of the stars can control one's fate, and alchemy can turn lead into gold or make someone immortal. The characters make burnt offerings to propitiate the gods of war and death before battles, pray for endurance and pleasure during sex, sacrifice animals to celebrate milestones, leave trophies at altars to mark victories, and so forth; they practice what is to them a real and effective religion.

The ritual sacrifices performed in Artesia's world — the very first images of the first graphic novel are of Artesia conducting a pre-battle sacrifice — conform to the near-universal standards of ancient sacrifice: the procession leading the sacrificial victim, the climactic throat-cutting, the butchering of the victim, the examination of entrails for signs and omens, the ritual use of fresh blood, and finally the burning or cooking of the remains (and, ultimately, their shared consumption by the sacrificers). The ancient Greeks, as I understand it, required the consent of the sacrificed; this was achieved in the Greek sacrifice rite by sprinkling water upon the body of the sacrificial animal, with the shake of its body or head (the *hupokuptein*) being taken as a sign of its acquiescence — an act of fakery and sacred theater, designed to assuage the guilt of the participants.[6] In a fantasy world, however, people can actually speak to animals if you want them to, so it becomes possible as an author to speculate on what a world might be like in which animals have made a choice between being domesticated (and therefore ultimately sacrificed) and being wild (and therefore hunted, preferably and most properly within the context of the gods of the Hunt). In a fantasy world, animals can actually communicate their acquiescence to sacrifice, or their refusal, and thus by extension their consumers can be made guilty of a fundamental crime, the sacrifice of the unwilling.

As a fantasy author I can speculate about what might happen to the spirits of dead animals, killed and consumed by those that did not ask their permission to kill them and eat them (my answer: *they get very, very*

Figure 2

angry). That became for me one of the deep background conflicts of Artesia's world: the tensions between, on the one hand, a culture that believes you can only eat meat within a sacred context — in an act of religious sacrifice, and with the permission of the sacrificed and the consumed — centered on the goddess cult of Yhera, the Great Queen; and on the other, a culture (the precursor to our modern one, naturally) that believes that animals don't have spirits or feelings — that the consumption of the flesh of the once-living is the divine right of their murderers — centered on the patriarchal cult of Islik the Divine King. Indeed, the anger of animal spirits improperly consumed becomes one of the primary motivations for the creation of "Heaven" in Artesia's world. Islik makes his Palace in the Heavens a refuge for his followers, to save them from the ire of the animal spirits that fill the Underworld and seek judgment in the afterlife on those that killed and consumed them without sacred context and consent. This desire to escape judgment becomes the hidden motif/theme for an entire culture.

Fire-theft

At worst, this sort of fantasy-world-building is an exercise in pastiche — cobbling together bits and pieces of better thoughts, stealing what I can, indulging in an act of piracy: *take what you can, give nothing back.*[7] In particular, I drew upon the mythology and religion of the ancient Greeks, Romans, and Celts (at least as interpreted by modern academic writers), along with a healthy dose of the intersection between the ancient pagan world and monotheism as seen in both Mithras and its rival cult of Christianity (essentially as the roots of the cult of Islik). Indeed, the primary conception of the setting of the comic rose out of texts on medieval witchcraft and its persecution, and the schema of an older Goddess-oriented polytheistic religion encountering a newer upstart patriarchal monotheistic religion. So dogmatic an approach later seemed overly simplistic, and I'd like to believe it gave way to more nuanced conceptions of the rival religions of Artesia's world that tried to emphasize their connections rather than simply their differences. I found the research roots of those religions and cultures and the arcs that they would follow in what could largely be called speculative academic writing on religion (if indeed it can be called academic at all): Marija Gimbutas' work on a proto-European Goddess culture, Joseph Campbell's attempts at a syncretic approach to world religion, Sir James

Frazer's and Margaret Murray's writings on pan-European religion, Carlo Ginzburg's work on early European shamanic culture's relations to medieval witchcraft, and the religious archeology of Martin Bernal's *Black Athena.*

But unlike an academic who must be concerned with the truth-value of their writings and sources (for at least as I as a non-academic understand it, many of the authors I turned to are viewed with dismissive skepticism by their more mainstream colleagues), as a fiction writer I was free to find the ideas in their works that resonate with the world I wanted to create: an older religion of sacrifice and sacred meat-eating vs. a newer religion that believes in human supremacy over the animal world; an ageless chthonic religion vs. a newer sky/sun-oriented cult; cults of Dionysian ecstasy vs. the orders of sexual Puritanism; the freedom of song and dance and sex vs. the stricture/discipline of the word and text. Of course the real world is more complicated than that, and doesn't really fall into such neat polarizations, or for that matter such neat connections; the morphology of the hero-journey, the existence of an original Goddess culture, shamanism as the root of witchcraft: *all theories, and like all theories, all fundamentally false.* They are not the thing itself, but a signifier, a schematic, an interpretation, a simplification, a fiction, a wish to be fulfilled. I hope ultimately the make-believe of Artesia's world isn't that simple either, but in an exercise in world-building those schematics can be become useful building blocks; I can, as a fantasy writer, make "true" a theory, grant a wish or three, make the world how I want it to be rather than how it is.

Transfiguration

There was a phrase of Hélène Cixous' that I first stumbled across in Teresa de Lauretis' *Alice Doesn't: Feminism, Semiotics, Cinema*: "You only have to look at the Medusa straight on to see her. And she's not deadly. She's beautiful and she's laughing."[8] When I first read that a long time ago, I felt inspired by that line not only to begin looking at myth and fantasy from a new perspective (for at the time I had left the fantasy and comic book stories of my youth far behind), but also to recombine her deadliness back into her — to make a woman beautiful and laughing *and* deadly. Hence, eventually, Artesia — part Queen Medb, part Joan of Arc, perhaps a bit like Galadriel if she'd taken the One Ring: "In place of the Dark Lord you will set up a Queen. And I shall not be dark, but

Figure 3

beautiful and terrible as the Morning and the Night! Fair as the Sea
and the Sun and the Snow upon the Mountain! Dreadful as the Storm
and the Lightning! Stronger than the foundations of the earth. All shall
love me and despair!"[9]

I gave Artesia the markings of a heroic birth as explored by Rank
and Raglan — born with a caul (to mark her as a magician[10]) under a
blood-red moon, with wolves and ravens and owls gathered as witnesses;
born to a witch who had summoned ghosts and spirits to conceive her,
her birth midwifed by a mountain spirit/witch queen named Urgrayne
(more thefts: a version of the Wild Hunt goddess variously named Diana,
Herodiana, Holda, Madonna Oriente, etc., and envisioned as a dark
version of C. S. Lewis' White Witch) who is daughter of Djara Luna,
the dark part of the tripartite moon (a version of Hekate). I gave her
an ungrateful king, a cadre of loyal captains, an army of lancers and
halberdiers and mercenary pikemen, all armored in blue-black three-
quarter plate harnesses. I gave her a magic sword she knows nothing
about, bound spirits to serve her. And I gave her gods to worship and
sacrifice to.

Artesia's gods were designed to be at once familiar and, hopefully, just
different enough from their closest inspirations to allow readers to see
something new in them. Yhera, the ruling goddess of her pantheon, is
a Hera unbound and undiminished by marriage to a King, worshipped
by a hundred epithets, perhaps closer to Inanna in mythological role
than Hera's reduction to bitter shrew. Yhera is part of several tripartite
sisterhoods, ruling the Earth with her sisters Geniché and Geteema,
and the Moon with her sisters Adjia and Djara. Geniché (shades of
Ereshkigal) abandons the Earth and creates the Underworld. She
becomes the Queen of the Dead, instituting the First Law, that of death,
that all those born of her Earth must follow her into the Underworld

at the end of their lives, and thereby she sets history into motion. Djara is, as mentioned before, a version of Hekate, a goddess of the dark, of magic and enchantment, of terror and crossroads and transformation; and from somewhere in her dark brood come the most visible goddesses that Artesia will follow in her books — the Gorgonae, a reworked version of the Greek Gorgons, remade as goddesses of war.

Artesia is epic military fantasy; it's a book about war, inspired in part by watching the descent into savagery that marked the Balkan wars of the 1990s and the relative helplessness of the civilized Western world to find any meaningful or even useful response to religiously inspired bloodletting on such a scale. As such, gods and goddesses of war play a keen part in the narrative. Goddess trios abound in ancient mythology (and in Artesia's world), but I felt a particular desire to combine the Greek Gorgons' iconography with the Celtic triple war goddess, the Mórrigán, to give those Celtic ladies a slightly different look; or perhaps not so different, as Ginzburg postulated a connection between the Celtic Mórrigán and the Sicilian, pre-Greek *Morgana* and the *morg* toponym — once again that hint of a universal connectivity that can never be either true nor false, but that I felt comfortable in extending further east (it being but a hop, skip, and a jump from *morg* to *gorg*).[11] I kept the Mórrigán's connection to ravens and crows (what self-respecting war goddess would not be accompanied by carrion eaters, after all?), but visually, tied them to lions and to serpents in the Greek style. The stylized lioness markings on the Gorgonae of Artesia's world are inspired by A David Napier's suggestion of a correlation between the Greek Gorgons' iconography and that of Near Eastern and Indo-European (largely Scythian) lion goddesses and leonine demons — specifically the superciliary marks that tie the Greek Gorgons to lion representations throughout the Near East.[12] Free to steal and combine and recombine as I desired (if always with an eye towards Cixous' phrase), I then added the lower bodies of snakes (shades of both the ancient Greek *Lamiae* and the Type V Demon from *Dungeons and Dragons*) and weapons of iron and bronze.

As with the Mórrigán, the Gorgonae hover over battlefields (to those that can see them), are invoked in prayers and rituals, and receive cult sacrifice from the warriors and soldiers of cultures that recognize them. In exchange, they give their worshippers aid that affects the narrative of the story by helping one side win over the other in a battle (though they do so fickly). They are, in effect, an active force in the narrative:

Figure 4

participants and divine actors, not merely window-dressing to cover up a more modern and essentially secular sensibility.

It can be argued, I suppose, that ancient cultures, and the people of Artesia's world, offer sacrifices of meat to the gods because ultimately the gods are carnivores and predators: *don't eat me, eat this animal instead.* (Even YHWH gave the sign of the rainbow only as a result of his pleasure in smelling the burning meat of a sacrifice.) The warriors of Artesia's world perform blood sacrifices to celebrate and reenact the human transition from prey to predator (as in Barbara Ehrenreich's formulation in her study of war, *Blood Rites*), and burned offerings to propitiate and satisfy the cravings of some very dark and deadly war goddesses. Artesia and her captains function as priestesses and sacrificers when they are on campaign, and this is a fundamental part of their conception of warfighting, just as it was to the ancient Greeks. The guilt endemic to the act of sacrifice and meat consumption (the use of scapegoats in ancient Greece, for example, to help purge the taint of murder from the polis) makes sacrifice an appropriate war act, since war is — in Ehrenreich's phrase — "by any sane standard, a criminal undertaking."[13] But of course, in both the ancient world and Artesia's world, sacrifice is everywhere there is civilization; it's one of its hallmarks. As is, perhaps, war.

I followed Ehrenreich's notion that culture (humanity) arises out of a need for protection and defense against hunger and violence, out of the experience of being hunted, and that people learned to cooperate in groups because of their fear of predators (and each other). This experience was built into the origins of both religion (the initial offer of sacrifice, to predator and predator goddess) and of war in Artesia's world (the initial instinct to band together for self-defense): *when you are gripped with fear, you turn to your gods, your neighbors, and your weapons.* The originators of war in Artesia's world are the women of an ancient Amazon paradise called Ürüne Düré (an Amazon Atlantis, if you will, in keeping with Cixous' direction, or perhaps with Wittig's *Les Guérillères*), seeking a method of protecting themselves and their arts against the pillage and rapine of their barbarian neighbors.

An Old Düréan Tale [as told in the appendixes of *Artesia Afield*]

In the Golden Age, when the Düréans recreated Geniché's Garden on their isle, rumors of their wealth spawned jealousy and greed amongst

Figure 5

many outlanders. The strongest of the barbarians came together, and conspired to build a fleet, and sail to Ürüne Düré, and rob the Düréans of their wealth. The oracles of Düréa dreamed dark visions and learned of this raid, and they turned to their predator goddess, to the great consumer of sacrifice, to Dread Yhera, for deliverance, asking her to show them how to defend themselves from the raiders.

Yhera called the other devouring beasts — first Adjia and Irré, the sun-masked archers, the huntress and the hunter, the javelin-wielding killer of women and the bow-bearing killer of men; then Hathhalla, the Devourer, the goddess of grief and vengeance; and her hunter and animal keeper, her consort Ammon Agdah. And she set them and their Companions to defending the Düréans. The raiders came and many died, stalked by Adjia, and Irré, and Agdah, but still they pillaged the Isle of many of its treasures and left triumphant with slaves and booty. Yhera looked down with sadness at the destruction they had wrought, and was filled with the grief of her children. Hathhalla came to her then, and whispered in her ear, and awoke the secret in her heart.

Yhera summoned Ariahavé, her brightest daughter, and bade her make unbreakable chains, and sent her to capture three of the fiercest half-mad daughters of Djara, who were the mothers of the Galéans and called the Gorgonae. So Ariahavé searched the dark places of Düréa, and found the Gorgonae hidden in their daughters' shame, and bound them, and brought them to Yhera: Mogran, the Riot Goddess and Queen of Discord; Halé, the Goddess of Rage and Fury; and Médüre, the Cunning One. And Yhera consumed them, chains and all, and then she gave a great cry and she disgorged them from her belly, and Yhera gave bloody birth to War.

Soon the raiders returned, unsatisfied with their first plunder. Yhera unchained the Gorgonae and they went amongst the Düréans, and taught them the secrets to transform themselves and become warriors, the ways to harness din and discord, rage and cunning. They danced, and drummed, and drank potions, and marked themselves and donned masks, and the Düréans armed themselves to war. And they greeted the raiders with the howls of lions and the speed of serpents, and drove them back across the sea. The Düréans pursued them into the outlands, and slew their families, and freed the slaves they had taken. And when they had returned to Düréa, the Gorgonae showed them how to purify themselves and take off their masks and stop being warriors, and become themselves again.

So the Gorgonae were the first goddesses of War and Battle, the goddesses of warrior transformation, who invoked war and ended it, and first made it an art. Yhera held their chains, and became Yhera Anath, the Queen of War and Victory, Dread and Unconquered. Adjia and Irré came and learned from them, and Adjia became the initiator, the first to take a child and show them the ways of war, and Irré became Lykeios, the old wolf, the destroyer prayed to by gray-haired veterans. Agdah and his hunting band came too, and they learned to become a warrior band, the Consort-Defender and his companions.

But Ariahavé, the goddess of civilization, had been midwife at the birth of War, and she learned better than them all. She went to her forge, and made skins and scales of metal for the Düréans to wear, and made the first sword, and shared her secrets with Bragea [the Smith]. She taught them the arts of forage and supply, so that warriors could go where they wanted when they wanted. She taught the Düréans how to take the dances that they loved so much, and turn them to war and give battle a rhythm: how to make many move as one, and make one part of many, how to make warriors into soldiers. And for all these things Yhera made Ariahavé her general, and gave her the chains of the Gorgonae for safekeeping.

War (as opposed to merely violence committed en masse by a group) becomes, by definition, an act of civilized peoples, in which in defense of and for the sake of their culture and society they allow themselves to be transformed, to become predators, to become animals — to kill, to sacrifice, to consume, on a grand and epic scale. Civilization, in Artesia's world, is perhaps ultimately defined by sacrifice, war, and religion, the acts which make all other acts possible (or perhaps the acts which make all other acts permissible). They are intertwined, inseparable: all part of the same theory, the same act of fiction.

Elixir

Weren't you paying attention? There's no such thing.

Notes

1 In the sense of stories about characters blessed with unusual powers in comparison with everyone else around them, who choose to use their powers to safeguard their fellow citizens in what is usually a vigilante manner.

2 I suppose it is also now commonplace for writers, musicians, and actors (or

essayists) to view the production of the written word or other kinds of art as a sort of hero journey, which may explain the autobiographical nature of much of modern literature or the compulsion of authors to shape their own biographies — shades of James Frey — as tales of trauma and tragedy, in which the tests they have allegedly undergone (addiction, abuse) in their personal hero journeys help prepare the elixir (the text) which shall transform the world and the reader.

3 Joseph Campbell, *The Hero With A Thousand Faces* (Princeton University Press/ Bollingen, 1973).

4 Indeed, in so far as superheroes tend be owned by corporations, there's always a new editor or writer to revive a dead superhero with some impossible, nigh-miraculous, and (to faithful readers) inevitably non-canonical explanation as to how he or she cheated death.

5 Unless it is some presentation of Catholicism, which seems to be the universal stand-in for an organized religion in both comics and horror movies.

6 See Louise Bruit Zaidman and Pauline Schmitt Pantel, *Religion in the Ancient Greek City* (Cambridge University Press, 1992).

7 Captain Jack Sparrow in *Pirates of the Caribbean* (Walt Disney Company, 2003).

8 Cited in Teresa de Lauretis, *Alice Doesn't: Feminism, Semiotics, Cinema* (Indiana University Press, 1984). Originally appeared in Hélène Cixous, "The Laugh of the Medusa," *New French Feminisms* (University of Massachusetts Press, 1980).

9 JRR Tolkien, *The Lord of the Rings* (Ballantine Books, 1965).

10 See Carlo Ginzburg's work on the *benandanti* in *Ecstasies: Deciphering the Witches' Sabbath* (Pantheon, 1991).

11 Ginzburg, *Ecstasies.*

12 A David Napier, *Masks, Transformation, and Paradox* (University of California Press, 1986).

13 Barbara Ehrenreich, *Blood Rites: Origins and History of the Passions of War* (Metropolitan Books, 1997).

Present Gods, Absent Believers in *Sandman*

EMILY RONALD

EIL GAIMAN'S *THE SANDMAN* SERIES is set in a world that mirrors our own. Hidden within his ordinary "waking world," however, are numerous supernatural beings: ghosts, fairies, demons, and the Endless (personifications of concepts such as Dream, the Sandman). The list of supernatural beings also includes gods, who move among humans and through the world: arguing at feasts, dancing at strip clubs, and working as CEOs. While a human within our ordinary world might wonder about the existence of God or gods, within the *Sandman* universe they are present and active. Even the Creator, though never pictured and present only by allusion and revelation, unquestionably exists in this realm. The presence of divinities is a given in Gaiman's universe.

But while the world of *Sandman* mirrors our own in many ways, there is an absence in the lives of its human characters that is thrown into sharp relief by the plethora of gods. Of all the human characters, very few are religious adherents of any kind. The number of characters that follow a religious tradition familiar to those in our world outside of the comic book can be counted on one hand. A few more follow a less-defined spirituality, some questing, some bargaining. Yet those who interact with divinities rarely benefit from it. The only instances of effective worship in the series emphasize the weakness and death of the goddess to whom they are directed.

Why is this the case? In a series where the existence of gods is reality — hidden to the inhabitants but clearly present to the reader — why do so few characters pay attention to them? This essay will begin by looking at the humans in *Sandman* as religious adherents, members of institutions, seekers, or magicians, then consider the objects of these religions, the gods of Gaiman's setting. Finally, a review of the kinds of human-divine interaction within the series suggests a philosophy of wonder that emerges as a quasi-theological argument within *Sandman*. *Sandman*'s setting ends up displaying a peculiar double effect of simultaneously making religion, or any interaction with divinity, irrelevant and disenchanted, while also encouraging wonder at the re-enchantment of the world. Gods as characters lose their divine wonder, but that wonder is instead distributed throughout the ordinary world of the *Sandman* setting. The intervening structures between gods and humanity (churches, ritual, laws) disappear or are devalued in favor of an embrace of wonder, and gods themselves change in order to survive among humans.

To explore this religious universe, I start from Paul Ricoeur's study of hermeneutics, the interpretation and reading of texts. In his *Interpretation Theory*, Ricoeur roots his hermeneutics in Christian study of the Bible, but he extends them to apply to any narrative text. The reader's work, suggests Ricoeur, is not to decipher or unveil the "true" meaning covered and hidden by the text. Instead, the act of reading opens up a world *in front of* the text, "a disclosure of a possible way of looking at things."[1] This world is not identical to the author's intention, but is rather a project, a proposition that suggests new "modes of being" or "a new capacity for knowing himself" to the reader.[2] Although there will be differences in each reader's encounter with the text, this essay looks at some of the elements that *Sandman*'s world in front of the text might contain. What ideas, moods, moments, or challenges does it invite the reader to reconfigure into her own life? Within this setting, what stories, gods, and symbols are made available to the reader? What does *Sandman* offer the reader, either as a full world disclosed in front of the text, or as a collection of separable, mobile symbols?

Sandman is not a single linear narrative running through 75 issues, but rather a series of related stories that center around the title character Dream of the Endless, his captivity on Earth, his kingdom of dreams, and his interactions with siblings, lovers, and subjects. Despite its many non-human characters, *Sandman*'s stories are set within a world that strongly resembles our own. This mingling of an ordinary human setting and the extraordinary non-human characters joins readers' expectations of the familiar with the fantastic. Gaiman ensures that humans are at the core of even the most fantastic conflicts and adventures. Human dreams, human motives, and human actions are driving forces of the stories and the setting within which the extraordinary powers of the Endless, the fairies, and the forces of Hell emerge. A few stories take place in settings outside the human world, but remain connected to human concerns. The longest time away from the human world is the story arc *Season of Mists,* in which Lucifer closes down Hell and gives the key to Dream to dispose of as he sees fit. Even there, one of the eight issues is devoted to the consequences for the human world. This waking world (as opposed to Dream's kingdom The Dreaming) is nearly congruent with our non-fictional one, sharing events such as World Wars, historical personages such as Augustus Caesar and Emperor Norton I, and locations such as the Taklamakan Desert and Central Park.

Within this mirrored world, however, there are very few characters that are identifiably members of a religious tradition. One is a nameless Jewish man in New York, introduced in "The Sound of Her Wings" as Death, Dream's Endless sister, visits him. He recognizes her as Death, and after a brief protest, says the *Sh'ma Yisroel* as he dies. "It's good I said the Sh'ma," he tells her posthumously; "my old man always said it guaranteed you a place in heaven. If you believe in heaven."[3] Another set of believers is the family of Wanda Mann, who appear at the end of *A Game of You.* They are conservative Kansas Christians who have rejected their transgender child and remade her corpse into the good, clean-cut, God-fearing boy she was supposed to be. These characters express no doubts about their faith, and they even assert that the hurricane that killed Wanda was a sign of God's judgment on New York.[4] They are intended to be unsympathetic and cold, especially in contrast to Wanda's protective, kind, and humorous personality. A few other nameless characters appear, such as the end-time preachers in a single panel of *Preludes and Nocturnes.*[5] In a brief moment during the serial-killer convention in *The Doll's House,* one panel includes three believers (or rather, two believers and one person claiming to be God), each of whom claims religious justification for their murders.[6]

The story entitled "Ramadan" centers on the Caliph Haroun al-Raschid. An invocation in the name of Allah opens the Middle Eastern setting, and statements such as "Allah alone knows all" throughout demonstrate a Muslim identity for several characters. Yet ultimately,

Ramadan serves as a setting rather than a motive for al-Raschid. Gaiman portrays him as a thoughtful and wise king over a city full of wonders. However, al-Raschid seems to break the Ramadan fast by eating grapes and offering to share them with Dream; when Dream reminds him of the holy fast, he responds "It is no matter," and continues his negotiations.[7] He is more sympathetic than the Manns, more dedicated than the Jewish man, but not especially observant.

Some characters reject all religion vehemently, taking on a quasi-religious atheism instead. Faith in secularism has a few adherents, but they clash badly with the supernatural and extraordinary qualities of the *Sandman* universe. In "Thermidor," set during the French Reign of Terror, Maximilien François Marie Isidore de Robespierre proudly proclaims that he has founded a new religion, "based on reason, celebrating an egalitarian supreme being, distant and uninvolved."[8] The miracles and superstitions of the past come back to haunt him, however, when the living head of mythic Orpheus sings with a chorus of the decapitated victims of Robespierre's regime. The song immobilizes Robespierre, and it is hinted that his swift fall from power is a result of Orpheus's enchantment. In the *Sandman* universe, to embrace reason to the exclusion of wonder is a dangerous position to take.

The volume *World's End* takes place outside of the human world that reflects our own, but features travelers from worlds like and unlike our own sheltering and sharing stories. "Cluracan's Tale" involves one of the few religious organizations mentioned in *Sandman*: the Universal Aurelian Church, which happens to be led by a corrupt priest, the Psychopomp. In Aurelia, among the crumbling statues and the corrupt dealings of the Psychopomp, we see more religious adherents than in the settings that are intended to reflect our own world. The priests and believers in Aurelia seem to take the Church of the Holy Twins seriously — enough so that Cluracan can use their outrage over the Psychopomp's religious scandals to start riots. But we never see the Holy Twins, the deities of this religion, and the temporal leader is unfit to safeguard the sacred.[9]

Far more common than worshippers, spiritual devotees, or even casual adherents are the magicians of *Sandman*. These magicians bargain with demons and strive to coerce powerful beings, but they do not worship. Instead of the development of a reciprocal relationship between deity and worshipper, these interactions are bribes and coercions, intent on a tit-for-tat exchange. This relation with divinity is purely instrumental.

Foremost among the magicians is the witch Thessaly, and her ritual for drawing down the moon in *A Game of You* bears some resemblance to Goddess spirituality of our world — though she harrumphs at the idea of the ritual as "empowering" rather than effective. It is hard to call this a relation of worship, however: Thessaly bargains with and threatens Trioditis, the triple goddess, and approaches her/them coolly or with harsh words, which Trioditis seems to resent. "Just as I pulled you down from the heavens, you are mine to dispose of, mine to command," Thessaly declares. The faces of the moon recall that Thessaly's kind "commanded, directed, ordered," instead of worshipped. "One day you will be ours, as they are," threatens Trioditis, though they agree to Thessaly's demands.[10]

Although the lines are often blurry between magic and religion, Thessaly's activities seem to match the idea of magical practice — individual, gain-oriented, and requiring skilled knowledge — than the idea of reverence, devotion, or patronage that theistic religion connotes. But Thessaly alone seems to have any prolonged interaction with the divinities that permeate the *Sandman* universe, and it is one of negotiation and détente.

Demons and devils are no more likely than gods to provide assistance to humans. Those few mortals who successfully bargain with them find their benefits short-lived and poisonous. Like Thessaly, these people are skilled enough with secret knowledge, proper rituals, and magical power to bind or coerce demons, for a little while at least. In *Season of Mists*, however, we see an example of what unskilled humans might do. Three deceased upperclassmen, returned from Hell after Lucifer has emptied it, reinhabit the boarding school where they sacrificed another student to the Devil. The intended benefits of this murder never materialized; "Nobody in Hell gave a toss." "We burned anyway."[11] Magic, it seems, is not especially beneficial for most of humanity.

Among humans, then, the range of religions Gaiman portrays is small. Individual adherence to a known tradition is rare, and the few believers are almost all casual in their attitudes. Religious institutions are corrupt or irrelevant to the concerns of most characters. Pursuing the attention of extra-human beings outside of institutions or traditions is at best useless and at worst dangerous to one's body and spirit. Are there more "religious" models among the deities and spirits themselves?

The beings to whom worship might be directed vary between named gods with a history of worship; angels and demons that fit within the

Christian mythos; and ineffable, mysterious figures and deities with limited power over specific worlds. The gods of the various pantheons are anthropomorphic deities who argue and flirt. They possess power beyond human capability; for example, Odin has created alternate worlds in which to observe Ragnarok, and Bast communicates with the ghosts of cats. When readers encounter the gods in conjunction with the human world, though, their powers seem sad and weak. The Egyptian sun god Ra in "Façade" has enough power to create champions in his fight against Apep, the serpent that never dies, but he lacks enough wit to know that Apep has long since passed away.[12] Bast inhabits a cold temple somewhere outside of the Dreaming and away from human reality; from there, she can hear the "handful of instants of halfhearted worship" directed to her.[13] The difference is pronounced between the sleek cat goddess who appears young and beautiful in the Dreaming and her waking appearance as old and tired, "her fur thinning, her eyes milky and dim." But Bast does still interact with humans as a goddess, returning prayers and receiving worship, even as it shrinks daily.

Without worshippers, gods fade; to survive, they can choose to transform themselves to live among humans. In *Brief Lives*, two Sumerian gods have turned to hiding their divinity in this way. Pharamond has become Mr. Farrell, changing from a god in charge of travel to a powerful businessman. Dream has helped extend his life by "suggest[ing] that he find another occupation."[14] Ishtar, once queen of love and beauty, is now working as a stripper. The strip club sustains her with a little worship, but also becomes her funeral pyre as she performs one last dance. Ishtar's final speech clarifies godhood within the Sandman universe: "I know how the gods begin . . . We start as dreams. Then we walk out of dreams into the land. We are worshipped and loved, and take power to ourselves. And then one day there's no one left to worship us. And in the end, each little god and goddess takes its last journey back into dreams . . . and what comes after, not even *we* know."[15] Being a pantheon god is not eternal; it comes with no guarantee against old age, weakness, loss, or death. In some ways, to be a pantheon god is to be a human writ large: more power, more life, but subject to the same suffering as humanity.

A less mortal and less vulnerable god appears in another alternate world from *World's End*. The charismatic young leader Prez is tempted three times during his youth and presidency by a mysterious figure named "Boss Smiley," who is "the prince of that world." Smiley offers Prez temptations eerily similar to the Devil's offers to Jesus, and Prez refuses each one. When Prez meets Death after his own demise, he remarks, "So there really is a watchmaker," eager to see who has created his world. Death responds, "I don't think this guy *made* the watch, Prez. He just runs the local franchise." Indeed, the deity on hand is not the ineffable Creator, but Boss Smiley himself. Boss Smiley has stereotyped attributes of the Christian God: he sits on a great white throne in a cloud-filled heaven, he is attended by angels, and he suggests that Prez, as a Christ-figure, sit at his right hand and sing hosannas.[16] But although Smiley has the clichéd costume of God, he's neither the Creator nor the Devil, just the local god-in-charge. He has no authority over Prez, no knowledge of where the dead go, and no power to compel Dream, who steps in to remove Prez from Smiley's realm. Unlike the pantheon gods, Boss Smiley has not needed to change to survive, but his power and jurisdiction are very limited. He ends up seeming distasteful and petty rather than awe-inspiring and divine.

The aforementioned Triple Goddess, Trioditis, makes several appearances throughout the series, from the first story arc to the last. Unlike the Creator, she's actively involved in the world of humans, and her powers shift from every encounter. In *Preludes and Nocturnes*, she (or more accurately they, for Trioditis is a three-part manifestation of female power) manifests as three witches: maiden, mother, and crone. In *The Kindly Ones*, they are the title characters; in *A Game of You*, Thessaly summons the threefold aspect of the moon. The three can be the Fates, the Furies, or the Graces, and it is strongly implied that they are all of these aspects simultaneously. Their interactions with humans take place in two ways: first, via magical transactions such as Thessaly's invocation, and second, as three human women who seem to draw down or evoke the three aspects of the Goddess in conversation with others. They are powerful, devoted to their own ends, and have limited concern for humanity. In some cases, their power seems to outweigh that of the Endless, such as following through on their purpose as the Furies to avenge kin-murder; in others, they seem deferential to Death or Dream. But aside from the magical compulsions of Thessaly and allusions to others like her, Trioditis lacks devotees and religious institutions. The three may be powerful, but they are not worshipped.

The presence of demons and angels in *Season of Mists* seems to suggest that the religious universe actually centers on God as traditionally understood in monotheistic traditions, as the omniscient and omnipotent Creator. The demons and angels derive from the Christian mythos of the fall of Lucifer and the war in Heaven. Their existence might imply that although "lesser" gods and spirits exist, the real power in the universe is a Creator with power over all other beings. The representations of the Silver City in the same story arc also evoke this conception of God. It is neither Paradise nor Heaven, but "outside the created order of things."[17] The Creator sends two angels to observe Dream's deliberation over who should receive the key to Hell, and ultimately, to bear a message about the Creator's will. Yet, the Creator intervenes only once in the entire comic, blasting an unseen message into the angel Remiel's consciousness: that the angels themselves are to take possession of Hell. The Creator's will is unknown even to those who will bear the message and the consequences; the maintenance of the status quo of Heaven and Hell must be preserved. Remiel receives the Creator's message in a flare of light that leaves him stunned, gasping out His command, and when he cries out against the unfairness of being sent to take charge of Hell and exile from the Silver City, there is no answer.[18]

Is this the Christian god? The plaintive cries of Remiel, rebelling against his exile into Hell, meet with no response — not in his first plea, nor ever again in the series. This Creator is beyond understanding, beyond contact; if he has a plan, it is beyond human comprehension. Do prayers reach him? Does he have wishes for humanity? Did he send his only Son to Earth, commandments to Moses, revelation to Mohammed? All of this is unknown. This God is without qualities, immeasurably distant, and if he acts in history, as monotheistic religions claim, it is so subtle as to be imperceptible.[19] The resulting image is closer to the *deus otiosus*, the absent god, who, having created the world, retreated to a faraway spot to observe, or the watchmaker god of the Deists, who exists primarily as a first cause for the universe and not as a being with whom to interact.

What about the Endless themselves, Dream and his siblings, including Destiny, Destruction, Desire, and Delirium (née Delight)? They are "not gods, and will never die like gods";[20] broader in influence and more powerful than the pantheon gods, they are more directly involved in human affairs than the Creator. The Endless occupy a strange realm between the inert, distant Creator and the intimate, personal, even meddlesome lower gods. Their realm, however, is placed outside religion. Only one of the Endless has a definite association with religion and worship: followers of Despair once proclaimed her to be a goddess, and the sect lasted two years before its last member committed suicide.[21]

While people have at times brought the Endless offerings, no system of worship has developed for them. Although the Endless spend a great deal of time with humans, watching them, changing them, loving them, or tormenting them, they do not seem to be interested in any form of religious interaction, and they reject the label of "god."[22]

What is the result of this universe of divine–human interaction? How are humans in the *Sandman* universe supposed to react to the world that contains so many divinities? Taking the antagonistic position will not end well, as Robespierre shows the reader. Bargaining is possible but risky, provided that the humans are already ritually skilled; Thessaly ends up making more bargains with Trioditis to "forget some old scores."[23] Worship might be personally meaningful, but it has few effects in the world. At best, a human worshipper within the *Sandman* setting might feel good for saying prayers that she's been told are good; at worst, one may end up under the thumb of a cruel religious despot who cares little for one's faith — either temporally, like the Psychopomp, or after death, like Boss Smiley. The "joys of belief" might also be manipulated without religion; in *Preludes and Nocturnes,* Dee uses the power of dreams to inspire his victims to put out their own eyes.[24] If an individual is lucky, she may receive the thin blessings of the weakening ancient pantheons, or see a vision of Bast or gain a merciful death for her injured cat. If people are unlucky enough to receive a more direct experience of the supernatural in *Sandman,* such as Ishtar's final dance, they may end up in a frenzy of worship that destroys them.

One answer to the initial question of this essay comes from a functional point of view: people are not religious in *Sandman.* There is no reason for the humans of *Sandman* to react to the gods of *Sandman* with much more than casual, off-hand worship. Prayers rarely work, the forces that act in one's world are dangerous to interact with and should not be worshipped, and the ineffable Creator is so remote that the results of any human petition are completely unknown. If the Creator does not answer the angels, why would he intervene for a human? According to the rational-choice theory of religion, humans worship divine beings because of anticipated spiritual gains such as eternal life or temporal blessings. Adherence to tradition is a result of making a rational calculation, consciously or unconsciously, that the sacrifices one makes in this lifetime are worth the benefits promised by a powerful God.[25]

But in this setting, religious adherents don't take up this calculation of tit-for-tat. Within the *Sandman* universe, the rational-choice theorists are not the adherents but the magicians, making a bet that they can gain benefits from controlling and bargaining with deities. Those who are religious within the *Sandman* world must be looking for something other than the functional benefit of interacting with existing supernatural forces. If the presence of the gods has derailed the functional rationale for religion, then other reasons must be sought. The Manns use their religion as a line of demarcation between purity and corruption, reinforced by the rural/urban divide; the old Jew in New York uses his for comfort and the signification of his identity at the end of his life. The active supernatural elements of *Sandman*'s setting, visible to the reader, have changed nothing for the believers within the story who do not encounter them.

Yet there is another religious component to the *Sandman* universe, one that rests in the hidden nature of the supernatural and its collision with the waking world, one that is, as a result, offered only to the reader and not to the inhabitants. Looking at this conjunction between the extraordinary and the everyday reveals the reasons why the *Sandman* religious universe is so slim despite the gods. The gods, spirits, demons, and angels are the key to this core theme of *Sandman*, one that can even be called Gaiman's basic theological argument and the main result of the world in front of the text: the philosophy of wonder.

This notion of wonder rests on the combination of an ordinary world with an undercurrent of the extraordinary. *Sandman* is filled with subway rides, office parties, stilted conversations on plane rides, and "seemingly ordinary" events. The key is the "seeming": over and over, this human-centered setting is revealed to be hiding a bizarre realm of non-human actors and events. The potential is always there for the ordinary person to be caught up in the extraordinary. A late-night dash for the subway can leave the rider stranded in the dream of a city; a dull patent lawyer may actually be hundreds of thousands of years old. Throughout the series, Gaiman calls this to the reader's attention, as over and over the most ordinary things reveal their extraordinary qualities. In *The Kindly Ones*, Lyta Hall's journey through the city streets is simultaneously a journey through mythic motifs as a stoplight becomes an ogress, a stray cat Puss in Boots, and scavenged trash the apples of the Hesperides.[26] A minor character in *Brief Lives* recounts a "real-life" encounter when a conversation partner at a cocktail party turns out to be a celebrity.[27] Indeed, Dream himself is a representation of the "flip side" of reality within *Sandman*,[28] defining it by embodying its opposite: dreams, visions, and illusions do not negate the reality of the everyday but inform it, permeate it, and give it wondrous life.

On one hand, this series of encounters might seem like a string of hierophanies, moments where the sacred breaks through into the profane. But Gaiman's divine encounters are not simply irruptions of divine power into human existence: again, they are "seemingly ordinary," this time with the emphasis on "ordinary." The sacred always has an ordinary face — a stripper, a CEO, a lounge pianist — and the transcendent nature of the divine is muted under the everyday nature of the encounters. Those supernatural beings who do not appear in the waking world among humans are represented as human-like: they age and lose their memories like Bast, get foolishly drunk like Thor, love passionately but not wisely like Dream, or suffer uncertainty and rebellion like Remiel. In part, this is the effect of the form in which Gaiman tells these stories, since the art and arc of a graphic novel require some consistency of representation and sense of dramatic character. But the results of these depictions go beyond simple representation and make the divine more human and humane.

In the *Sandman* universe, divinity is immanent within the world, either in the concrete figures of deities in various occupations and places or in the dream-realm that provides a counterpoint to "reality." In translating the divine into characters, Gaiman removes the otherness that gives deity power and authority surpassing human calculations. The Creator comes closest to being a transcendent figure, but instead seems merely otiose and unresponsive. Gaiman has populated the immanent world in *Sandman* by emptying out the transcendent, leaving only the distant Creator. There are hints of laws that not even the Endless may break, suggestions that there are motivating forces beyond any being's control, but no encounter with the divine surfaces akin to Moses' conference with God at Sinai, or Krishna's revelation of his infinity in the Bhagavad Gita, or the revelations to Mohammed. If the gods of *Sandman* are connected to transcendence, they say nothing of it.

The faith of the Manns, in this context, seems ignorant: they are dedicated to the Creator who sends angels, but they would not be able to recognize wonder if they saw it. Al-Rashid and his brethren seem far more rational and realistic. Because they directly encounter the supernatural, they know that reality expands far beyond the everyday world of rules and doctrines, and so they take a casual attitude. "It is of no matter," says Al-Rashid, and, compared to conjuring the Lord of Dreams or hatching the Second Egg of the Phoenix, a grape on Ramadan can seem a small thing. The actual processes of worship, ritual, teachings, community — in short, the things that make up the tangible features of a religion — are irrelevant next to the divine–human encounter that lies potential in every moment. Gaiman manages to de-emphasize religion while emphasizing its objects: the mystic, the supernatural, the wondrous, and the divine, all of which have ordinary and often human faces.

From one standpoint, the presence of gods can make the practice of religion irrelevant. The setting of *Sandman* is both filled with gods and empty of religion. The effect of the plethora of divinities is to elevate the ordinary to the level of wonder, but also to diminish the ineffable into the everyday. It seems that the re-enchantment of the everyday world also constitutes its disenchantment, and mixing the two risks making the extraordinary ordinary. At the same time, the flooding of the everyday world with the extraordinary constitutes an optimistic response to the potential of the supernatural. The humanizing of the gods makes them easier to understand, even as the traditional mechanisms mediating between divine and human disappear. The philosophy of wonder is the result of the mingling of the extraordinary and supernatural masked in the everyday. Its message is both unsettling, since any wrong turn, any casual encounter within the *Sandman* setting could lead a character into the wildness of Fairy or the dreams of cities, and comforting, since any beings that character might encounter share, to some extent, human qualities and human motivations. The ordinary is a disguise, but it is not false.

It is possible to read *Sandman*'s present gods and absent believers pessimistically, as a disenchantment paradoxically rooted in increased supernatural activity. Beings with control over life and death, over reality and illusion, are thereby tamed by their depictions in the art of the graphic novel and the plot of the story, reduced to mere characters — part of the array of potential symbols for the reader's taking. But it is also possible to read this depiction of human–divine interaction and the philosophy of wonder as an expression of what Lynn Schofield Clark terms "the religion of the possible." Clark's study of religion and media use by American teenagers included a group of men and women who, though well aware that supernatural-themed television and films are fictional, also entertained the possibility of "what if?" in their discussions about religion. This "what if" became a way of thinking about religions' claims to truth — sometimes for challenging them, sometimes for exploring them. This use of the category of the supernatural allowed for an intrigued tolerance of different faiths as equally possible, and equally fictitious.[29]

If the world that *Sandman* opens to the reader offers this option, how might it be applied or configured into her life? The very ordinary nature of the human setting within *Sandman* invites the reader to consider "what if?" within her own everyday life. Readers are offered the philosophy of wonder as a way to approach their own world, with the tentative suggestion that what they see might also be only "seemingly ordinary." Taking the philosophy of wonder into the reader's life provokes two questions: what if the gods were among us, and what if they were like us? It suggests a radical pluralism, an embrace of potential and possibility, but a concomitant devaluation of claims to the transcendent or to something that might stand beyond human experience. *Sandman*'s enchantment offers a reader a way to live in which the possibility of divine existence is never closed off, but the practicality of interacting with any divine is discouraged. The reader is invited to join in wondering "what if," to begin a speculative process that may or may not become religious faith. Wonder starts a reader on this path even as religions themselves are downplayed. *Sandman*'s religious universe seems designed to evoke this questioning, speculation, and wonder about the nature of reality without having to engage the real-life consequences of a proven religious claim. The resulting world "in front of the text" offers this dual vision for the reader, holding out a new way of seeing the world outside the text that enhances the ordinary and makes the transcendent intimate.

Notes

1 Paul Ricoeur, *Interpretation Theory: Discourse and the Surplus of Meaning* (Fort Worth: Texas Christian University Press, 1976), 92.

2 Ricoeur, 94.

3 Neil Gaiman (w), Sam Keith (a), Mike Dringenberg (a), and Malcolm Jones III (a), *Sandman: Preludes and Nocturnes*, "The Sound of Her Wings," Issues 1–8 of *Sandman* (New York: Vertigo-DC Comics, 1991), 14. (For citation purposes, I have used the page numbering from the collected graphic novels when available, and listed the issue number or title when the collection's number was omitted.)

4 Neil Gaiman (w), Shawn McManus (a), Colleen Dobran (a), Bryan Talbot (a), George Pratt (a), Stan Woch (a), and Dick Giordano (a), *Sandman: A Game of You*, Issues 32–7 of *Sandman* (New York: Vertigo-DC Comics, 1993), 178.

5 *Preludes and Nocturnes*, "Sound and Fury," 2.

6 Neil Gaiman (w), Mike Dringenberg (a), Malcolm Jones III (a), Chris Bachalo (a), Michael Zulli (a), and Steve Parkhouse (a), *Sandman: The Doll's House*, Issues 9–16 of *Sandman* (New York: Vertigo-DC Comics, 1991), 157.

7 Neil Gaiman (w), Bryan Talbot (a), Stan Woch (a), P Craig Russell (a), Shawn McManus (a), John Watkiss (a), Jill Thompson (a), Duncan Eagleson (a), and Kent Williams (a), *Sandman: Fables and Reflections*, Issues 29–31, 38–40, and 50 of *Sandman*, *Sandman Special 1* and *Vertigo Preview* (New York: Vertigo-DC Comics, 1993), 252.

8 *Fables and Reflections*, 60.

9 Neil Gaiman (w), Michael Allred (a), Gary Amaro (a), Mark Buckingham (a), Dick Giordano (a), Tony Harris (a), Steve Leialoha (a), Vince Locke (a), Shea Anton Pensa (a), Alec Stevens (a), Bryan Talbot (a), John Watkiss (a), and Michael Zulli (a), *Sandman: World's End*, Issues 51–56 of *Sandman* (New York: Vertigo-DC Comics, 1994).

10 *Game of You*, 87.

11 Neil Gaiman (w), Kelley Jones (a), Mike Dringenberg (a), Malcolm Jones III (a), Matt Wagner (a), Dick Giordano (a), George Pratt (a), and P Craig Russell (a), *Sandman: Season of Mists*, Issues 21–28 of *Sandman* (New York: Vertigo-DC Comics, 1992), 133.

12 Neil Gaiman (w), Kelley Jones (a), Charles Vess (a), Colleen Doran (a), and Malcolm Jones III (a), *Sandman: Dream Country*, Issues 17–20 of *Sandman* (New York: Vertigo-DC Comics, 1991), 109.

13 Neil Gaiman (w), Michael Zulli (a), Jon J Muth (a), and Charles Vess (a), *Sandman: The Wake*, Issues 70–75 of *Sandman* (New York: Vertigo-DC Comics, 1997), 35.

14 Neil Gaiman (w), Jill Thompson (a), and Vince Locke (a), *Sandman: Brief Lives*, Issues 41–49 of *Sandman* (New York: Vertigo-DC Comics, 1994) 3, 21.

15 *Brief Lives* 5, 20.

16 *World's End*, 110–11.

17 *Season of Mists*, 104.

18 *Season of Mists*, 175–6.

19 Gaiman takes a different tack on the representability and agency of the Creator in the graphic novel *Murder Mysteries*, set in the Silver City before the fall of Lucifer, and a still different approach to the ineffability of a seemingly distant Creator in his collaboration with Terry Pratchett, *Good Omens*.

20 *Doll's House*, 25.

21 *Season of Mists*, 21.

22 It is also hinted that human-Endless interaction is doomed: mortals are forbidden to love the Endless in *The Doll's House* (21), and Delirium muses that the Endless "deform the universe" (*Kindly Ones* 8, 8) and thereby endanger others. Neil Gaiman (w), Marc Hempel (a), Richard Case (a), D'Israeli (a), Teddy Kristiansen (a), Glyn Dillon (a), Charles Vess (a), Dean Ormstrom (a), and Kevin Nowlan (a), *Sandman: The Kindly Ones*, Issues 57–69 of *Sandman* (New York: Vertigo-DC Comics, 1996).

23 *Kindly Ones* 9, 20.

24 *Preludes and Nocturnes*, "24 Hours," 21.

25 Rodney Stark and Roger Finke. *Acts of Faith: Exploring the Human Side of Religion* (Berkeley: University of California Press, 2000), 88.

26 *Kindly Ones* 4, 8–10.

27 *Brief Lives* 3, 22.

28 *Brief Lives* 8, 16.

29 Lynn Schofield Clark, *From Angels to Aliens: Teenagers, the Media, and the Supernatural* (New York: Oxford University Press, 2003), 228.

Tell-Tale Visions:
The Erotic Theology of
Craig Thompson's *Blankets*

STEVE JUNGKEIT

E ROS, CAVES, AND DREAMS ARE central motifs of Craig Thompson's beautiful 2003 graphic novel *Blankets*, his autobiography of growing up
in rural Wisconsin within the strict confines of a fundamentalist/
evangelical version of Christianity. Indeed, a retelling of Plato's allegory
of the cave is the hinge upon which the story turns: a dream of Plato's
cave provides the initial impetus to discard a version of religion that
proved alienating. But it is the journey toward another kind of cave, this
one existing in the recesses of memory, that allows for a creative retrieval
of that religion later in the story. Thompson's graphic novel puts these
images to work in an explicitly theological way, one that is in keeping
with some recent scholarship reclaiming the role of eros in Christian
theology. God and sex belong together in this understanding, like two
estranged antagonists who have discovered an unexpected passion for
one another. What if this strange pair, God and eros, actually desired
one another, got off on one another, inflamed one another, found
themselves in one another? That's an unlikely alliance that's bound to
send the religious right into yet another moral frenzy, even as advocates
of free love would prefer to leave religion well enough alone, given how
theology has been used to police erotic affections. Nevertheless, there

is a strange desire smoldering here, one with which Thompson and the newer theologians of the erotic are flirting — and even consummating from time to time.

It is an erotic dalliance that I, too, want to flirt with in the coming pages, allowing this desire to erupt by exploring how *Blankets* plays with those themes and draws God and eros into a deeper relationship. The primary site of Thompson's innovation lies in the use of graphic literature as a form of expression, one that insists on the priority of visual images in achieving both its theological and erotic effects. In the tradition of the best erotic dalliances, there will need to be some build-up and development, and so it will first be necessary to explore the recent theological literature on eros. As we shall see, *Blankets* extends and supplements those works through its use of erotic projection as both a literary and theological tool. But a further piece of this build-up and development is provided by the feminist critic Luce Irigaray, particularly in the analysis of Plato's cave in the well-known essay "Plato's *Hystera*." Indeed, Irigaray's essay provides an invaluable lens for understanding Thompson's work, where layers of dreams, fantasies, and desires that usually remain hidden in the recesses of the mind are externalized (projected) in visual form. The very medium of the graphic novel allows these insights to emerge, thus opening up new avenues of communication in theological and religious rhetoric, revealing truths that are often obscured in written expression.

Erotic Theologies

The publication of *Blankets* coincided with a renewed interest in the topic of eros among many academic theologians. These writers were beginning to question the ways in which the erotic had been devalued in Christian theology and forced to play a subservient role to that of agapic love, a more chastened form of love that involves self-sacrifice and self-denial for others' benefit. To cite a representative sample, works such as Grace Jantzen's *Becoming Divine* and Graham Ward's *Cities of God*, as well as Marcella Althaus-Reid's *Indecent Theology* and Mark Jordan's *Blessing Same-Sex Unions*, all seek to retrieve eros as a central theological virtue. But it is a volume edited by Virginia Burrus and Catherine Keller, *Toward a Theology of Eros*, that provides the most helpful overview of this literature. In that volume's introductory essay, Burrus notes the dominance of Anders Nygren's 1953 book *Agape and Eros* over subsequent discussions of the erotic in Christian theology. Nygren famously argued that the form of love proper to Christianity was agape, and that eros itself was a vestigial trace of Greek paganism that needed to be carefully controlled, if not outright expelled from Christian theology. For Nygren, agape can best be seen in St. Paul's "hymn to love" in 1 Corinthians 13: love is patient, kind, and self-sacrificial, a series of attributes that Nygren thinks originates in the selfless giving of God. Agape, in other words, comes down from on high, enabling humans to love one another in sacrificial selflessness.[1] Eros, on the other hand, is understood as a lack, an unfulfilled desire ever in search of greater plenitude, always on the move, consuming the objects of its desire in search of greater satisfaction. On Nygren's reading, then, eros moves up, attempting to ascend to a more complete sense of fullness, the ultimate ideal of which is to be found in God. Because of these opposing directions, Nygren would have us believe that agape and eros "belong [. . .] to two entirely separate spiritual worlds, between which no direct communication is possible."[2] As he writes in a later passage, "There is no way which leads over from Eros to Agape."[3]

Drawing upon a variety of different sources from within and without the Christian theological tradition, all of the abovementioned authors raise questions about the viability of Nygren's analysis. They point out that Nygren's binarism neglects the productive role of the erotic in many strands of Christian theology, even as it ignores the multiple meanings of eros discovered in a source such as Plato's *Symposium*, to say nothing of theological appropriations of Platonic eros.[4] Using texts and figures such as the Johannine letters, Augustine's *Confessions*, Pseudo-Dionysius, Margarete Porete, Julian of Norwich, and others, they show that eros has always played a pivotal role in the Christian tradition, however subservient it may have been to agapic versions of love. These ancient and medieval writers are all mystics, lovers of the Divine and of the world. Their writings frequently resort to vivid erotic metaphors to capture what the love of God might be like, a fact often ignored by later generations of interpreters who were evidently uncomfortable with the sensual dimensions of these sources. That insight entails the recognition among the contributors to Burrus and Keller's volume that eros is the site of an ongoing form of divine revelation.

For most of these contributors, however, it is not merely contemplative eros and its ascent to God that needs to be revalued; it is rather the erotic in all of its bodily forms that must be revalued, a passion having to do with flesh and sexual desire, passion and incarnation. With this understanding of eros in mind, Burrus suggestively writes,

> if 'God is eros' as Pseudo-Dionysius insists in his erotic transposition of I John 4:8 and 4:16, then perhaps *eros is God*. Or rather, eros is the power or process of divine self-othering through which creation is ever emerging . . . A God in and of between-spaces, then, and also a God always incarnating, always subjecting itself to becoming-flesh.[5]

Stated differently, Burrus compels us to ask whether God is to be found in the pleasures of erotic desire and play, in the bodily passions existing between bodies and within them, rather than in the sublimation of that pleasure. That is the very question that Thompson's *Blankets* takes up. My argument is that Thompson's book can profitably be understood as belonging to this broad spectrum of texts seeking to salvage the role of the erotic in Christian theology. It is both a critique of the ways in which bodily eros has been marginalized within the Christian tradition (and more particularly within American evangelicalism) and a rediscovery of a different sort of God, precisely within and through the energy of that erotic passion, a God very literally "in and of between-spaces." Thompson's graphic novel, however, offers a subtle extension of the aforementioned works, for its form, *as a graphic novel*, insists on the priority of the visual — the authority of projected images. As such, the work of theologians such as Burrus and Keller or Jordan and Jantzen may yet remain too centered on the priority of words and abstract conceptuality, subtly directed away from the very materiality of the visible world.

Words have their own materiality, of course, and their own form of pleasure as well — that much is clear. But the medium of a graphic novel, in which narrative storytelling is accomplished via the interplay of text and images, allows for a different kind of erotic and theological performance than that which is scripted in academic theology. Thompson's *Blankets*, then, can be understood as an intervention in the *form* of theological communication. It insists that, if one is to retrieve an understanding of eros in theology, one might do so through a retrieval of the visual as well, those images projected onto the blank screen of the wall of a cave, the blank screen of a panel in a graphic novel, or the blank screen of the human psyche.

Ascent: The Light of the Sun

At its most literal level, *Blankets* is Craig Thompson's coming-of-age story about the casual traumas and humiliations of adolescence. It has to do with the fervency of adolescent faith and the awakening of sexual long-ing in the midst of a religious environment that seeks to suppress those impulses. Craig is ensconced in a hyper-masculinized culture of deer hunting and All-Terrain Vehicles. He is teased at church and school alike for his sensitivity — his love of art, his skinny frame, his piety, his lack of athletic prowess — and for having a father who, the story alludes, may or may not be an immigrant.[6] In short, Craig fails to conform to the strict masculine norms of his world, and it regularly earns him the epithets of "Girl!" or "Faggot!" from the other kids he encounters (see Figure 1). This treatment hints that the social space Craig occupies throughout the book is more queer than straight, despite his heterosexuality.[7] The centerpiece of the story has to do with Craig's romance with Raina, a fellow misfit whom he meets at a church youth retreat. Their romance is kindled by means of letters, drawings, and packages, long-distance flirta-tions that continue to stoke their emerging desire for each other. The story culminates when Craig travels some 400 miles to stay with Raina's family on the Upper Peninsula of Michigan for two weeks in the middle of winter. It is there that Craig is drawn out of his lonely isolation, and it is there that he begins to yield to his repressed sexual passions, learning to trust what his body loves.

Not surprisingly, what Craig loves are the nightly entanglements of his body with Raina's, pleasures stolen in secret after the rest of the house has gone to bed. Significantly, that sexual awakening takes place against the backdrop of Craig's evangelical piety, which taught him to view his body with suspicion and disdain. Night after night, Craig and Raina sleep in the same bed, setting the alarm for 6 a.m. so Craig can sneak back to his own room before anyone else is awake. On the final night of his visit, their passion reaches a crescendo. In contrast to the realism characteristic of much of the artwork in *Blankets*, Thompson's panels become intensely stylized during these erotic scenes, packed with intertwining vines, chutes, branches, flowers, circles of light, snowflakes, and other indeterminate shapes, all of it surrounding Raina and Craig's embrace (see Figure 2).[8] In Thompson's world, these ornate designs signify the space of dreams, of the imagination, of the unconscious unleashed, of the sheer energy of the erotic. Importantly, and rather humorously, in this moment of sexual ecstasy, Craig glances at Raina's

Figure 1. **Rednecks calling Craig "Faggot."**

wall, where she has an image of Warner Sallman's *Head of Christ* tacked up. Rather than staring unctuously up to heaven or turning his back in disgust, however, Craig is surprised to find Jesus smiling back at him in approval.[9]

It is here that a second, more subterranean layer of Thompson's graphic novel emerges, for this process of sexual awakening has the unexpected effect of unsettling both Craig's religion and, ironically, his relationship with Raina. Indeed, Craig begins to suspect that the impulses behind those phenomena (which are often equated throughout the book) are born of the same childlike naïveté, one that he must outgrow if he is to enter the realm of adult freedom. This process is narrated using the allegory of the cave found in Book Seven of Plato's *Republic*, which in Thompson's hands becomes a symbol of the unconscious as well. In this respect, *Blankets* bears a startling resemblance to Luce Irigaray's retelling of the same story in her essay "Plato's *Hystera*," a feminist rewiring of the allegory that becomes especially helpful in understanding much of what occurs in the latter half of *Blankets*. Indeed, Irigaray's essay is an indispensable tool in uncovering the subterranean layers concealed throughout Thompson's book.

Figure 2. **Craig and Raina in bed, surrounded by florid images.**

In a richly allusive reading, Irigaray characterizes the cave in Plato's allegory as a feminine space — literally a "hystera" or womb — in which human beings are enclosed in a den-like environment beneath the folds of the earth. Though Irigaray's reading stays close to Plato's text, she reads between the lines of that allegory, such that in the end the essay becomes a kind of hybrid, written in the margins of *The Republic*. The story is familiar enough: within that darkened space, prisoners of unspecified sex watch images projected onto a screen, which they mistake for reality itself. On Irigaray's reading, one prisoner (if that is what he is) is unchained in the name of truth, and is ushered out of the cave and into the light of day, where he is dazzled and blinded by the brightness of the sun. Irigaray notes that all of the preceding perceptions seen in the cave, those projections on the wall, "must be abandoned as childishness, dreams, insanity. One must turn around toward something else, cut short the childish beliefs and language, make a clean break between fantasies and reality . . . This is the price paid for the *reason* to which the prisoner is now converted."[10] Importantly, on the following page, Irigaray adds desire itself to the list of abandoned attributes. She suggests the ways in which eros, too, is relegated to this forbidden maternal sphere, discarded as something that at its very best is childish and at its worst is politically dangerous. It is a process that Craig himself enacts in his own emergence from the world of the cave.

For a time, Irigaray insists that the fight will go on between reason and dreams, between the rational and the unconscious. Even though the elements of fantasy and projection are ostensibly mastered under the tutelage of reason and enlightenment, Irigaray insists that the "discourse of reason [. . .] will never oust the fantasy structure of the cave completely."[11] Amidst the sun-drenched regime of this masculinized authority, Irigaray suggests that traces of the cave remain, "cracking open the fiction of the present."[12] But as the essay continues, the child of the maternal and earthly womb gradually learns to ignore those signs, forgetting his origin within that enclosed space, forgetting the projections and dreams cast upon the wall/screen/page of the cave. The child now becomes wholly oriented toward the noonday sun of enlightenment, which Irigaray equates with the rule of masculine logic or, in her language, the rule of the Father. Desire remains, to be sure, but it is channeled away from the body and into the realm of ideas. Ideas, in turn, become the feature of human life that are most valued, and the freed prisoner begins to associate himself with the highest point of the human body, the head, since the mind is that portion of the body that most closely resembles God.[13] This is the version of God most familiar from classical metaphysics and theology — omnipotent, omniscient, and omnipresent, sovereign, distant, and abstract. If one is not to fall back into the lower states of human life, i.e., into the realm of the body, matter, and the earth itself, where illusion resides, this God must be imitated and obeyed at all costs.

And yet, as we shall see in *Blankets*, those earlier memories of the cave do continue to intrude, no matter how fiercely they are repressed and policed. In Plato's allegory and Irigaray's retelling alike, the story ends with the former prisoner returning to the cave as an apostle of the light, delving into the depths once again in order to convince the remaining prisoners of their illusions, beholden as they are to fantasies, dreams, and bodily passions. On Irigaray's telling, this return trip is undertaken in order to confirm the self-identity of the converted prisoner as a child of the light, as the offspring of reason. The memories of the cave and its projections are anarchic intruders in the orderly world of enlightened life, and so the prisoner makes the return trip as a means of organizing and mastering those disorderly elements associated with dreams and the unconscious.[14] It goes without saying that the trip does not go according to plan, for the remaining prisoners reject the apostle and condemn him to death. Irigaray ends her essay by questioning whether the one put to death was not already dead, having long ago left the realm of the body. As such, there seems to be an irreconcilable split between these two orders, for it would seem that neither can tolerate the existence of the other. Nevertheless, Irigaray's rereading of Plato's allegory suggests the possibility of construing things otherwise, of revalorizing the feminine dream space of the womb, where eros and a different kind of theological desire than that of the abstract and sovereign lawgiver might be glimpsed. I would suggest, in turn, that Thompson's graphic novel accomplishes that task beautifully. There, a return to the cave does not result in violence, but it instead constitutes a rediscovery of the maternal womb as a kind of sacred site.

Blankets contains a number of glancing images of caves along the way, from a snow fort created by Craig and his brother as an image of childhood intimacy, to the internal warmth of Raina's room while huddled under a blanket in the middle of a snowy winter.[15] The first explicit treatment of Plato's cave is found shortly after Craig has returned from Raina's home in the latter portion of the book. Cast once more among his high school tormentors, Craig feels lost and alone. When he was with Raina, by contrast, he had experienced a degree of safety and acceptance, to say nothing of intense longing. Upon his returning home, realism pervades the frames of the book once again, as if the dream world of Raina's bed has been banished. It is here that the cave is introduced, narrated by a high school teacher as the waking realities of loneliness, boredom, and detachment from the body begin to dominate

Craig's life once again.[16] Craig imagines himself as one of the prisoners, trapped in a stock, gazing incessantly at the images dancing on the wall of the cave. Thompson renders those images in a manner akin to earlier instances of Craig's (the character's) drawings, as if to suggest that the art and imagery that had provided comfort and stability through the agonizing years of childhood and early adolescence had kept him trapped (see Figure 3). Indeed, the artwork of these panels suggests that the art of comics actually functioned to imprison Craig, for the wall of the cave doubles as the kind of panel witnessed in a comic book or graphic novel. As the memories of eros fade, as the images projected onto the screen of the cave and the page begin to seem dubious, so too religion begins to seem like a suspicious figment of the imagination, an adolescent dream best left behind.

Craig begins the slow journey upward, out of the cave, and into the sunnier pastures of enlightenment where clear and distinct thinking

Figure 3.   **Plato's cave, prisoners in stocks watching images on the wall.**

holds sway and both the unreliable dream world of the unconscious and its projections are held in abeyance. Craig looks away from the images projected on the wall of the cave, and he learns to distrust what he had once discerned there. Here, Thompson's art conveys the receding of eros, religion, and images themselves by depicting the gradual melting of the blankets of snow, as winter gives way to spring and summer (see Figure 4).[17] Childhood constructions vanish, and his relationship with Raina comes to an abrupt end. So, too, does his belief in God, for some rudimentary Bible study reveals textual inconsistencies that his fragile structure of faith can't sustain.[18] Craig packs his Bible away, making a self-conscious effort to leave his childhood faith behind. Not only that, he impulsively burns everything that Raina had ever given him, creating a harsh light that enables him to discern the newfound world of adult enlightenment where imagination and dreams do not intrude. And yet even here, Thompson's image of the fire links back to the fire inside Plato's cave, the one responsible for the shadows cast upon the wall. That ambiguity raises the question of where the illusion actually resides — in this newfound world of enlightenment, with the dazzling light of fires and suns, or within the cave itself? It is a question that returns throughout the remainder of the book.

Craig seems to welcome this new form of enlightenment, though he also mourns something that has been lost, something he cannot quite name. As the sun of adult life melts the snowy blankets of adolescent yearning, Craig surveys the landscape around him. Places that used to be accessible in the winter snow have now been made inaccessible by brambles and thorns. Whereas under all those blankets — the blanket he once shared with his brother, the blanket he shared with Raina, the blankets of snow — everything seemed connected, now the world seems disjointed (see Figure 5).[19] Craig begins to wonder what all the feelings that he experienced with Raina were. And what exactly had he wanted when he prayed to God and read his Bible? Were eros and faith both deceptive illusions, projected onto the wall of the cave, in order to confuse him, to keep him in shackles?

Descent: The Return of Eros

Time passes, and Craig moves away from his small town. He abandons his religion, disgusted at the ways it kept him isolated from the rest of the world in a ghettoized subculture. He reads books and works odd jobs.

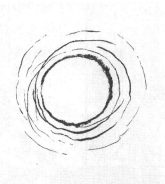

And slowly the snow began to melt.

First, doing a number on childrens' constructions;

Then retreating to the foundations of barns and other buildings.

Figure 4. **Sun melting children's constructions and house foundations.**

Figure 5. Craig in spring, daydreaming about snow — "Nothing fits."

And yet, traces of that womb-like cave keep returning, seen fleetingly in the brief erotic charges of chance encounters, but not strongly enough to launch the tangle of branches and flowers and snowflakes signifying the erotic and the divine.[20]

Enlightenment prevails. When Craig returns home after an absence of three years, he and his brother Phil walk through a field trading childhood memories. Phil recalls a long-forgotten moment when they were exploring the thawing fields around their home and discovered a giant cave, somehow created by the shifting mud of the spring thaw, one that quickly disappeared as the snow and ice melted. It is a visual metaphor that Thompson uses to forge a link between caves, eros, memory, and the unconscious. For Craig, the mud-cave had existed as a vague dreamscape but not as something that had actually occurred, not as something factually true or real. The startling memory of the mud-cave provokes a flood of desire in Craig, complete with the snowflakes, the flowers, a distant vision of Raina, and the salamander itself, an ancient symbol of Christ (see Figure 6). Thompson's association of all these images in one panel suggests that the cave shelters both erotic and theological imagination, hinting that where one is found, the other must be close at hand. Just as slowly as Craig had ascended from the cave years before, he now gradually begins a descent back into it.

The cave returns again when Craig travels home for the holidays years later. One night he begins digging through the boxes that he had stored in his parents' house, and he rediscovers a blanket that Raina had made for him during his visit, the one object he hadn't had the heart to burn years earlier. He finds his old Bible buried at the bottom of the same box, and he begins to read it again, this time with different eyes. The passage he reads is from Luke's gospel, where Jesus tells his followers that "the kingdom of God is within you." But Craig notes a textual variant at the bottom of the page, suggesting that it might also read "the kingdom of God is among you." Here, the page bursts to life as the curlicues and chutes of the erotic pour forth from Jesus's body.[21] At the bottom of the page, Craig opens the blanket that Raina made for him, a quilt composed of alternating squares that depict those same flowers and curlicues and snowflakes that emanate from the body of Jesus, though in a slightly altered form (see Figure 7).

The blanket symbolizes the raw desire of erotic passion, but it also stands in both for the blankets of snow that once allowed the world to connect meaningfully for Craig and for the deep sense of connection

Figure 6. **Craig, salamander, and Raina; Craig and brother.**

he experienced while sharing that blanket with Raina. So, too, it symbolizes the bond he felt with his brother Phil when they shared the same bed and blanket as children. But more importantly than any of those references, Raina's blanket stands for the enveloping folds of the cave, covered over by the layers of memory, seemingly inaccessible from the remove of adult skepticism. That night, as Craig buries himself in Raina's blanket for warmth, he reenters a version of the cave in his dreams.[22] As he drifts off to sleep, he falls off the edge of reality and back into an imagined embrace with Raina, where the florid patterns of erotic desire take over the page once again. Gravity pulls Craig downward toward snapping jaws with jagged teeth, but Raina's embrace keeps him aloft, floating above the troublesome creatures. The page bursts to life once

Figure 7.   **Jesus, ambiguously translated from the gospel of Luke.**

more as eros overwhelms whatever demons may have lurked at the edges of the dream. This time when Craig wakes up, it is the dream itself that overwhelms waking life, casting its spell over the routine interactions of his morning.[23]

The Authority of Projected Images

The blanket that Craig finds in his parents' storage closet has another important symbolic connotation as well, for Thompson explicitly compares its quilted panels to the composition of a comics layout. He imagines Raina sewing the squares into a sequential narrative that tells a kind of story.[24] Raina's blanket, then, is another instance of images projected onto a screen. Each of the quilted panels bears an image of the florid patterns used throughout the novel when eros or a sense of the divine is accessed (see Figure 8). When Craig wraps himself in that blanket at the end of the novel, he is enfolding himself within the erotic projections of this divine narrative, embracing them even as they embrace him, keeping him warm on a wintry night. As such, we can understand Craig's rediscovery of Raina's blanket as a descent back into the cave, reclaiming those elements he had dismissed or forgotten after the sun had melted his winter dream space. Moving back into the cave enables him to rediscover both a sense of the erotic and a renewed sense of the divine. Importantly, it also enables him to rediscover the power of his art.

The association of Raina's blanket with the art of comic books and graphic novels themselves invites us to understand *Blankets* as its own kind of blanket, performing for its readers all the symbolic connotations that the various blankets depicted in the story accomplish. In much the same way that Craig's depiction of the shadow images on the wall of the cave resemble a comic book drawing and that Raina's blanket resembles a narrative told in abstract images, *Blankets* is, in its very material form, a version of those same projections, shadow images cast upon a blank screen. The panels of each page become one of those subterranean projections on the cave wall. To read the book's beautiful interplay of words and images is thus to be ushered into the very dream space of that cave. In the very act of reading the book, which here involves discerning the complex interplay between text and image, readers are invited into the semi-conscious between-space constituted by dreams and reveries.

Thompson uses the medium of the graphic novel to perform an act

Figure 8.   **Raina, arranging blanket/comics panels.**

of seduction, one that can't be duplicated by even the best and most creative theological writers, since they remain bound to a particular form of language and communication. His images lure readers back into their own dream spaces, where they experience again the first flush of erotic desire. It is a desire that pulses at and between the edges of religious passion and the passion of bodily eros, blending the two such that they can barely be distinguished. Thompson invites his readers to reflect on what sorts of passions were at play in those moments and whether it might be possible to loosen those erotic dreams from the thicket of brambles and briars that often block them, rendering them inaccessible. Stated differently, the very act of reading *Blankets* gently compels readers to rejoin the prisoners in Plato's allegory, this time not as one duped into sleepy illusions, but as one harnessing those dream images for a different project, one that works to connect human beings to each other and to the world around them. In Thompson's dream vision, that means realizing that the hopeful power of erotic projection is overlaid upon the workings of something divine, and vice versa. The art of graphic novels becomes a redemptive cultural therapy in Thompson's hands.

Conclusion

Comic books and graphic novels have long been marginalized (in America, at least) as a juvenile or adolescent artistic medium that one should outgrow for the sunnier pastures of rigorous intellectual thought and more "serious" artistic interests, like those on display at MoMA or the Met. Until very recently, the only comic book images to be found in such institutions were the ironic appropriations of comics seen in Warhol or Lichtenstein. Thompson harnesses such prejudices in his art and turns them on their head. The effect of *Blankets* is to provoke a series of questions about what precisely we give up when we leave "childish" things behind. What sorts of embodied truths do we risk missing? Beneath the chagrin and embarrassment of childhood constructions of things such as faith, love, or even comics, might there be something lurking that is deeply revealing and deeply true? Even if one might not believe in the same God or fall in love with the same abandon, might the very desire for such things tell us something profound about our own human needs? What if the very form of comic books and graphic novels were a way to access some of those buried feelings and desires?

Among other things, Thompson suggests, attending to those buried feelings and desires might bring with it a renewed sense of the Divine. Chances are, it will have little in common with the very masculine judge, lawgiver, and power source that Craig encountered as a child. That God is a masculine fantasy that he can live without, and perhaps the rest of us can as well. The image of Jesus that Craig rediscovers in the dream space of the cave exists as an erotic projection, this time as the ultimate horizon of human beings and of the world, one that lures and seduces with a vision of the interconnectedness of all things and all people, releasing women and men from a privatized self-enclosure. The images of Jesus and Raina explicitly seep into one another, such that it becomes possible to understand Craig's sexual desire as opening up to a wider vision of plenitude and flourishing for all.

Whereas in the nineteenth century, Ludwig Feuerbach warned against the alienating effects of projection, Grace Jantzen, one of the key figures in the revitalization of erotic theologies, uses Irigaray's essay on the allegory of the cave to suggest that projection might have a liberatory quality as well, as women and men begin to trust their own deepest desires and their own most valued instincts. In Jantzen's accounting, men have always projected onto the divine, creating a situation of alienation for women and of disenfranchisement for men alike. For Jantzen, then, the problem is not so much projection itself, for projective imagination will always play a pivotal role in human life. The problem is what it is that gets projected and whether or not humans can become conscious of those projections.[25] That would circumvent Feuerbach's charge that religion is alienating, for on his telling, humans project qualities that they themselves lack onto a divine being, such that, in Feuerbach's words, "to enrich God, man must become poor; that God may be all, man must be nothing."[26]

Irigaray, Jantzen, and Thompson all suggest that liberating images of human flourishing and erotic interconnectivity are most often discovered in the liminal spaces where dreams and waking life somehow shade into one another. In this regard, learning to trust eros as a theological virtue would lead us through the thicket of enlightenment and into the maternal enclosure of the cave, where it is not the irrational that is discovered but rather a different form of the rational, a different form of logic and a different kind of visuality as well. Here, it becomes possible to imagine a world enchanted by the Divine, where human beings are seduced into a liberatory vision of a this-worldly redemption. It is a vision where men and women are invited to live more fully into their own bodies and into the body of the earth, a vision where no one is forgotten and all are drawn into the kingdom of this strange, maternal God, which, of course, cannot be a kingdom in any real sense at all.

Blankets is a beautiful and welcome intervention in a theological conversation about eros, a conversation that, for all its vigorous energy and creativity, betrays a subtle sublimation of that eros in its form as written theology. *Blankets* insists that, if the erotic is to be reclaimed as a site of theological authority, it will be necessary to insist on the priority of the visual, attending to the sites where our own projections are inscribed onto the blank surface of the screen, the page, the earth, and our bodies. At the conclusion of *Blankets*, shortly after Craig's rediscovery of Raina's blanket and his dream of religious ecstasy, the snow begins to fall once again, covering the surface of the earth in a hushed and tender embrace. Craig steps out of his family's house and marvels at this newly reenchanted world. He begins to create fresh new marks upon the blank surface of the snow[27] (see Figure 9). The image suggests that he is free to begin imagining the world along the lines of his own deepest desires, a desire for erotic bodies, a desire for a sense of the Divine, and a desire for a sense of connection with the world around him. Craig has somehow found a way back into the maternal cave, and he takes joy in the creative possibilities afforded him by the screen of the cave wall, depicted here as a fresh field of snow.

The final image in *Blankets* is one of Craig admiring the falling snow,

Figure 9. **Craig in snow, making his mark on the blank surface.**

the very element that creates the possibility of the final blank screen found in the story.[28] But between that final image and the acknowledgment pages, three entirely blank pages have been inserted, as if to invite the projected images of readers as well, a liminal space between Thompson's imagination and our own. *Blankets* has all along been performing its narrative, drawing its readers down into the cave itself, where dreams and desire reside. Whether intentional or not, those blank pages become a kind of screen for readers, for at precisely the point that Thompson's images end, dissolving into a field of white, the lost and forgotten images of his readers have a chance to begin. As *Blankets* testifies, discerning those images is hard and difficult work, but Thompson's graphic novel charts a way forward. Amidst the incredible proliferation of theologies of the erotic, *Blankets* joins Irigaray's essay and Jantzen's feminist theology to become a provocation to project our own images of the erotic and the divine onto the screen of the world.

Notes

1 Anders Nygren, *Agape and Eros* (London: SPCK Press, 1953), 210, as quoted in Virginia Burrus and Catherine Keller (eds.), *Toward a Theology of Eros* (New York: Fordham University Press, 2006), xiv.
2 Nygren, 31, as quoted in Burrus and Keller, xiv.

3 Nygren, 52, as quoted in Burrus and Keller, xiv.
4 See Mark Jordan's essay "Flesh in Confession: Alcibiades Beside Augustine" in Burrus and Keller, 23–37.
5 Burrus and Keller, xxi.
6 Thompson, Craig, *Blankets* (Marietta, GA: Top Shelf Productions, 2003), 21.
7 Thompson, 53.
8 Thompson, 437.
9 Thompson, 431.
10 Luce Irigaray, *Speculum of the Other Woman* (Ithaca: Cornell University Press, 1985), 273.
11 Irigaray, 274.
12 Irigaray, 287.
13 Irigaray, 324.
14 Irigaray, 342.
15 Thompson, pages 75 and 417, respectively.
16 Thompson, 496–500.
17 Thompson, 504–6.
18 Thompson, 550.
19 Thompson, 506.
20 Thompson, 552.
21 Thompson, 565.
22 Thompson, 568–71.
23 Thompson, 572.
24 Thompson, 566–7.
25 Grace Jantzen, *Becoming Divine: Towards a Feminist Philosophy of Religion* (Bloomington: Indiana University Press, 1999), 88–95.
26 Ludwig Feuerbach, *The Essence of Christianity* (New York: Harper & Row, 1957), 26, as quoted in Jantzen, *Becoming Divine*, 90.
27 Thompson, 578–9.
28 Thompson, 582.

Appendix A

The following entry comes from the Journal page at
ScottMcCloud.com and was written by the writer/artist/theorist
on the release of R. Crumb's *The Book of Genesis Illustrated.*

"Visualizing Religion" http://scottmccloud.com/2009/10/19/
visualizing-religion/
October 19, 2009

Today is the release date for R. Crumb's massive, fleshy, and strangely
literal adaptation of the book of Genesis. It will make some people
happy, other people mad, and still other people shrug, but from a purely
comics perspective, all you really need to know is that it's 224 pages
of new Crumb artwork. (Hell, I'd buy it if it was the official R. Crumb
adaptation of the Boise, Idaho Yellow Pages).

Coincidentally, on NPR this morning, I heard this depressing story
about "feuding" atheists. Apparently, even though I'm a sometimes
"angry" atheist myself, I would actually be classified as "old school" according to this story. The idea of going out of one's way to offend believers
seems pointless and self-defeating to me — a resounding demonstration
of how religion can dominate a person's life instead of a good case for
a compelling alternative.

I don't know about you, but I always thought the alternative to blind
faith was *knowledge*. If some people insist on ignoring scientific evidence
(150 years of research on evolution for example), maybe it's because

we've done such a bad job of *teaching* that science. There are no quick fixes, but I can't help thinking that simply getting knowledge out the door by any means necessary is our only way out of the swamp.

In a way, Crumb's *Genesis* is a step in that direction, because it makes visible a document that even the faithful are sometimes a bit sketchy on as they cherry-pick the lessons that sound warm and fuzzy and conveniently forget all that weird, crazy, ancient gibberish. I can think of one instance, profiled on *This American Life* episode #290, where actually *reading the Bible* finally convinced one Catholic to give it all up.

Note that I have no idea if that was Crumb's intent or not. All I know is that I'd be much happier if everybody had a fuller understanding of *all religions* and *all sciences* and could simply make up their minds based on information instead of merely taking sides among warring tribes of fanatics.

I've said it about art, but I guess it applies here too: We can't define ourselves by what we're *not*.

Appendix B

The following two-part profile of Gary Panter's *Jimbo's Inferno* originally appeared online as part of *Broken Frontier.com*'s "Library of Babble" columns by Beth Davies Stofka.

"*Jimbo's Inferno*: Caveat Emptor" http://brokenfrontier.com/columns/p/detail/jimbos-inferno-caveat-emptor/
October 29, 2006

Jimbo's Inferno stands in a long and honorable tradition of comics artists exploring hell, and among them, Jimmy Hatlo (*Hatlo's Inferno*) and Mike Peters (*Mother Goose and Grimm*) have provided some truly nutty hilarity. Like Dante, Hatlo and Peters take their readers to a distant and terrible terrain — hot, rocky, and painful — to skewer the ironies, irritants, and hypocrisies of their times. In sharp contrast, Gary Panter sends Jimbo no further than a shopping mall called Focky Bocky.

But Focky Bocky is no ordinary shopping mall. Between cantos 17 and 18, on pages 22 and 23, Panter includes a map of Focky Bocky, a "Gloom-Rock Life-Style Mall-Scape . . . that exists to serve only you, and you, and you." Panter is famous for his graphic design, and this map does not disappoint. A continuous outer wall encloses a seven-pointed moat. The moat surrounds the mall, which is shaped like a seven-pointed star. Each arm of the star has a tower at its point, and an intricate monorail system connects the towers and then zooms to every corner of the mall in bewildering triangular patterns. The monorail's star pattern is reflected by a star-patterned "people mover" near the center of the mall. At the very center of the mall, nine concentric rings descend into the underground, each ring smaller than the one above it. At the bottom is the "Bottom-Most Pit of Focky Bocky."

The outer edges of the mall are full of fast food, where cotton candy, fudge, and chips compete with chicken-fried steak and enchiladas for the consumer's attention. As the mall visitor moves closer to the center, however, the landmarks become less familiar. "Cerberus," says one label, and another reads "Dr. Pepper River." The forest and the desert seem out of place, and the strip clubs and the chicken ranch seem completely unlikely attractions for a mall. What is this place? An utterly wacky riff off of the ubiquitous labyrinth of consumerism, Focky Bocky is uniquely Panter, yet, as Panter says, "engorged with Dante's hell."

Indeed, *Jimbo's Inferno* is very faithful to Dante's epic poem. Following Dante closely, Panter organized his comic into 34 cantos. Dante's cantos are roughly 135–155 lines each, and Panter's cantos are normally 6 frames organized on one page, although occasionally he uses only 3 frames. Panter helpfully numbers many of his cantos by inserting the Roman numerals into one of the frames. He also titles his cantos in ways that call Dante's to mind.

Panter's cantos are economical, adapting only the barest of key themes and plot developments from each of Dante's, and mystifying the reader with original dialogue, sometimes pious and sometimes obscure. Panter preserves the key relationship, that between pilgrim and guide. In Dante's *Inferno*, Dante himself is the pilgrim, while Virgil is his guide. In Panter's *Inferno*, Panter's signature character Jimbo is the pilgrim, while his robot parole officer Valise is his guide. Just as in Dante's poem, Jimbo converses with people he meets in the mall, at times heckling them and trading insults, at times making pious and judgmental speeches, and at times succumbing to fear or disgust. Both works are defined by their forceful and unforgettable imagery.

Dante's *Inferno* is one of the seminal works of Western culture, telling a story of a poet who, on the Good Friday before Easter in the year 1300, goes on a journey through the Christian hell guided by another great poet of the Western tradition, Virgil. The poem is devout, heretical, and direct. Dante skewered the political and religious pretensions and hypocrisies of his day. He also named names, showing characters from the past, and his own personal enemies in various torments, condemned for their sins.

Through his poem, Dante has had lasting influence on how we think about hell, sin, and punishment. It was Dante who organized hell into nine circles and who made us believe that each circle is lower than the last, containing sinners worse than the last. It was Dante who bestowed a permanent sense of hierarchy on sins. It was also Dante who gave us the notion of symbolic retribution, the idea that sinners are not only punished for their sins, but also by their sins. One of the best examples of symbolic retribution came from Mike Peters, who in a *Mother Goose and Grimm* Sunday strip portrayed the guy who invented plastic wrapping for CDs, doomed for all eternity to try unwrapping them.

Even if we haven't read Dante, his influence is so great that, when we encounter a work of art like *Jimbo's Inferno*, we look for certain elements. We expect a cautionary tale, one that will define our sins and the sinners, too. We willingly join the protagonist on his journey, reading it as a pilgrimage and anticipating the spiritual enlightenment that comes at the end. And we look for paradise, a sense of divinity and salvation embedded in the bleakness of punishment and pain.

"*Jimbo's Inferno*: Paradise Lost"
http://brokenfrontier.com/columns/p/detail/jimbos-inferno-paradise-lost/
November 5, 2006

Now, to consider the moral meaning of Jimbo's visit to Focky Bocky. Unlike Dante, who infused sin and punishment with terrifying order and pitiless justice, Panter presents an ambiguous hell, one that replaces Dante's efficient regulation with chaotic, disgusting ickiness. While Dante's poem conveyed a warning to the reader to avoid sin and thereby avoid punishment, Panter's comic replaces such moral instruction with intensely hideous scenes drawn with thick black lines and tortuous detail. The dialogue is obscure, full of inside jokes, and nearly incomprehensible. The imagery is blunt. While we may not understand how the suffering characters in Panter's hell got there, we know we don't want to go.

Dante's *Inferno* contains impressive moral instruction. Sin and punishment figure prominently in the poem, and the punishments uniquely fit the crimes. Scandalmongers and gossips, divisive individuals in life, are continually, and physically, sliced apart for eternity. Liars, impostors, and counterfeiters, who were corrupting influences in their time, suffer corrupted and diseased bodies and minds. Diviners, who in life claimed to be able to see the future, are condemned forever to walk with their heads twisted painfully backward on their necks, only able to see behind them. In Dante's hell, the relationship between the sin and the punishment is painfully and efficiently logical, and the message is clear: don't commit this sin unless you want to end up like this.

Panter's *Inferno* contains impressive imagery. Suffering figures prominently, but in contrast to Dante's account of hell, the sin is absent. Drug addicts die in their own filth. A weeping man is torn open by a lizard, his entrails removed and spun into elaborate patterns. A man with no skin uses his own sword to cut himself open and cut off his own head. In a strange flat plain, people are buried up to their necks. They chew on each other's heads. One character is repeatedly incinerated, only to rise from the ashes to be incinerated again. "Don't watch: it's humiliating," he tells Jimbo. "May you die of grief."

Dante explains the sins of the condemned sufferers encountered on the journey through hell, but in *Jimbo's Inferno*, there are no tales of sin to give sense to the suffering. Jimbo chats with the suffering people, but the dialogue is impenetrable. In Canto X (p. 14), Jimbo and his guide Valise visit Kilroy's Fifth Amendment Bottom-Lit Spa-Bar. (In Dante's tenth canto, Dante and his guide Virgil visit the tombs where the Epicureans are buried.) Jimbo discovers some friends there.

> Drunk #1: Hey, Jimbo. You know me! Have a drink with Zipper and Gruden. Hell, we're drinking with a firm resolve, Jimmy.

> Drunk #2: H-How's Bob War, Dimbo? Hic!

> Jimbo: Why doesn't he just call Bob up on his comtat?

> Drunk #1: He threw the phase out on the tatcom. He wet it.

> Valise: Time to move onward.

> Drunk #1: You fucker, stay here and drink with me. Are you too good for us?

> Jimbo: Thy obdurate rages profit thee not. Now I must away. Tell him Bob lives in Garcia's pool.

Similar dialogue occurs throughout Jimbo's trip through Focky Bocky. The conversations between Jimbo and the sufferers, and the commentaries from Jimbo's guide Valise, do little to make sense of the suffering of those trapped in the mall's nine infernal circles. Indeed, the only moral discernment comes from Jimbo, whose pious pronouncements make him sound like a member of the Moral Majority. When a trio of young women die of an overdose, Jimbo comments, "An unthinkable waste of cute girls." When he encounters a prostitute covered in shit, he says, "I hope you are using condoms." Much like his model Dante, Jimbo has little pity for the suffering souls he meets in Focky Bocky.

The obtuse dialogue helps create a sense that *Jimbo's Inferno* is a confusing series of repulsive vignettes with no obvious meaning. Are these people dead? Are they in Focky Bocky by choice, or sentenced there by divine judgment? Are they being punished? Are they unlucky? Or is this all a part of a normal day at the mall?

The moral clarity of Dante's *Inferno* is lost in the chaos of Focky Bocky. You may not want to end up like this, but you're not sure what these people did to deserve their pain. In this respect, *Jimbo's Inferno* neatly captures our contemporary moral malaise. Suffering is arbitrary, its intensity and duration unmitigated by innocence or goodness. No one seems to be in charge. But because of the meaninglessness of it all, Panter's comic is unsatisfying. The confusing dialogue reduces the comic to something idiosyncratic, and ultimately forgettable.

Appendix C

GRAVEN IMAGES:
RELIGION IN COMIC BOOKS & GRAPHIC NOVELS

APRIL 11-13, 2008
BOSTON UNIVERSITY
ELIE WIESEL CENTER FOR JUDAIC STUDIES
147 BAY STATE ROAD - BOSTON, MA

SPONSORED BY
The Luce Program in Scripture and Literary Arts
The New England-Maritimes American Academy of Religion
The Boston University Department of Religion
The Boston University Graduate Student Organization

From the performance of religion in comics, to religious or mythic traditions among the elements of various works, to the use of comics by religious practitioners themselves, the relationship between comics and religion is dynamic and evolving. Given the increasing seriousness with which the public has come to view comics as an art form and Americans' fraught but passionate relationship with religion, "Graven Images" will provide an opportunity for discussion of cutting- edge artistic and social issues by exploring the roles of religion in comic books and graphic novels.

LEAD CHAIR: A. David Lewis
ASSOCIATE CHAIR: Christine Hoff Kraemer

FRIDAY, APRIL 11
Keynote Address
6:00 pm - 7:30 pm
"Comics: Finding My Religion"
James Sturm, Center for Cartoon Studies
Xeric Award and Eisner Award-winning author of *The Golem's Mighty Swing* and *James Sturm's America: God, Gold, and Golems*

The lecture will be followed by a light reception. Copies of Mr. Sturm's works will be available for purchase at the reception.

SATURDAY, APRIL 12
Opening Remarks
8:30 am - 9:00 am

Panel 1: Missionizing with Comics
9:00 am - 10:30 am
"Liber Corpus: Grant Morrison's Reflexive Relationship with his Invisibles"
Megan Goodwin, University of North Carolina at Chapel Hill
"A Hesitant Embrace: Comic Books and Evangelicals"
Kate Netzler, Boston University
"From Bambi to Buddha: Manga's Amazing Spiritual Search"
Rene Javellana, Boston College

Panel 2: Literary Applications of Religion
10:45 am - 11:45 am
"London as Sacred and Desecrated Space(s) in Alan Moore's From Hell"
Emily Merriman, San Francisco State University
"Eros and Visuality: On Blankets, Caves, and Theological Desire"
Steve Jungkeit, Yale University

Lunch Break
11:45 am - 1:30 pm

Panel 3: Judaism and Identity
1:30 pm - 3:00 pm
"Representing Jewish Identities in Joann Sfar's Graphic Novel The Rabbi's Cat"
Marla Harris, independent scholar
"Three Faces of the Comic Book Rabbi"
Laurence Roth, Susquehanna University
"Why Not, in Time, a Judeo-American?"
Vincent Gonzalez, University of North Carolina at Chapel Hill

Panel 4: Comics and Pedagogy
3:15 pm - 4:45 pm
"'To Learn of Magic is Not Hard': Teaching Tarot in Comics"
Jason Winslade, Northwestern University
"American Catholic Citizenship: Prescriptions for Children from Treasure Chest of Fun and Fact (1946-1962)"
Anne Blankenship, University of North Carolina at Chapel Hill
"Religion & Comics: Theoretical Connections and Pedagogical Benefits in an Undergraduate Honors Seminar"
Darby Orcutt, North Carolina State University

Sandman Round-Table
5:00 pm - 6:00 pm
Respondents:
Emily Ronald, Boston University
Joshua Cohen, Mass College of Art & Design

SUNDAY, APRIL 13
Panel 5: Scripture and Theology
9:00 am - 10:45 am
"Gold Plates, Inked Pages: The Authority of Graphic Storytelling"
Graham Stott, Arab American University - Jenin
"Killing the Graven God"
Andrew Tripp, Boston University
"The Devil's Reading: Revelation and Revenge in the Comics "
Aaron Ricker Parks, McGill University
**"Puritanism in Spandex: Puritan Ideological Apotheosis into
Popular Culture Superheroes and Villains"**
Nicholas Yanes, Florida State University

Creator Q&A
11:00 am - 12:30 pm
Panelists:
A. David Lewis (*The Lone and Level Sands*), Saurav Mohapatra (*India Authentic*), Steve Ross (*Marked!*), Mark Smylie (*Artesia* series; Publisher of *The Long Count* and *Some New Kind of Slaughter*), and G. Willow Wilson (*Cairo, Air*)

Closing Remarks
12:30 pm – 12:45 pm

Please visit our exhibitors and publishers in the Judaic Studies Library

All questions or comments about the conference can be directed to ADL@bu.edu.
"Graven Images" icon by J.T. Waldman

Selected Bibliography

Comics Scholarship

Abbott, Lawrence L. "Comic Art: Characteristics and Potentialities of a Narrative Medium." *Journal of Popular Culture* 19.4 (Spring 1986): 155–76.

Baetens, J., ed. *The Graphic Novel.* Belgium: Leuven University Press, 2001.

Barker, Martin. *Comics: Ideology, Power and the Critics.* Manchester: Manchester University Press, 1989.

Benton, Mike. *The Comic Book in America: An Illustrated History.* Dallas: Taylor, 1989.

Bettley, James. *The Art of the Book: From Medieval Manuscript to Graphic Novel.* London: V&A Publications, 2001.

Bongco, Mila. *Reading Comics: Language, Culture, and the Concept of the Superhero.* New York: Garland Publishing, 2000.

Carrier, David. *The Aesthetics of Comics.* University Park: Pennsylvania State University Press, 2000.

Chute, Hillary. "The Changing Profession: Comics as Literature? Reading Graphic Narrative." *PMLA* 123.2 (March 2008): 452–65.

Cohn, Neil. *Early Writings on Visual Language.* Boston: Emaki, 2003.

Daniels, Les. *Comix: A History of Comic Books in America.* New York: Outerbridge & Dienstfrey, 1971.

Di Liddo, Annalisa. *Alan Moore: Comics as Performance, Fiction as Scalpel.* Jackson: University Press of Mississippi, 2009.

Duncan, Randy and Matthew J. Smith. *The Power of Comics: History, Form, and Function.* New York: Continuum, 2009.

Eisner, Will. *Comics and Sequential Art: Principles and Practices from the Legendary Cartoonist.* New York: W. W. Norton, 2008. Includes *Comics and Sequential Art* (1985) and *Graphic Storytelling and Visual Narrative* (1996).

Estren, Mark James. *A History of Underground Comics.* 1974. 3rd edn. Berkeley: Ronin Publishing, 1993.

Ewert, Jeanne C. "Reading Visual Narrative: Art Spiegelman's *Maus.*" *Narrative* 8 (2000): 87–103.

Fletcher, Robert P. "Visual Thinking and the Picture Story in *The History of Henry Esmond.*" *PMLA* 113.3 (May 1998): 379–94.

Gravett, Paul. *Graphic Novels: Stories to Change Your Life.* New York: Collins Design, 2005.

Groensteen, Thierry. *The System of Comics*. Trans. Bart Beaty and Nick Nguyen. Jackson: University Press of Mississippi, 2007.

Hajdu, David. *The Ten-Cent Plague: The Great Comic Book Scare and How it Changed America*. New York: Farrar, Straus & Giroux, 2008.

Harvey, Robert C. *The Art of the Comic Book: An Aesthetic History*. Jackson: University Press of Mississippi, 1996.

Hatfield, Charles. *Alternative Comics: An Emerging Literature*. Jackson: University Press of Mississippi, 2005.

———, ed. *Arguing Comics: Literary Masters on a Popular Medium*. Jackson: University Press of Mississippi, 2004.

Heer, Jeet and Kent Worcester, eds. *A Comics Studies Reader*. Jackson: University Press of Mississippi, 2009.

Horrocks, Dylan. "Inventing Comics: Scott McCloud Defines the Form in Understanding Comics." *Comics Journal* 234 (June 2001): 29–39.

Inge, M. Thomas. *Comics as Culture*. Jackson: University Press of Mississippi, 1990.

Iser, Wolfgang. *Prospecting: From Reader Response to Literary Anthropology*. Baltimore: Johns Hopkins University Press, 1989.

Johnson-Woods, Toni, ed. *Manga: An Anthology of Global and Cultural Perspectives*. London: Continuum, 2009.

Jones, Gerard. *Men of Tomorrow: Geeks, Gangsters, and the Birth of the Comic Book*. New York: Basic Books, 2004.

Kannenberg, Gene Jr. "Graphic Text, Graphic Context: Interpreting Custom Fonts and Hands in Contemporary Comics." *Illuminating Letters: Typography and Literary Interpretation*. Ed. Paul C. Gutjahr and Megan L. Benton. Amherst: University of Massachusetts Psres, 2001. 165–92.

Klock, Geoff. *How to Read Superhero Comics and Why*. New York: Continuum, 2002.

Kunzle, David. *The Early Comic Strip: Narrative Strips and Picture Stories in the European Broadsheet from c. 1450 to 1825. History of the Early Comic*, vol. 1. Berkeley: University of California Press, 1973.

Kurtzman, Harvey and J. Michael Barrier. *From Aargh! to Zap!: Harvey Kurtzman's Visual History of the Comics*. New York: Prentice Hall Press, 1991.

Lefèvre, Pascal. "Recovering Sensuality in Comic Theory." *International Journal of Comic Art* 1.1 (Spr/Sum 1999): 140–9.

Lewis, A. David. "The Shape of Comic Book Reading." Conference paper. 2–4 October 2004. International Comic Arts Conference, Georgetown University, Baltimore, MD.

Magnussen, Anne and Hans-Christian Christiansen. *Comics and Culture: Analytical and Theoretical Approaches*. Copenhagen: Museum Tusculanum, University of Copenhagen, 2000.

McAllister, Matthew P., Edward H. Sewell and Ian Gordon, eds. *Comics and Ideology*. New York: Peter Lang, 2001.

McCloud, Scott. *Making Comics: Storytelling Secrets of Comics, Manga and Graphic Novel*. New York: Harper, 2006.

———. *Reinventing Comics: How Imagination and Technology Are Revolutionizing an Art Form*. New York: Perennial, 2001.

———. *Understanding Comics: The Invisible Art*. New York: HarperCollins, 1994.

Ndalianis, Angela, ed. *The Contemporary Comic Book Superhero*. New York: Routledge, 2009.

Nyberg, Amy Kiste. *Seal of Approval: The History of the Comics Code.* Jackson: University Press of Mississippi, 1998.

Pustz, Matt. *Comic Book Culture: Fanboys and True Believers.* Jackson: University Press of Mississippi, 1999.

Rhoades, Shirrel. *A Complete History of American Comic Books.* New York: Peter Lang Publishing, 2008.

Sabin, Roger. *Adult Comics.* New York: Routledge, 1993.

———. *Comics, Comix & Graphic Novels: A History Of Comic Art.* New York: Phaidon Press, 2001.

Saraceni, Mario. *The Language of Comics.* New York: Routledge, 2003.

Simon, Joe and Jim Simon. *The Comic Book Makers.* Lebanon, NJ: Vanguard, 2003.

Talon, Durwin S. *Panel Discussions: Design in Sequential Art Storytelling.* Raleigh, NC: TwoMorrows, 2003.

Varnum, Robin and Christina T. Gibbons, eds. *The Language of Comics: Word and Image.* Jackson: University Press of Mississippi, 2001. ix-xix.

Versaci, Rocco. *This Book Contains Graphic Language: Comics As Literature.* New York: Continuum, 2007.

Wolk, Douglas. *Reading Comics: How Graphic Novels Work and What They Mean.* Philadelphia, PA: Da Capo Press, 2007.

Wright, Bradford W. *Comic Book Nation: The Transformation of Youth Culture in America.* Baltimore, MD: Johns Hopkins University Press, 2001.

Religion and Comics

Baskind, Samantha and Ranen Omer-Sherman, eds. *The Jewish Graphic Novel: Critical Approaches.* Piscataway, NJ: Rutgers University Press, 2008.

Brewer, H. Michael. *Who Needs A Superhero?: Finding Virtue, Vice, And What's Holy In The Comics.* Grand Rapids, MI: Baker Books, 2004.

Buhle, Paul, ed. *Jews and American Comics.* New York: New Press, 2008.

Coogan, Peter. *Superheroes: The Secret Origin of a Genre.* Austin, TX: Monkeybrain Books, 2006.

Fingeroth, Danny. *Disguised as Clark Kent: Jews, Comics, and the Creation of the Superhero.* New York: Continuum, 2007.

Fowler, Robert B. *The World of Chick?* San Francisco: Last Gasp, 2001.

Garrett, Greg. *Holy Superheroes! Revised and Expanded Edition.* Louisville, KY: Westminster John Knox Press, 2008.

Kaplan, Arie. *From Krakow to Krypton: Jews and Comic Books.* Philadelphia: Jewish Publication Society of America, 2008.

Lewis, A. David, ed. "Ever-Ending Battle: A Symposium." *International Journal of Comic Art* 8.1 (Spring 2006): 163–282.

Knowles, Christopher. *Our Gods Wear Spandex: The Secret History of Comic Book Heroes.* San Francisco: Weiser Books, 2007.

Lawrence, John Shelton and Robert Jewett. *The Myth of the American Superhero.* Grand Rapids, MI: William B. Eerdmans, 2002.

LoCicero, Don. *Superheroes and Gods: A Comparative Study from Babylonia to Batman.* Jefferson, NC: McFarland, 2007.

McLain, Karline. *India's Immortal Comic Books: Gods, Kings, and Other Heroes.* Indiana: Indiana University Press, 2009.

Morris, Tom and Matt Morris, eds. *Superheroes and Philosophy: Truth, Justice, and the Socratic Way.* Peru, IL: Open Court, 2005.

Oropeza, B. J., ed. *The Gospel According to Superheroes: Religion and Popular Culture.* New York: Peter Lang, 2005.
Reynolds, Richard. *Super Heroes: A Modern Mythology.* London: B.T. Batsford, 1992.
Strömberg, Frederik. *The Comics Go to Hell: A Visual History of the Devil in Comics.* Seattle, WA: Fantagraphics, 2005.
Weinstein, Simcha. *Up, Up, and Oy Vey.* Baltimore: Leviathan Press, 2006.
White, Mark D. and Robert Arp, eds. *Batman and Philosophy: The Dark Knight of the Soul.* Hoboken, NJ: John Wiley & Sons, 2008.
——, eds. *Watchmen and Philosophy: A Rorshach Test.* Hoboken, NJ: John Wiley & Sons, 2009.

Journals
Ault, Donald, ed. *ImageTexT: Interdisciplinary Comics Studies.* http://www.english.ufl.edu/imagetext/.
Groth, Gary, ed. *The Comics Journal.* Seattle, WA: Fantagraphics Books.
Lent, John, ed. *International Journal of Comic Art.* Drexel Hill, PA.

Websites
Adherents. "The Religious Affiliation of Comic Book Characters." http://www.adherents.com/lit/comics/comic_book_religion.html/.
Bergeson, Steve. "Jewish Comics." http://jewishcomics.blogspot.com/.
Davies Stofka, Beth. "Holy Heroes!!" http://holyheroes.blogspot.com/.
——. "Library of Babble." http://brokenfrontier.com/columns/p/column/library-of-babble/.
——. "Religion and Comics." http://www.comicbookbin.com/religioncomics.html/.
Kannenberg, Gene. "ComicsResearch.org: Comics Scholarship Annotated Bibliographies." http://comicsresearch.org/.
McCloud, Scott. "ScottMcCloud.com." http://scottmccloud.com/.
Wilson, Willow. "Idle Worship." http://brokenfrontier.com/columns/p/column/idle-worship/.

Index

Made in the USA
San Bernardino, CA
28 January 2018